Strategic
Database
Marketing

For Helena

Also by Arthur Middleton Hughes

The Complete Database Marketer
McGraw-Hill Publishing Company, 1991

The Complete Database Marketer, 2nd Edition
McGraw-Hill Publishing Company, 1996

Strategic Database Marketing
McGraw-Hill Publishing Company, 1994

Strategic Database Marketing, 2nd Edition
McGraw-Hill Publishing Company, 2000

The Customer Loyalty Solution
McGraw-Hill Publishing Company, 2003

*Don't Blame Little Arthur; Blame the Damned Fool Who Entrusted
    Him with the Eggs*
Database Marketing Institute, 1998

The American Economy
Norvec Publishing Company, 1968

Strategic Database Marketing

Arthur Middleton Hughes

Third Edition

McGraw-Hill

New York   Chicago   San Francisco   Lisbon   London   Madrid
Mexico City   Milan   New Delhi   San Juan   Seoul
Singapore   Sydney   Toronto

The **McGraw·Hill** Companies

Copyright © 2006, 2000, 1994 by Arthur Middleton Hughes. All rights reserved. Printed in the United States of America. Except as permitted under the United States Copyright Act of 1976, no part of this publication may be reproduced or distributed in any form or by any means, or stored in a database or retrieval system, without the prior written permission of the publisher.

5 6 7 8 9 0 DOC/DOC 0

ISBN 0-07-145750-X

Printed and bound by R. R. Donnelley.

McGraw-Hill books are available at special quantity discounts to use as premiums and sales promotions, or for use in corporate training programs. For more information, please write to the Director of Special Sales, McGraw-Hill, Professional Publishing, 2 Penn Plaza, New York, NY 10121-2298. Or contact your local bookstore.

Contents

Acknowledgments

Virtually all the ideas that you will read in this book have occurred to me as a result of stimulating contact with the many master database and Internet marketers quoted in these pages. If you find useful concepts in this book it comes about because in writing it "I stood on the shoulders of giants." I particularly want to acknowledge a debt of gratitude to several who helped me in special ways:

Paul Wang, Associate Professor of Marketing, Northwestern University. Paul and I gave 32-day seminars together to more than 1,200 database marketers over a five-year period. Paul, more than anyone except Helena, is responsible for what success I have had in this field.

Frederick Reichheld, author of The Loyalty Effect. This amazing book, filled with wonderfully insightful ideas, has been an inspiration to me. Reichheld's book had such a powerful effect on my thinking that I sought a contract with McGraw-Hill to produce the second edition, updating many of my concepts to square with Reichheld's principles.

Brian Woolf, President of the Retail Strategy Center and author of Customer Specific Marketing. Brian understands supermarket marketing better than anyone in America. His helpful comments on the first edition of this book were largely responsible for its success.

Bob James, formerly with Centura Bank. Bob was the first to teach me the science of bank profitability analysis. He is an excellent marketer and a good teacher.

Randall Grossman, Senior Vice President of Bank One in Columbus, Ohio. Randall, formerly with Fleet Bank, pioneered in linking profitability analysis with lifetime value and potential lifetime value to create a super bank customer marketing system.

Bruce Clarkson of Sears Canada. Bruce is one of those people who can see the forest when he is walking through the trees. He explained the principles involved in Sears Canada marketing reorganization in a way that universalizes the general principles involved.

Paula Hart, former Marketing Director at Dayton Hudson and author of the Regards Program. Paula is an extremely creative marketer who knows how to win customer loyalty.

Judd Goldfeder, President of The Customer Connection, who took an obscure subject, restaurant customer loyalty, and showed what could be done to build repeat business and sales.

Bill Moore and Andy Zeigler of KnowledgeBase Marketing who taught me much about modern file processing which is reflected in this book.

Gary Laben, CEO and **Dennis Kooker,** COO of KnowledgeBase Marketing, who invited me to join a highly advanced team at KBM that carries out professionally the principles described in this book.

Database Marketing and the Web

Introduction

The second edition of this book went to press just before the stock market crash and the 9/11 tragedy. In those days, we still thought that dot coms were the wave of the future and that CRM was going to be a success. We have learned a lot.

The Internet has turned out to be a tremendous winner as a tool for getting information and communicating with customers. It has not been so successful as a sales medium. CRM has been a gigantic waste of capital resources—producing increased profits in a minority of applications.

Many of the early dot com enterprises, except for Amazon, Ebay, Google, and a few others have mostly gone out of business—and good riddance to them. They were based on false premises: that clicks were more important than profits, that being the first mover was important, that Web advertising and sales were going to be huge, and that young, inexperienced technical people could beat experienced businessmen.

On the other hand, because of database marketing and the Internet, we are on to something very big and no one knows where it is going. At first companies began collecting data on their customers and learning about their preferences and life styles so that they could make relevant offers to them. It worked. Companies began to compute customer lifetime value and use the numbers to measure their success in various marketing strategies.

The Old Corner Grocer

Back in the days before there were supermarkets, all the groceries in America were sold in small corner grocer stores. In many cases, the proprietor could be seen at the entrance to his store, greeting the customers by name. "Hello Mrs. Hughes. Are your son and his family coming for Thanksgiving again this year?"

These guys built the loyalty of their customers by recognizing them by name, greeting them, knowing them, doing favors for them. They helped by carrying heavy packages out to customer's cars (there were no shopping carts in those days). These veterans no longer exist. The super-markets put them out of business. Prices came down. Quality went up. The corner grocer had 800 SKUs in his store. Supermarkets today have more than 30,000 SKUs. He had a few hundred customers. Companies today have hundreds of thousands or millions of customers.

As a result, the familiarity of the old corner grocer that produced loy-alty in the old days has become much more difficult to create and sus-tain—until database marketing came along. Using the techniques in this book, it is now possible for a large corporation with a marketing data-base to build a relationship with customers that recreates the recogni-tion and loyalty of the old corner grocer. We do this over the phone, through creative use of a Web site and e-mails, and by providing our employees in marketing, sales, customer service, or at retail counters and teller windows with the kind of information about their customers that the corner grocers used to keep in their heads. We are returning today to methods that worked wonderfully in the old days. They work. They build loyalty, repeat sales, cross sales, and profits. This book explains the principles and provides scores of examples.

What Do Customers Want?

What has been happening is that the customers are becoming dominant. Companies are discovering what their customers want and selling them that. It is customer-based marketing. But it is really more than that. What customers want today can be summed up in a few general concepts:

- *Recognition.* They be recognized as individuals, with individual desires and preferences. They like being called by name.

- *Service.* Thoughtful service provided by knowledgeable people who have access to the database, and therefore know who they are talking to, and what these people are interested in.

- *Convenience.* People are very busy. They do not have time to drive a couple of miles to do business. They want to do business from where they are by phone or using the Web, with companies that remember their names, addresses, credit card numbers, and purchase history.

- *Helpfulness.* Anything that you can do to make customers' lives simpler is appreciated. Merchants have to think every day, "How can I be more helpful to my customers?" Only those who come up with good answers will survive.

■ *Information.* Customers are more literate today than ever before. They use the Internet. Technical information is as important to many of them as the product itself.

■ *Identification.* People like to identify themselves with their products (like their cars) and their suppliers (like their country clubs and condominiums). Companies can build on that need for identification by providing customers with a warm, friendly, helpful institution to identify with.

The Importance of Price

Many company managements think that price is the most important factor in the sale of a product or service. They argue that when the products are on sale, more people buy. When the competitor is on sale, less people buy. Does that not prove that price is central to profits? Not at all. There are two kinds of customers: transaction buyers and relationship buyers. Transaction buyers are interested in price. They have no loyalty. They will leave you for a penny's difference. Relationship buyers are looking for a reliable supplier with friendly, helpful employees. They will stick with you even when the competitor is on sale.

The reason for the gain in customers when products are on sale is that the transaction buyers are moving from company to company to take advantage of the sales. The relationship buyers are staying right where they were. Here is a big secret: you cannot make much money from transaction buyers. The money is in the relationship buyers. You should design your customer contacts to maximize the services and attention to the relationship buyers and ignore the transaction buyers. Through database marketing we will identify our most profitable customers and build lasting relationships with them, increasing their retention rates, spending rates, and referral rates.

Database marketing and Internet commerce are primarily aimed at making customers happy and loyal. They are built on the theory that if—in addition to providing a quality product at a reasonable price—you can find a way to provide recognition, personal service, attention, helpfulness, and information to your customers, you will build a bond of loyalty that will keep them coming back for a lifetime. Database marketing, therefore, is a way of providing service that is focused on the customer, not on the product.

Modern computer technology is used to create a relational database that stores a great deal of information on each household (or company, in the case of a business-to-business product). Retained is not just the name and address, but also

- e-mail address plus the cookies that keep track of their Web visits;
- complete purchase history;
- customer service calls, complaints, returns, inquiries;
- outgoing marketing promotions and responses;
- results of a customer surveys;
- household (or business) demographics: income, age, children, home value and type, etc.

Through database marketing it is now possible to determine the profitability of every customer in the database. Presented in this book is a fairly universal way of calculating lifetime value that has become standard practice in most modern database marketing situations. Using this method, new strategies in marketing can be tested before serious money is committed.

Two Kinds of Databases

There are really two different kinds of databases in any company that is engaged in direct marketing of products and services. One is an operational database and the other is a marketing database (Figure 0-1).

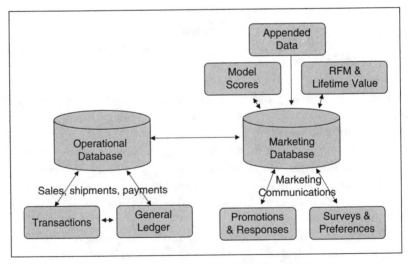

Figure 0-1. Operational and marketing databases.

An *operational database* is used to process transactions and get out the monthly statements:

- For a cataloger, this database is used to process the orders, charge the credit cards, arrange shipment, and handle returns and credits.
- For a bank, the operational database processes checks and deposits, maintains balances, and creates the monthly statements.
- For a telephone company, the operational database keeps track of the telephone calls made and arranges the billing for them

A *marketing database* gets its data from the operational database, if there is one. These data consist of a summary of monthly transactions. But the marketing data also include much more. It gets data from:

- preferences and profiles provided by the customers;
- promotion and response history from marketing campaigns;
- appended data from external sources such as KnowledgeBase Marketing, Donnelly, Claritas, etc.;
- lifetime value and RFM analysis, leading to creation of customer segments;
- modeling for churn and next best product.

The marketing database passes data back to the operational database. It may advise the operational database:

- Which segment each customer has been placed in, which may lead to operational decisions. Gold customers, e.g., may get different operational treatment.
- Expressed customer preferences leading to different operational treatment: smoking or non-smoking rooms assigned automatically.

The *operational database* is run by IT. It is run on accounting principles and balances to the penny, since there are legal and tax aspects to its data. It is audited by external auditors. It contains only current data on customers. Old data are archived. There are no data on prospects until they make a sale.

The *marketing database* is managed by the marketing department. It is usually out-sourced. It is not run on accounting principles and does not need to balance. There are few legal or tax aspects. It contains current customers, prospects, lapsed customers, and communications with them. It may retain data stretching back over a period of several years.

What about CRM?

Before implementing a CRM package it is necessary to understand why nearly half of U.S. implementations and more than 80% of European implementations are considered failures. It's difficult to fathom failures of such monstrous proportions, especially when complete CRM installations can cost millions of dollars and then hundreds of thousands of dollars more per annum. John_taschek@ziffdavis.com

Database Marketing became known by some as Customer Relationship Management (CRM) in the late 1990s, to emphasize the fact that successful database marketing looks at the transactions from the customers' point of view rather than the company's. Unfortunately, CRM enthusiasts assumed that the CRM software used would build customer loyalty and profits. In most cases that was a mistaken view. What builds customer loyalty and profits are creative marketing strategies using customized communications based on a database. Sophisticated software is used, of course, but the marketer, not the software, does the thinking and develops the strategy.

The focus of database marketing is the development and testing of various marketing *strategies*, as outlined in this book. The focus of CRM is *automation of customer relationships*. The strategy is supposed to be embedded in the CRM software which, it is assumed, will produce increased sales and profits. The National Retail Federation Annual CRM Conference survey of North American retail companies found that 69 percent of the respondents said they had gained little or no benefit from their CRM investment.

In this book, we are concentrating on customer marketing strategy based on a customer marketing database. Software is used, to be sure, but the software is not supposed to do the job by itself. Database marketing requires the work of intelligent, imaginative, and resourceful marketers who keep trying new strategies in a constantly changing market.

Where We Are Going

Although database marketing was invented in the late 1970s, with the advent of constantly reducing costs of computer storage and retrieval, it only began to take root actively in major American corporations in the late 1980s.

There is one factor that is often missing from database marketing as it is being practiced today. That factor is strategy. We have learned how to build customer databases, store information, and retrieve it at will. What most companies have not yet learned is how to make money with a database. That is the main objective of this book, Strategic Database Marketing, 3rd ed. In these pages we will show the techniques whereby many companies have successfully built profitable relationships with their customers. We will explain exactly how to compute customer lifetime value and how to use it to evaluate strategies before thousands or millions of dollars are wasted on them.

A Sense of Balance

There is something else that is needed, which this book provides. That is a sense of balance. Database marketing is not helpful for every product and service. Unless they are proprietors of an office supply store, who wants to get letters from the people that make our paper clips? To visit their Web site? To build a relationship with them? Life is too short. We do not have time to build up a relationship with the producers of many of the thousands of products that we use every day. There are some products where database marketing will not work and should not be attempted. In these pages you will find many examples of failure as well as methods of determining in advance whether your great strategy will succeed or fail. This book, therefore, concentrates on the strategy that underlies successful database marketing.

Conclusion

Database marketing and the Internet are not just ways to increase profits by reducing costs and selling more products and services, although those things are, and must be, the primary results. They are tools that provide management with customer information and provide customers with information as well. This information is used in various ways to increase customer retention and increase customer acquisition rates— the essence of business strategy. The database combined with the Web provides both the raw information you need, and a measurement device essential for the evaluation of strategy.

Looked at from the customers' point of view, database marketing and the Web are ways of making customers happy, of providing them recognition, service, friendship, and information for which, in return, they will reward you with loyalty, retention, and increased sales. Genuine customer satisfaction is the goal and hallmark of satisfactory database marketing. If you are doing things right, your customers will be glad that you have a database and that you have included them on it. They will want to log on to your Web site. They will appreciate the things that you do for them. If you can develop and carry out strategies that bring this situation about, you are a master marketer. You will keep your customers for life and be happy in your work. You will have made the world a better place to live in.

1

Strategic Database Marketing and the Web: An Overview

Accountants have developed sophisticated techniques for appraising capital assets and their depreciation; they have learned how to monitor the constantly changing value of work-in-progress; but they have not yet devised a way to track the value of a company's customer inventory. They make no distinction between sales revenue from brand-new customers and sales revenue from long-term, loyal customers, because they do not know or care that it costs much more to serve a new customer than an old one. Worse, in most businesses, accountants treat investment in customer acquisition as one more current expense, instead of assigning it to specific customer accounts and amortizing it over the life of the customer relationship.

FREDERICK REICHHELD
The Loyalty Effect

Somewhere in the middle 1980s some marketers discovered that customer retention was more profitable than customer acquisition. It always was, of course, but most companies were not organized to do anything about it. In his lectures, Paul Wang, a great expert on database marketing, illustrates the point by saying money spent on acquisition seldom pays for itself. The customers become profitable only if they stick around for repeat purchases. Money spent on customer retention, on the other hand, is usually much more profitable.

Conclusions similar to these have been replicated in study after study in many industries. Most marketers today are aware of the significant profits involved in retention programs. Despite this recognition, most companies are still spending about 90 percent of their marketing budgets on acquisition and only about 10 percent on retention. This situation, and what to do about it, is a central theme of this book.

Why is most of the money spent on acquisition? There are a number of very valid reasons.

Acquisition is Easier to Measure than Retention. You can count the number of new customers that you acquire. It is not as easy to count the number of customers that you have hung on to through your retention programs. The critics will always say, "They would have kept on buying anyway. You just wasted your money and resources being nice to them."

Acquisition is Easier to Carry out than Retention. With acquisition, we use mass marketing and other impersonal means to bombard prospects with offers. We do not have to know very much about these prospects. If one method does not work well (the return on investment is low) we shift to another method until we get one that works. Retention, on the other hand, is more difficult. Here, we are dealing with our existing customers, people whom we have sold something to and whom we (theoretically) know. If we want to retain them, we must recognize them as individuals and show them that we remember and appreciate their business. This is much more difficult than sending promotions to prospects.

Acquisition Involves Product Managers. Retention needs segment managers. For acquisition, you put someone in charge of selling a new line of tractors, credit cards, or computers, and you provide bonuses and incentives for success. The process is easy to measure and understand. For retention, you should create customer segment managers whose job it is to reduce attrition and build loyalty and sales to customers in their segments. Once you have segment managers, you cannot really abolish the product managers, however. Retention involves creating a new layer of managers whose responsibilities and success measures are not obvious.

Retention Involves Maintaining a Database. You must create a database to keep track of your customers: who they are, what they have bought, and what their preferences are, etc. You need this so that you can engage in meaningful dialog with customers. You need the database to provide recognition, create segments, and provide rewards. The process is expensive and complex. It costs money that has to come out of some budget somewhere. Many companies find it difficult to justify these expenses.

To Measure Retention, you must have Test and Control Groups. To deal with the "They would have bought anyway" argument, you must set aside customer control groups who do not get the rewards that you shower on the customers that you are trying to retain. If you do it right, you will lose a lower percentage of the customers in the test group than you do in your control group. This is excellent database marketing but it is difficult to carry out in practice and sell the idea of setting up control groups to management.

Becoming Customer Centric

The core idea behind strategic database marketing and the Web is that the behavior of customers can be changed by things that you can do. By recognition, relationships and rewards, you can get customers to be more loyal. The charts and case studies in this book show that long-term loyal customers:

- buy more often and spend more on each purchase;
- have higher retention and referral rates;
- are less costly to serve;
- are willing to refer others who become loyal customers.

Customers respond to friendship and recognition. They like to be greeted using their names. They like to be thanked. They like to build relationships with your sales and service personnel. The old corner grocers used to provide this friendly contact automatically. It is more difficult with the large numbers of customers that most firms have today. How can you possibly recognize and build a relationship with tens of thousands or even millions of customers? Add to that problem the fact that you have a large number of customer contact personnel: they cannot possibly know more than a small fraction of the customers.

Database and the Web to the Rescue

The answer, of course, is a database aided by personal contact over the Web. Companies today are building user-friendly customer databases, loaded with actionable personal information, that permit customer contact personnel to recognize and quickly establish rapport with each customer, even though they personally have never met them or talked with them before:

"LL Bean. May I help you?"
"Oh, Hello. This is Norah Webster."
"Mrs. Webster. Glad to hear from you again. How did your grand-daughter like the sweater you sent her last October?"

Wow! How would that be possible? LL Bean has caller ID on their telephone system. Their customer service representative knew that it was Norah Webster before she even answered the phone. Norah's entire database record was put on the screen electronically before the representative said the first word. What would this do for relationships between Mrs. Webster and LL Bean? What would it be worth to your company to be able to hold conversations like this? This is strategic database marketing. This is how you build customer loyalty.

The same thing is happening on the Web. Using Web page cookies, companies are able to keep track of customers that come back a second time, saying "Welcome back, Arthur" whenever they click on the site. Using their customer databases created from prior visits and purchases, companies are able to replicate the friendship and relationships of the old corner grocers on the Web as well as on the phone. They populate any ordering forms with names and addresses already filled in, so the customers know that you remember them.

Avoiding Discounts

Discounts do not build loyalty. They destroy relationships. Once you give a customer a discount, you send a number of messages:

- Our regular product is overpriced. If you pay full price, you are being ripped off.

- You focus the customers on what they are paying, rather than what they are getting.

- You encourage your customers to shop around. Discounts can be copied by the competition. Solid relationships are hard to copy.

One of the key reasons for database marketing and creating personalized Web sites is to avoid having to give discounts. The loyalty created by the relationships insulates your customers from the blandishments of the competition.

How the Web Changes Things

The Web gives us an opportunity to invite customers into the interior of our company. In the 1980s all companies learned that they had to have a toll-free number so that customers could contact them. It was new and expensive. Eventually, call centers developed sophisticated software so their employees could answer customer's difficult technical questions by reading the answers off a screen. With this system, companies at their answer centers are paying for the toll-free call. They were paying a good salary to an employee to talk to you, operate a computer, and read information off the screen to you. The Web has eliminated the need for the phone charge and the cost of the employee. Savings to companies today? Millions of dollars per year. Advantage to you as a customer? Easy access to information whenever you need it. When Sears Canada put their big catalog on the Web, they found that 97 percent of the customers ordering products from the Web site had the paper catalog in front of them. Each page of the catalog had the toll-free number on it. Some customers prefer to use the Web rather than talk to a live operator. This is how the Web is changing things.

One word of caution: the Web is where it is at. The Web is the future of marketing. If the design and operation of your company's Web site is not under the control of the marketing department, you must fight very hard to get it, or you will be swept aside in the very near future. Do not let it be the province of some "technical" arm of your company. It is a marketing technique.

Getting the Right Customers

Frederick Reichheld in his wonderful book, *The Loyalty Effect,* pointed out that some customers are loyal and some are not. He described a customer "loyalty coefficient." His ideas suggest that, rather than starting by spending money trying to change customer's behaviors, we should begin by trying to attract the right kind of customer to begin with. Analysis of customers who defect in many companies shows that loyalty and disloyalty can be predicted early in a customer's career. Disloyal customers, e.g., for some products and services in some industries may be found to be:

- transient individuals;
- young people, rather than older people;
- single people, rather than married people;

- renters, rather than homeowners;
- people who respond to low-ball discount offers;
- people who respond to temporary sales.

Your customer retention programs will be much more successful if you begin with potentially loyal customers in the first place. The way to begin is to build a database, retaining in it both loyal customers and the records of those who have left you for any reason. Careful analysis of the loyalists and the defectors can lead you to develop rules for acquisition that may, in some cases, be more powerful in terms of profits than retention programs aimed at existing customers.

Creating Customer Segments

Central to strategic database marketing is the creation of customer segments or status levels. The typical status level system looks like Figure 1-1.

We will be using this diagram throughout the book. These status levels do not have to be of equal size. Typically the Gold customers at the top are a small percentage, such as 5 percent, of the customer base. The losers at the bottom may represent more than half of all customers. The point in such a segmentation scheme is to direct your marketing dollars where they will do the most good.

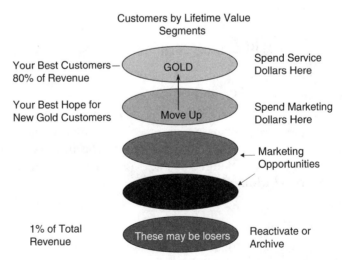

Figure 1-1. Segmenting customers by lifetime value status level.

Many companies have discovered that they cannot profitably market to their Gold customers. These are their best customers who are placing their entire category spending with your firm. They represent 80 percent of your revenue or profits. Do not market to them. Provide special services to them and build profitable relationships with them. The ones you should be marketing to are in the second, third, and fourth segments. Work to get them to migrate up to Gold status. Provide recognition, relationship, and rewards.

Do not waste your retention dollars on the losers at the bottom. These customers are typically not only not profitable but also represent a loss of profits. They should have their products and services re-priced or they should be dropped, if you can do it gracefully without adverse PR.

Building a database and a Web site and identifying customer segments is a key first step in strategic database marketing. Developing separate marketing programs for each segment is what it is all about. This is an area in which database marketing really can affect the bottom line.

Selling the Database and the Web Site to Management

There are a lot of people who have not yet read this book. This group probably includes the senior management of your company. Most of them have come up the hard way, selling products and services without a database or a Web site. They do not know why a database or an Extranet is necessary. How can you prove it to them?

Your first step, as soon as you have built a database, is to determine the lifetime value of your customers. You will learn:

- the retention rate;
- the referral rate;
- the spending rate;
- how costs go down with loyal customers;
- how to create customer segments;
- how the lifetime value varies by segment;
- how to identify Gold customers and develop strategies to keep them loyal;

- how to identify worthless customers who are losing your company money;

- how to modify customer behavior with recognition, relationships, and rewards and how to determine the return on investment for your efforts.

You will need to educate management to understand these things. Once you have done this, you must develop an action plan designed to change customer behavior to improve customer lifetime value. Then you demonstrate, in a lifetime value spreadsheet, how your strategic database marketing programs will increase company profits. In this book, you will learn how to determine customer lifetime value and use LTV charts in your work.

Benefits to the Customer

In any free market transaction, both parties always make a profit—both the buyer and the seller—because they receive something which they value more than what they give up. To assure that there are lots of transactions (sales), therefore, a marketer needs to be sure that his potential customers are making what they consider to be a profit.

In today's world, profit for the customer is not necessarily measured in dollars. For most of today's busy customers, time—even leisure time—has a high value. In many cases, they value convenience and time-saving delivery processes more than a lower price. Today's customers place a high value on recognition, service, helpfulness, information, convenience, and identification. The database can help make this possible.

The 24 Essential Techniques

We have learned a great deal from database marketing in the last two decades. The following is a list of the 24 essential techniques used in database marketing. After reading this book you will be familiar with and able to use all of these techniques:

LTV. Customer lifetime value can be calculated in any industry, business to business or business to consumer. It is used to direct marketing strategy. In the early days of database marketing few knew how to calculate it or how to use it. Today it is widely practiced. It is powerful and it works.

RFM (*Recency, Frequency, Monetary Analysis*). It is a highly successful way of predicting which customers will respond to promotions. It has been around for 50 years, but even today many marketers do not understand it or use it properly. It is a versatile tool that has helped to make database marketing successful.

Customer Communications. Personalized customer communications, based on data in a database, can be shown (using tests and controls) to increase customer retention, loyalty, cross sales, up sales, and referrals. They are effective and they work. They are the principal reason why you build a marketing database.

Appended Data. It is possible today to append data to any name and address file to learn the age, income, home value, home ownership, presence of children, length of residence, and about 40 other valuable pieces of information about any household. This information can be used to create customer segments and guide strategy designed to create powerful customer communications. Similar information can be appended to business-to-business files: SIC code, number of employees, and annual sales.

Predictive Models. Using appended demographic and behavioral data, it is possible to create models that predict, accurately, which customers are most likely to defect and which customers are most likely to respond to new initiatives. Modeling, combined with customer communications, can be a very powerful technique that can increase response and reduce your attrition rate.

Relational Databases. Putting customer databases in a relational form makes it possible to store an unlimited amount of information about any customer or prospect and retrieve it in an instant in a hundred different ways. Relational databases are essential to modern database marketing. Marketers need to understand the principles involved.

Caller ID. Set up originally as a call-routing device, caller ID linked to a customer marketing database permits customer service to get a customer's complete record up on the screen before taking a call. As a result, the CSR can speak to the customer as if she knew her, bonding with her and building close rapport. This helps deliver the promise of database marketing.

Web sites. The Web has revolutionized database marketing. A modern Web site, with cookies, can do almost everything that a live operator can do and much more, showing and enabling customers to print pictures of the product, maps, instructions, background information, and details. Web sites are not wonderful at selling. They are a tremendous research tool and customer bonding and ordering tool. No database marketer can be successful without a personalized Web site with cookies.

E-mail. Despite the SPAM, e-mails have emerged as a powerful database marketing tool. The ability to contact customers immediately: "Your product was shipped today. Here is the tracking number..." makes for vastly improved customer relationships leading to retention and increased sales.

Tests and Controls. Since 1980, marketers were sending out direct mail and measuring the response to each campaign. Today, we can use our database to measure much more. Setting aside customers in a control group, we can measure with pinpoint accuracy the short and long-term effects of any marketing initiative.

Loyalty Programs. Most customers are delighted to participate in well-designed loyalty programs. Airlines have been outstandingly successful in these programs. Their use has spread to supermarkets, hotels, retail stores, banks, and a variety of industries. They are part of the mix of retention-building services that database marketing has made possible.

Business Intelligence Software. Previously, after a campaign, you got canned printed reports showing what happened. Today, marketers have very sophisticated analytical software linked to their database so that each analyst can do any type of standard or ad hoc report before, during, and after a campaign, with the results printed on his PC printer. We have "hands on" marketing, which has made database marketing very powerful.

Web Access. Today, the marketing database is in a relational format on a server, which is accessed online over the Web by anyone in the company, in any location. Instead of a couple of analysts working with the data, it is available to management, sales, customer service, marketing, and market research. Web access has made marketing databases a useful tool throughout the enterprise.

Rented Lists. In the past, most companies kept their customer lists strictly private. Today, most lists are shared, exchanged, or rented. As a result there are more than 40,000 lists on the market, including data on more than 240 million American consumers and millions of businesses. Sharing of lists created the catalog industry and has spurred the growth of hundreds of other direct response industries.

Campaign Management Software. Direct marketing campaigns used to be generated by memoranda to a service bureau: "Select these groups, divide them into these segments with these codes, and fax me the counts." The process of getting the mail out the door took three to six weeks. Today, marketers have campaign management software linked to their database so that they can do the planning and actual selections themselves in an afternoon. It cuts weeks off the direct mail time, resulting in higher response rates.

Address Correction Services. Modern service bureaus can take any large or small file of customers or prospects, reformat them to a common format, correct the addresses to USPS standards, consolidate the duplicates, apply National Change of Address (to determine the new address if people have moved), and get the records ready for mailing or storage in their marketing database in one or two days after receipt of the data. This service has made modern database marketing possible.

Profitability Analysis. We used to know that some customers were more profitable to us than others, but it was hard to measure. Today banks, supermarkets, insurance firms, business-to-business enterprises, and many others can compute the monthly profitability of each customer. They have discovered that many customers are unprofitable. As a result they have changed their marketing and pricing strategy to increase their profits. The Wall Street Journal reported that Best Buy had identified 100 million out of its 500 million customer visits each year as unprofitable and undesirable.

Customer Segmentation. With small retail stores of the past, marketers could keep needed information about their customers in their heads. Today, companies have many more customers—some in the millions. A database is needed to store the information. To develop marketing strategies for all these customers, you have to divide them into segments usually based on demographics and behavior. Success comes from creating useful segments and developing customer marketing strategies for each segment.

Status Levels. The airlines started it: Platinum, Gold, and Silver. It has spread to other industries. Customers now understand their status and work to move up to a higher level. Companies provide special benefits, rewards, and services for higher status customers. In a democracy, it is an egalitarian method of customer differentiation that assists in building customer loyalty and company profits.

Multichannel marketing. Customers buy through multiple channels: retail, catalog, and the Web. We have learned that multichannel customers buy more than single-channel buyers. To be successful, you need a database that provides a 360-degree picture of your customer, coupled with strategies that recognize and communicate personally with the customer when she shows up in any of the three channels.

Treating customers differently. All businesses have Gold customers—a small percentage that provides 80 percent of your revenue and profit. With a marketing database, you can identify these Gold customers. Then you develop programs designed to retain them. You use resources that you could not afford to spend on all of your customers. Profits come from working to retain the best and encouraging others to move up to higher status levels.

Next Best Product (NBP). The database is used to determine what customers in each segment normally buy. From this, you can determine anomalies: customers who are not buying what the others are buying (usually because they are buying this product from somewhere else). This is their NBP. The NBP is put into the customer database record and used by customer service and sales in communicating with customers. It can be a powerful tool.

Penetration Analysis. Using a database and online analytical software, marketers can do their own penetration analysis. What percent of sales do we have in each zip code, SIC code, income level, or age group? This is a versatile tool that can help you to locate retail stores, place advertising, and direct your sales force.

Cluster Coding. Claritas and others have divided U.S. (and Canadian) consumers into 60 or more different clusters with catchy names and similar spending habits. In many industries, using clusters with penetration analysis can help you identify who is buying your products and who is not. It can be a creative tool to use in improving your marketing and sales.

Why Databases Fail

It is not all beer and skittles in the database marketing and Internet world. There have been some notable failures, involving hundreds of millions of dollars plus hundreds of smaller database and Web site projects that have not panned out as planned.

This book provides many case studies in a variety of fields, both business to consumer and business to business which document the successes and the failures. More important, there is an analysis of why databases fail and what you, as a marketer, can do to avoid failure in your work.

Failures come from both faulty planning and faulty execution. Planning success comes from creative strategy development based on sharp-pencil lifetime value calculation.

Executive Quiz 1

"What are these quizzes doing in this book?" you may ask. "Is this supposed to be a text book?" Actually, this book is used as a text in many university courses throughout the world. But for the general reader, these quizzes are here for enjoyment. Database marketing is supposed to be fun for the customers. If you do not like quizzes, ignore them. The quizzes are in here to make the book more interesting. Some people like to do crossword puzzles. Some people like quizzes. If you are one of them, then try your luck. The answers can be found in Appendix B.

Put the appropriate letter before each correct definition	
Term to be defined	**Correct Definition**
a LTV	Access to the database by many company units
b RFM	Ad hoc back end analysis
c Relational Database	Add age and income to a name file
d Profitability	Affluent buy in several ways
e Predictive Modeling	Customer learn about your company
f Next Best Product	Customers like to build equity in your company
g Caller ID	Don't waste resources trying to retain losers
h Penetration Analysis	Instant customer contact
i Cluster Coding	Main use for a database
j Segmentation	Make sure mail gets delivered
k Multi Channel Marketing	One purchase = ten catalogs
l Address Correction	Plan and select for a mailing in an afternoon
m Campaign Management Software	Predict future profits
n Rented Lists	Predict who will respond
o Tests and Controls	Prove that what you are doing is working
p Analytical Software	Senior Citizens, College Students
q Websites	Shotguns and Pickups; Furs and Station Wagons
r Email	Silver, Platinum and Gold.
s Customer Communications	Talk on the phone as if you really knew them
t Appended Data	Unlimited storage of data about a customer
u Web access	What percent of all law firms buy your product?
v Loyalty Programs	What should we sell them today?
w Treating Customers Differently	Which are the best customers today
x Status Levels	Who is most likely to leave?

Figure 1-2. Quiz 1.

2

"The Vision Thing"

As electronic commerce booms, it's not just middlemen who will find creative ways to use the Internet to strengthen their relationships with customers. The merchants who treat e-commerce as more than a digital cash register will do the best. Sales are the ultimate goal, of course, but the sale itself is only one part of the online customer experience. Some companies will use the Internet to interact with their customers in ways that haven't been possible before and make the sale part of a sequence of customer services for which the Internet has unique strengths.

BILL GATES
Business @ The Speed of Thought

What is database marketing, and how does database marketing work? How does it relate to the Internet? This chapter is aimed at answering these questions. We will be taking a broad look at the customer's situation today, in contrast with the situation in earlier times—decades and centuries. We are going to attempt to place database marketing and e-commerce in their historical perspectives as evolutionary forward steps. This chapter is what former President George Bush would have called "the vision thing."

If the first President Bush were to read this book, he might skip this chapter entirely. Compared to the rest of the chapters, which describe practical applications of database strategy and the Web, this chapter is filled with history and philosophy, and my personal views, which may well be wrong. I, personally, love to explore the ideas of the past, wonder about how we got where we are now, and speculate about what future generations will think about what we marketers are doing today. So that is what we will be doing.

Lets settle back, therefore, and see ourselves as painted figures on a grand historical canvas leading from the earliest Sumerian traders of 5000 B.C., up through the Industrial Revolution, past the electric age, the automobile age, the nuclear age, the jet age, the computer age, and on into the twenty-first century.

What Drives Industry?

Let us begin with a basic question. What drives industry—production, or marketing? In general, are products manufactured first, and then marketed? Or are they marketed first, and then manufactured to meet the needs of the market?

This is an important question for economists and marketers. It goes to the heart of the whole philosophy of marketing, particularly of database marketing and e-commerce. To answer it, let us go back to the Industrial Revolution—an epoch that changed the production system, and led to our present affluence. Let us examine the role of marketing in this revolution.

The Industrial Revolution

For thousands of years before 1760, productivity in industry and agriculture was stagnant. Roughly the same number of bushels of grain per acre or bolts of cloth per worker per year was produced in 1700 A.D. as was produced in 1700 B.C. Things stayed the same from year to year, and from century to century.

In the period after 1760 in England, however, an unusual series of events occurred that changed the world forever. For the first time, entrepreneurs began to combine significant amounts of capital—machinery and raw materials—with labor, in large factories devoted to the mass production of goods. By 1800, thousands of people were organized into enterprises which mass produced cotton thread, pottery, iron products and other items. For the first time in the history of mankind, mass production, making extensive use of capital, increased the productivity and brought the price of consumer goods down dramatically. It led to England's dominance of world trade for a century. Owing to the system which evolved in the Industrial Revolution, the average person in developed countries today can expect to live a longer and much more satisfying life than the average person has ever been able to do since the world began.

The Central Role of Marketing

Why have we become so wealthy in the last two centuries? Is it our production methods or our marketing skills? Most writers have concentrated on the factories as the places that have produced the wealth. In concentrating on the factories alone, however, they have overlooked the main reason the Industrial Revolution was possible: the expansion of the market system and trade.

Adam Smith pointed out in 1776 that mass production was the product of the division of labor: many people working together successfully in a common enterprise, producing much more than the same people could produce working independently. But Adam Smith said something else: "The division of labor is limited by the extent of the market." Where the market is small, the gains from the division of labor are correspondingly small. The larger the market, the more the possibility of efficiencies: greater productivity, greater profits, greater affluence.

Marketing is the key. Producing a million pounds of cotton thread would not have been possible if marketers had not found a way to sell a million pounds of cotton thread. Marketing is not something that happens after the goods are produced. Marketing is the reason the goods are produced in the first place.

The reason why cellular phones, VCRs, and personal computers have been manufactured in hundreds of millions is not primarily because of the activity of inventors and investors—although they are essential to the process—but primarily because of the activities of the marketers that have made the public aware of the products, created the demand for them, and set up the distribution channels.

New and unknown products—plus new versions of old ones—have to be introduced to the public in a way that creates the orders for factories. Marketing comes first.

The American Market

From 1900 to the present time, America has had the largest single market on Earth. Everywhere else, cultural restrictions, political systems, or physical boundaries combined with poor transportation to limit most markets to comparatively small areas. America has spent the last 200 years breaking down barriers, building waterways, railroads, telegraph, telephone and electronic communications systems, superhighways, airports, and massive delivery systems which link all parts of our market together in a freely competitive order.

The result has been the greatest outpouring of production, affluence, and personal freedom ever known. The process has not been directed or controlled by government. Instead the driving force has been free competitive market activity: each entrepreneur trying to satisfy the public best so as to realize his own personal dream.

Marketing has been the means whereby the division of labor has expanded. Individual marketing heroes have provided the leadership. From 1812 to 1860 Frederic Tudor, one of our first mass marketers, built his fortune by shipping blocks of ice from Boston to the south and the outside world. He taught the middle class how to store ice and to preserve food. He changed the way people ate and drank. A hundred years later, another hero, Frank Perdue, taught us "It takes a tough man to make a tender chicken." His chicken empire was not so much a triumph of production—which was superb—but of marketing, which was even better. Jeff Bezos, the creator of Amazon.com, figured out how to sell books and scores of other things on the Web—before most people even knew what the Web was. Americans as a people are master marketers. Our marketers have educated the public and provided the means whereby fantastic new products can be developed, mass produced, and delivered at lower and lower prices.

The Growth of Mass Marketing

From 1950 to 1980, mass marketing predominated. The growth of television built on the solid foundation of national print advertisements and radio to create mass audiences for national advertising. National brands, sold in supermarkets, department stores, fast food restaurants, and franchised outlets everywhere, homogenized the contents of the American home. Mass marketing makes mass production possible. This combination resulted in a constant reduction in the cost and improvement in the quality of most products, and a vast increase in the real income of the average American consumer.

The American consumer has steadily become more and more affluent. The market has been changing, and our marketing methods have to adapt. The growth in real income conceals another trend which is hard to display in graphic form: the products that Americans are buying with their income have become a lot more efficient and sophisticated.

One result of this productive system is that the middle class has grown from being about 15 percent of the population in 1920 to being 86 percent of the population in 2005. While some of the population always seem to live at the poverty line, the vast majority of Americans today are affluent compared to their grandparents. They have the money to buy the products produced by American industry. In the process, the definition of poverty has changed. The vast majority of Americans who are classified by the government as living at the poverty level have color television sets, air conditioning, washers and dryers, microwaves, automobiles, and access to free health care through Medicaid. They are also a significant buying group.

We have arrived at the situation where more than 85 percent of the American households have discretionary income: not all of their take-home pay is required to pay for food, clothing, rent, and transportation. In 1950, the average American family was spending 31 percent of their household income on food. Today they are spending less than 14 percent on food, and the food they are getting with that 14 percent is better in quality and quantity than what they were spending 31 percent for in 1950. We have all gained. Our basic needs are met. We want something more.

What the Market Consists of Today

We are not at the end of a long evolutionary process. Instead, we are today right in the middle of a vast program of change that is leading us on to new levels of wealth and affluence. Our market is still expanding. Look at some of the features of this market:

Consumers became owners of the economy. An amazing development took place in the late 1990s. The average household acquired mutual funds. By the end of the decade, almost 60 percent of American households owned stocks, either directly or indirectly. Consumers began to look on American industry from the standpoint of being owners of it, rather than as just employees. It changed their attitude as shoppers. They were not tied down to their neighborhood. They began to use the Internet to see what was available.

New products were created at an accelerating rate. If you look at the U.S. market in the last two centuries there was a steady acceleration in innovation. A graph of patents issued during the past 200 years shows a staggering increase during the past decade. There were more patents issued in the 20 years from 1995 to 2005 than in the first 200 years of our nation.

The pace of new product introduction and expansion is staggering. It is not possible for anyone to keep on top of even a small percentage of the new developments today. As a result of this constant innovation, the market is much more complex for the consumer than it once was.

Why the U.S. Economy Is So Successful

Despite temporary setbacks, America has been going through an unprecedented boom that never seems to stop, while most of the rest of the world does not do as well. Why is that?

Freedom to produce. We are successful primarily because of freedom. Unlike most of the rest of the world which is burdened with high taxes, heavy governmental regulation, and a culture that frowns on personal advancement at all levels, American business is freer to innovate, hire and fire, and produce. We learned to understand the customer, and to design products and services not only to meet the customer's needs but also to continually delight the customer with new products and services that the customer had not even imagined.

Freedom to market. In a trip to Germany, I was astonished at the governmental restrictions on the marketing of products and services there. Stores are closed on Sundays and holidays and at 6:30 every evening *by law!* In the U.S., our biggest sales come on weekends and holidays. Every evening billions of dollars change hands when American shoppers visit shopping malls. Why were the German stores closed during these peak shopping days and hours? *Because of the workers!* German stores are not run for the customers. They are run for the workers in the stores. American stores are run for the customers. We keep the stores open at all hours to make our customers happy. By having two shifts we provide more jobs and money for our workers and convenience for the customers. In Germany, keeping the stores closed means fewer jobs and money for their workers and great inconvenience for the customers. Marketing freedom is central to our prosperity. Anyone can manufacture products. Only Americans know how to market them. We let the Chinese and other Asians make our products. We sell them.

Low inflation due to our trade deficit with the rest of the world. The trade deficit came about because Americans bought more every year from abroad than foreigners bought from us. The result: prosperity for America. It is a wonderful system! We give China, Taiwan, Singapore, and many other countries dollars which are created by our banking system and really cost us almost nothing. They give us millions of valuable products which they have to work very hard to produce and ship. How did this system result in American prosperity? The flood of inexpensive foreign goods was why we were able to hold inflation in check here for many years. Low inflation was central to our success. Some American workers were displaced by the flood of imports, of course, but most of them soon found jobs in an economy that keeps growing and growing.

High investment. There was a second benefit from the foreign trade deficit: *those dollars in New York banks owned by foreigners*. The foreigners were not content to let the dollars just sit there. From the first moment, they wanted them earning interest. So the dollars were invested in American business: stocks, bonds, mutual funds, and other investments. These were not temporary investments. The trade deficits went on for decades. They fueled the boom in the Dow Jones and American industry.

Meanwhile, American consumers, benefiting from this prosperity, became affluent and changed their buying habits.

Customers buy products to reduce uneasiness. Why, after all, does anyone buy anything? There is one basic reason which is always true: people purchase products because they think that their life will be better with the products than it was without them. This is true of both consumer and business customers. They do not *know* that their life will be better with the products. They just make that assumption. Sometimes they are wrong.

The value of products is subjective. The market value of products and services is determined primarily by the customers. A computer, for example, has no value at all unless someone wants it. The money that went into its production is totally ignored by potential customers. They simply see it as a way to relieve uneasiness. If it will not relieve their uneasiness more than some competing product of which they are aware, they will not buy it, and it will have, essentially, no value at all for them. Obsolescence is an ever-present worry for any business holding inventory. Constant obsolescence is the result of constant innovation.

In free market exchanges, both parties make a profit. It is often over-looked that the consumer makes a profit as well as the supplier. Each party to a trade gives up less than he gets—or why would he trade? Money has exchange value. Purchased products seldom do. If you sell a consumer a computer for $1,000 it must be worth more to the consumer than $1,000, or he would never buy it. By doing so, he gives up $1,000, which he could use to buy anything he wants, for a (now used) computer which will be hard to trade for anything. For you as a retailer, the computer must be worth less than $1,000, or why would you sell it? The fact that both parties always must make a profit is essential to understanding the market, and particularly to the strategy for database marketing.

Purchase decisions cause internal conflicts in potential customers' minds. All customers are torn between their desire for a product or service on the one hand and their desire to retain their money stock on the other. Acquiring a product tends to reduce uneasiness; dissipation of one's personal money stock tends to increase uneasiness. Life is a balancing act between the two desires.

The internal struggle affects different sides of the brain. Research on the hemispheres of the brain has made us aware that we possess two different and complementary ways of processing information—a linear, step-by-step style that analyzes the parts that make up a pattern (the left hemisphere) and a spatial, relational style that seeks and constructs patterns (in the right). It is the left hemisphere that controls our language. It is here that we do our mathematics, and calculate prices and bank account balances (Figure 2-1).

The right brain constructs patterns and recognizes relationships. It is most efficient at visual and spatial processing. It is here that we visualize what our life would be like if we were to acquire a new product. It is the source of our imagination and our *desire*.

It is the complementary functions of both sides of the brain that gives the mind its power and flexibility. We do not think with one hemisphere or the other; both are involved in the decision-making process. Any significant decision is often preceded by a good deal of logical, linear thinking as a person defines and redefines a problem. This linear verbalized thinking goes on in the left hemisphere. Then there comes a moment of insight when an answer presents itself. This answer occurs when the right side combines all the pieces together into an image of the solution to the problem. Finally the mind tackles the difficult job of evaluating the insight and putting it into a form in which it can be communicated and applied to the problem.

The purchase decision process

Right Hemisphere

Patterns, and
relationships. Visual
and spacial processing.
Imagination and desire.

"If I had that product, I
would be handsome,
cultured, sophisticated
and popular. I must
have it."

Left Hemisphere

Language, linear
thinking. Mathematics,
accounting, and logic

"I have only $X in my
bank account as a result
of yesterday's
extravagance. I must
resist the right side's
customary exuberance."

Figure 2-1. The purchase decision process.

Advertising can appeal to either side of the mind. It is well known in retailing that *buy one, get one free!* out-pulls *50 percent off!* Why should that be? There seem to be several reasons:

One reason is that you can get the 50 percent reduction by buying only one, instead of two, so purchases could prove to be less.

The second reason is that, even today, many people are insecure about the meaning and method of computation of percentages. Everyone, however, understands the meaning of *free!* It is a wonderful word.

The third reason is basic to database marketing. Wanting products is a right brain function. Calculating money is a left brain function. *Fifty percent off* requires a left brain calculation plus a right brain stimulus: a complicated mental sleight of hand, which is hard to process. *Buy one, get one free* is pure right brain. You not only get what you want, but you also get two of them.

Marketers are faced with a dilemma on the approach. Should they base their message on the price (a left brain argument) or on the benefits of the product (which appeals to the right brain)?

Products Tend to Become Commodities

There is a problem with both marketing approaches today. Prices tend to become similar as each airline, computer company, and automobile manufacturer rushes to match every price move of the competition.

The consumer knows that price changes are temporary, and seldom fundamental. Many consumers, moreover, being relatively affluent, are less interested in price than in quality and service.

Product quality also tends to be uniform. Avis, Hertz, National, Budget, Dollar, and Alamo all rent brand new cars. Detergents, yogurts, canned goods, tires, television, phones, and toilet paper are all getting better and better and more similar: each manufacturer produces equally good, high-quality products that do the same thing. Every improvement is immediately matched by the competition.

The Importance of Time

Price and quality have been the staples of marketing for years. Today, there is a new dimension entering into consumer decision making that is of equal importance. It is time. People have less and less time available for shopping (or for anything).

Products that can be purchased for $100.00 and a one-hour round trip to the supermarket or the mall are perceived to cost more than the same products that can be purchased for $120.00 and a telephone call or an Internet click. Our leisure time has acquired a monetary value that it never had before.

To the monetary cost of any transaction, therefore, we must add the cost of the time involved in completing the transaction.

If we can make a purchase more convenient and less time consuming for customers, we make the product more attractive to them. They are more likely to buy it. In many cases, making this purchase more convenient costs us less than the increased value to the consumer: both of us make a profit by the change in delivery methods.

What we marketers are selling today, therefore, is more than the product. It is the product, plus the delivery method. The convenience and service is part of what we are selling. The real decision-making process required for a purchase (from the customer's point of view) looks something like this:

$$\text{Customer Profit} = a \text{ (utility of product)} + b \text{ (value of brand)} - c \text{ (money cost)} - d \text{ (time)}$$

The numbers a, b, c, and d are *weights* which vary with each customer. Lower income customers place a higher value on c, and a lower value on d (since money is worth more to them and time is worth less). Busy people place the highest value on d. This was illustrated in the 1970s during the energy crisis. Gasoline prices were controlled at low levels by the government. As a result there were regional gasoline shortages and long lines at the gasoline stations. Across the Texas border in Mexico gasoline cost much more, but there were no lines and unlimited supplies. For a number of months, Texans drove south of the border to fill up their gas tanks at high prices, while Mexicans came north across the border to wait in lines for the cheap gas.

Providing Information

The fact that the market today is filled with change, uncertainty, lack of information, and ignorance is a wonderful opportunity for marketers. Millions are refinancing their homes at lower and lower interest rates. Interest rates used to be a mystery. Today, owing to the Internet, you can find them out with a click of a mouse. We live today in a world in which customers have as much information about products as the suppliers. This is what is happening today through the Internet.

The American market is not only huge, but gigantic. It is filled with millions of businesses and hundreds of millions of consumers, each looking out for themselves, pursuing subjective goals of their own. Before the Web came along, no one could possibly know all the commodities and services that were available, their respective benefits and features, and the prices at which they could be obtained. Now, much of that information is at your fingertips.

How Database Marketing Solves Customers' Problems

Database marketing and the Web came along just when they were needed. They solved the information problem; they provided recognition, personal service, and a profit to the customer. The Web is an extension of that database, providing recognition and helpful information.

Database marketing is possible, of course, because of the development of computers with advanced software. We can store scores of facts about every customer, and retrieve them in seconds when we need them to provide information and services to each customer. We can use this customer information to create personalized communications that customers like and respond to. Let us take a concrete example. Read this letter (originally created by Thomas Lix):

Ridgeway Fashions
404 Main Street
Leesburg, VA 22090

Dear Mr. Hughes:
    I would like to remind you that your wife Helena's birthday is coming up in two weeks on November 5th. We have the perfect gift for her in stock.
    As you know, she loves Liz Claiborne clothing. We have an absolutely beautiful new suit in blue, her favorite color, in a fourteen, her size, priced at $232.
    If you like, I can gift wrap the suit at no extra charge and deliver it to you next week so that you will have it in plenty of time for her birthday, or, if you like, I can put it aside so that you can come in to pick it up. Please give me a call at (703) 754 4470 within the next 48 hours to let me know which you'd prefer.

Sincerely yours

Robin Baumgartner, Store Manager

What is my reaction to this letter? Halleluiah! Helena is a Catholic. She has two birthdays a year: her Saint's Day is August 18th and her birthday is November 5th. I have to buy her something for both days. What should I get for her? She is a very stylish, fashion conscious businesswoman who always wears the latest clothes. I, on the other hand, am color blind and hate to shop. I wander around the malls, "What? What? What?" These people know. "Liz Claiborne"—what is that? I don't know, but Helena does and she likes it. If the database has the correct information in it (about Helena's tastes and my pocket-book), I will snap at this opportunity to remove my uneasiness, and save myself time.

This letter can also be quite effective as an e-mail on the Internet. Scores of stores and catalogers are now encouraging consumers to record their important events. They provide reminders, like this one, in time to help the consumer make up his mind before the event. This is classic 1:1 marketing. This is strategic database marketing. This is what it is all about.

Database marketing and the Web are designed to reduce ignorance and lack of information: bringing a very particular buyer with unique subjective goals together with a specialized solution to the customer's problem.

Database marketing and the Web, of course, are not universal solutions. They will be effective only in situations in which a continuing relationship between a seller and a buyer is *profitable for both parties*. If either one or the other finds that they can do better without the relationship, the database or Web project will fail—and they should.

Collecting Information

How would Ridgeway Fashions get the information necessary to send me such a personal letter? It should not be from analyzing purchases. That is too much like the CIA, snooping through personal files. It would be an invasion of privacy. To collect this information, a Ridgeway clerk, when Helena was shopping, should ask her, "Would you like to be in the Birthday Club?"

"What is the birthday club?"

"Well, you tell us your birthday, your preferences and sizes, and your husband's business address. Then a couple of weeks before your birthday, we will write to him and give him some hints on what to buy."

"Hints? He needs hints. OK. Where do I sign up?"

Additionally, Ridgeway could collect the same information by listing their birthday club on the Internet. The information is stored in the customer's database file. The data go to the merchandise buyers who have to buy clothing that the customers want. Then, once a month, the computer scans the file for people who have a birthday coming up. They check the warehouse to see if what the customers want is in stock. Then they can write these 1:1, powerful, personal letters.

Event-Driven Personal Communications

To create these letters, you need to store a lot of information about your customers and their preferences in your database. The database software will:

- sweep the database weekly to determine relevant targets for communications;
- determine which product type represents a match;
- calculate the expected value of each target, recipient, merchandise, and occasion combination;

- select the winning possibility;
- generate inputs for the communication package;
- monitor the results of each communication; update the database with the results.

Lifetime value. To know if this club is going to work you have to compute the lifetime value of each customer. Lifetime value permits calculation. It permits you to figure out the amount of money which is practical to expend on maintaining your relationships with your customers.

Building the database necessary to send that letter to Arthur Hughes was not cheap. The store had to collect a lot of information about Helena and me: sizes, styles, birthdays, budgets, ages, fashions, interests, and preferences. The software had to use all of that information to match this data with the products that Helena had already bought at the store and the thousands of products currently available, so as to produce the perfect letter at the right time to the right person.

Capturing the information has a cost. Maintaining the database and producing the monthly output has a cost. Mailing the letters has a cost. E-mail would be much cheaper. Most of the letters or e-mails will not result in a sale. Balancing all of these costs are the potential profits that will come from the actual sales (less the returns), which the system produces.

The way to know whether you have built a successful database marketing system is to compute the lifetime value of the Hughes family and all of the other families on your database. Each time you introduce another innovation (sending out a gift suggestion before a wedding anniversary or child's college graduation, for example) you recompute the lifetime value. If the value goes up, you should do it. If it goes down, you should not.

In the next chapter, we will build a lifetime value table for Ridgeway Fashions to show how you would go about costing out the birthday club to determine whether it will pay dividends.

Do Database Marketing and Web Commerce Always Work?

No, they definitely do not. There are tens of thousands of products, particularly packaged goods, where database marketing or the Web will never work. Too many articles have been written which imply that database marketing or Web sites are panaceas, and that those who fail to use them are blockheads. Do not be fooled. Work out the economics. The next chapter, on lifetime value, will give you a solid tool to determine whether database marketing and a customer Web site will work in your situation.

Is Mass Marketing Ending?

Of course not. It is alive and well. Smart mass marketers will include a Web site in their advertisements so customers can get more information, locate dealers, or buy products directly. Mass marketing will always be essential to make the public aware of new products, and old products for which database marketing and the Internet will not work well. Will most toothpastes ever be sold by database marketing or the World Wide Web? Never. Manufacturers of packaged goods will be using mass marketing plus retailers' shelf space long after the people reading this book have been shipped off to a nursing home, located through the Internet.

Summary

America is unique and fortunate. Working in a land of freedom and opportunity, a nation of immigrants built a continental market with few political and economic restrictions. For the last century we have had the largest and freest market on Earth.

In this free market, entrepreneurs and marketers seek better and better ways of making the customers happy. Customer happiness means purchases, and purchases mean profits for both the buyer and the seller. The size of our market has resulted in economies of scale from mass marketing, mass production, constantly lower prices, constantly increasing per capita income.

Database marketing and the Web are aimed at the customer's right brain. Instead of being bombarded with discounts, the customer is showered with attention, recognition, friendship, and service. Why these things? Because that is what the customer wants. Furthermore, database marketing and the Web are the only way to start a two-way dialog in which the customers are able to tell you what is on their minds, and you are able to react to their thoughts by varying your services and product mix.

Database marketing and the Internet work for some products because they are uniquely qualified to meet today's customers' requirements, just as mass marketing was the ideal marketing solution for these same products in previous decades. Companies that recognize this shift and take advantage of it will prosper. Others may be consigned to the dustbin of history.

We Americans do have a "vision" which directs our market and our economy. The vision is freedom and control by the consumers. It works.

Executive Quiz 2

Answers in Appendix B.

Put the appropriate letter before each answer		
	Questions	**Answers**
a	The Left Brain	Amazon
b	Both buyers and sellers make a profit	August 18th
c	Stores in Germany	Basic principle of free market
d	Annual productivity gain 1700 BC - 1700 AD	Blocks of ice
e	Key reason for success of US economy	Close at 6:30 every night
f	Average income of Americans today	Computes Mathematics
g	Trade deficit with China	Determined by the customers
h	Why do customers buy products	Eighty-six percent
i	Value of most products	Higher than their parents
j	When is Helena's Saint's Day ?	Increases investment in US business
k	The source of our desire	The consumers
l	Middle class percent in 2005	The extent of our market
m	Profit = utility + brand - Cost - ?	The right brain
n	Who controls the US economy ?	Time
o	Frederick Tudor	To reduce uneasiness
p	Jeff Bezos	Zero percent

Figure 2-2. Quiz 2.

Marketing Strategy Development

3

Lifetime Value—
The Criterion of Strategy

*One of the most powerful, but surprisingly under-
utilized, tools is the referral program. For generations,
companies have witnessed the power of satisfied customers referring products or services to someone they
know. However, most companies do not actively pursue
referrals, thinking customer advocacy is a phenomenon
that occurs naturally, not one that can be encouraged.
This "hands-off" approach to referrals is being pushed
aside for something more proactive. In many industries
the cost of acquiring customers via traditional marketing efforts is four times what it is to acquire customers
through referrals. Renowned business author Frederick
Reichheld believes the number of people who are willing
to refer your product or service is the single most important customer metric in determining a businesses success. He quoted Enterprise Rent-A-Car's CEO Andy
Taylor: "The only way to grow a business is to get customers to come back for more and tell their friends."*

CHRIS MOLONEY
Parago, Inc.

Most marketers today talk about lifetime value. A growing number are
calculating it and using it in their marketing strategy. You do not need
to feel badly if you have not used it yet. It takes an understanding of
some basic concepts that—once you know them—are not difficult, but
until you do, may seem quite mysterious.

In this chapter, you will find a complete explanation of how lifetime value can be worked out. Once you get through it, you will be able to use it in your marketing planning. This chapter is detailed. If you stick with it to the end, however, it will change your life as a marketer and make you a better person. Who could ask for anything more?

Definition of Lifetime Value

First, a definition—lifetime value is the net present value (NPV) of the profit that you will realize on the average new customer during a given number of years. Lifetime value can be used in the development of marketing strategy and tactics. At any given time it is a specific number, but it will change from month to month. There are many different things that cause lifetime value to change, some of which are under your control, many of which are not.

What a Lifetime Value Table Looks Like

Let us begin with a basic lifetime value table. After you understand it, we will explain:

- How you can modify it
- How you can use it to test strategy
- Some of the technical details

For this table, we are going back to Tom Lix's example at the end of the previous chapter. We will look at Ridgeway Fashions before and after they adopted the new strategy of writing letters to husbands before their wife's birthday. We will see how they costed out the Birthday Club, and determined whether the strategy would work, using a lifetime value table. While this is a retail example, the principles apply to any type of industry: financial services, telecommunications, business-to-business situations, as well as consumer marketing. Lifetime value is a universal measurement system. This book contains more than a dozen different lifetime value tables for a variety of industries. You will probably find your business represented on one of more of these charts. For now, however, study this particular table, because you will learn the basic principles of lifetime value from it (Figure 3-1).

Lifetime Value Without the Birthday Club	Acquisition Year	Second Year	Third Year
Customers	200,000	80,000	36,000
Retention Rate	40%	45%	50%
Visits Per Year	1.10	1.30	1.50
Spend Per Visit	$120	$130	$140
Total Revenue	$26,400,000	$13,520,000	$7,560,000
Variable Costs %	60%	56%	55%
Variable Costs $	$15,840,000	$7,571,200	$4,158,000
Acquisition Cost ($40)	$8,000,000	$0	$0
Card Database Costs ($2)	$400,000	$400,000	$400,000
Total Costs	$24,240,000	$7,971,200	$4,558,000
Gross Profit	$2,160,000	$5,548,800	$3,002,000
Discount Rate	1	1.16	1.35
Net Present Value Profit	$2,160,000	$4,783,448	$2,223,704
Cumulative NPV Profit	$2,160,000	$6,943,448	$9,167,152
Lifetime Value	$10.80	$34.72	$45.84

Figure 3-1. Customer lifetime value.

In this table, we are looking at a group of 200,000 Ridgeway Fashions customers over a three-year period. Let us assume that prior to this time, Ridgeway Fashions issued a plastic membership card to many of their customers, or with customer permission, recorded customer's credit card numbers so that they could find out who was buying what, and could store that data in a simple database. This chart is based on the data available on these customers in the database. It does not include other Ridgeway Fashions customers who pay cash, or otherwise cannot be tracked. The first year is the acquisition year of the 200,000 customers. We are following these specific people over three years. The store will be acquiring other customers during this time. We are not tracking them on this chart. This is the way lifetime value tables are constructed.

The Retention Rate

You will note that of the 200,000 customers who were acquired in Year 1, only 80,000 of them came back to make purchases in the second year. That means that Ridgeway retained only 40 percent of the customers that they acquired in Year 1. The retention rate is the single most important number in a lifetime value table. It is a measure of customer loyalty, and is something that you, as a marketer, can modify by your marketing strategy and tactics.

The retention rate is easily calculated by a simple formula:

$$RR = Year \times Customers/Previous\ Year\ Customers$$

$$RR = 80,000/200,000 = 40\ percent$$

Year × Customers represent those previous year customers who are still buying in the later year. In the appendix to this chapter, we cover the interesting problem of computing the retention rate of people who do not buy from you every year—such as automobile purchasers. There is a simple formula that converts their spending pattern to an annual figure.

What do we do with new customers who wander in to the store and begin shopping in the second year? We can develop a LTV table for them. That is their acquisition year. In your table, you do not need to select 200,000 as your group for study. You could select 59,102, or any number that you might have in the database. The only requirement is that we are taking snapshots of the performance of a specific group of consumers or companies over their first several years as a customer. Later, we will be developing the lifetime value of customer segments, not of all customers, as we are doing here. For now, however, let us stick with looking at all the customers in the database who were acquired together, to see what we can learn about them.

What do we do with lapsed customers who did not buy in Year 2, but came back in Year 3? They are in there. They are part of the 36,000 who are shopping in Year 3. The fact that some of the lapsed customers may be reactivated leads companies to keep these customers on their books for a couple of years. There is always hope. Of course, since they are on the database, we will have to keep track of them and send them occasional messages. This costs money. Database marketing is not free.

In this chart, we have shown the cost of the card database as $2 per card holder per year. We keep this database going for the three years, even though more than half of the customers have left us forever. The reason is that we still have hope that they will return to shop again.

The Visits per Year and Spending per Visit

We are tracking each visit to the store. Many come once, and never come again. Some come many times. In the first year this averages out to 1.1 visits per year. We are also tracking the spending per visit. Both of these numbers tend to go up over time. The disloyal customers have left, and the loyal ones who remain visit more often and spend more per visit. You will have the same experience. Typically, the longer customers are with you, the more they will spend per year, per visit, per order. The second year represents the activity from the customers who are still active out of the original group acquired in the Acquisition Year.

Variable Costs

Direct costs are computed in a wide variety of ways in different industries. To determine costs in your industry, you should consult the finance department in your company. These costs include the cost of the products or services provided, plus the variable administrative costs such as customer service, debt collection, deliveries, returns, credits, etc.

What you will notice, and will be true of your situation as well, is that the costs of servicing a customer tend to decrease with the number of years that the customer has been buying from you. This is true in business to business as well as in most forms of consumer marketing situations. If you are selling software, for example, the customers are likely to tie up your customer service lines during the first 60 days until they learn how your software works. For the next 60 months, you may never hear from them again. This is true in a wide variety of industries, and helps to reduce costs and increase lifetime value.

Computation of costs should not be made into a major problem. If you develop a consistent system and stick to it consistently, that is all you need. The reason? We are going to look at the effect of a new strategy on lifetime value. If both tables use the same cost percentages, what that percentage is may not be of crucial importance. So do not worry whether your costs are 50 percent or 60 percent or 70 percent. If you come up with a good number, stick with it, and use it in all your LTV charts.

The Acquisition Cost

Most companies are geared for acquisition. They spend a lot of money to get customers. To compute the acquisition cost, simply add up all the money you spend on your advertising and marketing efforts during the year (exclusive of retention programs, which we will discuss later). These marketing efforts can include advertising, sales commissions, sales salaries, etc. Then divide this total by the number of new customers who actually make purchases from you each year. That is your cost of acquisition.

Computing this number is very important. It may drive your whole marketing strategy. You will find that money spent on acquisition does not pay as well as money spent on retention. Lifetime value computation is the first opportunity most companies have to find that out.

Gross Profits

Gross profits are easy to compute. They are equal to the total revenue less the total costs. We need to spend some time on the discount rate, however, since that is the most complicated part of the entire lifetime value analysis.

The Discount Rate

The reason why we need a discount rate is simple: the profits you receive from your customers come in over several years. Money received in future years is not worth as much today as money received today.

If I owe you $1,000 right now, but pay you the $1,000 a year from now, I have gypped you out of the interest you could have earned on that $1,000 if I had paid you right away. Future money is worth less than present money. To estimate the value of future money, we must discount it by a certain amount, so we can equate it to present money, and add the two totals together.

 How much should you discount future revenue? There is an easy answer: you use the market rate of interest. As I write this today, 7 percent seems like a reasonable market interest rate. Ten years ago, 12 percent was what businesses were paying. The amount varies with the general market conditions. You should use a number which corresponds with your current situation. In this book, I am using 8 percent throughout, as being a nice round average number.

In reality, however, I am doubling that 8 percent to get 16 percent. Why is that? Because I am including risk. In any long-term business transaction, like lifetime customer value, there is always a serious risk. What are the risks?

- Interest rates could go up.

- *Obsolescence.* Your product could become obsolete in the next few years, and wipe out your expectation of further sales.

- *Competition.* In most industries, competitors always make marketing a risky business. They could steal your expected customers.

- *Other business risks.* In each business situation, there is many a slip twixt the cup and the lip. Your business is no exception.

For these reasons, in this example, I have doubled the interest rate to get the discount rate. The risk factor (rf) is two. You may be able to develop more sophisticated risk factors than (rf = 2), based on your business history. We will discuss the risk factor in Chapter 14 on Business-to-Business.

Computing the Discount Rate from the Interest Rate

Once you have decided on a market interest rate—such as the 8 percent that I have used—you need to compute the discount rate that applies to amounts to be received in each year. There is a simple formula that is used to compute the discount rate. It is

$$D = (1 + (i \times \text{rf}))^n$$

where D is the discount rate, i, the interest rate, rf, the risk factor, and n is the number of years that you have to wait. The discount rate in Year 3, for example, (two years from now) is computed like

$$D = (1 + (0.08 \times 2))^2$$

$$D = (1.16)^3 = 1.35$$

It is possible to be much more precise in your discount rate calculation. You can worry about whether you have to wait several weeks or months, on the average, to be paid. This is true in most business-to-business operations. In this case, we can make "n" into a fractional amount, like 3.25. We will use this type of system in calculating lifetime value for a business-to-business situation in Chapter 14.

Net Present Value Profits

Once you have the discount rate, each of your expected profits must be discounted so as to arrive at the NPV of these future profits. The process is a simple one:

NPV profits = gross profits/discount rate

The NPV of the $3,002,000 profits expected in Year 3 is $2,223,704 which is the result of dividing $3,002,000 by the discount rate of 1.35.

Cumulative NPV Profit

We must now add together the NPV of all the profits in the present year, and each previous year. The NPV of profits realized by the third year, for example, is equal to sum of the NPV of the profits in the Acquisition Year + Year 2 + Year 3.

Lifetime Value

The lifetime value is simply the Cumulative NPV Profit in each year, divided by the original group of customers (in this case 200,000). It really means this:

The NPV lifetime value represents the average profits which you can expect to receive, after a given number of years, from the average new customer that you can sign up. The lifetime value of the average new customer for Ridgeway Fashions in the third year is $45.84

LTV = CUM – NPV/acquired customers = $9,167,152/200,000 = $45.84

This is a very important number. It is the most important number in your entire database. It can be used to develop your entire marketing strategy. We will be using this number throughout this book. Built into this number are all of the other numbers in the LTV table: the retention rate, spending rate, the acquisition cost, marketing costs, product costs, and discount rate.

Strategy Development

Developing your customer lifetime value table is the first step in the development of strategy. The second step is to get a great idea, and test it out—in theory—using your lifetime value table as the measuring stick. Let us do this right now.

Strategy always begins with some assumptions. "If we do this, then the customer will do that." We will learn that customer relationship building strategy can affect five (and only five) basic things:

1. *Retention rate.* Building relationships increases customer loyalty, and augments the retention rate. Increases in the retention rate will reduce the costs of servicing customers, and increase the revenue per customer.

2. *Referrals.* Relationship building activities can turn your customers into advocates and lead them to suggest your company to their friends, co-workers, or relatives. This works in business to business as well as consumer marketing. Referrals typically have higher retention rates and spending rates than other newly acquired customers.

3. *Increased sales.* Database activities can lead to increased visits, larger average purchases, cross-selling, or upgrades.

4. *Reduced direct costs.* Database activities can reduce costs, in some cases, by changing the channel of distribution. Once you have customers on your database, you can learn more about them, and can increase your channels to reach them. You can send them e-mails. You can call them on the phone.

5. *Reduced marketing costs.* Well-planned database activities are often much more cost effective than mass advertising. Once you have your customers on a database, you will develop innovative ways to market to them. For example, you will find that some customers have a negative lifetime value. They are costing you profits. Why spend a lot of money trying to build a relationship with these losers? Save your marketing money for people who can do you some good.

For Ridgeway Fashions, let us imagine a creative Director of Database Marketing whom we will call Robin Baumgartner. Robin decides to test out the idea of a Birthday Club: to ask women customers to provide information about their sizes and preferences, their birthday, and their husband's business address. This information will be put into the database, and supplied to the merchandise buyers who have to buy what the customers want. Then, each month, Robin will send letters to husbands about their wives birthdays providing hints on what to get.

Here is what Robin's idea might do to the lifetime value of customers who decide to join the Birthday Club (Figure 3-2).

Included in the LTV table are many individual number revisions that Robin estimates will occur as a result of the Birthday Club.

Retention Rate

In the previous example, the retention rate for Ridgeway began at 40 percent. In drawing up this new table for the Birthday Club, Robin makes the assumption that her programs can increase that to 50 percent—with further increases as the remaining customer base becomes composed of more and more loyalists. Where did she get the 50 percent

With the Birthday Club	Acquisition Year	Second Year	Third Year
Customers	200,000	100,000	55,000
Retention Rate	50%	55%	60%
Visits Per Year	1.20	1.40	1.60
Spend Per Visit	$130	$140	$150
Total Revenue	$31,200,000	$19,600,000	$13,200,000
Variable Costs %	60%	56%	55%
Variable Costs $	$18,720,000	$10,976,000	$7,260,000
Acquisition Cost ($40)	$8,000,000	$0	$0
Card Database Costs ($2)	$400,000	$400,000	$400,000
Birthday Club ($15, $2)	$3,000,000	$400,000	$400,000
Total Costs	$30,120,000	$11,776,000	$8,060,000
Gross Profit	$1,080,000	$7,824,000	$5,140,000
Discount Rate	1	1.16	1.35
Net Present Value Profit	$1,080,000	$6,744,828	$3,807,407
Cumulative NPV Profit	$1,080,000	$7,824,828	$11,632,235
Lifetime Value	$5.40	$39.12	$58.16

Figure 3-2. Lifetime value with the Birthday Club.

number from? She estimated it, based on some tests that she had conducted. One objective of any new strategy will be to make customers happier, and thus to increase their retention rate. What that increase will be you will have to estimate. Lifetime value is a forward-looking concept. You use it to predict your future revenue and profits.

What determines the retention rate? A great many things, only some of which are under the marketer's control. Factors that marketers usually cannot control include:

■ The strength of the competitor's marketing strategy.

■ The saturation of the market for their product.

■ Macroeconomic events like recessions, booms or changes in interest rates which affect the overall demand for most products.

The factors that marketers can control that affect the retention rate, however, are quite impressive:

■ The type of customer that you acquire in the first place

■ The price charged for the product

■ The efforts made to build a relationship with the customers

■ The way you treat your customers

Certainly, the Birthday Club will appeal to some customers. It will result in some husbands, who have never bought women's clothing before, ordering a birthday gift for their wives, based on the information which she has provided to the store. As a result of these additional sales, we can assume more visits (or orders) and a higher average order size.

The Spending Rate

Robin is assuming that the Birthday Club will increase the acquisition year average visits (or orders) from 1.1 per year to 1.2, with additional increases in the second and third years. She estimates that Birthday Club members will buy an average of $130 dollars worth of clothing in the acquisition year instead of $120. How does she know that it will be $130? She can do little tests using test and control groups (see Chapter 11). Database marketing offers a tremendous opportunity to conduct mini-experiments prior to your major rollouts. Robin has done her home-work. Her estimate is, clearly, a testable proposition.

Her assumptions in the next two years also follow from database mar-keting theory. Loyal customers always buy more than new customers. As customers drop out, those who are left are the more loyal customers. It is safe to assume that the average annual purchases will go up. If you keep track of customer spending in your database, you can prove, easily, to yourself that loyal customers tend to make more purchases per year, that they buy more on each visit, and that they tend to buy higher priced items.

Birthday Club Costs

In planning her variable costs, Robin assumes the same cost structure that applied for her customers in general. The costs for the Birthday Club can be calculated with some precision. To set the club up in the first year will cost $15 per customer. This includes the cost of training the clerks to ask people to join the club, giving the clerks a commission of $5 per customer signed up, getting the survey data, keypunching the data, putting it into the database, creating the Birthday Club software, and writing one letter to each member's husband at birthday time. In Years 2 and 3, the costs are set at $2 per year. This covers the generation of the birthday letters. You will note that she is sending out birthday let-ters to all club members, even though many have already stopped buy-ing in the store. This is an excellent strategy. The club communications, alone, may serve to reactivate some lapsed customers, and are well worth the investment.

Resulting Lifetime Value

Lifetime value for club members is computed exactly as it was for regular store customers. It shows that lifetime value in the third year rises to $58.16. To show what has happened, we use a third chart which compares the bottom line on both tables (Figure 3-3).

What this shows is that in the first year, the Birthday Club will reduce lifetime value. In old-fashioned direct marketing programs, one might use this initial loss as a reason to abandon the club as being a loser. But with database marketing we can look at the impact of a new strategy several years ahead. What this shows is that by the third year, the Birthday Club will increase Ridgeway profits by more than $2.4 million. Bear in mind that this $2.4 million is not sales, it is net profits, after all costs have been subtracted including the loss of $1 million in the acquisition year. It is a real number that can be measured. It shows that the Birthday Club is a profitable strategy for Ridgeway Fashions.

Referral Rate

Almost any company can get some satisfied customers to become advocates. It is possible that the Birthday Club will be so successful that she can persuade (or incentivize) 3 percent of her customers to recommend Ridgeway to their friends or relatives. As a result, we will have 3 percent more customers in Year 2 than we otherwise would have had. The same thing can happen in Year 3.

Is Robin correct? Can she really increase her customer base by 3 percent in Year 2 through a referral program? Who knows? That depends on many things, including the success of Ridgeway as a store, the execution of the marketing plan, etc. But it is certainly a reasonable goal to build in to a marketing plan. It is also a testable proposition. If the plan does produce 3 percent new customers, the database will show it. If it brings in 6 percent, or only 1 percent, the plan can be modified. This is the beginning of good strategy development. The MCI Friends

Results of new Strategy	Acquisition Year	Second Year	Third Year
Base LTV	$10.80	$34.72	$45.84
New LTV	$5.40	$39.12	$58.16
Difference	($5.40)	$4.41	$12.33
Times 200,000 Customers	($1,080,000)	$881,379	$2,465,083

Figure 3-3. Gain from the Birthday Club.

Including Referrals	Acquisition Year	Second Year	Third Year
Referred Customers (3%)	0	6,000	3,180
Customers	200,000	106,000	61,480
Retention Rate	50%	55%	60%
Visits Per Year	1.20	1.40	1.60
Spend Per Visit	$130	$140	$150
Total Revenue	$31,200,000	$20,776,000	$14,755,200
Variable Costs %	60%	56%	55%
Variable Costs $	$18,720,000	$11,634,560	$8,115,360
Acquisition Cost ($40)	$8,000,000	$0	$0
Card Database Costs ($2)	$400,000	$400,000	$400,000
Birthday Club ($15, $2)	$3,000,000	$400,000	$400,000
Total Costs	$30,120,000	$12,434,560	$8,915,360
Gross Profit	$1,080,000	$8,341,440	$5,839,840
Discount Rate	1	1.16	1.35
Net Present Value Profit	$1,080,000	$7,190,897	$4,325,807
Cumulative NPV Profit	$1,080,000	$8,270,897	$12,596,704
Lifetime Value	$5.40	$41.35	$62.98

Figure 3-4. LTV with 3 percent referrals.

and Family program was one of the most successful referral programs in the history of marketing. It showed what can be done (Figure 3-4).

Just adding these 3 percent referrals in the second two years has made a major change in the overall success of the Birthday Club. Look at these numbers (Figure 3-5).

Our overall profits have gone from $2.4 million to $3.4 million. Generating referrals is a really valuable strategy.

There is one issue here that we should note. These referred customers are really new acquisitions. Why do not we just tuck them into the numbers in the Acquisition year the way we do with other new acquisitions. Why do we show them as a separate category on a lifetime value chart? There is a very important reason. Research shows, and your

New strategy with Referrals	Acquisition Year	Second Year	Third Year
Base LTV	$10.80	$34.72	$45.84
New LTV	$5.40	$41.35	$62.98
Difference	($5.40)	$6.64	$17.15
Times 200,000 Customers	($1,080,000)	$1,327,448	$3,429,552

Figure 3-5. Gains from referrals.

database records will prove it, that referred people are more loyal, have a higher retention and spending rate, than the average new acquisition. They are better people than the average customer. Why this is so, no one really knows. But the fact that they are linked to an existing customer results in their being more valuable than many other customers. You list them separately because you want to track them, you want to measure their purchasing habits, and devise special programs to increase their number. You may want to create a special lifetime table just for them. Do not lose track of them. In your database, you put the ID number of the referred person in the referrer's record, and vice versa. That way you can track referred people and those who refer them, to determine their lifetime value. Research shows that those who refer other customers are also better customers. They are advocates. They spend more, and are more loyal. If you have enough of them, you may want to create a special "advocates group," giving them special attention

Lessons Learned

What lessons can we draw from what we have learned already?

- Lifetime value is a practical, hardheaded technique for determining the effectiveness of various marketing strategies. It can, and should, be applied to any marketing program to test it before any significant amount of money is spent. Before we act on our hunches and prejudices, we can do our homework and prove to ourselves, at least theoretically, whether any proposed program has the possibility of success.
- Lifetime value is future net profits computed in today's dollars using the NPV calculation method.
- Lifetime value grows with the number of repeat customers and referrals.
- Lifetime value increases with the number of years that customers continue to buy.

The basic idea is to come up with strategies that increase lifetime value by as much as possible. If we set up a matrix showing lifetime value each year for three years (as we have already done), then we can use our imagination, and do "what if" analysis to see what can we do to increase lifetime value. The results of each possible action can be calculated to determine whether the effect on lifetime value is worth the effort and resources that went into it.

Looking at Customers as Assets

Most businesses list buildings, machinery, and cash as assets. But when a business is sold, "Good Will" is often what the buyer pays the most for. Good will is nothing other than the value of the customer base that the company has built up over the years, and currently is holding on to. Lifetime value is a way of quantifying the value of the good will represented by the existing customer base.

Economists and accountants often talk as if the main problem of any business is to find the most efficient way to produce products and services. It is not. The main problem of any business is to find the most efficient way to sell its products and services. Customers provide the cash flow that keeps any business alive.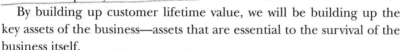

By building up customer lifetime value, we will be building up the key assets of the business—assets that are essential to the survival of the business itself.

The Computation Period

In this example, we have shown the results of lifetime value in the acquisition year and after one and two years. Why stop there? Why not compute it over 10 years? Which is the right number of years to look at? Throughout industry there is a lot of confusion over this question. When you think about it, however, it is not that complicated.

Some customers stay with you for years. Others buy once, and drop out. The remainder drop out at various intervals—and some drop out and then come back. The lifetime value is a function of the length of time that you use for measurement. The longer period of time you use, the greater the lifetime value. That being the case, which is the correct length of time: one, two, three, five, or ten years?

Paul Wang has what I consider to be the best answer: all of them are correct. Lifetime value, for Paul, is always tied to a number of years: Lifetime value after two years is X; Lifetime value after 3 years is Y. You look at all the numbers, and say to yourself: "How long is a reasonable period for our business?" If, for instance, you are a consumer cataloger or are selling on the web, long-term lifetime value may be self-delusion. Catalog and web customers tend to come and go quite rapidly. If you are a bank or an insurance company with long-term retention rates in the 90 percent range, a 10-year LTV table may be quite feasible.

You have to look realistically at your product, your competition, and the market and say, "How long are customers likely to stay with us?" After that you can ask, "How long can we afford to wait?" The answer will be quite different for each product in each industry.

The lesson: compute lifetime value for each of several years. Use the period of time that makes the most sense to you based on your particular product situation.

How Do You Calculate LTV for a Single Customer?

For any individual customer you can learn the customer's demographics, transaction history, spending rate, and frequency of spending. These are solid facts which, mostly, will be true today and next week. What you cannot know is this customer's retention rate. Any given customer could be gone tomorrow. She could die, move, or shift to the competition. No one, even the customer, can really predict these things. This presents a problem in calculating the lifetime value of an individual customer, as opposed to the lifetime value of a group of customers. How can you get a single number that you can put in each individual customer's record?

To begin with, you create realistic customer segments (see Chapter 8). In business to business, the segments may be based on SIC code and size of company based on number of employees or annual sales. For consumers, your segments may be based on gender, age, income, lifestyle, family composition, type of home, etc. Then you calculate the LTV of each segment.

Although you create a segment and work out its lifetime value, you cannot do the same thing for a single customer. Why not? Because lifetime value always includes the retention rate. I cannot pick out one customer and tell you that she will be here next year. But I can pick out 1,000 customers who are members of a segment and say, with some confidence, based on recent experience with that segment that 600 of them will be here next year. This is what insurance actuaries do. The success of the entire insurance industry is based on the findings of actuaries. They separate out a group, such as male non-smokers age 67, and can look you in the eye and tell you how many will die within the next year. We can do the same thing with lifetime value, if you create meaningful and predictive customer segments. To determine the LTV of a single customer, you include her in a valid segment or group; determine the LTV of the group, and then attribute to her the LTV of the group

Lifetime Value of Teenage Customers	Acquisition Year	Second Year	Third Year
Customers	200,000	60,000	24,000
Retention Rate	30%	40%	50%
Visits Per Year	1.10	1.30	1.50
Spend Per Visit	$80	$90	$100
Total Revenue	$17,600,000	$7,020,000	$3,600,000
Variable Costs %	60%	56%	55%
Variable Costs $	$10,560,000	$3,931,200	$1,980,000
Acquisition Cost ($30)	$6,000,000	$0	$0
Card Database Costs ($2)	$400,000	$400,000	$400,000
Total Costs	$16,960,000	$4,331,200	$2,380,000
Gross Profit	$640,000	$2,688,800	$1,220,000
Discount Rate	1	1.16	1.35
Net Present Value Profit	$640,000	$2,317,931	$903,704
Cumulative NPV Profit	$640,000	$2,957,931	$3,861,635
Lifetime Value	$3.20	$14.79	$19.31

Figure 3-6. LTV of teenage segment.

members. This can be varied with the individual customer profitability or spending rate.

For example, assume that we have determined the lifetime value of our teenage customers. Their spending rate in the third year is $100 and their LTV in that year is $19.31 (Figure 3-6).

What is the LTV of Eliza Hughes, a member of this group, whose personal visits per year and spending per visit are known? Based on the group she is in (teenagers), we can redo the LTV chart using the group's retention rate, and cost structure, but using Eliza's ordering and spending rate. We can then determine that Eliza's LTV in the third year is $33.71. We can tuck this number into her database record and use it in future marketing strategies involving Eliza (Figure 3-7).

To compute this table, we used the LTV table developed for the segment (teenagers) that includes Eliza. Then we inserted Eliza Hughes actual visits and spending into the teenage LTV table, as if there were 200,000 teenagers just like Eliza. Doing that, we find that Eliza clones have a LTV in the third year of $33.71. We put that number into Eliza Hughes database record. We do the same thing for each one of the 200,000 teenage customers. We can then use these numbers to rank these customers by their lifetime value. We will use this concept in developing a risk revenue matrix later in the book.

Lifetime Value of Eliza Hughes			
	Acquisition Year	Second Year	Third Year
Customers	200,000	60,000	24,000
Retention Rate	30%	40%	50%
Visits Per Year	1.00	2.00	1.00
Spend Per Visit	$105.31	$91.34	$150.03
Total Revenue	$21,062,000	$10,960,800	$3,600,720
Variable Costs %	60%	56%	55%
Variable Costs $	$12,637,200	$6,138,048	$1,980,396
Acquisition Cost ($30)	$6,000,000	$0	$0
Card Database Costs ($2)	$400,000	$400,000	$400,000
Total Costs	$19,037,200	$6,538,048	$2,380,396
Gross Profit	$2,024,800	$4,422,752	$1,220,324
Discount Rate	1	1.16	1.35
Net Present Value Profit	$2,024,800	$3,812,717	$903,944
Cumulative NPV Profit	$2,024,800	$5,837,517	$6,741,461
Lifetime Value	$10.12	$29.19	$33.71

Figure 3-7. LTV of Eliza Hughes.

To do this, you write a computer program that creates the lifetime value table shown here. You feed into this program the facts about the visits per year and spending per visit that you know about a particular customer, and substitute these known facts for the group estimates. This yields a different number for each individual customer.

Does LTV Predict Success?

In this chapter, we compared the lifetime value of all Ridgeway Fashions customers with those who join the Birthday Club. This is an excellent use of LTV, since it tells us whether the Birthday Club can be a success. It does not, of course, tell us that the Birthday Club *will* be a success. Success depends on execution, and on guessing the situation in the market at the time. Maybe the competition already has a birthday club. Lifetime value analysis will tell us that the club could be a success, if all other factors are favorable. There are plenty of marketing strategies that could not work out even in theory because the costs would exceed possible increased profits. The LTV table will show this clearly, and should be calculated before any new strategy is undertaken.

Possible Strategies

What can you do to increase your profits by increasing customer lifetime value? Throughout this book, we will explore a number of techniques including:

Retain existing customers:

- Provide strategies that encourage customers to renew or retain their membership.
- Build a relationship with customers to make them more loyal.
- Segment the database and target the company's relationship to the appropriate groups of customers, rather than treating them all alike.
- Establish special groups: a President's Club, a Gold Card Group to build loyalty and encourage people to buy more to belong.
- Set up a frequent buyer/flyer/traveler/shopper club.
- Increase renewal or reactivation efforts.

Add new customers:

- Study existing customers who have stayed with you, and those who have left. Use the analysis, plus a model to determine the type of customer most likely to stay. Then devise strategies to acquire that kind.
- Determine the customer acquisition budget with more precision.
- Profile existing customers and use the profiles to find new customers.
- Use the database to qualify prospects.

Increasing Retention Efforts

Magazine owners have renewal down to a science. Newsweek, for example, grips on to their customers like a pit bull. Before the subscription is due to expire, they have a series of reminders and increasingly strident warnings of impending doom. After the subscription has expired, there are a continuing series of reactivation messages. They just cannot accept the idea that anyone would ever want to drop their subscription to Newsweek.

This is great marketing. Most companies do not do this because they do not know how to do it. Magazines do it because they are in the habit of corresponding with their customers, and have developed lifetime value down to a fine science.

How to Do Your Own Calculation

Lifetime value calculation as a base for strategy development, therefore, is not as difficult as you may have thought. Follow these simple steps:

1. Use your database to select a group of customers all of whom came on board at about the same time in the past. Depending on the size of your customer base, you could use any number from 1,000 to 1 million or more.

2. Determine how many of *these particular customers* are still buying a year later to figure your retention rate. If you have enough data, determine the second year retention rate as well. If not, estimate it for subsequent years. Fifty percent attrition of newly acquired customers is not unusual. If you have a rapidly moving type of business, you can compute LTV based on quarters or half years rather than annual numbers.

3. Estimate the money that you spent in acquiring these customers by advertising, direct mail, promotions, etc. This is your acquisition cost.

4. Determine the average amount of money that these customers spend with you in a single year so as to compute their spending rate.

5. Determine the discount rate that applies to your business: adjust this rate for risk.

6. Put all of this data into a spreadsheet, projecting your customer lifetime value out for three or more years.

7. Try out some "what if" scenarios, experimenting with the costs and effects of relationship building activities, with the goal being to build the long-term customer value to as high a level as possible. Predict the results of each major marketing initiative before you implement it.

8. Keep your LTV spreadsheet active. After you have tried a few marketing initiatives, check their results against your spreadsheet. Improve your predicting ability. Become a master marketer. If you need help in creating your spreadsheet, you can download a sample spreadsheet from the Database Marketing Institute's web site: www.dbmarketing.com. It is free.

Selling Your Marketing Program to Management

Every year you have to justify your existence to some flinty eyed CFO. Now that you have calculated lifetime value, it will become the centerpiece of your budget justification. Suppose you are Robin Baumgartner, trying to get the money for her Birthday Club from her management. What she will do is to say, "If you can give me this budget, I can turn the club into a $3.4 million profit in the third year."

The CFO will be skeptical. "Prove it to me", he will say.

Robin then produces her revised lifetime value chart, showing the referral rate, the retention rate, and the spending rate once the Birthday Club is in full operation. "Where did you get these numbers?" he will ask.

"I ran some tests in our stores in Braintree and in Danbury. The numbers are the result of these tests. Do you want to see the details?"

If the CFO finally gives Robin the money she needs, there will be a problem. The CFO will save her revised spreadsheet in his desk drawer. Next year when Robin comes up for a budget review again, he will produce the sheet and ask: "OK, now tell me. What was your actual retention rate with the club? What was your referral rate and your spending rate?"

The problem, of course, is that lifetime value tables represent real numbers that can be audited by any accountant. Database marketing is an accountable art. It is not like mass marketing where you use "awareness" or customer satisfaction as a measure of success. What is awareness? It is a vague, indefinable number, which may be in no way related to real sales. Customer satisfaction is also often a fuzzy number that can be manipulated by your sales force. In the automobile business, for example, the percentage of those who are satisfied or very satisfied is often about 90 percent. The repurchase rate (of the same make) is around 35 percent. How satisfied really are these customers if they do not buy the same make when their current car is turned in? Lifetime value is a solid, testable number. You can use the database to prove whether your numbers are valid or not.

Because of this, Robin should be cautious in providing spreadsheets to management. If I were her, I would prepare the sheets, but then discount them before she makes them public. If she is sure that her retention rate will be 50 percent, she should put 48 percent on the chart. If she is sure that the spending rate will be $180, she should say it would be $176. Always under-promise and over-deliver. That way, next year, she will come off as a heroine when her actual performance beats her projection.

Keeping Management Informed

Now that you know how to compute lifetime value, you should create meaningful customer segments, compute the lifetime value for each of them, and then append lifetime value to every record in your database. You should let top management know what the overall retention rate is for your customers as a whole, and for each segment. Let the CEO know what the LTV and retention rates are on a monthly basis. These numbers are more important to the company than the stock value or any of the other measures that are currently on the CEO's desk. You and you alone can produce such numbers. It will make you an information power-house within the company.

Summary

1. More and more marketers today are computing the lifetime value of their customers as a basis for their marketing programs and strategic planning.

2. NPV is a way of determining the value today of money that you will receive or expend at some dates in the future. It discounts future money by the assumed market rate of interest plus risk. The formula is $NPV = Amount/D$. $D = (1 + i)^n$ where i is the interest rate plus risk, and n is the number of years.

3. Customer lifetime value must be recalculated from month to month, because conditions are always changing: competitors come up with new initiatives, products become obsolete, some customers improve their LTV, and the market becomes saturated. The marketplace is always filled with uncertainty and lack of information. There are no eternal truths.

4. The retention rate is a measure of how many of last year's customers are still buying from you this year. It varies with things you cannot change like type of product, competitor's strength, public perception, and macroeconomic trends. There are many things you can do to affect your retention rate: type of promotions, pricing, renewal efforts, and relationship building.

5. The computation period defines how far out you must go to define the lifetime customer value. It varies by industry. The longer the period, the greater the lifetime value.

6. Calculate lifetime value for different customer segments. Lifetime value may be different for different types of customers. You should think this through before you lump all customers together.

7. For lifetime value purposes, you need to estimate your variable costs. The easiest method is to compute them as a percent of revenue. The amount depends on your industry. Variable costs (for this purpose) include everything except marketing and database costs and fixed costs.

8. Cumulative NPV profit. To compute lifetime value for a given group of customers, add together the net profit from prior years to the net profit from the current year. This gives you the cumulative profit up to that year. This number is divided by the original number of customers.

9. Good will. Customers are assets, the same as buildings or cash. Another name for lifetime value is good will. LTV is a way of measuring the value of your customers.

10. Marketing. Customer lifetime value calculations will also help to determine how much effort to put into acquisition, referral programs, and reactivation programs.

11. Customer lifetime value also helps to determine the cost and the value of database marketing relationship building efforts.

12. New strategies, such as gold cards, president's clubs, newsletters, can and should be tested by measuring lifetime value before and afterwards. If your calculations do not show an increase in future years, drop or modify your strategy before it is too late.

Technical Appendix

Computing the Retention Rate for Infrequent Purchasers

Background. The retention rate is the most important single number in a lifetime value table. It is typically calculated on an annual basis. A 60 percent retention rate means that of 10,000 customers acquired in the acquisition year, there will be only 6,000 of these particular customers still remaining as active customers in Year 2. This is easy to compute for cellular phones or credit cards. But what is the annual retention rate if

50 percent of the customers buy the same make of automobile after four years? Here a formula is necessary. The formula is

$$RR = (RPR)^{(1/Y)}$$

where RR is the annual retention rate, RPR, the repurchase rate, and Y is the number of years between purchases. Here are several examples of the use of the formula.

1. *Automobile purchase by one segment:* A segment of Buick owners buys a new car every four years. About 35 percent of them buy a Buick, and the balance buys some other make of car. What is their annual retention rate?

$$RR = (RPR)^{(1/Y)}$$

$$RR = (0.35)^{(1/4)}$$

$$RR = 76.9 \text{ percent}$$

2. *Automobile purchase by several segments:* Buick owners can be divided into four segments: those who buy a new car every one year, two years, three years, and four years. Their respective repurchase rates are given in Figure 3-8.

This chart provides some interesting information. The repurchase rate of those who buy a Buick every year seems much higher than that for those who wait four years between automobile purchases. Their annual retention rate, however, is far lower. That is because those who wait four years to buy are still driving their Buick for four years. You can sell them tune-ups and spare parts.

3. *Restaurant patrons by week:* A businessman's restaurant had a regular clientele of patrons who ate there almost every day. They decided to try database marketing. They set up a system to gather the names of their customers, and gave points for each meal. They discovered that

Segment	Years Between Purchase	Repurchase Rate	Annual Retention
A	1	55.00%	55.00%
B	2	45.00%	67.08%
C	3	40.00%	73.68%
D	4	35.00%	76.92%
Total			68.17%

Figure 3-8. Repurchase rate and retention rate.

they were losing about 1 percent of their clients every week. What was their annual retention rate? The formula is the same:

$$RR = (RPR)^{(1/Y)}$$

In this case, the repurchase rate is 99 percent, and the period involved is 1/52 of a year. So the formula becomes

$$RR = (0.99)^{(1/(1/52))}$$

$$RR = 59.3 \text{ percent}$$

This tells us that the restaurant's annual customer retention rate was 59.3 percent.

Including Payment Delays in the Discount Rate

Payment delays are typical in business to business, where the customer often pays in 30, 60, 90, or even 180 days. The complete formula for the discount rate, including payment delays is

$$D = (1 + (i \times \text{rf}))^{n + \text{pd}}$$

where i is the market rate of interest; rf, the risk factor (rf = 1 means that there is no risk factor); n, number of years to wait for payment; and pd is the fraction of a year delay in customer payment. If the market rate of interest is 7 percent and the risk factor is 1.5, and the number of years to wait is 3 and customers typically pay in 90 days, the formula becomes

$$D = (1 + (0.07 \times 1.5))^{2.25}$$

$$D = 1.25$$

Executive Quiz 3

Answers to quiz questions (Figures 3-9 and 3-10) can be found in Appendix B .

Put the appropriate value in each box.

Customers	Sample LVT Table Acquisition Year	Year2	
Referral Rate	3.00%	4.00%	
Referred Customers	0		a
Retention Rate	50.00%	60.00%	
Retained Customers	0		b
Total Customers	16,988	9,514	
Spending Rate	$200.00	$220.00	
Total Customer Revenue	$3,397,600		c
Expenses			
Variable Cost Percentage	60.00%	55.00%	
Variable Costs	$2,038,560		d
Acquisition Cost $40	$679,520	na	
New Strategy $15	$254,820		e
Referral Incentive $20	0		f
Total Costs	$2,972,900	$1,304,097	
Profits			
Gross Profit	$424,700	$788,983	
Discount Rate	1.00	1.20	
NPV Profit	$424,700		g
Cum NPV Profit	$424,700		h
Lifetime Value	$25.00		I

Figure 3-9. Quiz 3-1.

Put the appropriate letter before each answer

	Questions	Answers
a	NPV of $4,000 in 3 years. int = 8%, rf = 1	53%
b	Int = 14% Wait 4 years for money. Disc. Rate=	73.91%
c	Why include risk in the discount rate?	1.69
d	Retention Rate = Customers this year /	$6.10
e	2000 customers last year. 1060 today. RR=?	$3,175.33
f	Disc. Rate 1.8 Revenue $142,846 NPV=?	$79,359
g	80,000 cust yr 1. Cum NPV yr 4 = $488,219 LTV=?	Customers last year
h	Cust buy cars every 3 years. RPR = 40%. Annual RR=?	Obsolescence of product

Figure 3-10. Quiz 3-2.

4

Designing a Successful
Customer Strategy

*The greatest obstacle to growth is not ignorance, but the
illusion of knowledge. The illusion of knowledge exists
because large amounts of data provide security. The
reality, though, is that the data is never looked at or
used. Why? Because most times there is no technology
in place what can do anything meaningful with the
data or find the patterns in the data that will energize
it and make it come alive to answer our questions.
Data alone is not enough. This suggests strongly that
we need to change the way we think about and look at
information.*

*By thinking of database-marketing in broader terms,
you can integrate into your business decision-making
based on new technology that finds the patterns in
your information, that gives you, with laser-beam precision, a complete understanding of where you are in
your marketplace, what your prioritized opportunities
are, why they are best for you and how and who to target for maximum return. And maybe most importantly,
you get the ability to answer those questions now!*

ROBERT POSTEN

The Landis Group

Finding Profitable Customers

The ideal customer is one who is highly profitable, and stays with us for a lifetime. The best marketing strategy is to attract such customers and to keep them loyal. In the real world, such customers are hard to find. We make our success by managing the customers we have, using marketing strategies that help to nudge them into behavior that is satisfying for the customer and profitable for us.

There are really two behaviors that we can influence here: profitability and loyalty. They are not the same.

- Some customers are highly profitable, but disappear after a single purchase. One example is new homebuyers. No matter how satisfied these buyers may be, it is almost impossible to maintain a profitable long-term relationship with these customers so that we can sell them their next home, 10 or 15 years later when they retire, get promoted or have another child.

- Some customers are only mildly profitable, but they are very loyal. They continue to stay with us for years and years. Banks and utilities have thousands of such customers. Many of these customers will never be very profitable, but they can be very loyal.

In between these two extremes are the vast majority of customers who exhibit behavior that can be modified by conscious database marketing strategies. Some are profitable, and some are very unprofitable. Some are loyal, and some are very disloyal. The combined measure of both characteristics is customer lifetime value, which we explained in the last chapter. In this chapter, we will discuss strategies and tactics for managing customer behavior to improve lifetime value. Let us begin with profitability.

Measuring Profitability

Profitability usually measures activities in the recent past, whereas loyalty measures future long-term activity. Profitability is measured by adding up recent receipts from a specific customer and subtracting the costs incurred by this customer in the corresponding period. We measure profitability by saying, "Did we make money on this customer last month? Or last year?" In Chapter 15, we cover in some detail how banks measure profitability. Insurance, transportation, utility and telecommunication companies can do the same thing. Most other companies, however, cannot do profitability analysis on a customer-by-customer basis because of the difficulty of allocating costs to each customer. How can Sears Roebuck, or General Motors, or Dow Chemical allocate their costs back to each customer? They cannot. For the vast majority of customers, therefore, companies have to use net revenue, balanced off against a rough cost percentage as a measure of profitability. That is ok, however, and works just fine.

When they do this, however, they discover something very interesting. Most companies break their customers down into five groups, based on profitability or net revenue. The top group—the Gold customers—usually produces 80 percent or more of their profits or net revenue. The bottom group—the losers—often produces zero profitability or a net loss. Here is a typical layout, which we first saw in Chapter 1. The number of customers in each group does not have to be equal to the other groups. Typically, the number in the top group is quite small—sometimes as small as 5 percent or 6 percent. The number in the bottom group can be 35 percent or higher. You will have to decide how to make the divisions based on lifetime value, revenue, or some other measure (Figure 4-1).

My experience with American Airlines serves to illustrate this chart. I do a lot of traveling making speeches. When I started out I had never made Gold status on an airline. So, I picked American Airlines to get Gold status. To achieve Gold on American you have to fly 25,000 miles in a calendar year. January 1, the clock starts all over again and you lose the Gold qualifying miles you had the year before. That year, I flew everywhere on American. I went several times to Orlando via Miami, for example. It is the wrong way to go and takes much longer but you get more miles that way. On Christmas day I called American Airlines to see how many miles I had.

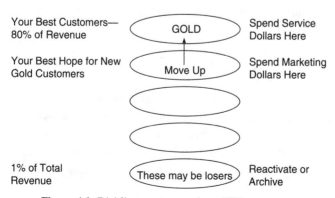

Figure 4-1. Dividing customers into LTV segments.

"Mr. Hughes, you have 24,600 miles."

"I'm so close! You are going to give me the Gold, aren't you?"

"No, Mr. Hughes. You have to have 25,000 miles."

"But I have only a few days left. Can I pay you for the 400 miles?"

"No, Mr. Hughes. You have to fly them."

So, the day after Christmas, I went to American Airlines, and for $44 I bought a round trip ticket to Raleigh Durham because it was close and inexpensive. At 7:00 a.m. I flew down there. At 9:00 a.m. I flew back. I was in my office in Reston, VA by 11:00 a.m. Since then I have been Gold, or higher.

What did it mean to me to be Gold? I got to fly first class without having to pay very much for it. I got to go on the plane first, with the little children and the old people. I got GOLD printed on my boarding passes. I was given 25 percent bonus miles every time I flew. I got a special toll free number to call for customer service. This number was just for the Gold people. And, finally, I felt Gold. I had worked hard for that status, and I enjoyed it. I felt that I deserved it. American found ways to provide little services for me that had me completely dedicated. They provided status levels that I could work towards. A couple of years later, I achieved Platinum Status and finally I became a Platinum Executive, with 100,000 miles on American in one calendar year. With each upgrade in status came special additional services. I loved it.

What did American get out of it? They had Arthur Hughes hooked. I flew all of my discretionary flights on American. We took vacations in Chile and Germany on American. I asked the promoters of my speeches in Brazil, Tokyo, Australia, and London to let me fly American. I flew American with stopovers in Dallas or Chicago, taking a couple of extra hours in the process, when I could have taken shorter direct flights on other airlines. I dreamed about the miles. Without my fixation on airline status, I would probably have flown half as many miles on American as I actually did.

Gold Customers

Every business has gold customers. Most companies have not identified them. This is a pity. These customers are the backbone of any business. You absolutely must maintain this group if the company is going to be a success. Many marketers who have identified their Gold customers think that they should single them out for special marketing promotions. This is probably a mistake.

Gold customers are often maxed out. The reason that they are gold is that they are probably giving you all of their business in your category. That was certainly true of me with American Airlines. I could not possibly have flown more with them, no matter what offers they might have made. What should you do for Gold customers? Find ways to reward them, to let them know that they are important to you. Provide services to them. Make it so attractive for them that they would not think of switching.

Fleet bank did an analysis of their customers, and divided them into segments similar to the chart above. They discovered that it was almost impossible to profitably cross-sell their Gold customers. Most new sales to this group cannibalized profitable existing business. They decided that their marketing efforts to their best customers should be restricted to retention building programs.

Take heed of Fleet Bank's findings. In most cases, do not market to your Gold customers. Provide special services for them.

Marketing to Those just below Gold

This is where your marketing dollars should be concentrated. These are the people with 24,600 miles. You should let them know that they are on the verge of qualifying for Gold status. Just buy a few more times, and they will be up in Gold Heaven, getting all the rewards that come with that status.

The three middle segments are where your marketing programs can do the most good (Figure 4-2).

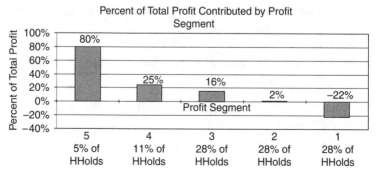

Figure 4-2. Household profitability segments.

This chart was developed by a bank in the southeast. It shows the profitability of their retail customer households. The chart shows that 105 percent of their profits came from the top two groups, representing only 16 percent of their customers. The bottom 28 percent represented a loss of 22 percent of their profits. Their marketing goal, as a result, was to increase their profits from the middle three quintiles, and to re-price the services rendered to the bottom quintile.

They discovered, like Fleet, that marketing to the Gold customers was an unproductive exercise. Fleet found that:

- Nearly half of their customers were unprofitable. The bottom 20 percent were very unprofitable. Half of the customers currently being acquired would never be profitable.

- However, there was considerable profit potential among many of their low-profit customers. Fleet could gain an increased share of wallet from some of them. Others could be converted to other products that were more profitable for the bank, and more satisfying for the customers.

Dealing with the Losers

What can you do with the bottom segment—the group that, in most industries not only does not pay their way, but also robs you of your profit?

The first step is knowledge of what is going on. Few companies today have that knowledge. You can gain the knowledge only by building a customer database, which includes purchase history, and grouping customers into revenue segments. Next you determine the lifetime value of each segment using the methods found in the previous chapter.

Once you have isolated and identified the profit losers, what can you do about them? You need analysis and strategy.

The analysis will help you separate those who are unprofitable for temporary reasons from those who are going to be permanently unprofitable. What are the temporary reasons?

- Some losing customers may actually be doing a lot of business with your competitors. You have a small share of their wallet in your category. If you can learn this fact, then your goal is to find those hot buttons, which will shift their business to you. The money is there. You just have to get it redirected. Do not give up.

- Others are losers because they are just starting out in life and currently have a small income. The business customers may consist of small but growing companies that will soon be able to buy much more from you. Find this out, and develop a long-term strategy to wait until they are profitable, but avoid losing much money while you wait.

- Still others may be losers because they are buying the wrong products. You may be able to change their price plan, or product mix in a way that will make them happier, and improve your profits.

- The final group contains the true losers. These may be transaction buyers who only buy from you when you are on sale. They may be people with bad credit, or those who have excessive claims or returns. What can you do about these people? One strategy is to give them your competitor's 800 number. You might even call your competitor and say, "We are really swamped with work here. Can you handle some of our overflow?" They will take your customers and thank you for it.

Your employees can be very helpful in solving the loser problem. Once you have identified your profit quintiles, let your employees know who the Gold customers are, and also the profit quintile of the other customers. Let your employees help by providing super services to the Gold customers, and by re-pricing the services given to the losers.

For example, if losers tie up your customer service lines, or waste time in branch visits, offer them a reduction in price if they buy through the Internet, or use an ATM.

Choosing a Marketing Strategy

All marketing involves some strategy, even if it is as simple as providing quality merchandise at low prices in a convenient location. For many years TROY-BILT had the strategy of coming out with a new model Roto-Tiller each year, concentrating on a better and better product with more and more features. The strategy failed. The company went on the rocks in the late 1950s. In 1962, the new managers developed a different strategy: focused on what the customer could do with the product, reaching him directly. The new strategy, based on database marketing, turned the company around.

How can you decide what is the best marketing strategy for your product? There is no single answer that has universal validity. For some products, mass marketing through retail stores is the best possible strategy. For some business-to-business products, a Web site that lets customers rummage through the inventory and warehouses beats all other methods.

There are thousands of situations where database marketing—relationship building—in conjunction with other methods, is the most profitable solution. If you have such a product or service, you must devise an effective method of using your database to build profits. This chapter contains guidance on the development of this strategy.

To develop a workable strategy, each marketer must come up with clever ideas, using, among other things, the hundreds of ideas being tested by others. Each clever idea should be examined to determine to what extent it would modify customer behavior to improve lifetime value.

Strategy Development Steps

The steps in strategy development are these:

- Group your customers into profitability, demographic or behavioral segments (see Chapter 8).
- Determine the lifetime value of each segment.
- For each segment, determine whether you can modify their behavior to make them more profitable or to increase their retention rate.
- Put yourself in the shoes of the members of the segments whose behavior you want to change. Think like a customer saying: "What would I want to receive in the way of information, communications, rewards or services from this company? What could I get from them that would make me spend more money, or be more loyal?"
- From the answers to these questions, develop a list of possible services, benefits, rewards, premiums, or relationships that you could develop with the customers in the segment that the customers would value, and which would nudge them towards greater lifetime value.
- Imagine that you have implemented these new strategies. Visualize how the strategies would affect the customer's spending habits, retention habits, or referrals. Put those changed behaviors *and their costs* into a lifetime value table. See whether lifetime value goes up or down. Play with the benefits until you have maximized lifetime value.

■ Run little tests to make sure that you are right: that the rewards and relationships really do change customer spending and retention. Make sure that you test before you do a rollout.

Designing a Strategy

Let us apply these principles to the marketing of American magazines. The magazine business in America exploded in the last decade. Hundreds of new magazines appeared.

Each magazine had almost the same problem: high cost of renewals and low retention rates. Most of them were in a discount trap. They offered substantial discounts to new subscribers, and then attempted to get them to renew at the higher (regular) rate. Most subscribers were too smart for that. They realized that they could let their subscription lapse, and then renew at the discounted new-subscriber rate. Magazines spent considerable sums on mailings before and after the subscription expired offering more and more frantic "your last chance!" appeals to renew.

Meanwhile, some magazines, for example those sponsored by American Express, were having a much easier time of it. They billed their subscribers one time per year on their American Express card. To avoid renewing automatically, subscribers had to contact the magazine in advance, or when they saw the renewal on their American Express monthly bill. Most people did not bother, and let the renewal stand. Result: renewal costs and hassles were almost eliminated, and the retention rates were way up. Outside of American Express, however, most magazines used the old-fashioned system, asking subscribers to send in a check or call a toll free number with their credit card to renew.

How profitable would it be for a magazine to shift to the negative option system, letting readers pay with an American Express, Master, Visa or other credit card? Let us look at a typical magazine, and analyze their lifetime value before and after adopting this and some other strategic database marketing strategies.

To begin with, let us create a lifetime value table for a typical magazine (Figure 4-3).

We have 100,000 subscribers acquired from a variety of sources at a heavy discount from the regular price of $39.95 per year. Subscriptions represent about a quarter of the magazine's regular revenue, with advertisers making up 75 percent. In addition, most magazines derive revenue

	Acquisition Year	Second Year	Third Year
Subscribers	100,000	30,000	12,000
Retention Rate	30.00%	40.00%	50.00%
Price Paid	$19.95	$39.95	$39.95
Advertising (3XRate)	$120	$120	$120
Name Rental & Misc.	$20	$22	$24
Total Revenue	$15,995,000	$5,458,500	$2,207,400
Cost Percentage	70.00%	69.00%	68.00%
Direct Costs	$11,196,500	$3,766,365	$1,501,032
Acquisition Cost $40	$4,000,000	$0	$0
Renewal Costs $8	$0	$800,000	$240,000
Total Costs	$15,196,500	$4,566,365	$1,741,032
Profit	$798,500	$892,135	$466,368
Discount Rate	1.00	1.16	1.35
NPV Profit	$798,500	$769,082	$345,458
Cum. NVP Profit	$798,500	$1,567,582	$1,913,040
Lifetime Value	$7.99	$15.68	$19.13

Figure 4-3. Magazine subscriber lifetime value.

from renting the names of subscribers to other businesses. The renewal rate is about 30 percent, at a cost of about $8 per renewal, including a series of letters and, in some cases, frantic phone calls.

The resulting lifetime value is very low in the first year, rising to about $19 in the third year.

New Strategies

Let us apply some of the ideas developed in this book, many of which are practiced by advanced magazine marketers.

The Web site. We will create a Web site for the magazine which

- Has a personalized page for each subscriber, using her name
- Takes credit cards and new subscriptions
- Sells additional related and unrelated products

- Provides access to all the archives of back issues of the magazine going back for several years

- Partners with other magazines owned by the chain, selling subscriptions to these magazines as well

- Partners with advertisers to the magazine, linking to their Web sites and featuring their products

To do it right, the magazine assigns a unique PIN number to each subscriber, printed as a part of the label affixed to each copy of her magazine. We post the Web site name (URL) all over the magazine: on the cover and at least once on every page. We provide incentives for the reader to go to the Web site. After every magazine article, we tell the reader that there is more information about the article or the author available on the Web site. This will drive some readers to visit the Web site.

When the reader logs on to the Web site, using her PIN number, she sees a page that says:

Welcome Susan! If you're not Susan, click here.

Once she has logged on, we will use Cookies to identify her in the future. Cookies are better than a PIN, because they are more like the Old Corner Grocer. He did not ask the customers for their PINs when they came into his store. He knew them by sight.

The Web site home page is designed for Susan with the results of any survey and preference information that she filled out in the past. It contains a new survey for her to complete in case she has not already filled one out. She will receive something free (provided by an advertiser) if she completes the survey. The page will have the features that Susan wants.

Her page becomes the entrée to a whole new Web magazine, created especially for Susan. For each article in the regular magazine, there is a brief bio of the author with a picture. There is material that was left out of the article because of space limitations. There are few space limitations on the Web. There is a search button to look for similar subjects covered by the magazine in the past. There are things for Susan to do, and to buy.

How expensive is it to create such personal pages? It is not expensive at all. Once you have a Web site, programmers can quickly add the software that creates personalized pages based on subscribers' preferences on Web survey forms. If Susan never looks at her Web site (which will be the case in a high percentage of the magazine readers), there is nothing lost. Susan's page was a couple of lines of computer code that were created automatically when she subscribed. Susan's page never actually exists until she logs on to it for the first time. Even then, it disappears into cyberspace when she logs off, with the results of her visit stored in her database record. Her database data becomes more and more valuable and sophisticated, the more she uses the magazine's Web site.

Negative Option Renewal. When Susan's subscription was taken in the first place, the agent took her credit card number. She was told that the renewal cost would be billed automatically to the credit card when due, unless she notifies the magazine by phone or through the Web site in advance (or right afterwards). Experience in other magazines shows that when presented in the right way, this negative option system was accepted by between 70 percent (American Express) and 69 percent (Toronto Globe and Mail) on the first telephone call.

The significance of this initiative is that the renewal process and problem almost completely disappears. No more threatening or plaintive letters "This is your last chance, Arthur Hughes!" Furthermore, the renewal rate in many cases zooms from 30 percent or lower to 60 percent or higher. The system really works.

Referral System. We will set up an organized referral system on Susan's page on the Web. We use viral marketing to help Susan to nominate other people as subscribers to the magazine. There is a simple Web form for her to fill out. We can send Susan's friend a letter, or, if Susan provides an e-mail, we can send an e-mail to the person (shown to Susan in advance on the Web site so she can edit it) saying:

> "Susan Webber suggested that you would be interested in reading Arizona Highways. As a result, we would be delighted to send you a free trial copy. If you are interested, <u>click here</u>. We hope that you will try our great magazine, but even if you don't, Susan says Hi!"

If Susan's friend signs up, we will give Susan a $15 gift. Perhaps we should be even more generous to Susan. After all, new subscribers are costing us $40 each. Referred subscribers have a higher retention rate, spending rate, and referral rate than the average new subscriber, so they are worth more.

Why do we encourage Susan to edit the letter? This will make Susan happy and may make the letter much more powerful. Susan may take the opportunity to add some personal greeting which may make all the difference.

Additional Products. We will go all out to sell Susan some new products associated with the magazine. What could they be? Let us provide a list:

- Books related to the subject of the magazine
- Subscriptions to publications from the same chain
- Related products: health magazines sell vitamin pills, sports magazines sell sports clothes, travel magazines sell cruises, etc.
- Emblems of the magazine: hats, scarfs, pins, tee shirts, etc. with the magazine's logo on them.

Why is it so important to sell Susan these additional products? Because we know, from prior experience, that the subscriber's retention rate is a direct function of their participation in the content of the magazine. The more products they buy related to the magazine, the more likely they are to remain as committed subscribers. It does not matter if we make a lot of money, or very little from these extra products. They will help us achieve our overall objective of building the retention rate, and therefore making the magazine a success.

Personal Communications. We will send Susan an e-mail or direct mail birthday card on her birthday. In addition, we may send her a Thanksgiving Day card, or a Christmas card or Valentines Day card. Most important, we will send her a simple thank you after the annual renewal. Not a pitch for more money, or anything commercial. Just a simple letter on company stationary signed by the Publisher or Editor which says:

> "I want to thank you for renewing your subscription to Better Homes & Gardens. You have been a loyal subscriber since 1994. I want you to know that we really appreciate having you as a reader. It is good people like you that make our magazine a success. Thank you, Susan."

Discounts Abolished. We are going to abolish subscription discounts as a policy. If you want Architectural Digest, you will pay full price, or you cannot get it at all. "Won't that kill our acquisition program?" you might well ask. Answer: Of course, it will ruin any program that is based on discounts. But let us see what is wrong with discounts as an inducement for subscribers.

- *Discounts bring in the wrong kind of subscribers.* Some people are interested in buying magazines cheap. Some people want the magazines to read them, and possibly, to see what is advertised in them. The first kind of people will not stay with us. The second kind, if they like the magazine, will stay for a long time.

- *Discounts send the wrong message.* We want readers to concentrate on the value of the magazine to their lives, not to their wallets. We do not want them to begin comparing magazines based on price, but based on content.

- *Discounts cost a lot of money.* Millions of dollars are wasted in attracting and signing up the wrong kind of people. Good, serious readers subsidize temporary, disloyal readers. This is wrong.

If we end the discount policy, subscriptions will decline at first. We will have to change our whole approach to acquisition to stress the value of the magazine, the Web relationships, and additional benefits and bonuses, which come with subscriptions. There is, for example, nothing wrong with premiums for subscribers. A premium does not discount the value of the magazine. It is something extra. Also, we can give premiums to subscribers who adopt negative option. But, we will never offer discounts.

Effect of the New Strategies

Here we are looking at the same 100,000 subscribers, but assuming that the new strategies have been applied to them (Figure 4-4). A number of significant benefits have come from these strategies. In the first place, the renewal rate has gone up from 30 percent to 60 percent. A dramatic gain of this sort is often the result of shifting to a negative option. The Toronto Globe and Mail went from 12 percent to 69 percent renewals with negative option. American Express had even higher rates.

Since we have abolished discounts, the price paid is the standard price, not a discounted price. This will save us $20 per subscriber, or $2 million. We can spend the extra money on premiums for subscribers. Most of the premiums, however, are paid by advertisers through a partnership program.

Our cost of acquisition has gone up from $40 to $50. Why? Because without discounts getting 100,000 subscribers is more difficult. We have to be very creative in our messages to surmount the difficulty of not buying the subscribers' votes.

We have added a referral program that will bring in 3,000 new subscribers in Year 2. These referred people will have a higher renewal rate

Magazines With Strategy	Acquisition Year	Second Year	Third Year
Referral Rate	3%	3%	3%
Referrals	0	3,000	1,890
Subscribers	100,000	63,000	42,840
Retention Rate	60.00%	65.00%	70.00%
Price Paid	$39.95	$39.95	$39.95
Advertising (3XRate)	$120	$120	$120
Name Rental & Misc.	$20	$22	$24
Product Sales	$12	$14	$16
Total Revenue	$19,195,000	$12,344,850	$8,565,858
Cost Percentage	70.00%	69.00%	68.00%
Direct Costs	$13,436,500	$8,517,947	$5,824,783
Acquisition Cost $50	$5,000,000	$0	$0
Renewal Costs $0	$0	$0	$0
Credit Card Costs 3%	$119,850	$75,506	$51,344
Web Site Costs $4	$400,000	$189,000	$128,520
Relationship Comm. $3	$300,000	$315,000	$214,200
Referral Incentives $15	$0	$45,000	$28,350
Total Costs	$19,256,350	$9,142,452	$6,247,197
Profit	($61,350)	$3,202,398	$2,318,661
Discount Rate	1.00	1.16	1.35
NPV Profit	($61,350)	$2,760,688	$1,717,527
Cum. NVP Profit	($61,350)	$2,699,338	$4,416,864
Lifetime Value	($0.61)	$26.99	$44.17

Figure 4-4. Lifetime value with new strategies.

than the average new subscriber. How do we know that? We can keep track of them, and we can prove it in subsequent years. We will incentivize our referrers an average of $15 each.

We have sold some new products to subscribers. These new products, as already noted, are not as valuable as revenue earners, as they are in building the renewal rate. Every new product sold binds the average reader to the magazine more.

Many of these new benefits are balanced by new expenses. The Web site is not free. Credit card processing costs have to be accounted for. Referrals have to be paid for. The relationship building cards and messages cost money. When we get finished, lifetime value in the first year has gone down. But look at what has happened to lifetime value in future years (Figure 4-5).

The total impact of the changes we have suggested will be to increase customer lifetime value by more than $2.5 million in the third year. This is $2.5 million pure profit. All the costs have been subtracted including the loss in the acquisition year. If we had been doing direct mail alone, the loss of $860,000 in the first year would have ruled out such a program.

Magazines With Strategy	Acquisition Year	Second Year	Third Year
New LTV	($0.61)	$26.99	$44.17
Old LTV	$7.99	$15.68	$19.13
Difference	($8.60)	$11.32	$25.04
With 100,000 Subs.	($859,850)	$1,131,756	$2,503,825

Figure 4-5. Gains from the new strategies.

Since we are doing database marketing, we can look two years ahead and see the value of this program.

What to Do with the Charts

Once you have thought up your great new strategies and developed life-time value charts that cost them out, you have several additional steps.

■ Try adding some customer benefits (and associated costs) and see if LTV goes up or down. Maybe there is more you can do.

■ By testing, see if you can eliminate some customer benefits (and costs) and still keep LTV up. We are trying to build profitable relationships here. But keep the word profitable in mind. That is the point of the relationship building process.

■ When you have developed a benefit (and cost) package that you think is a winner, then discount your resulting LTV growth estimates by a percentage. Things seldom work out as well in practice as they do in a test or in your planning process.

■ Use these charts as a basis for getting your marketing budget approved. Explain the retention and referral rates to management. Explain the basis of the numbers. Show that with the budget you have requested you will generate $2.5 million in increased profits in the third year.

Strategy Based on Cross Sales Predictions

A major magazine company published over a dozen magazines in several major categories.

The publisher had been conducting cross-sell campaigns for many years, but had failed to maximize their opportunities for a number of reasons:

- Selections were done for each mailing from the individual magazine lists.

- Information on multiple subscriptions was not used.

- Lapsed subscribers were rarely given a chance to try a magazine other than the one to which they originally subscribed.

- Outside data such as demographics and behaviors were appended to their subscriber database, but were not used—this is an old story in database marketing.

To solve these problems, the publisher asked KnowledgeBase Marketing to develop a suite of cross-sell models to identify the individuals most likely to respond to each campaign. The data for the cross sale models came from multiple sources. Over 400 potential predictors were created.

For each magazine published, the objective was to select the best individuals from the database for promotion. For each magazine they found different variables in those factors determining customer behavior. For example:

Home Magazine A: Key variables:
Interest in Home Decorating
# Magazines Ever Active
# of Prior Orders for Magazine A
$ in Food Magazine B
Age
Interest in Crafts/Garden

Fashion Magazine C: Key variables:
Women's Magazines Ever Active
Orders in Latest Year
Months since Latest Order
Income
Age
Urban Single ZIP Codes

Before this information was available, cross sales were based on the "offer of the month." With this data, the publisher identified those customers most likely to respond to each particular cross-sell promotion, and which offer to make to each customer. They began to think, "What will appeal to Lydia McCabe?" instead of, "How can we sell more subscriptions to House and Garden?" Using that information the publisher was able to make more cross sale promotions and to increase the response rates to the promotions by a significant amount.

The Importance of a Relational Database

To do database marketing properly, you want to collect data on your customers, and use that data to measure their lifetime value and to communicate with them. The messages can be personalized because you have stored information properly so that the database can enable you to have meaningful dialog with hundreds of thousands of customers, just as the old time corner grocers had with their individual customers.

Database marketing today is usually based on relational databases maintained on servers (or in the case of very small databases, on PCs). A relational database consists of fields, tables, and records.

A *field* is the smallest structure (the atom) of the relational database. Examples are: A last name, a date, a dollar amount, a product number. There may be a hundred fields in a database. Properly designed fields have only one value: Wrong: Arthur Hughes. Right: two fields 1) First Name 2) Last Name. They should not contain data that changes or calculated values: Wrong: Age. Right: Date of Birth.

Fields are grouped into *Tables*. A Table is the chief structure in a relational database. A table always represents a single specific subject which can be either an *object* or an *event*. Object Example: Customers. Event Example: Orders.

Keys are special fields used to uniquely identify a record within a table. Every table contains a primary key field and may have one or more foreign key fields. A primary key field for the Customers table would be the Customer Number. A foreign key field for the same table would be an Order Number field (which is the primary key in the Orders table). Other fields in the Customer Table could be data fields, such as name, street, city, state, zip, etc.

Records are the structures in a table that represent unique instances of the subject of the table. An example is Arthur Hughes, one of the records in the Customers table. A purchase that Arthur Hughes made on August 12th could be an example of a record in the Orders Table.

Relationships are connections established between pairs of tables (Figure 4-6).

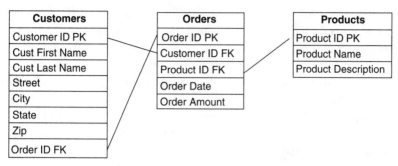

Figure 4-6. Tables, fields and keys in a relational database.

PK = Primary Key for that table. FK = Foreign Key (the Primary Key of another table)

Why Should You Care?

Why is this technical detail important to database marketers? Because, in many cases today, their databases are not designed properly. They are old-fashioned mainframe flat files. The update process is slow. Adding or changing data in a flat file is a difficult process. What are the advantages of a relational format to a marketer? A modern relational database:

- Is easy to update—either in real time, or in periodic batches
- Permits ad hoc drill down queries and reports
- Allows you to store an unlimited amount of data about any customer
- Permits you to add fields without redoing the whole database
- Makes it easy to modify the data and to retrieve information
- Makes it easy to develop and carry out personalized customer communications
- Permits the inclusion of business rules in the database design

Because many marketers do not know how relational databases are constructed, they tend to be dominated by IT professionals who tell them what can and cannot be done. IT professionals explain how difficult it is for them to do whatever the marketers want done. To be an effective database marketer today, therefore, marketers must learn some of the basics described above so they can understand what IT is saying, and get out from under their thumbs. They must look at the tables set up by their IT design team to be sure that they are well constructed to carry out their marketing programs.

Business Rules are central to marketing use of a relational database. They are built into a relational database structure. Business rules can dictate not only the correctness of data stored in records (dates in correct format, product ID's are correct, zip codes consistent with city and state, for example), but they can also permit marketers to create event driven communications. What are these?

- Letters sent to customers on their birthday
- Thank you messages sent for orders
- Automatic responses to customer surveys (stored in the database) when the response indicates that the customer is bothered by something

A *view* is really a virtual table. It usually contains data from many tables arranged like a report or a screen shot. Typically, you may want your customer service people to see a view of each customer while they are talking to them on the phone. The view includes not only the customer's name and address, but their most recent purchases, their total purchases, and, probably, their complaints or preferences. For you, as a marketer, the view is probably the most useful part of the database. The view can contain calculated values. Date of Birth is converted into age in a typical view. Total number of orders and dollars purchased in the past 12 months is another useful field to show in a view. Views make the database come alive for you, for customer service, and for management. Screen views are often called dashboards.

Access to Your Customer Information

Once you have a relational database set up, how do you use it for marketing? In most modern applications, you use access software like E.piphany or Hyperion (there are many others) that enable you to work with your database over the Web. You will use a "Thin Client" application. Thin Client means that your users will have only a browser on their PCs. All the data access and processing will be done on a server at your data center. You may have a half a dozen marketers each of which needs only Web access and a (free) browser to look simultaneously at your customer database and:

- Do counts, selects, drill downs, downloads
- Plan and carry out marketing campaigns
- Do back end analysis of any campaign
- Determine customer lifetime value
- Create customer communications programs
- Do graphs and charts for management that tells them what is happening

When you log on to this software, you will see on your screen the tables in your relational database. You can pick out any fields of interest to you and create queries that result in reports or customer segments. The results should be ready in a few minutes. If you do not like what you see as a result of a query, you can redo it. You will have the power to get information out of your customer database, and create action programs that communicate with your customers and get them to buy more, visit your retailers more often, and be more loyal.

Summary

- Profitability and loyalty are different customer attributes. They can come together in lifetime value.
- Banks and insurance companies can measure customer's profitability exactly. Most companies cannot. They have to estimate costs.
- Gold customers are very valuable. Efforts should concentrate on retaining them, not marketing to them.
- Concentrating on the losers can have a big impact on the bottom line. Re-price their services, move them up, or get rid of them.
- Magazines can boost lifetime value using Web pages, negative option renewals, referrals, sale of secondary products, personal communications, elimination of discounts and advertiser premiums.
- LTV charts can be used to sell management, but only if they have been discounted first.
- Put your data on a relational database format.
- Provide access to it with web based thin client analytical software.

Executive Quiz 4

Answers to quiz questions (Figure 4-7) can be found in Appendix B.

	Put the appropriate letter before each definition	
	Term	**Definition**
a	Why not market to gold customers?	A screen view
b	How AMEX helps magazines	A virtual table
c	Why cookies beat a PIN	Add fields without redoing the database
d	Getting subscribers to find others	Automatic billing
e	The value of a second product	Chief structure in a relational database
f	Globe and Mail renewal rate after	Customer Age
g	Personalized offers are better than?	Dictate data correctness
h	Dashboard	Higher loyalty to the first product
i	View	More like the Old Corner Grocer
j	Relational Database	Need only web access and a browser
k	Table	Offer of the month
l	Record	Primary key of another table
m	Field	Sixty nine percent
n	Primary Key	The atom of any database
o	Foreign Key	The sales will cannibalize existing business
p	Business Rules	Unique instances of a table subject
q	Event Driven Communications	Uniquely identifies a record within a table
r	Thin Client Application	Viral Marketing
s	Calculated Value	Your order has shipped

Figure 4-7. Quiz 4.

5

Building Profits with Recency, Frequency, Monetary Analysis

Being measured continually is a tough lesson. In direct, its cost-per-lead, or cost-per-sale, not some art director's squinty-eyed aesthetic standard that counts. And you learn very quickly that you can be wrong about how you think people will react. When you put it on the line this way, you become a different kind of creative person.

MIKE SLOSBERG
Wunderman Worldwide

Never assume a CHAID program or even a regression model will outperform an old-fashioned RFM analysis if the RFM has been refining the model for more than 20 years.

DAVID SHEPARD

Direct marketers have been using Recency, Frequency, and Monetary (RFM) analysis to predict customer behavior for more than 50 years. It is one of the most powerful techniques available to a database marketer. It is the basis for any predictive model of customer behavior, yet differs from traditional modeling in that it requires no knowledge of statistics. It does not require any appending of data. If you have a database of your customers, with their purchase history, you can use RFM analysis right now at virtually no cost. You do not need to hire a statistician.

There are two types of facts that you can learn about customers: who they are (demographics) and what they do (behavior). In marketing, we are usually trying to predict behavior. Accurate behavior predictions are important for making profitable marketing decisions. The best predictor of future behavior is past behavior. It beats demographics every time. If you are planning to sell something to your customers, knowing that some of them have bought several items worth $100 by mail recently is worth much more than knowing their age, income, home value, presence of children or any other demographic information. RFM is pure behavior.

RFM only works with customer files. It cannot be used with prospects, because it requires knowledge of the customer's prior purchase history with you. Prospects, by definition, have no such history. Use of RFM to guide your communications will *always* improve profits over any other method. RFM works with consumer and with business-to-business customer files. It works with any type of industry in which you communicate with your customers for marketing purposes.

In this chapter, we will cover everything you need to know to make serious money using this technique. If you do not already use RFM, you will emerge from this chapter a much more professional marketer who can make your company a lot of money. We will begin by describing each of the three components of RFM, and then show you how you can increase your profits by segmenting your database into RFM cells and using these cells to direct your customer communications.

How to Code Your Customers by Recency

To code your customer base for recency, you need to store one vital piece of information in every customer's database record: the most recent purchase date. Every time you update your database, be sure that this date is updated as well. To create the recency code, you sort your entire database by this date, with the most recent at the top. Then you divide the database into five exactly equal parts—quintiles, which you number from 5 (the most recent) down to 1 (the most ancient). The coding process looks like Figure 5-1.

Once you have done this, you append a "5" to every record in the top group, a "4" to the records in the next group, etc. Every record in your database is now coded as a 5, 4, 3, 2, or 1 for recency. This method of creating the five divisions, each of exactly equal size, i.e., 20 percent of

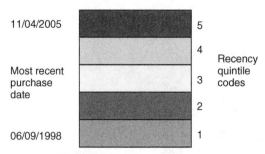

Figure 5-1. Sorting by recency.

the entire database, is called "exact quintiles." There is another way of doing RFM, which has been around for a long time. This method is called "hard coding." Using hard coding, the top quintile is set as being some arbitrary date range, such as 0–3 months. The next is 3–6 months, etc. That method works, and is in active use in direct marketing operations all over the world. What is being explained here, however, is another, and more accurate method, also widely used, which you will see produces RFM cells of exactly equal size.

Using exact quintiles, there is a certain arbitrary quality in the divisions. The recency dividing line between 5 and 4, for example, may occur on February 12th. Because of the sorting process, some customers with a most recent date of February 12th may show up as 5's. Others with the same date can show up as 4's, yet they have exactly the same date! Do not worry about it. Just do it. We are going to recalculate RFM codes every month, so any arbitrary number assigned this month will be corrected next month. Adjusting the boundaries every month is not worth the effort, and ruins the accuracy of the result.

Now that your file is coded for recency, go ahead and do a promotion to your customer base. Not a special test promotion, but some communication that you had planned to do all along which calls on customers to respond or make a purchase. Keep track of which quintile every customer is in and which ones respond. If you do, you will have a response picture that will look very much like Figure 5-2.

The customers coded with a "5" will respond much better than the "4"s, who will be better than the "3"s etc. The recency code will accurately predict who is most likely to respond. These numbers, and all those used in the first part of this chapter, are from an actual promotion done by a database marketer who had a customer database of 2.1 million names, going back over a five-year period. They were offered a video

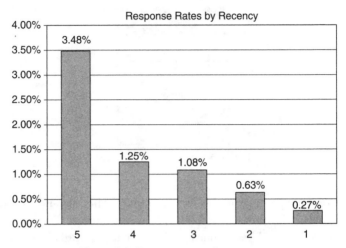

Figure 5-2. Response rates by recency.

package that cost them about $100 including shipping and handling charges. The charts represent the responses to a test mailing to 30,000 of these 2.1 million names.

If you add these response rates together, you will note that only 402 people or 1.34 percent of the customers responded to the offer. The percentages in the five columns add up to 6.71 percent. Dividing this by five, gives you the 1.34 percent for the overall response. This means that 98.66 percent of the customers did not respond. This is normal. You will experience the same type of response rates, somewhat better or worse, unless you have a highly unusual offer. What this marketer found, and you will also find, is that recency is a very powerful predictor of response. The 5's responded almost three times better than the 4's.

Why is recency so powerful in predicting behavior? Think about it. I recently bought a new Honda Odyssey—a really great car. I am out on my first day on the road in this wonderful vehicle. I am looking all around. What am I looking for? Another Honda Odyssey! If I see one, I want to honk my horn and wave, "Hey, I've got one too! Aren't they great?"

Everyone in the world feels a rush of enthusiasm when he purchases a new car, house, suit, or dress. The feeling lasts for a while. If you were to take out a checking account with the Fleet Bank this week, and next week you get a letter from the Fleet Bank, you are going to open that letter. Maybe it is something about your new account. But if you have had an account with Fleet for the past five years, and next week you get a letter from Fleet that is obviously not your monthly statement, you may well chuck it out. It is just another credit card solicitation. In other words, recent buyers will respond. Ancient buyers may not. Recency works. It is a universal human emotion that we may count on in designing our marketing programs.

If you are a telephone company, recency cannot be the last time the customer made a phone call or the last time they paid their monthly bill. Everyone would have the same date! Recency is the last time that they changed their service (added or dropped a line, or signed up for cell phone service). A bank has to count the last time a person opened up a new account or took out a loan. You will have to decide what constitutes recency for your business. You can experiment with different definitions until you get a graph that looks like the one above. It costs you nothing to experiment, and can produce very profitable results when you get the correct answer.

So we have learned how to code our database for recency. Just sort the files by the most recent date, divide it into five exactly equal parts. Code them as 5, 4, 3, 2, and 1, and check the codes on the responses after any promotion. We have learned something. But before we devote more time to exploring recency, let us explain frequency.

How to Code Your File by Frequency

To code a database for frequency we need another piece of information in every customer record. It is a number: the total number of times that the customer has made a purchase from you.

The chart in Figure 5-3 is compiled by sorting the database by the total purchases made by each customer from you. There are many ways

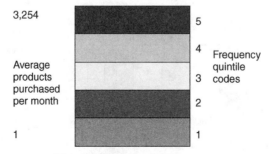

Figure 5-3. Sorting by frequency.

of measuring frequency. It could be the average number of purchases per year, the average number of products bought per year, the average number of telephone calls made per month (for a phone company), the total number of checks and deposits made during a month (for a bank). You may experiment to find the best measure for you. What you are looking for is a measure of how important doing business with you is in the minds of your customers, measured by the frequency of use of your products or services. Once you have such a code kept in each customer record (and updated on a regular basis), you should sort your database by that number, divide it into five equal parts, and put quintile codes into each database record. The process is identical to that for recency.

If, then, you do a promotion to your existing customer base and keep track of the frequency quintile that each customer belonged to at the time of the promotion, you will get a graph of response rates as given in Figure 5-4.

This chart shows the same 402 customers whom we graphed by recency in the previous graph, here graphed by frequency quintile. What this illustrates is that frequency is also a good predictor of behavior, but much less so than recency. If you look at the previous graph of the recency response, you will see how dramatic the response rate of the 5's was (three times the rate of the 4's). Here, the frequency slope from 5 down to 1 is much more gentle. This is generally true of frequency codes. That is why RFM is RFM instead of FRM or FMR. You put the most predictive variable first.

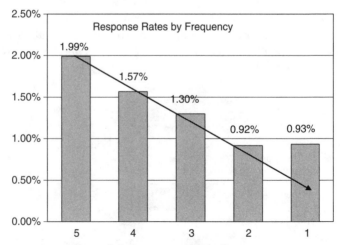

Figure 5-4. Response rates by frequency.

There is something else interesting here, shown by the diagonal line on the graph. There is something wrong with the lowest frequency quintile. The response rate is 0.93 percent. But if it were to follow the trend of the other frequency divisions, the response rate should be less than 0.5 percent. This is not an accident. You will undoubtedly have the same result when you graph your own customer response by frequency.

Why do the 1's on a frequency graph respond better than one would suppose? Because the lowest quintile on a frequency chart contains an abnormal number of recent buyers. A customer who just joined you yesterday is your most recent buyer. So his recency code is 5. Recent buyers are your best responders. But this recent buyer, being brand new, has not had a chance to become a frequent buyer yet, so his frequency code is 1. You probably cannot make any money with this universal fact, but it does serve to prove to you that you have done your RFM coding correctly. If your lowest quintile on frequency is not higher than the trend, as shown above, then you have probably done something wrong.

Response by Monetary Amount

Finally, let us graph these same people by their monetary spending. The method is the same. We keep in everyone's database record a single piece of information: the total amount spent on our products or services, either per month, per year, or in some other way. We are trying to determine the monetary significance of our company to each of our customers, as measured in dollars. We will take this data, and sort the entire database by this number, divide it into five equal groups, and assign code numbers: 5, 4, 3, 2, and 1.

In Figure 5-5 we have sorted the entire file by monetary amount and assigned monetary codes. The left axis represents the amount that each

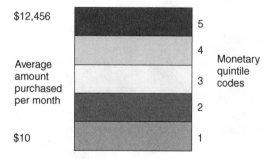

Figure 5-5. Sorting by monetary.

customer has purchased per month. The best customer has purchased an average of $12,456 per month. The lowest customer has bought only $10 per month. These amounts are stored in the customer's database record every time they make a purchase. We sort the entire file by this amount. Let us see what happens when we look at the monetary response rate of the same 402 people who we already graphed by recency and frequency.

When you look at this graph, remember that the 5's represent people who spend a lot of money with your company. The 1's spend very little. Monetary coding is far less predictive of behavior than either recency or frequency. While there is a gentle slope from the 5's down to the 1's, it is not really very dramatic. It is almost flat. What this means is that on small-ticket items, monetary is not very predictive. In today's market, a small-ticket consumer item would be something that sells for, say, $120 or less. A big-ticket item would be something that sells for $1,000 or more. This video, which sold for $100, is a small-ticket item. Let us see what the monetary response rate looked like (Figure 5-6).

To understand why monetary is not as predictive as recency or frequency, imagine two of your customers: one who spends a million dollars a year on your category of products, and one who spends only a thousand dollars per year. Is there any reason to believe that the million-dollar customer would be more likely to open your envelope containing your promotions than the thousand-dollar guy? No. In fact, I would say

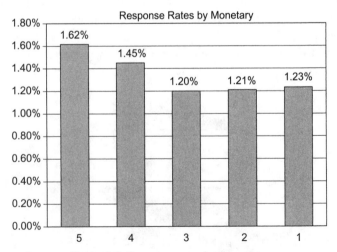

Figure 5-6. Response rates by monetary.

that the million-dollar customer would be *less likely* to open the enve-lope. Why? Because, as a million-dollar guy, he is on everyone's list. Everyone writes to him. He, or his secretary, checks his mail with the wastebasket near at hand. The thousand-dollar guy gets far less mail. He is probably much more likely to open the envelope. So if we go by propensity to open your envelopes (or read your e-mails or take your phone calls) the graph would have exactly the opposite shape, with the 1's having a higher response rate than the 5's.

But once the envelope is opened, the million-dollar guy can write out a check for whatever is in that envelope, but the thousand-dollar guy will have to think it over. It may not be within his budget. So, if we are going by the ability to pay, the 5's will have a very high response rate, and the 1's will be very low. So the final monetary graph is a combination of two opposite human emotions: willingness to open the envelope and ability to pay. That is why the monetary graph, for low-ticket items, tends to be almost flat. The money does not matter.

That is not true of big-ticket items. If you are selling something for $5,000, let us say, then the ability to pay will overwhelm the opening of the envelope and give you a completely different monetary graph. Figure 5-7 shows the response rate of a bank in New York, which made a $5,000 certificate of deposit offer to its 250,000 most affluent customers.

In this chart of response rates to a $5,000 Certificate of Deposit offer, the monetary response rates look almost like recency response rates. You will have the same experience. If you offer customers a commodity

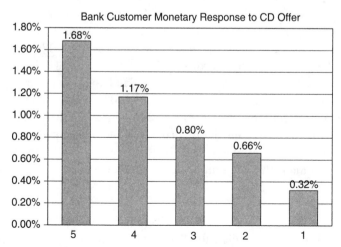

Figure 5-7. Response to bank CD offer by monetary quintile.

or service with a high price, the high monetary quintiles will respond much better than the low ones.

Putting It All Together

Thus far, we have learned the theory of RFM which is based on three aspects of customer behavior. The theory does not show how we can make money with this knowledge. That is what we are going to do right now.

When the coding process is finished, every customer should have in his or her database records three single digits: one for recency, one for frequency, and one for monetary. Every customer is either a 555, 554, 553, 552, 551, 545, 544,....down to 111. There are 125 RFM Cell Codes in all. (Later in this chapter, we will learn that you can work with higher or lower numbers than 125.)

When you do promotions to your customers, therefore, you keep track of the RFM cell code that each is occupying. The results can be very interesting. Let us see how the company we have been following so far in this chapter coded their database for RFM and did a test of its offer to 30,000 of its 2.1 million customers.

Selecting an Nth

The test group was selected using an Nth. An Nth is a test group that is an exact statistical replica of the full database. For example, if a database had 300,000 customers, and we wanted to select a test group of 30,000 using an Nth, we would divide the 30,000 into the 300,000, giving the result of 10. We need to select every tenth record from the master database to create the test group. We will select records 1, 11, 21, 31, 41, 51,...taking every tenth record. The resulting test file will have 30,000 members and will exactly mirror the main database. It will have the same percentage of people whose zip code is 22203, whose income is over $100,000, who have two children, etc., as the main database. It does not matter whether the main file is sorted in alphabetical order, zip code order, or customer number order; the results will be the same, provided we are dealing with large numbers, such as 30,000.

Results of the Test

When the company mailed the $100 offer to their 30,000 test group, they got the results as in Figure 5-8.

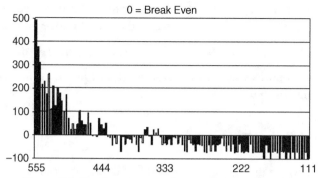

Figure 5-8. Results of test mailing to 30,000 customers.

On this chart, the bottom (*X*) axis represents the RFM cell codes of each of the 125 cells mailed in the test. The left (*Y*) axis represents the break-even index of each cell. Break-even is explained in the following paragraph. From this graph we can see that only 34 of the 125 cells did better than break-even. The remainder lost money. Let us take a moment to explain break-even.

How Break-Even Is Calculated

Break-even in direct marketing means that the net profits from sales to a test group exactly equals the cost of promoting that test group. If, e.g., we mail 400 people at a cost of $0.50 each, or $200, and the net profit from that group of 400 people (after credits, returns, cost of goods sold, shipping, etc.) is $200, then we have just broken even. Before we begin a promotion, we can calculate the response rate we will need to get from each cell to break-even. There is a neat little formula that tells us this break-even response rate. It is:

$$BE = (\text{cost per piece}) \ / \ (\text{net profit from a single sale})$$

In the case of the $100 video offer, the company we are studying calculated that they made $40 on each successful sale. The cost per piece of the mailing was $0.55. So the rate they needed for break-even on each RFM cell was:

$$BE = (\$0.55) \ / \ \$40 = 1.375\%$$

The *break-even index* is calculated by another neat little formula:

$$BEI = ((r - BE) \ / \ BE)) \times 100$$

In this formula, r is the actual response rate of the RFM cell. So if the response rate of one cell is 2.5 percent, then the break-even index is:

$$BEI = ((0.025 - 0.01375) / (0.01375)) \times 100 = 81.82$$

A break-even index of 0 means that the cell just broke even. A negative number means that the cell lost money.

Results of the Test

In summary, the test mailing to 30,000 had the result given in Figure 5-9.

They lost $420 on the test. Was that a failure? Not at all. For a net cost of $420 they learned how 30,000, an Nth of their 2.1 million database, would respond to this offer. Since the 30,000 was an Nth, these customers were completely representative of how the entire database would have responded to this same offer. The company then knew which RFM cells would be profitable and which RFM cells would be losers. As a result, they did not mail the offer to the entire database of 2.1 million. Instead, they selected customers from the 34 profitable RFM cells on the rollout. (They also selected a small number of customers from each of the unprofitable cells just to be sure that they had done the coding correctly.)

The selection process went like Figure 5-10.

	Number	Rate	Dollars
Sales	402	$40	$16,080
Mailing	30,000	$0.55	$16,500
Net Loss			($420)

Figure 5-9. Loss from test mailing.

	Test	Full File	RFM Select
Response Rate	1.34%	1.17%	2.76%
Responses	402	23,412	15,295
Average Profit	$40	$40	$40
Net Revenue	$16,080	$936,480	$611,800
No. Mailed	30,000	2,001,056	554,182
Cost per piece	$0.55	$0.55	$0.55
Mailing Cost	$16,500	$1,100,581	$304,800
Profit (Loss)	($420)	($164,101)	$307,000

Figure 5-10. Results of RFM select mailing.

The first column is the test file results. The second column shows what would have happened if they had mailed the full database of 2.1 million. They would have lost about $164,000. The appendix to this chapter explains why the response rate to the full file is estimated at only 1.17 percent instead of the 1.34 percent achieved on the test. The third column shows what the company actually mailed on their rollout. They selected customers out of the 2.1 million who were in the 34 RFM cells that were shown to be profitable on the test. There were 554,182 of these folks. Mailing only to them, they got an overall response rate of 2.76 percent and a net profit of $307,000. This shows the full power of RFM. You profit by *not promoting* people who you have learned are unlikely to respond.

What happened when they mailed these 544,182 people? That is the most exciting result of this entire case study. Look at the chart given in Figure 5-11, which compares the actual response rates of the 30,000 people in the 34 successful RFM cells on the test with the 554,182 people mailed on the RFM selected rollout:

The numbers on the bottom of this graph (the X axis) are the RFM cell code numbers of the 34 cells mailed on the test which were profitable. The percents on the left (Y axis) of this graph are the actual response rates of the profitable cells on the test and the corresponding cells mailed in the rollout. The vertical bars are the response rates of the 34 profitable cells in the test. The lines and dots are response rates of

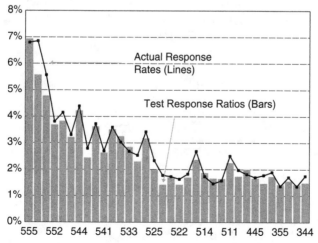

Figure 5-11. Test and rollout response rates.

the 544,182 people from those same profitable cells which were mailed on the selected rollout. It is uncanny how accurately RFM predicted the response of these people. This is why RFM through the years has been selected as the most profitable method for doing customer promotions. It works. And, it costs almost nothing to use. All the charts and methods explained so far in this chapter can be understood by any marketer with no knowledge of statistics. We do, however, have to let you in on a secret that we have been withholding up to this point.

How RFM Sorting Is Done

The RFM sorting is a little more complicated than the earlier sections of this chapter have implied. From the early sections, you got the idea that you would sort your database once for recency, once for frequency, and once for monetary. That is true, and it will work to produce the results shown on the R, F, and M graphs shown in this chapter. But when you come to create the three-digit RFM cells used in the test and rollout shown above, you use a slightly more complicated RFM sorting scheme. You have to sort your database 31 times. The scheme is given in Figure 5-12.

To create RFM cells, you sort the database once by recency, dividing the database into five equal parts. Assign a 5, 4, 3, 2, or 1 to all the members of each of the recency quintiles. Then sort each of these five quintiles by frequency, dividing each into five groups, and assigning the members of each group a 5, 4, 3, 2, or 1. Finally, each of these 25 groups is sorted again by monetary. It seems complicated, and it is. But computers can do this with ease. The result of this process is that every RFM

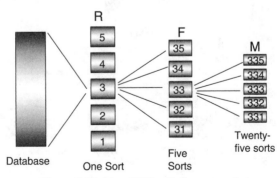

Figure 5-12. How RFM cells are created.

cell has exactly the same number of customers in it as every other RFM cell. This becomes very useful for comparing RFM performance and selecting the appropriate customers for promotions.

Paul Wang and I had been teaching database marketing principles, including RFM, in two-day seminars for The Database Marketing Institute for many years. In each seminar, marketers would ask us, "Is there software that does this RFM sorting job?" At first we said, "No," and told them to ask their MIS departments to do the job. But after a while it became obvious that many marketers could not get sufficient help to create RFM cell codes. We decided to create some software to help them out. The result is *RFM for Windows*, which is available from the institute (www.dbmarketing.com). Many alumni of the institute and others use this software in their work. They share with us reports of their promotions to customers. From these reports, we have learned a great deal about customer response. The data for all of the graphics in this chapter has been obtained from alumni who are users of this software. You can get a free copy of this software on the Internet by clicking on www.dbmarketing.com and downloading it. About 10 companies per week do this, and have been doing so for the past 10 years.

RFM with a Consumable Product

One alumnus worked for a company that sold personalized checks. They had a database of 600,000 customers. The alumnus coded the database for RFM using the methods shown in this chapter. Then he did a promotion to 45,000 customers selected using an *N*th. The results were very surprising (Figure 5-13).

As you can see, the response rates for the most recent quintile were lower than those for the second quintile. When I saw that, I wondered if there was something wrong with the theory. How could this be? Then I realized that this company sells a consumable product. The most recent buyers had not yet run low on the product, so they did not order as many. So, I wondered, did the company mail too soon? Should they have waited for these recent buyers to run low? To verify that, I looked at their total sales by recency quintile. The graph was gratifying (Figure 5-14).

These are the same people, arranged differently. The most recent buyers (5's) purchased even more than the next quintile (4's), even though their response rate was lower. What I had not counted on was that recent buyers tend to place larger orders. Since then, I have verified

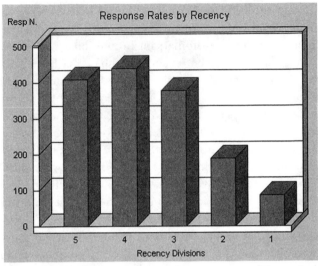

Figure 5-13. Response rates by recency for consumable product.

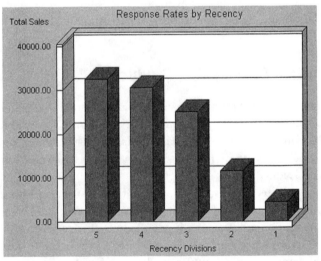

Figure 5-14. Total sales by recency for consumable product.

this finding with other alumni. Recent buyers not only have higher response rates, but also tend to buy more per order and higher priced options. Further analysis showed that both frequency and monetary could be used to increase profits for this company. We discovered that, in general, for most products:

- The highest frequency quintile buys much more than the lower quintiles.

- The highest monetary quintile places much bigger orders than lower quintiles.

This customer's break-even rate by RFM cell was quite different from the company with the video offer. They had 72 profitable cells out of 125 (Figure 5-15).

At this point, you understand the theory behind RFM. It helps you to determine which of your customers will respond, and how much they will buy. It is a wonderfully powerful tool.

RFM for Business-to-Business Files

RFM was originally invented primarily for consumer database files. It works well there. It also works with most business-to-business files. Federal Express, e.g., has made highly profitable use of RFM in segmenting its business customers. Most business-to-business files are much smaller than consumer files. Many business customer files are well below 20,000. How can such a company make profitable use of RFM? There are two factors to consider.

125 cells are too many for a small file. The number 125 comes about by multiplying 5 recency divisions by 5 frequency by 5 monetary. Dividing a small business file of 20,000 records by 125 gives you only 160 customers

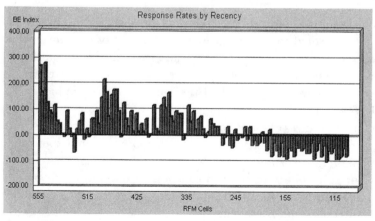

Figure 5-15. Break-even index for consumable product test.

in each cell. This is too small for accurate statistical results. For a business file of 20,000 records, therefore, there probably should not be more than 20 RFM cells, each one having about 1,000 companies in it. To get down to 20 cells, the RFM should be created by reducing the frequency and monetary divisions like this:

5 Recency × 2 Frequency × 2 Monetary = 20 RFM Cells

If experience shows that monetary is very important in the sales of the business (the company sells big-ticket items) then the division might be changed to:

4 Recency × 2 Frequency × 3 Monetary = 24 RFM Cells

There are many ways of doing RFM. The user will have to experiment to see which works best for their situation.

RFM does not beat a sales visit. RFM is not too useful for those customers being called on by the sales force. The sales force knows far more about the customers than can be learned from RFM analysis. However, most businesses have their sales force calling on only the top 20 percent of their customers, leaving the remaining 80 percent to be dealt with by catalogs, letters, e-mail, and phone calls. If this is the situation in your company, RFM is perfect for helping to manage the 80 percent who do not rate a sales visit. It will tell you which customers are most likely to respond to a phone call, an e-mail, a fax, or a letter.

RFM and Modeling

How does RFM compare with modeling? In this book we have a whole chapter devoted to modeling. Any good model of customer behavior always includes recency, frequency and monetary amount. They are the most important available measures of customer performance. Most models, however, go beyond RFM to include demographics, product selection, and other factors. Some of these other factors do help in predicting customer response, so a good model, properly run, can outperform RFM. The problem is that models are usually expensive and difficult for a layman to run. To run a model you usually have to hire a statistician or outsource your model. You have to buy or obtain demographic data and append it to your file. A good model takes a week or two to run—some companies have spent more than six weeks to get a perfect model run. The cost of the modeling professional, the data appending, and the modeling software, plus the time involved, may run the cost of a model from $5,000 to $200,000, depending on who is doing it, and what is involved.

To decide whether to use RFM or a model, you have to consider the economics. The purpose of both modeling and RFM is the same: to increase profits by deciding *not to mail non-responsive customers.* Modeling is usually expensive. RFM is almost free of charge. Any marketing professional can understand it and use it. The software for creating the RFM cells can be bought for permanent use for as little as $500. You can use it over and over again without paying any fee to anyone. Models quickly get out of date. A $25,000 model needs to be run every six months or more often as the market changes and competition heats up. So, to determine whether to use a model, you must accept the idea that the model has not only to be more accurate than RFM (which it probably is) but also that it gives you enough lift in response to pay for the model, plus beating the RFM lift. Except in the case of large databases, this may not be true.

Elsewhere in this book, you will find a number of case studies of companies that make major use of RFM in their marketing program. The studies include Sears Canada and Federal Express. RFM is being used by catalogers, retailers, hotels, airlines, banks, insurance companies, cellular phone companies, and high-tech manufacturers. There are tens of thousands of active users in the United States and Canada. If you have not used it yet, you should look into it, because it will definitely improve your response rates and build your profits.

When Not to Use RFM

Using RFM is like taking drugs. It gives you such a high that you want to use it all the time. That would be a mistake. If you use RFM to decide who to write to or who to call, some of your customers will never hear from you at all. The more responsive customers may suffer from file fatigue: you will communicate with them too often.

You should develop a customer contact strategy. Figure something valuable that you want to communicate to your less responsive customers once or twice a year just to let them know that you have not forgotten them. Birthday and holiday cards are useful. Thank you cards are always in season. But do not bother non-responsive people with continual offers if they do not respond.

Database marketing is meant to be profitable for both the buyer and the seller. If you lose money, it is not profitable for you. If your customers do not respond, you have wasted their time sending them something that they do not want. You have cheapened your reputation and relationship with them, forcing them to reject you. Save your promotional dollars for situations in which both you and your customers are likely to win. It is a favor to both the buyer and the seller.

When Should You Use RFM?

Now that you have learned about RFM and have coded your customer base with RFM cell codes, you are in a position to make serious money any time that you want. If management comes to you and asks you to introduce a new product, you know exactly which customers are most likely to respond to your offer, and which are less likely. You can amaze your management with your success rates.

Another time for RFM use is during budget season. Once a year, database marketers typically have to justify their marketing program to management for the coming year. One of the best ways to do that is by Customer Lifetime Value analysis described in Chapter 3. Another useful step is to do a customer promotion to high-responding RFM cells a couple of months before your budget comes up for review. You can bring in a lot of sales with very little promotional expense if you just promote the highest-ranking customers. RFM can open a whole new world for you, at very little expense.

Appendix: Frequently Asked Questions about RFM

How Big Do RFM Test Cells Have to Be to Get Accurate Predictions?

There are two contradictory goals in creating RFM cells. You want them as large as possible so that tests with the cells will be statistically accurate. On the other hand, you want them to be as small as possible to keep the costs of tests down. There is a simple formula that tells you the right size. The formula for the minimum test cell size is:

$$\text{Minimum RFM Test Cell Size} = 4 / \text{BE}$$

where BE is the break-even response rate. What is the "4"? It is a rule of thumb. Use it. It works. If your break-even rate on a promotion is 1.76 percent, then your minimum test cell size is:

$$\text{Test Cell Size} = 4 \,/\, 0.0176 = 231 \text{ customers}$$

Why Use Quintiles for RFM Cells? Why Not Deciles?

Deciles (creating 10 recency divisions, 10 frequency divisions and 10 monetary divisions) are a possible RFM method that some have used. It makes for a very large group of RFM cells ($10 \times 10 \times 10 = 1,000$), which can be used only for the largest consumer files. It has certain obvious drawbacks. Each test is very expensive. If your minimum test size is 231 customers in each cell, as shown above, then each test will require mailing to 231,000 people. That is too expensive a test for anybody. So, the answer to the question is that deciles are great for scientific accuracy, but useless for practical testing purposes. Stick to something simple that works. Use quintiles, or smaller numbers.

For many files quintiles may be too large. As already pointed out, for a business-to-business file of 12,000 names, e.g., you would not want to have more than about 20 cells, not 125. You can figure out your distribution by seeing which of the divisions turns out to be the most predictive for you. If monetary is very important, then $2 \times 2 \times 5 = 20$ might be the way to go.

I like to use a budget calculation. If you have a large file but management has given you a test budget of only $12,000, then I would figure my RFM cells this way. Suppose your mailing costs are $0.50 each. For $12,000 I can only mail 24,000 pieces. If my minimum test cell size is 240 customers, then I can have only 100 cells ($24,000 \,/\, 240 = 100$). So I would create my RFM divisions as $5 \times 5 \times 4 = 100$.

How Do You Measure Recency with Continuity Products?

Most people use their telephones, electric service, bank accounts, credit cards, and newspapers every day. Most people pay their bills once a month. What constitutes recency in such situations? The answer is different in each case. What we are trying to get at is "The last time that the customer made a business decision concerning your company's services." It could be the last time that they opened a new product account, changed their service, or moved. Keep your eye on the goal: we are trying to predict behavior. You will have to experiment with various events to determine which is the most predictive of response rates.

How Do You Measure Frequency of Purchase?

Frequency is the stepchild. Recency is independent. Monetary is independent. But frequency is closely related to both monetary and recency. It is half-way in between. One customer spent $2,400 two years ago and has not bought since. Another spent $100 per month for the last 24 months. They have both spent $2,400 with you. Which is the best customer? I would say that the second customer is far better. You are maintaining contact and have hope for future sales, and increased sales.

How is frequency measured? What units should be used? There are many possibilities:

- A cataloger or retailer can measure the number of purchases in a year, or the number of items ordered.

- A bank can measure the number of checks written and the number of deposits made.

- A hotel can measure the number of trips or the number of nights stayed.

- A telephone company can measure the number of calls or the number of minutes talked.

- An electric utility could measure the number of months in service or the number of KWH used per month.

Each of these industries has several possible ways of measuring frequency. *Which is the best frequency measurement?* There is no universal answer, but there is a universal method of finding the answer. The universal method is this: test each of several possible methods and see which of them does the best job of predicting actual response rates. The cost of testing is almost nothing:

- Identify two or more possible measurements of frequency, such as the number of purchases or the number of items purchased. Use each method to develop separate RFM scores. File both in your customer database.

- Carry out any regularly scheduled promotion to your customer base, but keep track of the frequency quintile that each customer is located in. When the responses come in, append them to the database and draw a graph of the results.

- The correct measurement is the one that produces the most predictive graph. A predictive graph is one in which there is a dramatic

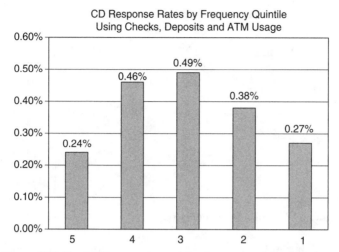

Figure 5-16. Bank CD response rates by frequency with ATM usage.

difference between the response rates of each quintile. Figure 5-2 is very predictive. Figure 5-6 is not.

You will get some very interesting results. The New York bank, which sold $5,000 certificates of deposit, was described earlier in this chapter. The marketing director tested one measure of frequency, and got the results as shown in Figure 5-16.

This chart makes no sense. Why would the best responders be those whose frequency is in the third quintile, and the lowest response rate be from those in the top quintile? When I saw this chart, I called the marketing director at the bank right away and asked her what she had done to create this monstrosity.

"I did just what you told me," she said, "adding together the number of deposits and checks written per month. Then, because the data was available, I added in the number of times that the customer had used the ATM each month. That was how I measured frequency."

At first, her explanation seemed to make sense to me, and I wondered if my understanding of frequency was flawed. But after a while, I figured it out. She was selling a product whose minimum price was $5,000. I asked her "Do people who can afford a $5,000 CD tend to make extensive use of ATMs?"

She pondered this question and did a little research. What she discovered was that higher income people tend to use ATMs less often than lower income people. By adding ATM usage as a frequency measurement,

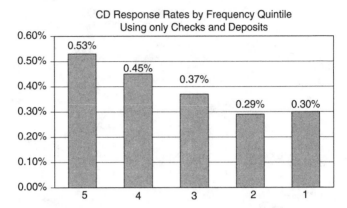

Figure 5-17. Bank CD frequency response rates without ATM usage.

she was mixing in a contrary factor: a behavior that was the opposite of the desired response—purchase of a high dollar CD. After learning this, we redid her calculations, taking out the ATM usage. We ended up with the chart given in Figure 5-17.

Why is this chart better? Because the measure selected for frequency of use more accurately predicted who actually responded to the offer. These response rates are low: the highest is only one-half of 1 percent. But, for the bank, the rates were high enough to make the overall promotion profitable. Their use of the correct frequency measurement enabled them to drop close to 100,000 customers from their next CD promotion, getting almost the same amount of sales, but greatly increasing the profits to the bank.

Does RFM Measure Profitability?

Only very indirectly. There are really two different customer behaviors: responsiveness and profitability (Figure 5-18).

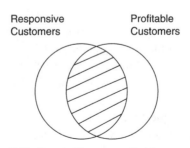

Figure 5-18. Responsive vs. profitable customers.

Some customers give you thousands of dollars worth of business every year, but they would not respond when you write to them. Other customers that are very unprofitable will answer all your surveys and buy your specials but still would not be profitable. RFM measures responsiveness but not, necessarily, profitability. Do not confuse the two. However, you can use monetary and frequency as a surrogate for profitability if you have nothing better to use.

Why Do Rollouts Not Do as Well as Tests?

In the example given in this chapter, the test of 30,000 had a response rate of 1.34 percent. The predicted rollout response rate was only 1.17 percent. Why was the rollout rate expected to be lower? In fact, most marketers find that rollout rates are quite often lower than test rates. There are a number of valid reasons, but the most compelling is that marketers just cannot leave well enough alone. Marketers hate to have unsuccessful tests. So, they do things for the test that they could not afford to do for the rollout. They may use the best list or mail first class or mail at the ideal time. When the rollout comes, they find that they have to economize, so they get a lower overall response rate.

Because that is so, when you are estimating your response rate after a test, be sure to discount it by a factor, such as 10 percent. If you do that, and the rollout is better than you predicted, you will look like a hero. If it is worse, people will think that you are not such a good marketer after all.

How Do You Know the Best Ways to Measure Recency, Frequency, and Monetary Amount?

This problem comes up a lot, and leads many companies to abandon RFM because they feel it will not work in their situation. For example, if you are a magazine with a standard subscription rate, everyone pays the same price. So how do you score monetary? Answer: keep track of other products that they buy from you. These will create differences in monetary amount.

For recency, electric utilities complain that everyone uses electricity all the time, so their most recent date for everyone is yesterday. No problem. Use other measures, such as "When was the last time that the customer changed his service, or bought some new product from you?" Use that as the recency date.

The basic rule is to be creative. You are trying to determine how important the products and services of our company are to each customer.

If you are debating between two possible measures, use them both and develop two RFM scores for each customer. Keep them in the customer's record. Then, the next time you run a promotion to your members, see which RFM system does the best job of predicting behavior. That analysis will tell you which method to use.

Executive Quiz 5

Answers to quiz questions (Figure 5-19) can be found in Appendix B.

Put the appropriate letter before each answer		
	Questions	**Answers**
a	Cost per piece = $0.72 Avg. Net Profit = $60 Break Even = ?	1.20%
b	Mail 30,000. Responders = 510. RR = ?	1.70%
c	Which produces best prediction: R, F, M, Demographics	219
d	Rollout response compared to test response is	31
e	Cust = 7,000 BE = 2.12 How may RFM cells can you make?	37
f	BE = 1.83% What is minimum test cell size	444
g	Best way to measure frequency	48
h	311, 444, 231, 211, 333. Which gives highest response?	Be creative
i	How to use RFM to increase the response rate	File fatigue
j	Divisions: R = 4, F = 3, M = 4 How many cells in all?	Recency
k	How many times sorts required to do RFM?	Skip low cells
l	Danger from overuse of RFM	Usually lower

Figure 5-19. Quiz 5.

6

Communicating with Customers

*Any communication, irrespective of whether or not
there is a promotional offer, will increase
visits...However, the right promotional offer to the
right recipient at the right time will dramatically
increase response.*

JUDD GOLDFEDER
The Customer Connection

*As our dialog program evolved, we learned to put
the best people in the call center into our Regards hot
line. We had to show the hot line staff the packages
before they were mailed to the customers, so they would
know what the customer was talking about when they
called. We learned the importance of investing time
and effort in our hot line people. We learned to share
with our hot line people what was working and not
working, and to take their suggestions on ways to make
the program better. We made many changes in the program based on the feedback from the hot line operators.*

PAULA HART
Former Director of the Dayton Hudson Regards Program

People call it database marketing, but that is not an exact description of
the process. The central idea is customer communications. These communications build relationships and repeat business. The database is
needed to make the communications personal and to keep track of
whether the communications are working correctly. Instead of sending

everyone the same mass message: "Buy our upgraded Model 6.0" you send a personalized message, "As you know, Mr. Hughes, you have been using Model 5.0 since May 2002. The new Model 6.0 should save you at least $240 per year, based on your current usage. The price of the upgrade is only $149.00…"

Communications with customers can be very profitable. One of the best examples of this was an experiment done with the customers of a manufacturer of lighting products. This manufacturer sold only to contractors and builders. He sent out 45,000 catalogs per year, receiving orders through a bank of operators on a toll free number. Business was good.

A consultant from Hunter Business Direct in Milwaukee persuaded the manufacturer to try a test. They took the top 1,200 customers and divided them into two exactly equal groups of 600 each. One was the test group, and the other was the control group. They set up a two-person staff to work with the test group. One person was a customer relations specialist and the other was a lighting engineer. The job of this two-person staff was to contact the decision makers at each of the 600 test companies to build a relationship with them. What did they offer?

- Following up on bids and quotes
- Scheduling product training
- Reminding them of product specials
- Asking about their customer's needs
- Product comparison information
- New product information
- *They did not offer discounts*

The 600 in the control group received none of these things. They got the same excellent treatment that all other customers had always received: an alert and helpful inbound order taking staff.

What was the result of six months worth of communications? In the first place, the retention rate of the test group was slightly higher. Seventy-six percent of the test group placed orders during the six-month period, while only 73 percent of the control group made further purchases. This 3 percent improvement in the retention rate, however, masked other, far more significant differences.

In terms of the number of orders placed during the six-month period, the test group placed more orders than they had before, while the control group placed fewer orders (Figure 6-1).

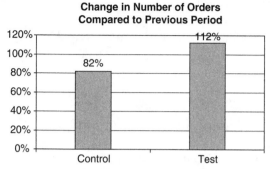

Figure 6-1. Number of orders placed by control and test groups.

Not only was the test group's average order size 14 percent larger than they had been placing before the test. The average order size of those in the control group was 14 percent smaller than their previous orders. The net result of the test was a gain of $2,600,000 in orders from the test group as compared with the control group (Figure 6-2).

What a success! You spend $70,000 to put two workers on the phone communicating with customers for six months. As a result, you produce $2,600,000 more in sales. Communications with customers work!

To prove that communications work, you *absolutely must have a control group.* Imagine this test without the control group. How would you be able to prove that the two-person staff had done any good at all? You could not. Management usually does not understand control groups. Executives of the lighting firm might say, "That consultant cost us $2.6 million dollars. If we had communicated with all 1,200 customers, instead of only 600, our overall sales would have been $2.6 million

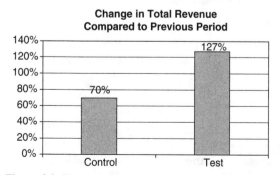

Figure 6-2. Total revenue from control vs. test groups.

higher. We cannot afford such expensive consultants!" In fact, of course, the control group was the only way that anyone could have known that the test was working. Without the test group, the executives might have thought that the entire project was a "feel good" worthless waste of money.

The Role of Customer Communications

There is no point in building a database, segmenting customers, and computing RFM and Lifetime Value if you do not communicate with your customers. Database marketing and the Web only work if the customer benefits from them. She has to say, "I'm glad I'm on that database because…" You will have to fill in the rest of the sentence. In communications today, you can use the Web, email, mail, retail contacts and phone. This chapter explains how to go about creating and profiting from personalized customer communications.

Let us start with the Web. For your company, you must use the Web to provide information and dialog with your customers. Why is the Web important to you? Let me count the ways:

- It is far cheaper than telephone customer service.
- It operates 24 hours a day, 7 days a week.
- It never puts customers on hold.
- You can know, instantly, which customer has read your message, and when.
- It enables customers to find out information for themselves—information that your customer service staff may not be briefed on, and may not have available.
- It can build a bond with customers that will keep them coming back.
- It can expand your trading area. You will have visitors from all over the country, and all over the world. Some of these visitors can become valuable customers.

In using the Web for communications, begin with this idea: "We are going to give our customers the same access we provide to our employees." Let them look into your warehouses to see what is in stock. Let them track delivery of packages. Let them look for discontinued items.

Use of an Extranet

An excellent way to communicate with customers using the Web is to create an Extranet for your customers. Anyone can log on to your Web site, but good customers are given an ID and password that enable them to see information that is just for them. Dell Computer created more than 40,000 "Premier Pages" for their best customers. Amazon says "Welcome back Arthur" whenever I log on. American Airlines uses a cookie to know who I am when I click on their site. Without entering a password, they tell me how many miles I have earned. Fedex lets customers track the status of all packages they have shipped. The reason why Web communications work so well is that they are:

- *Interactive.* Customers can talk to you, and you can talk back to them.

- *Inexpensive.* Message by message, the Web costs a very small fraction of the cost of any other communications media.

- *Addictive.* Once people have learned how to use your Web site, they become hooked. They do not want to go back to letters, statement stuffers, and phone calls.

How Travelers Property Casualty Retains Their Best Customers

Travelers is the second largest writer of auto and homeowners insurance through independent agents. They had a problem: customer attrition in the first year was higher than average. To solve this, Travelers developed a program that reduced this defection rate through agent direct mail communications. For more than a decade, Travelers has pioneered a One-to-One program for building customer loyalty. Every month, Travelers segments their customers based on a model that includes the number of years with Travelers, the premiums spent, and payment behavior. The program creates direct mail from agents to their Travelers policyholders. The letters include the agents' company logos. Agents who opt in to the program pay an average of $2.69 per year for each of their customers. Agents log on to a Web site where they can see their customers' segmented data. Agents choose their mail plans from a wide array of choices. The mailings are timed to be sent when each particular customer may be shopping for insurance.

One third of Travelers agents use the system. Result: customers who get the mailings renew their policies at a higher rate than those who do not. To illustrate this, here is what happens to two typical agents (Figure 6-3):

	Non One-to-One	One-to-One	One-to-One Gain
Customer Households	250	250	
% Remain after 1 Year	85.1%	90.7%	5.6 points
Policies after 1 Year	213	227	14
Premium for Retained Business	$213,000	$227,000	$14,000
Agent Commissions (17%)	$36,210	$38,590	$2,380
Annual One-to-One Cost & ROI		$672.50	$2.54

Figure 6-3. Agent gain from one-to-one communications.

The program gains Travelers $14,000 more in premiums that they would have lost without the program. The annual gain in commissions for agents is $2,380 for which they have to pay only $672, for a return on investment of $2.54 for every dollar invested in the program. For Travelers, expanding this example across the entire customer base has a tremendous impact on the bottom line. This long-term program shows the value of personalized custom customer communications.

This type of customer communications program has all the right attributes:

■ It is based on a customer database with purchase and response history.

■ It is based on measuring customer profitability, lifetime value and retention.

■ It creates custom communications from an agent that people know.

■ It was sold to the agents, involved them, and enlisted their enthusiastic participation.

■ It made customers happy, and Travelers profitable.

Getting Them to Eat More

The Customer Connection (TCC) in Escondido, California developed real proof that customer communications work.

In the beginning TCC began with birthday and anniversary cards. They developed dramatic results. For one 25-unit steak and seafood restaurant, they offered a $10 birthday discount to 215,600 customers who filled out a birthday club registration card. A database was created from these registrations. The birthday card mailings, over a year, cost $90,000. 41.1 percent of the cards were redeemed, producing overall sales of $2.9 million dollars. Each birthday patron brought an average of 1.8 other guests for the party who paid full price.

Building on the success of the birthday programs, TCC created permanent Frequent Diner membership cards for restaurant patrons. One restaurant chain had given its diners paper membership cards. Then TCC ordered plastic cards from a manufacturer. In June, TCC mailed out 24,725 of these permanent plastic cards. During the week before the cards went out, these patrons visited the restaurants 1,050 times. During the 13 weeks after receiving their permanent plastic cards, these same patrons visited an average of 1,400 times per week—an increase of 33 percent. They spent $156,000 more than they were spending before the cards were mailed. What is most significant is that there was no special promotion associated with the plastic cards. There was no additional discount offer. The plastic cards were simply a substitute for the paper cards. They were a form of customer communication. Communications programs work!

"They Would Have Come Anyway"

So how do communications really affect dining behavior? Programs like those run by TCC permitted managers to measure the impact of their communications in detail. Let us take a specific example:

A restaurant chain wanted to increase frequency and reactivate members who seemed to be "drifting away." TCC selected 4,000 members who had not earned any points during the previous three months. They sent them a letter offering a $5 discount on dinner. The offer was good for 35 days. The letter cost $1,800. What were the results?

- *Average member visits* went from 25 per day before the promotion to 42 per day during the promotion, and 29 per day in the 35-day period after the promotion was over.

- *Average visits per card* went from 1.18 before to 1.26 during and 1.22 after the promotion.

- *Incremental sales* were $17,100 during the promotion and $4,700 in the 35 days after the promotion was over.

In other words, by spending $1,800, this restaurant chain reactivated 599 people who were otherwise lost as patrons. The gain was not only during the promotion period, but had a lasting effect, with 147 of the reactivated people visiting the restaurant after the promotion was over. Relationship building works and has lasting benefits.

Boosting Retention through Targeted Communications

What do you do when you have a defection rate of almost 60 percent and falling revenue per customer in a highly competitive industry? This was the problem faced by a large Fortune 50 telecommunications company. The marketing staff turned to KnowledgeBase Marketing (KBM). KBM's first step was to identify strengths, weaknesses, opportunities, and threats. The KBM group interviewed customers and employees. Before KBM arrived the telephone company had a customer contact strategy that involved five communications per year:

- A welcome message
- A "how are you doing?" cross-sell piece at 90 days
- A retention piece after six months
- A referral piece after nine months
- An anniversary piece after 12 months.

Everyone got the same communications. They cost an average of $7.38 per customer per year. The customer satisfaction indexes showed very high satisfaction, but 4 out of every 10 of these satisfied customers were leaving every year—most of them to the competition.

The company had no marketing database, so KBM set about creating one to meet the needs of an enhanced program. They included in the database both current customers and those who had dropped the service during the past three years. They included calls to customer service and sales, and responses to marketing efforts broken into negative, positive, severe, and mild. KBM also appended demographic data, including age, income, education, and home value. Using this database with billing history going back for several years, the KBM team built predictive churn models that rated customers by likelihood of dropping the service.

A Risk Revenue Matrix

Once KBM had the database in place and had run the churn model, the team developed a current value algorithm and created a risk revenue matrix that looked like this (Figure 6-4).

	Likelihood of Churn		
Lifetime Value	High	Medium	Low
High	**Priority A**	*Priority B*	Priority C
Medium	*Priority B*	*Priority B*	Priority C
Low	Priority C	Priority C	Priority C

Figure 6-4. A risk revenue matrix.

The basic principle of this matrix was to determine which customers the company should work to retain, and which they did not need to bother with. Those in Priority C were either of low value to the company, or had a low probability of leaving. Do not waste money on these folks. Concentrate your resources on the valuable people (Priorities A and B) who might quit the service. This matrix reduced those customers included in the retention program from 100 percent to 44 percent—a tremendously cost-effective technique.

To determine the value of customers to the firm, KBM determined everyone's current lifetime value (LTV) and their potential lifetime value based on their demographics. For example, a woman in her twenties might be currently using 1,200 minutes per year. Looking ahead, as her family expanded and her income grew, her potential might expand to 1,800 or more minutes per year. These calculations were built into a program that stored LTV and potential LTV into every customer's database record.

A Customer Contact Strategy

The relationship marketing program consisted of a series of two way (survey and response) communications ranging from zero "touches" up to eight per year, depending on the priority of the customer and their personal preferences and demographics. For those people in the retention program, KBM devised a customer contact strategy that included the same elements the client was already mailing: a welcome package, an anniversary package, a retention questionnaire, and a cross-sell package. In addition, KBM introduced a rewards program for a very select group of high-value customers.

Once KBM had determined the appropriate communications, they had to test various combinations to be sure that they would be effective in modifying behavior. To do this, they created a communications testing matrix, which was tested on a relatively small number of customers. Senior management agreed to test four communication components: A, B, C, and D. There were three types of incentives: none, a few free minutes, and a lot of free minutes. Each of the test programs was compared with the behavior of a control group that received no communications at all.

How Big a Reward Do You Need?

One of the things that the team discovered in the testing phase was that the number of minutes given as a reward had little impact on behavior. People responded just as well to a reward of a few minutes as they did to a lot of minutes. As a result of this very valuable discovery, they scaled back the rewards to just enough to make a difference. They also learned that in communications, the slickness of the creative did not matter either. They tried two different creative approaches, one expensive and one inexpensive. Both worked equally well, so they retained the less expensive package.

With the testing completed, they were ready for the rollout, comparing always the behavior of the customers they were trying to retain with those of control groups that received no retention building communications at all.

The Results

In the first place, they were able to reduce churn. They brought the defections of the test group down by 3 percent per year that reduced the attrition rate from 39.27 percent to 38 percent annually. This translated into a $2 million annual increase in the bottom line (Figure 6-5).

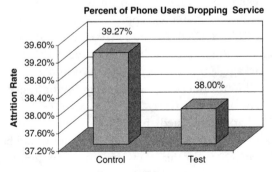

Figure 6-5. Increased retention rates.

Within the target groups, churn reduction was even more dramatic. The overall rate of churn in the control group of the four priority cohorts (A and B) was 24 percent. Of those in these cohorts who were mailed the retention program, the churn rate was 18 percent—a decrease of 25 percent. Most of the retention packages called for a response from the customer. Of those who responded positively—saying that they were happy with the service—the churn rate was only 9 percent. For those who responded that they were unhappy, a SWAT team worked to resolve their problems. Where the team was successful and the problem was resolved, the churn rate was also 9 percent. But response to the communications was not essential to reduce churn. *The churn rate of the non-responders to the messages was lower than the churn rate of the control group that received no communications at all!*

Increased Annual Revenue

Besides reducing the churn rate, the communications program also had a positive impact on phone usage and revenue (Figure 6-6).

The average annual revenue from those in the retention program was 5 percent higher: $707 as compared to only $678 from identical people in the control group that did not receive the retention communications. The phone usage for the targeted groups also increased by 15 percent—from 1,300 to 1,500 minutes per year (Figure 6-7).

Perhaps most surprising of all was the reduced cost of the communications. Previously every customer got five mailings per year for an average cost of $7.38 per customer per year. With the new retention program, they stopped mailing to everyone in Priority C. The number of people

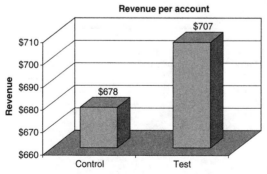

Figure 6-6. Increased phone revenue.

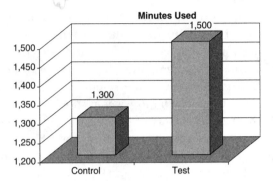

Figure 6-7. Increased minutes usage.

mailed dropped by 56 percent. The highest value, highest risk customers, Priority A, received eight messages a year, while Priority B customers received less. The overall cost per customer of the communications, therefore, in the third year came down to only $1.38 per total customer (including those that got no communications) per year (Figure 6-8). In other words, they got these great retention benefits, *and at the same time* reduced the cost of the retention program!

We can sum up the central lessons learned about customer communications from this program developed by KBM. To succeed you must:

- Interview customers and employees to come up with a plan that would work in the circumstances.

- Build a database that contains enough data so that you can determine two things: likelihood to churn, and lifetime value to the company.

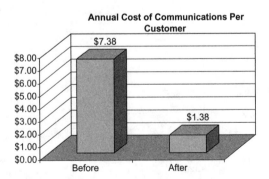

Figure 6-8. Reduced cost of communications.

- Run a churn model, and determine lifetime value and potential value.

- Create a risk/revenue matrix so that you can focus attention on only those customers who are most valuable and most likely to churn.

- Develop a winning series of communications designed to modify the behavior of the target groups.

- Test those communications against a control group so that you can be sure of what you are doing.

- Measure your success every step of the way against control groups so that you are sure that what is happening to churn, to usage, and to revenue is due to your efforts, and not to some market shift.

Communicating Using Emails

The Indiana Health Care Association lobbies on behalf of hospital-based nursing homes and assisted living communities in the state. For many years, the IHCA's primary means of communicating with members was via a printed, bi-monthly newsletter sent to several hundred members.

Art Logsdon, IHCA President, decided to experiment with email. "The cost effectiveness of email let us communicate with our members at a frequency impossible to achieve with printed pieces. Using ExactTarget's tracking features, we were able to tell which stories were of interest to our members. We tailored our communications by the feedback in our tracking reports. Before we used emails, with our printed newsletters, we had no way of knowing if our members were actually reading them, or what stories had the highest interest. Now that we're using email, we've been able to track the results and continually improve our messaging and the overall effectiveness of our newsletter."

With printing costs upwards of $2,000 for each newsletter, the email system saved IHCA over $50,000 per year. In addition to the newsletter, the Association began using the software to send legislation and educational updates to their members.

Turning Customers off

Be careful that your responses to inbound communications do not turn your customers off. Several years ago I spent $100 and became a member of a think-tank institute in Washington. It was everything

I wanted: they showered me with newsletters and policy papers on important public issues and invited me to a seminar at which I got to meet all the members of the staff. As a result, I increased my voluntary annual payment to $250. Here was the kind of institution that was interesting, and, I thought, was interested in me.

That was my big mistake. After a long overseas trip to a politically hot country, I sent the president of the institute a 12-page analysis of the political and economic situation in the country, asking for his views. He never answered. I sent a follow-up letter a month later.

Still no answer. Two months later I sent another follow-up letter. I finally received a letter after three months from a low-level staffer who said that he disagreed with my analysis. He did not thank me for preparing it. I got the impression that he thought that my letter was a nuisance and a waste of his time.

My mistake was thinking that they had me on a marketing database. Actually, they had me on a mailing list. It was intended to be a one-way communication. They sent out the policy papers, I sent in the money. My attempt to write a policy analysis paper just did not fit into the mailing list system that they had going. I cut my annual contribution back to $100.

My lifetime value to this institute went from about $2,500 to about $1,000 due to one unanswered letter. I would have been happy with a one-paragraph letter from the president (drafted by an assistant) saying, "Thank you for your very interesting letter on X. I am passing it on to our foreign policy group as input to their thinking on this very important country. I appreciate your taking your time to write to me."

The point: marketing databases permit any organization to maintain one-on-one communications with their customers or members in a mutually profitable relationship. They create the illusion of a close relationship. It lies in your hands to determine whether this illusion is to be maintained and supported, or shattered by your responses to customer input.

Once you have set up a database, many of your customers would like to feel that the flow of information and products from you to them and the orders and payments from them to you has created a friendly, close, mutual relationship between them and your company. But if in setting up your database you do not provide for two-way communication, customers will eventually realize that they are corresponding with a computer, not a person. The illusion of mutual interest will be shattered, and you will lose loyalty and sales or contributions as a result.

When Will They Buy a Second Product?

A major entertainment software company faced shrinking profit margins because of:

■ Price competition

■ Power struggles between software manufacturers, distributors and retailers

■ Rebates offered by the competition

■ The expansion of the Internet as a new channel and a "community base" for software purchasers

■ Increases in processing costs

KBM analyzed the company's sales during the previous two years to:

■ Assess the potential for increasing direct sales.

■ Identify current direct-purchasing customers and likely direct-purchasing customers to increase sales through the direct channel (as opposed to driving sales to the resellers).

■ Identify likely next purchases and cross-sell them to the customer base via direct contact.

■ Get a better understanding of the company's customer segments by brand, product, and channel purchase behavior.

The study concentrated on four analytical approaches:

■ Channel Analysis

■ Enhanced RFM Analysis

■ Purchase Interval Analysis

■ Product Path Analysis

Channel Analysis

There were three ways that the company's products were purchased: through retailers, through direct sales, and by a combination of the two. Retail sales predominated (94 percent) but the other channels were growing faster.

Analysis showed that people whose previous purchase was more than 10 months old were very unlikely to buy again.

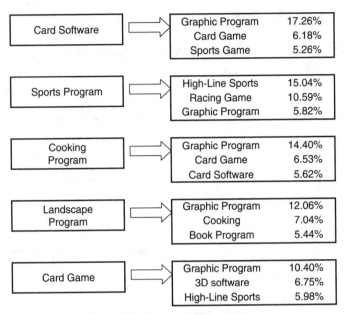

Figure 6-9. Cross-sales possibilities.

So, when was the best time to sell a second product? Twenty-three percent of all second product purchases were made on the same day as the original purchase, and 38 percent were bought within the next three months. After that, the possibility of a cross sale became less and less likely.

Knowledge of when to offer a second product was clear from this analysis. But what product should be offered? KBM looked at 94 different products and compared the cross-sale rates for each of them. Ninety-four product series were crossed against each other to determine the most likely next best product. This analysis produced a very detailed Next Best Product chart (Figure 6-9).

Results

Using this chart and many others like it for the 94 different products the software firm knew when to provide a cross-sell offer (the same day or within three months) and what product to offer to each customer. This information provided guidance for the retailers (in retailer instructions), for customers (in brochures included with products), and for the direct-sales staff (in terms of what offers to send to which registered customers). This was personalized information that had not been available to the company previously, which had been based on individual product promotions. The information provided a substantial lift in cross sales.

Summary

- Communications with customers can make the customers happy and increase retention and sales. You can only prove that communications work, however, if you have a control group.

- One of the fastest growing and least expensive ways to communicate with customers is by use of the World Wide Web. You create an Extranet, giving your best customers their own ID, personal page, and password. If you do it right, you will have them hooked for life.

- The Travelers communications program was successful in increasing customer retention. This program had some key features:

  - It was funded by the independent agents, not by Travelers.

  - The communications came from a local agent, not from a Travelers VP.

  - Its messages were personalized for each customer's situation.

  - It improved the retention rate by up to 5 percent.

- Birthday rewards from restaurants produce very significant sales annually at comparatively little cost.

- Points work in building interest and retention. Everyone opens the envelopes that tell them how many points they have accumulated.

- A revenue reward matrix can be very useful in deciding who to communicate with, and who to ignore. Use of such a matrix can be highly profitable.

- Giving free minutes as a reward can change behavior. The number of minutes given is not as important as the fact that you are paying attention.

- Slick, expensive, communications may do no better than less expensive communications. Do not waste money. Test.

- Successful retention communication programs not only improve retention, they usually increase sales and the average order size as well.

- The second product analysis is highly useful in certain situations. It tells you when people are most likely to buy another product, and what that product is most likely to be, based on the previous purchases. Knowing these two facts enables a company to create communications that are meaningful to the customers and profitable for the supplier.

Executive Quiz 6

Answers to quiz questions (Figure 6-10) can be found in Appendix B.

	Put the appropriate letter before each answer	
	Questions	**Answers**
a	Communicating with customers increases the?	38%
b	Needed to prove the value of a communication?	41.10%
c	In Travelers case, messages came from?	$2.54
d	In Lighting case, control group spent?	$2.69
e	Email messages compared to direct mail	$707
f	Ideal group to receive messages	1,500
g	How many birthday cards redeemed in case study	$50,000
h	Restaurant reactivation increased visits from 25 to	42
i	Which risk revenue cells should be mailed?	A and B
j	Travelers gain in ROI per dollar	Agents
k	How can Amazon say, "Welcome back Arthur"?	average order size
l	In telecom case, attrition rate reduced from 39.27% to	Control group
m	In telecom case, revenue per account increased to	Cookies
n	In telecom case, minutes used went from 1,300 to	Customer communications
o	Annual Indiana Health Care saving though emails	Failure to respond
p	Annual participating Travelers agent costs per customer	High LTV, High Churn
q	Who helped Dayton Hudson improve communications?	Hot line staff
r	Central idea in database marketing	Less than before
s	Result of giving customers access to a premier page	Lifetime Value
t	Risk revenue axes are likelihood of leaving versus	Lower response
u	The best time to sell a second product	Retention rate
v	Good way to assure envelopes get opened	Show accumulated points
w	Successful retention messages also increase	The next best product
x	What shatters the illusion of a close relationship?	The same day
y	Product path analysis helps to determine	They become addicted

Figure 6-10. Quiz 6.

7

Customer Retention and Loyalty

Loyalty is the result of our marketing efforts. It's an indicator of how successful we have been with our total marketing effort. We must never forget that loyalty is not the obligation of the customer. Rather, it's the result of us providing such a continuous set of positive shopping experiences for the customer that she chooses to keep returning to do business with us...

BRIAN WOOLF
Loyalty Marketing—The Second Act

The first step in managing a loyalty-based business system is finding and acquiring the right customers: customers who will provide steady cash flows and a profitable return on the firm's investment for years to come, customers whose loyalty can be won and kept. Loyalty-based companies should remember three rules of thumb:

- *Some customers are inherently predictable and loyal, no matter what company they're doing business with. They simply prefer stable, long-term relationships.*

- *Some customers are more profitable than others. They spend more money, pay their bills more promptly, and require less service.*

- *Some customers will find your products and services more valuable than those of your competitors. No company can be all things to all people. Your*

*particular strengths will simply fit better with
certain customer's needs and opportunities.*

FREDERICK REICHHELD
The Loyalty Effect

What constitutes customer loyalty? Is it a series of actions such as repeat purchases or an emotional bond such as recommending your company to a friend? I think that true customer loyalty is something like a successful marriage. It is a relationship in which both parties are satisfied with their relations with each other. They are not worried every day that their partner will stop loving them or run off with somebody else. They will come through misunderstandings and arguments with their relationship still intact, or even stronger. Developing a bond of loyalty between you and your customers is what database marketing is all about. Loyal customers are more valuable than the average customer. They tend to:

- have higher retention rates;
- have higher spending rates;
- have higher referral rates;
- have a higher lifetime value;
- be less expensive to serve;
- buy higher priced options.

There is one key measurement for loyalty. It is the retention rate (sometimes measured as the repurchase rate or the renewal rate). Retention is more important than the spending rate or the frequency of spending. Why? Because when they are gone, they are gone. It is hard to get them back. As long as you have them, there is always a possibility of working out any problems, and getting them to spend more or trade up to higher options.

The link between loyalty and database marketing is communication. Loyalty is built and maintained by two-way communications between you and your customer. Customers make purchases. You thank them for their patronage. You ask your customer for their preferences. They respond. You store their preferences in your database. Then you modify your services to make sure that their preferences are respected. Acting on these preferences involves a lot of little perks and services that show customers that you really are loyal to them. When they see the Wall Street Journal, instead of USA Today, on the doorstep of their hotel room door in the morning in some new city without having to ask for it the night before, they realize that you listened to them and are being loyal to their preferences. The database is central to the process: this is where the customer preferences and other data are stored. You use the database to create the personalized services and messages that build loyalty.

Loyalty-Building Communications

Customer Preferences. One of the most inexpensive but powerful customer marketing techniques is to get customers to enter their own preferences for services. This can be done in writing or over the phone, but today it is increasingly done on the Web. The advantages of creating a customer profile with preferences are twofold: you learn more about the customer, and the customer feels that he or she has been listened to by your company. Tests and controls can show that customers who complete a profile with preferences are more loyal than other customers. (Were they already loyal or did the preference creation process make them so?) For preferences to work, of course, you will have to modify your services or communications to customers based on their expressed preferences. That is where the database becomes important. With an automated system you can have a means of using the database-stored preferences on a daily basis to provide personalized services and communications. Employees throughout your company, all over America, have to be informed about these preferences and act on them day after day. Your Web site will have to be modified. Will the cost of collecting customer profiles and preferences and acting on them be justified by increased retention and increased revenue? This can be determined by setting up control groups that are not asked to complete preference forms.

The Importance of Caller ID and Cookies. When a guest calls room service today in most modern American hotels, the CSR says, "What can I do for you, Mr. Adams." This is superior customer service, and has become standard in hotels. What many companies have not realized is that the same principle that applies within a hotel can also apply to customers calling your customer service from their home or office. When a repeat customer calls your customer service, caller ID permits you to know who is calling before you answer the phone. The customer's entire record, from the database, should automatically show on the CSR's screen. The customer can be greeted by name with some personal information included in the conversation to make it clear to the customer that your CSR knows who the customer is and how important that customer's patronage is to your business. Using caller ID, it is not necessary for the customer to give her customer number, name, address, etc. To build loyalty, you set up an automated system that recreates the personal relationships that the old corner grocer used to maintain with his customers. The same benefits of caller ID on the Web are created by cookies. When customers come back to your Web site, the screen says, "Welcome back, Susan" and you populate the customer's name and address in any forms that she has to fill out to order products or services. The costs of caller ID and cookies today are very low. The cost of the software to provide the database information to the customer service representatives and the Web site is also comparatively low. Is this personalization worth it? Does it make a difference in terms of customer retention and spending? This can and should be tested using control groups.

Event-driven Relationship Messages. There are lots of ways to build loyalty with event-driven communications. These are not sales pitches. They are expressions of friendship. Some companies send birthday or holiday cards. Do such cards do any good? With a database, you can test this by not sending the cards to 20 percent of the customers. After a year, you measure the spending and retention rates of the two groups. You can see right away if they are making a difference, and how much. You can see if they are paying for themselves in terms of retention and sales.

Some companies use their database for trawling. They look for events. National Change of Address (NCOA^{LINK}) should be run on any database four times a year. Twenty percent of Americans move every year. When NCOA^{LINK} is run, you will know, every quarter, the identity of the 5 percent of your customer base that has just moved. You will have to decide what to say to the movers.

Other trawling results can be based on behavior. Did they just make a big purchase? Have they reached an anniversary with your company? "Congratulations on 10 years of loyalty! We want you to know that we value your business, Mr. Hughes. Ever since your purchase of a Kenmore dishwasher 10 years ago, we have been happy to have you as a customer. We are delighted that our relationship is continuing into another decade!"

Is this just a neat thing to do or are there solid economic benefits to be derived from it? Your database holds the answers.

Event-driven Marketing Messages. There are many loyalty-building marketing messages that can be driven by events. One example is the Birthday Club discussed in Chapter 3. Another is a follow-up on a customer request. For example, if you have a search box on your Web site and the customer enters "Lawn Furniture" but did not buy anything, you could send the customer an e-mail, out of the blue, that features lawn furniture. It does not have to say, "Since you were looking for this". This is particularly useful in business to business where executives are seeking specific products. To learn that you have something that you know they are looking for can make a real difference and make your company seem more interesting. Instead of the "product of the month" you can keep track of what customers are interested in and send them notices of what you think they might want. Customer service can keep track of what people have asked for in phone calls, but not bought. It will not hurt to have an e-mail about what they asked for which arrives within an hour of the phone call. If it comes the next day, it may be too late. You will have to set up an automated message system that can be triggered by your customer service representative with one click of her mouse.

Loyalty Programs

Finally, of course, you can build and maintain loyalty with loyalty programs. By a loyalty program, I mean a system whereby a customer has specifically signed up for a program. She receives a plastic card with her name on it. The card is used whenever she shops in a retail store, on the phone, or on the Web. The card does two things: it provides her with some benefit she could not get without the card and it provides you with valuable information that you can use to understand the customer and build her loyalty. Before you begin a loyalty program, you have to decide what you expect to get out of it and what role it will play in your total marketing program.

Brian Woolf made a detailed study of customer loyalty programs and customer behavior. He started out by asking, "What customer behavior do you want to reward?"

- Do we want *better* or *more* customers?
- Do we want *high* or *low*-spending customers?

- What is more important: increased sales or increased profitability?
- What changes in behavior are required to hold on to more of our good customers and lengthen their average stay with us?
- Of the behaviors we have chosen as our goals, which are the most profitable ones to be rewarding?

These are important questions to ask before we launch any program designed to maintain or increase loyalty. Loyalty programs require resources. They are not free. Money can be wasted unless we know what we are doing. As Brian notes: "We must water what we want to grow. But first we must decide what we want to grow... All customers are not equal. Behavior usually follows rewards."

Customer Registration

The loyalty program for a retailer, bank, or other service provider begins with a customer application or registration form. The idea is to capture not just the name and address, but some information about the customers, which is relevant to their purchasing decisions concerning your products or services. Be sure to get their e-mail addresses with permission to contact them through e-mail. You will also want to get age, income, home ownership, and length of residence. To get the customers to register, there has to be something in it for them. If they ask, "Why should I register?" your answer could be, "Because we want to reward our regular customers more." What are the rewards? You must determine that. They could be lower prices for card holders, access to information not available to others, or points towards achievable rewards. The rewards must be so compelling that most customers will want to register.

Loyalty and Affluence

Wealthy consumers are more loyal. A nationwide survey by Parago (www.parago.com) showed that high-income households exhibit greater loyalty and are influenced more by loyalty programs than average-income households. Even more influential than age, gender, or geography, household income proved to be the most indicative of the strength and impact of customer loyalty. In total, 94 percent of high-income households said their membership in a loyalty, rewards, or frequent customer program had a strong to moderate influence on their purchasing decisions vs. 78 percent of all consumers.

As income increases, so does the importance and impact of loyalty programs on consumers. Among loyalty program members, 92 percent of high-income households ($125K+) are actively enrolled in an airline frequent flier program, compared to 51 percent of all respondents. Hotel program membership showed similar income-dependent results, with 78 percent of high-income households enrolled in a hotel reward program, compared to only 35 percent of the general population.

High-income households also differed in the types of rewards they preferred to receive from loyalty programs. Compared to the general population, high-income households were less interested in price discounts and more interested in receiving both rewards and recognition for their loyalty. In the Parago study, 39 percent of high-income households named the "special treatment" they received from loyalty programs as one of their favorite things. Particularly among male travelers first-class upgrades, perks, faster check-in and boarding were more important to them than the free miles.

The loyalty programs affected consumer behavior. According to the survey, 93 percent of U.S. consumers were willing to depart 1 hour earlier than needed for a flight—if it meant they could fly on their preferred frequent flier airline. Sixty-seven percent of frequent flyers said they would be willing to pay $25 more (or 5 percent more) for a ticket on their frequent flier airline vs. a competitor.

Helena and I both have Citibank credit cards because they give us American Airlines miles. We dropped our Chevy Chase and MBNA cards that we had had for years when we decided to collect American miles. What Chevy Chase and MBNA should have done was to ask us what airline program we were members of. If they had offered us airline miles, pro-actively, we would have stayed, happily, as customers. Too bad for them.

How to Use Your Customer Database to Promote Loyalty

Once customers are registered and on your database, you can create periodic reports that will enable you to direct your loyalty program in profitable directions. There are dozens of things that can be done. In fact, just about all the loyalty-promoting steps described in this book are available to you now that you have a database rich with transaction history derived from customer's use of their cards.

I should note that, depending on your situation, you may not require customers to use their cards whenever they make a purchase. As a result of their registration for the card, you have their telephone number. You should have at least one credit card (Master, Visa, Amex, or your own proprietary card) registered with you with the card numbers in the database. Every night (or more often) when all your POS systems are polled to provide data for your database, you can run all the credit cards used and telephone numbers provided against lookup tables in your database, so you can record transactions in your customer's files even though they have not used their membership card or provided their card number when they made a purchase. Of course, with a good POS system connected with your database, just the entering of the phone number at the POS station will bring up a customer transaction history on a screen at the station, so that the clerk can talk to the customer as if he knew her.

With this data, you can create lifetime value tables as described in Chapter 3 or automated communications described in Chapter 6. You can do segmentation as described in Chapter 8. You can set up tests and controls as described in Chapter 11. You can do electronic marketing described in Chapter 12. The registration, therefore, is the entrance to the world of loyalty marketing.

Loyalty Cards

Loyalty programs begin with loyalty cards or the data related to them. Brian Woolf said on this subject: "The primary purpose of a business is to acquire, satisfy, and retain customers, profitably. The primary purpose of a loyalty card program is information, which then helps achieve the goals of the business. Customer information is used to help a business retain its customers (i.e. build loyalty). But it is also used to help accomplish the other business goals of customer acquisition; satisfying customers with the right location, product assortment, quality, service and friendliness; and doing so cost-effectively, by helping identify inefficient and wasteful areas of spending, particularly expenditure on low yield customers".

Brian gave as an example this quote from Steve Burrows, Director of Retail Operations of the Hale-Halsell Company, based in Tulsa, Oklahoma: "Some time after the card launch in our Super-H stores, we utilized our zip code report to more efficiently reach our customers and were able to cut 25 percent of our ad copies. We requested a name and address report for five area zip codes where we were sending 20,000 ads—and where we are now sending only 750 ads directly to our card customers in those areas. We will save $250,000 this year in our 14 stores—all previously wasted. This is just the tip of the iceberg. We had been sending out ads weekly, equal to three times our customer count. I am using 50 percent of this to finish paying off my program expense and the other 50 percent goes straight to my bottom line. After one year, advertising expense has been cut dramatically."

Bolstering Loyalty with Points

There is no question today that loyalty can be created or increased by awarding points or miles. The basic idea behind points is to avoid discounting your product. Points represent a gift or reward which cannot easily be related to the price of the product or service. Millions of Americans' loyalty to an airline is molded by frequent flyer programs. These airline points programs work. Do loyalty programs work for other products and services? The answer seems to be yes, but not as well. There are scores of other programs run by restaurants, retail stores, banks, hotels, credit cards, long-distance services, and others who reward customers with points. Many companies have been able to prove, using control groups, that these programs do build loyalty.

What Reward Should You Offer?

Chris Moloney of Parago offered this case study: "A large, national paint company wanted to develop a loyalty rewards program for their most valuable customers. Most of these customers were professional or semi-pro painting contractors. The program was designed to reward them for their paint purchases. Despite my strong recommendations to the contrary, the company insisted that the only reward would be more free paint and some paint-related products. The program launched rather poorly. Why? Our research indicated two main issues. First, painters were simply not motivated by free paint. It was far less interesting for them than a free airline ticket or a TV. Second, most of these painters passed through the cost of paint and materials, showing the receipts for the costs to customers. Free paint, therefore, provided almost no financial value to the contractors. As a result, with no financial or personal motivation surrounding the rewards, the program did not modify customer behavior. In a short time we changed the program to offer items like portable CD/radios designed for "on the job" usage and leather portfolios for contractors to use in writing bids. Within three months, the company saw exponential growth in program enrollment and activity. The return on investment was significant."

Be careful with points, however. If you are a supermarket or discount retailer with a very low profit margin, the points can eat you alive. A better strategy would be to provide card holders with reduced prices on certain featured items, rather than awarding points at all. Many stores set up their POS systems to record the savings on selected items at the bottom of the cash register receipt, "Today you saved $6.71 by using your Wynn Dixie Card." This, you can afford. It is a form of communication. It builds loyalty. It is much less complex than a points program which requires monthly statements and redemptions.

Is Loyalty Inherent in the Customer or Can You Create It by Your Actions?

Frederick Reichheld's book, *The Loyalty Effect,* burst on the database marketing industry like a welcome rainstorm. When I read it, I learned a lot. His ideas are so important that they permeate every chapter of this book. If you have not already read it, you should run out right now and buy a copy yourself.

As you can see by the quote at the beginning of this chapter, Reichheld identified loyal customers (and loyal employees) as central to the success of any enterprise. To be successful, therefore, you have to recruit the right kind of customers (loyal ones) to begin with and then develop programs to foster and maintain that loyalty by the way you treat these customers. Loyalty is a two-way situation: if you want customers to be loyal to you, you must be loyal to them.

How Customers Are Recruited

Reichheld pointed out that your method of attracting and supporting customers may be the most important factor in maintaining customer loyalty. Customers acquired through discounts tend to be less loyal than those acquired through the promise of excellent service. As I have already pointed out, discounts do not foster loyalty. They make customers think about what they are paying instead of what they are getting.

The Importance of Loyal Employees

Another key contribution of Frederick Reichheld is recognition of the importance of employee loyalty to customer loyalty. He pointed out that many, if not most, customers are loyal not to the brand or the firm, but to the people who serve them at the firm. When you lose employees, you often lose customers as well. Any marketing program aimed at customer retention must begin with looking at employee satisfaction and retention. This is not normally an issue dealt with in marketing books, like this one. It should be. The problem is that employee retention throughout a company is seldom something that the marketing department can influence directly. If they want to retain customers, however, marketers must recognize that customer loyalty and employee loyalty are usually tightly linked.

Acquiring the Right Customers

Given that loyal customers are better to have and more profitable than others, what can you do about it? Until Reichheld's book came along, there was one universal answer: figure out who the loyal customers are and treat them well. Provide the things we have discussed in this book: gold cards, President's clubs, advisory panels, member nights, special toll-free phone lines, and hundreds of special services that will encourage these loyal people to stick around for a long time.

There is nothing in Reichheld's book that disagrees with these recommendations. But there is little to support them either. Reichheld simply changed the subject. The route to loyalty, he explained, is to recruit loyal people to begin with. "Some customers are inherently predictable and loyal, no matter what company they are doing business with. They simply prefer stable, long-term relationships."

His book provides dozens of examples of companies who have figured out the characteristics of their loyal customers. They have developed simple rules that aid them in attracting the right kind of customer and avoiding the wrong kinds. Some of his examples are:

■ An insurance company discovered that, for them, married people were more loyal than singles. Mid-Westerners were more loyal than Easterners. Homeowners were more loyal than renters. Once they found this out, they used the knowledge to guide their acquisition strategy.

- MBNA discovered that people reached through an affinity group—such as doctors, dentists, nurses, teachers, and engineers—were more loyal credit card holders than people reached through general direct mail campaigns.

- Many companies used their databases to learn that customers attracted by low-ball discount offers were more likely to disappear than customers attracted using non-discounted offers. They tended to leave as soon as the competition made them an even lower ball offer. Were they different people or had the offer made them think of the company's products in terms of price, rather than value? Who knows? It really does not matter. Discounting is not a profitable long-range strategy.

Reichheld pointed out that satisfaction scores may be worthless as a means of measuring customer loyalty. In the automobile industry, American cars typically have satisfaction scores in the 90 percent, but the repurchase rates hover around 35 percent. Repurchase is the best indicator of loyalty, he concluded.

The Importance of Sales Commissions

An important part of employee loyalty is the employee compensation system. Reichheld pointed out that "There is always a tension between commission sales and customer loyalty because a sales force paid on commission and hell-bent on customer volume generally finds that the easiest prospects to sell are the ones whose loyalty is low." In many industries the acquisition process has become so costly that customers who defect after the first year are unprofitable. A way has to be found to recruit the right kind of customers: loyal customers who last several years. It is possible that this can be done only by modifying the way customers are acquired in the first place and the way they are maintained during the first couple of years.

Insurance Illustration

Let us apply the loyalty principle to life insurance. First-year attrition in life insurance is usually high. In some companies, a life insurance agent receives a large commission on the initial sale and reduced commissions on the next few years' premiums. Let us see how we could increase

40/4/4 Commission Plan		Acquisition Year	Second Year	Third Year	Three Year Total
Retention Rate		65%	70%	75%	
Customers		400,000	260,000	182,000	
Average Premium		$1,600	$1,600	$1,600	
Revenue		$640,000,000	$416,000,000	$291,200,000	$1,347,200,000
Commissions(40/4)	40%	$256,000,000	$16,640,000	$11,648,000	$284,288,000
Reserve for Claims	40%	$256,000,000	$166,400,000	$116,480,000	
Administration (20/15)	20%	$128,000,000	$62,400,000	$43,680,000	
Total Costs		$640,000,000	$245,440,000	$171,808,000	$1,057,248,000
Profit		$0	$170,560,000	$119,392,000	$289,952,000
Discount Rate		1	1.07	1.14	
Net Present Value		$0	$159,401,869	$104,729,825	
Cumulative NPV		$0	$159,401,869	$264,131,694	
Lifetime Value		$0.00	$398.50	$660.33	

Figure 7-1. Lifetime value under the 40/4/4 commission plan.

customer loyalty by changing the commission structure for the agent. Suppose, initially, that agents get a commission of 40 percent of the first year's premium and 4 percent of the premiums paid in the second and third years. Figure 7-1 is an illustration of the resulting lifetime value.

In this example, 35 percent of the customers defect after the first year. Administrative costs are 20 percent the first year and 15 percent each subsequent year. The profit to the company in the first year is zero. The lifetime value of newly acquired customers in the third year is $660. With this system, we are down to less than half of the originally acquired 400,000 customers in the third year. Future profits have to come from this group.

Let us look at this picture and see how we could improve customer loyalty. Customers respond to contacts with agents. In this picture, the agent gets most of his commission in the first year. The agent receives about $200 in the first year for signing up a new customer. Commissions in the next two years are about $40 per retained customer per year. If the agent is aggressive, in the second and third years he is busy hustling up more business @ $200 each, rather than spending a lot of time communicating with his existing customers in the next two years @ $40 each (at least half of which will come in without any significant effort on his part). The way he sees it, one hour spent on new business pays him five times as much as an hour spent with a prior year customer—and he is right.

Suppose we were to change the commission structure. We will offer agents 20 percent on the initial sale and 20 percent on each of the next two years' premiums. The effect of the new commission structure is to get agents to focus more on customer retention and loyalty. Customers respond to communications. There is no question that the retention rate will increase. Why does it increase? For two reasons: (1) the agent will consciously or unconsciously recruit people who will last for two or more years; (2) once customers have taken out a policy, the agent will contact them frequently to make sure that they do not defect. In Figure 7-2, we show the retention rate increasing by 5 basis points in each of the three years. As a result, the insurance company has 210,000 premium-paying customers remaining from the original 400,000 in the third year, rather than the 182,000 resulting from the old system. How have the insurance agents made out?

As you can see from Figure 7-2, the agent's revenue per newly acquired customer has grown by $192. Total company profits have increased from $290 million to $324 million.

Why did the retention rate go up? Because the agent realized that the second and third year premiums were vital to his success as an agent and his ability to maintain his standard of living (Figure 7-3). Under the new system, agents will both seek out loyal customers to begin with and maintain active contact with customers once they have 40/4/4 system may be difficult. You might start by using the new system for new agents, rather than old veterans.

Getting Customers to Be Loyal

No matter how you measure it, loyal customers are more profitable. So how do you get loyal customers? There are really three ways:

- We can treat loyal customers better.
- We can reward loyalty with points or benefits.
- We can vary our customer acquisition methods to attract good customers and avoid the bad ones.

Agent Commissions		
	Before	After
Year 1	$640.00	$320.00
Year 2	$64.00	$320.00
Year 3	$64.00	$320.00
Total	$768.00	$960.00

Figure 7-2. Agent commissions under two compensation schemes.

20/20/20 Commission Plan		Acquisition Year	Second Year	Third Year	Three Year Total
Retention Rate		70%	75%	80%	
Customers		400,000	280,000	210,000	
Average Premium		$1,600	$1,600	$1,600	
Revenue		$640,000,000	$448,000,000	$336,000,000	$1,424,000,000
Commissions	20%	$128,000,000	$89,600,000	$67,200,000	$284,800,000
Reserve for Claims	40%	$256,000,000	$179,200,000	$134,400,000	
Administration 20/15/15)	20%	$128,000,000	$67,200,000	$50,400,000	
Total Costs		$512,000,000	$336,000,000	$252,000,000	$1,100,000,000
Profit		$128,000,000	$112,000,000	$84,000,000	$324,000,000
Discount Rate		1	1.07	1.14	
Net Present Value		$128,000,000	$104,672,897	$73,684,211	
Cumulative NPV		$128,000,000	$232,672,897	$306,357,108	
Lifetime Value		$320.00	$581.68	$765.89	

Figure 7-3. Lifetime value under the 20/20/20 commission system.

Treating Loyal Customers Better

The 80/20 rule applies in all industries. The top 20 percent of your customers give you 80 percent or some other large percentage of your total revenue. Banks compute this by measuring profitability on a monthly basis. We will return to a familiar chart (Figure 7-4) showing how one bank divided their customers into five segments with this result.

In this example, the top two segments totaling 16 percent of the customer households produced 105 percent of the profits. The bottom 28 percent of the customer households were losers. Many companies have an idea that their customer value looks something like this, but few have taken the time actually to do the analysis, and figure out who their

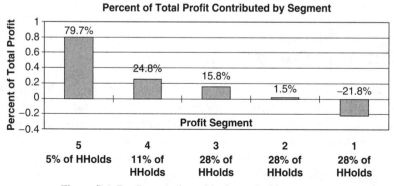

Figure 7-4. Profit contributed by household segments.

loyalists are and who are the others. As already noted, Best Buy found that 20 percent of their customers were unprofitable.

Once you have determined customer profitability segments, however, there are many things that you could and should do to retain your best customers. Here is what some people do:

- special customer service lines, Web sites, or phone numbers for Gold customers putting their best agents on these lines;
- create advisory panels made up of their best customers;
- have special member only nights for Gold customers;
- have special seminars or reports;
- in business to business, host an annual retreat at a resort for the CEOs of their best customers.

Dropping the Losers

In addition to keeping your loyal customers, you should do something about the losers. If these customers are actually costing you money and eating up profits that other customers are creating, you must do something about it.

The first step is to identify these people. Once you know who they are, you can re-price their services or move them towards the door. One bank lets all their employees know which segment each customer falls into. For those customers at the bottom, who are losing money for the bank, the employee screens suggest re-pricing of products. Their loans are renewed at a higher rate. Waivers are not granted. Even more interesting, using caller ID, the call center software makes losing callers wait for five or six rings before anyone from customer service picks up. Gold customers are answered by a special Gold Team on the first ring.

Does Price Cutting Create Loyalty?

Brian Woolf, in his insightful book, *Customer Loyalty—the Second Act*, explains, "Sales always grow when prices are cut. Unfortunately, we now know that new customers attracted by such promotions typically exhibit low loyalty and require constant 'price feeding' to keep returning which means continued lower gross margins. Heavy promotional pricing is not a recommended tactic for building loyalty. Offers to existing customers that reward frequency and spending are far more effective in achieving that goal... Several years ago one major US retailer was suffering from the sales doldrums. To address the problem, it reduced prices in its weekly circulars from previous levels. As expected, this triggered higher sales and transactions—but also less customer loyalty. Its best customer numbers, already down 10 percent from the previous year, continued to fall during the promotional period despite the increased foot traffic. The promotion simply resulted in gaining low margin sales rather than building customer loyalty."

To illustrate how companies go about creating and benefiting from loyalty programs, here are two different case studies from similar companies in the cell phone field:

Case Study: Cell Phone Customer Loyalty #1

A cellular telephone company had a high rate of attrition and declining revenue per subscriber. They had a high proportion of low-end customers within their customer base. Their competitive environment was changing rapidly with price wars, new competitive technology, and alternate distribution channels. They decided to institute a loyalty program designed to:

- reduce customer attrition;
- increase customer lifetime value and customer loyalty;
- get a greater share of their customer's spending;
- make a more effective allocation of their marketing budget.

They asked KnowledgeBase Marketing to conduct two studies:

- *A segmentation and customer satisfaction study.* This showed that the best customers perceived the least value and were the least satisfied with the company's service.
- *An attrition study.* This showed that:
  - □ Defectors expressed low satisfaction months before the decision was made to defect.
  - □ If a customer complained, the odds of defection quadrupled.
  - □ If the customer was "very satisfied" with how a problem was handled, they were quite unlikely to defect.

To identify potential defectors, the analysts:

- developed 68 models in all;
- rated the models based on performance vs. the control group;
- selected a neural network for the final segmentation job which had the ability to handle a large volume of variables.

The key findings of the neural network model were:

- Two-thirds of all defections occurred within 15 months.
- Approximately 4 out of 10 defections were preventable.
- 53 percent of preventable defections occurred before the seventh month.

A quadrant analysis showed the segments of most concern to the company (Figure 7-5).

Creating the Rewards Program

Based on the models, the company created a rewards program focused on Group A: the high risk (high potential for attrition) with the highest current revenue. Other rewards programs were created for the other groups. The strategies were to:

- identify key customer segments;
- allocate marketing investment based on revenue and profit;

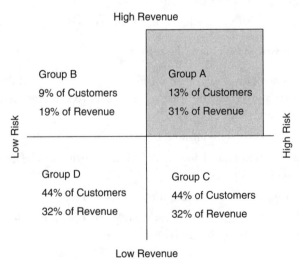

Figure 7-5. Quadrant customer analysis.

- provide different treatments for each segment within the loyalty program;
- provide super services to the best customers;
- provide individual loyalty rewards based on a customer's life stage, needs, and value;
- use models to trigger proactive communications to customers with high attrition risk;
- establish a system to detect problems and resolve them before the customer headed for the door.

After a year into the loyalty program, the company found that:

- The program generated a return on investment of $2.09 for every $1 invested.
- Attrition of those customers receiving the rewards communications was 1.27 points lower than those in a control group.
- Average revenue ($1,412) in the rewards test group was 5 percent higher than in the control group ($1,358).
- There was an increase of $19.6 million dollars in annual sales to those 13,881 customers who were retained by the loyalty program (compared to a control group).

Cell Phone Loyalty Program #2

Another cell phone company analyzed their customers for the purpose of creating a loyalty program. They found that (Figure 7-6):

- The top 5 percent of membership generated 78 percent more revenue and 103 percent more profit than the next 6–10 percent
- The top 10 percent had 38 percent greater tenure than the average member
- The bottom 15 percent was unprofitable—yet was receiving same communications, benefits, etc., as all other customers.

To reward and retain their best customers the company divided their customers into three segments based on monthly profitability:

- Less than $15 per month profits—These received no rewards at all.
- $15–$49 per month profits—These received rewards.
- $50+ per month profits—These were the Gold customers who received very valuable rewards.

Telecom Customer Ranking	Average Monthly Revenue	Average Monthly Gross Profit
Top 5%	$125	$69
Top 10%	$70	$34
Top 15%	$55	$25
Top 20%	$45	$20
Top 25%	$39	$17
Top 30%	$33	$14
Top 35%	$29	$11
Top 40%	$25	$10

Figure 7-6. Revenue and profit from the top four deciles.

With the help of KnowledgeBase Marketing, the company overlaid AmeriLINK data to get a customized view of each customer. Based on this view, they developed a number of individual communications tactics customized for the segment involved. After a year, the company assessed the payoff from the new system:

Gold customers ($50+ per month) compared with controls (Figure 7-7):

- 37.65 percent reduction in revenue churn (due to customer attrition);
- $3.15 MM saved revenue;
- 33.94 percent reduction in customer attrition;
- 27,420 accounts saved.

Customers below Gold (less than $50 per month) (Figure 7-8):

- 21 percent reduction in revenue churn;
- 40 percent reduction in account churn (customer attrition).

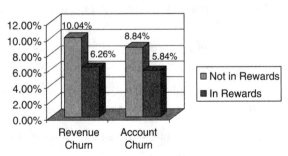

Figure 7-7. Revenue and account attrition difference in rewards and non-rewards customers.

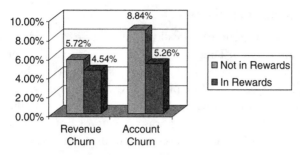

Figure 7-8. Below Gold loyalty improvement.

The Hallmark Gold Crown Loyalty Program

There were 5,000 independently owned Hallmark Gold Crown Stores. Few people buy cards only at these stores. People are busy. They buy where it is convenient. To protect these Gold Crown stores, the Hallmark marketing staff created a special loyalty program. At the inception of the program the Gold Crown stores did not think of themselves as a network. They thought of the Hallmark Card store down the street as their competition. The Hallmark marketing staff had to teach them that their competition was the mass markets.

How the Program Was Developed

The Laurie Broderick of The Carlson Marketing Group in Minneapolis developed the initial plan working with Cindy Jeffreys of Hallmark Cards in Kansas City. The test was not difficult to sell, but the rollout required that thousands of individual store owners had to agree to the program, fund it, participate, and carry out all the rules of the program.

The test was done in 16 stores in two cities, Kansas City and Denver. These stores were chosen because they had the point of sale technology that made it possible to track behavior at the consumer level—what products were purchased in detail. In the test, the consumers enrolled in the stores and immediately got a sequentially numbered temporary card. Customers earned 10 points for every dollar they spent, with a reward certificate for every 100 points. Hallmark issued a permanent card after each consumer had earned 500 points. Reward certificates were issued quarterly as they were earned. The test was measured by comparing total store sales, transactions, and the individual average transaction of each customer, with similar statistics from the national average.

Lessons Learned from the Test

The test resulted in increased call volumes that exceeded anything that had been anticipated. There was a backlog. The service center could not call customers back fast enough. There was a backlog in the enrollment process and in getting out the plastic cards. Another problem was in the creation of control groups. Hallmark marketers soon realized that to prove that what they were doing was working or not working, they had to set up a control group for every single program: every bonus offer, every customer segment.

For the rollout, Cindy and Laurie revised the base reward structure to 200 points for a $1 reward. This lowered the payout to 5 basis points. They added points for cards and bonus offers. They offered 25 points for every greeting card purchased—the key behavior they wanted to drive. They added unique seasonal bonus offers, ornament offers, and still had the flexibility to give special offers and stay within a profitable financial reward structure.

They lowered the hurdle rate to get a permanent card to 200 points. They learned that once you have a consumer who has raised her hand and who wants to be included, you should not keep her waiting too long. The sooner you get that plastic card in her hands, the sooner you get her actively engaged in the program and get her using it. They capped the quarterly reward certificate at $20. If the consumer earned more points they just banked them to the next quarter.

After consumers earned 200 points, they were sent a welcome kit including a 100-point bonus, a plastic card, and a description of the system. Every letter was personalized with their transaction balance and the stores where they shopped. The letter included a product brochure announcing all of the new Hallmark product lines for the season.

The result: after three years, there were 13 million members in the program. It became the largest active member database loyalty program in the world. Ten million customers used the card every year. The Hallmark Gold Crown stores became very successful. The dollars per transaction, the number of trips customers made, the total store sales, and total store transactions were all up, compared to controls. The program grew to the point where a quarter of all the transactions and a third of all card shop dollars were on the card.

Challenges

As the program matured, Hallmark accumulated greater point liabilities and therefore dollar liabilities. They had to combat "Loyalty Fatigue" by trying to make the program seem fresh and new to customers, illustrating to them the benefits of being in the program so that they did not tire out. New members were excited at first with a lot of activity which then tapered off. Hallmark had to be constantly working on doing new creatives and making fresh new offers to keep members' interest.

Hallmark soon learned to create customer segments based on behavior. Some members came in once a week to buy one card. There were lots of little transactions. Others came in once a year, at Christmas, spent a lot, and did not come back for a year. It was important to understand customer behavior and treat each segment differently. If you are someone who comes in just once a year, there is no economic sense in mailing you a Valentines, Mother's Day, and summer mailing, if you are really just a Christmas shopper.

Interviewing the Defectors

Probably the most important names on your customer database are those of the people who have recently deserted you. These people are valuable. They provide important clues as to what you are doing right and wrong. You should set up an ongoing program to interview them to determine why they left. To make the most of the situation, you should determine the lifetime value of each customer and keep it in the customer's database record. When you lose customers, therefore, find out if their lifetime value is higher or lower than the LTV of your existing customer base.

Summary

Long-term loyal customers are more profitable than regular customers. They:

☐ spend more, buy more often, buy higher priced options;

☐ are less expensive to serve;

☐ have a higher retention and referral rate;

☐ There are three ways in which you can increase the number of loyal customers:

    ☐ we can treat loyal customers better;

    ☐ we can reward loyalty with points or benefits;

    ☐ we can vary our customer acquisition methods to attract good customers and avoid the bad ones.

The first step in treating customers better is to identify who they are. The retention rate is the key measurement of loyalty:

☐ Since your top 20 percent of customers usually give you 80 percent or more of your revenue you must develop programs to reward and retain these people.

☐ You may also want to find ways of dropping the losers.

Airline miles programs have proved to be an excellent method for retaining and building customer loyalty.

As important or more important than customer recognition and rewards is recruiting the right kind of customer to begin with. Reichheld pointed out that the type of customer acquisition system can be a key element in building customer loyalty. He also pointed out that employee loyalty is central to customer loyalty.

Executive Quiz 7

Answers to quiz questions (Figure 7-9) can be found in Appendix B.

Put the appropriate letter before each answer		
	Questions	Answers
a	Higher insurance customer retention	13 members in the program
b	Loyal Customers	About twenty percent.
c	Why insurance retention rate went up	Acquire loyal customers
d	Primary purpose of loyalty card	Affluent customers
e	Reichheld's Discovery about Loyalty	Agents sought better customers
f	Which customers like loyalty programs	Buy higher priced products
g	Why Helena & Arthur dropped MBNA	Cookies
h	Caller ID on the Web	Customer communications
i	Link between loyalty and database marketing	Didn't offer American Miles
j	How you measure loyalty	Don't answer the phone right away
k	Those who give you their preferences	Dropped 37.65% with communictions
l	How many Americans move each year	Get information about customers
m	How to know if birthday cards work	High revenue high risk
n	Why the paint companies did not want paint	Increase commissions for renewals
o	How one bank discourages unprofitables	Long term loyal customers
p	Most important quadrant for retention	More loyal than those who don't
q	Cell Phone Loyalty #2 Gold Churn	One third
r	Hallmark Gold Crown after 3 years	Tests and controls
s	Very important names in a database	The defectors
t	How many Gold Crown dollars on the cards	The retention or renewal rate
u	A higher retention and referral rate	Their customers paid for it.

Figure 7-9. Quiz 7.

8

Customer Segmentation

*In the past, we would look at a direct mail campaign
and see the response rate and what it yielded as the primary measure of our effectiveness. Now, we are willing
to live with lower response rates if the responders are
more likely to stay. That, in turn, helps us target better
next time.*

VP of a major telecommunications firm

*Market segments are not neat and tidy. ... The same
consumer may enjoy shopping in both Neiman-Marcus
and K-market.*

WILLIAM H. DAVIDOW
Marketing High Technology

Customer segmentation is essential for successful database marketing.
Segments are groups of customers with similar interests in your products
or services which you have created based on their demographics and
lifestyle. Your messages to customers in each segment should reflect
these differing interests if you want to find a receptive audience. The old
corner grocer had a couple of hundred customers. He could keep their
data in his head. His loyalty strategies, if they were any good, were based
on what he could learn from the customers by trial and error.

Today we have thousands or even millions of customers. To manage
them we cannot create a million different marketing programs. We create a few segments, and create a marketing program for each segment.
The programs can be personalized, of course. They can say something
different to each person (based on what we know about them, their

159

behavior, etc.): "Since you have been a loyal customer since 1992, Ms. Hopkins…" or "Since you took a cruise with us to Alaska last year…" To create these communications, you need to have several things: a database with data about the customer that can be used for personalization, a segment that the person is in, a marketing plan for the segment, and an automatic system to produce the communications that uses all of the above. Let us take an example:

Segment. Retired couples who visit their children and grandchildren.

Strategy. Get them to register their children's and grandchildren's cities and birthdays. Suggest air packages to the proper destinations a month in advance of each date.

Communication. "We can fly you both from Atlanta to Portland Maine next month to visit David and Tracy for Tracy's birthday. The price is only $189 each round trip. If you are interested in learning more, click here."

The goal of customer segmentation is to develop database marketing action programs that lead to measurable increases in retention, cross sales, up sales, and referrals. Wherever possible, these action programs should operate automatically with outgoing messages sent based on dates or transactions. Some of the examples in this chapter are from the travel industry. But segmentation is required for any sort of industry: insurance, retailing, financial services, etc. As you read this, substitute your industry for the travel and other examples (Figure 8-1).

Segment Definition

An ideal segment is one which:

■ *has definable characteristics* in terms of behavior and demographics: e.g., retired couples, business travelers 30–60, college students, families with young children, etc. Business customers should be segmented by SIC code, annual sales, and number of employees.

Figure 8-1. Segment strategy concepts.

- *is large enough* in terms of potential sales to justify a custom marketing strategy with appropriate rewards and budget.

- *has members who can be motivated* by cost-effective rewards to modify their behavior in ways that are profitable for your company.

- *makes efficient use of available* data to support segment definition and marketing efforts.

- *can be measured in performance*, with control groups.

- *justifies an organization* devoted to it. The managing organization can be a single person, or part of a person's time, but there should be someone definite in your company who "owns" each segment.

Defining the segments requires insight, analytics, and anecdotes:

- *Insight* requires experienced marketing strategists who develop hypotheses about each possible segment including the rewards necessary to modify member behavior.

- *Analytics* involves using statistical analysis which supports or rejects each hypothesis: Does such a segment exist? How much are they spending now? What is their income? When do they purchase in our category? How much will it cost to change their behavior?

- *Anecdotes* are success or failure stories that illustrate what your company or other companies have done to modify the behavior of segments like this one. They offer a clue as to what is likely to work in terms of an actionable strategy. You start with an anecdote, and develop a hypothesis which can be tested before any rollout.

Strategy

Each defined segment requires a custom marketing strategy. One size may not fit all. Some people are motivated by premiums or discounts, others by perks, others by exotic destination packages, etc. For example, a businessman whose travel is paid by his company may not be primarily interested in discounts. He may be interested in perks that give him status or make his travel more relaxing.

A valid strategy for each segment involves:

- *communications* to the segment (direct mail, e-mail, on-location personal attention);

- *rewards* designed to modify behavior;

- *controls* to measure the success of the strategy;
- *a budget* for implementation of the strategy;
- *specific goals* and metrics for engagement: for behavior modification;
- *an organization* that accepts responsibility for the segment.

Infrastructure

Segment marketing strategy involves a database infrastructure with a user-friendly analytical and campaign management front end, which can be accessed by authorized personnel. To support the strategy the infrastructure should be:

- Available to all authorized users 24/7 over the Web.
- Updated frequently to keep it current and fresh with feedback from actions of the segment members.
- Designed to permit the development of automated segment campaigns, event-driven communications, back-end analysis, creation of control groups, measurement of success.
- Easy for marketers to understand and use in their work.
- Capable of supporting multi-channel communications: e-mail, direct mail, point of sale communication, personalized Web, inbound and outbound telephone contact.
- Capable of supporting standardized segmentation applications.
- Able to support automated customer contact strategies without extensive manual intervention.
- Able to support central marketing programs, while assisting decentralized branch initiatives. In other words, you set up a system whereby you can run programs centrally, but you let regional managers create their own marketing programs at the same time.
- Able to provide speedy evaluation of campaigns to support continuous improvement.
- Capable of moving from ad hoc analysis to automated marketing programs.
- Designed so that top management can learn, on a regular basis, whether the segment strategy is working—and where it falls short.

Action Plan

The action plan should show how we get from here to there. It guides the development and implementation of the segmentation strategy. It includes:

- A roadmap showing what will happen, when. "Send each policy holder a birthday card and a policy review 45 days before their policy renewal date."

- A budget for the infrastructure and for the segment marketing plans.

- Standard application of segmentation—how to maintain consistency and control while providing flexibility and localization power.

- An organization chart that shows who is responsible for each segment.

- Specific goals to be achieved with milestones for measurement of success

Segmentation Enhancement, Hypothesis and Analysis

Development of segments begins with the dreaming up of segment hypotheses. "I think that such a segment exists (retired people who visit their children and grandchildren and who would be willing to register this information with us). I think that the segment spends a significant amount of money each year. I believe that we can come up with some cost-effective marketing strategies that will move the behavior of segment members in directions that are profitable for our company. I want to do the analysis to see if I am right." Typically, you would use analytics to go into your database to determine the characteristics of the segment you have dreamed up: its size, spending habits, demographics, history, etc. The result of the analytics will feed into automated strategy development concepts for each segment. "There are X number of retired people on the database. Some tests were run to see if they would register their travel objectives for the coming year. Twelve percent of those approached, registered. The 12 percent across our entire database amounts to about 82,000 people (Figure 8-2)."

Not every segment that you can think up will be a profitable one to pursue. Some segments may be too small in number. Others may have very low revenue potential. Others may be very infrequent in their propensity to spend in your category. Finally, others may not be responsive to any sort of communication you might send. The analytics are

Segment	Estimated Quantity	Strategy	Cost Per Message	# / Year	Cost per Year	% Resp.	Sales / Resp	Annual Sales	Profit @13%	ROI
Retired visiting children	82,000	Trip Offers	$0.12	4	$39,360	12.0%	$478	$18,814,080	$2,445,830	62.1
College Students	420,000	Spring Break	$0.08	2	$67,200	4.0%	$205	$6,888,000	$895,440	13.3
Business Travelers	390,000	Miles	$0.22	12	$1,029,600	6.0%	$420	$117,936,000	$15,331,680	14.9
Bargain Hunters	370,000	Last Minute	$0.04	52	$769,600	3.0%	$178	$102,741,600	$13,356,408	17.4

Figure 8-2. Segments.

essential to test typical segments on real data to find out the correct methods for identifying the segments worth pursuing. Investment in communications to unprofitable segments should be minimal.

Strategy Development

Each segment will need to have its own marketing strategy with different messages and rewards. Segments differ in profitability as well as needs. Segment strategy development begins by understanding each customer segment, its size, potential value, and the best way to reach them. Then you start mapping the content, the offers, the channel and the contact strategy with that segment. You should build testing and learning steps into this process so that all the decisions can be refined and optimized along the way. The strategy for each segment should involve:

■ *Targeted communications to the segment.* Communications should support both your short-term sales and long-term marketing objectives. These may differ. For example, if you have a segment that normally pays full price, it may not be in your long-term best interest to send them bargain offers, even though your message may generate some immediate sales. You may be training them to wait for bargains. You may lose their normal full price business.

■ *Using the channel that works best for each customer.* E-mail messages, of course, are less expensive than direct mail. Some direct mail recipients may be stimulated to buy more if they get an e-mail saying "Look in your mailbox this week for a special catalog from us with photos of the new fall fashions. Ponchos are definitely "in"."

Profitable database marketing segment automation initiatives will be based on successful customer communications in the broad sense: e-mails, direct mail, customer service phone conversations, web site personalization, brochures, direct staff communications, and on-site literature and services.

Content and Offer Development

Your first job in developing content is to determine the overall marketing strategy that includes positioning, targeting, segmentation, testing, and measurement plans. The content, messaging, and offers then have to be developed consistent with your business goals.

Content and offer development have to be based on data and insights from research and analysis. You want to ensure that what you say is relevant to the audience and works to motivate them to do what you want. You will be using multiple channels: direct mail, phone, e-mail, Web contact, point of sale literature, and personal contact. How can you get the content across these multiple channels to be consistent? In many companies, each channel operates independently. The Web group has little contact with customer service, or those designing direct mail pieces. This practice has to be changed if you want to provide a customer experience that resembles the close bond that the old corner grocer had with his customers.

While the central marketing staff is developing a corporate marketing initiative, regions and retail locations should also conduct their own local programs. Quite often, what is of interest at the local level seems unimportant to central marketers. But where the rubber meets the road may be where really great ideas are created. Central database marketing research should collect and analyze the lessons that come from regional experiments.

Rewards Designed to Modify Behavior

Rewards may have to be varied consistent with what the customers want. What do they want? A free night in a hotel or a free air fare? Points towards a long-range goal? Recognition and status when they show up at a retail location? If your program is not working, it may be because you are not offering the correct rewards. At one bank, branch managers were trained to recognize their best customers by sight. When one of these customers came in to the branch, the manager would jump out of his chair, and walk into the lobby to greet these customers. It did not cost much to do this, but it was a very effective reward for boosting retention of those people that the bank had determined most important to retain.

Using Test and Controls to Measure the Success of a Strategy

As you will learn in Chapter 11, setting up control groups for each marketing initiative is very important, but also very hard to do. Let us continue our grandparent segment idea. To prove that it works, you need to set up a segment of grandparents who have registered, but to whom you do not send any messages about traveling to visit their grandchildren. If they call up to book a flight, of course, you give them super service. But you hold out 10,000 that do not get the messages, and have 70,000 that do get them. After a while, you compare the performance of the two groups.

To create the control groups, you have a field in your database record that is set aside for control group codes. The code indicates the initiative for which it is a control, the date it was put into the control group, and the date on which the customer can be moved back into the regular participating segment. This should probably be a year or 18 months later. Of course, some of those in the control group will discover that others are getting these messages, and will complain. Your customer service response: "It must be a computer error. I am so sorry. I will see that you get these messages from now on, starting today." Customer service must be empowered to change the control group codes then and there without going through any approval process.

Why Segments Should not Be Based on Spending

It may be self-defeating to segment customers by total sales. Silver, Gold, and Platinum may be great for *status levels* for customers—it gives them something to work towards. It may not be useful for you in planning your marketing campaigns. What do you say to the Silver people? "Buy more." What do you say to the Gold people? "Buy more." How can your marketing programs be personalized when they all have the same message?

A better way of segmentation is by demographics and lifestyle. Helena and I have been saving money in the last 30 years. We have money in mutual funds and no mortgage on our condo. We have no payments on our cars. We are totally debt free. You could not sell me anything that involves financing: a credit card, a home equity loan, or cash back on buying a car. On the other hand, 30 years ago, I had five credit cards which were maxed out. I had a mortgage and second trust on my house and monthly payments on both of our cars. I had four children in college or about to go to college. I was teaching university courses three nights a week in addition to my full time job so that I could make ends meet. I was a different guy. You could have sold me anything with lower interest rates or lower monthly payments. What this means is that your segments should reflect the lifestyle and attitudes of the people you are dealing with, at their particular life stage.

Appended data and customer profiles are the keys to understanding the psychology and interests of your customers and prospects. In the rest of this chapter there are some great ideas for creating meaningful segments, including lists with attitude or cluster descriptions such as those used for PRIZM or Mosaic clusters. See if combining some of the appended data with the actual behavior of your customers (Silver, Gold, or Platinum) cannot give you a workable segmentation system that will enable you to speak to your customers in language that they will understand and respond to.

Status Levels and Segments

Segments are different from status levels. You can look at a *segment* as a marketer, trying to build loyalty and repeat sales. You can look at a *status level* as a customer trying to earn recognition, increased status, and perks.

For an airline customer, for example, Silver, Gold, or Platinum status can have real value. You get preferential treatment in upgrading, or choice of seating. You get to go on the plane first. On a recent trip, for example, my flight was cancelled. I rushed to get a seat on another flight. There were only two seats left, and eight people trying to get on the plane. Since I and another passenger were "Platinum" status, we were the only two of the eight who got on the plane. Airline passengers that have achieved these status levels usually like them. Some customers work hard to achieve them. Your literature to them has to refer to their status. But within Gold customers, for example, you can still have different segments. Look at these two Gold members of an airline:

Jim Jones (32) successful salesman with a wife and two young children. He flies a lot on business. His travel is paid by his company.

Sam Wilson (72) and Janet Wilson (70), retired businessman and wife. They fly a lot to visit grandchildren and take vacations in Europe.

They pay for their travel themselves from accumulated savings and their pensions.

Both have the status of Gold but they have very different lifestyles and interests. They should be put in different segments. Marketing offers that will tempt the Wilsons to visit Vienna in October will not tempt Jim Jones who hates being away from his wife and children and could not easily take them to Europe in the middle of the school year (Figure 8-3).

Your segmentation scheme should not be too complex and expensive. One high-priced consulting team developed an elaborate marketing program for a large corporation. The plan, which went from marketing planning through execution and post execution, involved 35 separate steps, including establishing contact strategies, developing metrics, closed loop tracking, monitoring progress, and socializing. It was a good plan, but it was cumbersome and expensive. It lacked the close touch with the market that real database marketing involves.

A more successful segmentation scheme was developed by a retailer based on consumer behavior. They looked at not just how much the customer spent, they looked at when they bought and what they bought. Some customers bought only once a year—at Christmas. Others bought only necessities. Some bought only items on sale. On the other hand, there were customers who were fiercely loyal to the chain. Others who

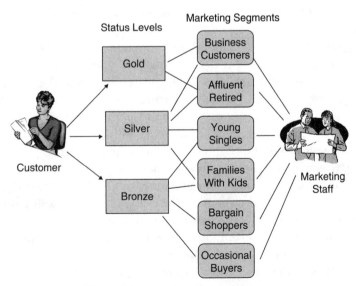

Figure 8-3. Status levels and segments.

wanted to be the best-dressed people on the planet. In total, the retailer broke their customers down into three large groups: Gold, Silver and Bronze, each divided into three smaller segments. The following picture makes the segmentation scheme clear (Figure 8-4).

The segments were developed based on a very sophisticated analysis of their customer's habits. They looked for the answers to the following questions:

- Who are my best customers?
- What percent of sales do they generate?
- How big is their clothing budget, and the chain's share of their wallet?
- What are their demographic characteristics?
- When and what do they buy in our category?
- Who buys full price versus only items on sale?
- When and what do they buy from the competition?

Armed with lots of statistics from their marketing database, they went through five steps to create the segments:

- Determine the behavior that drives each segment.
- Identify naturally occurring clusters of customers each with a unique buying pattern based on 24-month purchasing history.

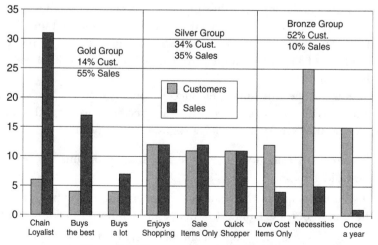

Figure 8-4. Nine segments in three groups.

- Enhance these clusters with lifestyle data and demographics.
- Conduct an in-depth survey of each cluster for competitive information and fashion attitudes.
- Emerge with a multi-dimensional picture of each customer segment.

Once the segments were identified and backed up with statistical analysis, they had to develop a marketing strategy for each segment. In essence, they decided to put their marketing money where it would do the most good. They allocated their marketing budget to each of the major groups.

For the Gold group (14 percent of the customers with 55 percent of the sales) the goal was retention. These were the most valuable individuals to the chain. They allocated 60 percent of their marketing budget to programs designed to retain this loyal group. They let them know how valuable they were to the store, and provided special services and status perquisites.

For the Bronze group (52 percent of the customers and 10 percent of the sales) they decided that they should not waste resources. These people did not spend much money in the store. $1 spent here would not do anywhere near as much good as $1 spent on the Gold customers. So, they allocated only five percent of their entire marketing program to these Bronze customers.

The Silver group was right in the middle. Here, the goal was to encourage them to move up to Gold status. They felt that they could motivate those who enjoyed shopping to spend more time in the store. They could encourage the sale shoppers with sale offers. They experimented with special programs for the quick shoppers so that they could find what they wanted quickly—more quickly than their competitors. They allocated 35 percent of their marketing budget to these 34 percent of the customers.

So how did they measure their success? By measuring retention and migration using control groups. They had specific goals for each group. How could they see whether their programs were working?

- Attrition and retention—were the retention programs working on the Gold group?
- Migration upward and downward—how many of the Silver people could they get to become Gold? How many slipped down to Bronze status?
- Incremental sales per program and per season—the store had regular seasonal programs. They could measure the effect of these programs on each of the nine segments.

- Frequency of seasonal purchases—Christmas was always the big season. But what about spring and fall buying? How did each segment respond to those seasons?

- Dollars spent per trip and per season—the shopping basket was a key measurement of success.

- Number of departments shopped per trip and per season. It was possible to take people who had only visited one or two departments, and make them an offer that would get them to go to a new department for them. The measurement is: did they keep buying in the new department after the promotion was over.

- Share of customers' wallet—here they conducted a continual review of share of wallet to see how it varied with each segment.

Segmenting by Prizm NE Cluster Codes

Claritas (www.claritas.com) has been developing consumer segments since 1974 when the PRIZM lifestyle segmentation system was first introduced. The segments have catchy names and are based on such factors as income, age, lifestyle, and purchasing habits. The current version, PRIZM NE, contains 66 clusters organized into 14 groups.

Here are some examples of the descriptions of some of the clusters within these groups (Figure 8-5).

How You Can Use the Claritas System

Service bureaus, such as KnowledgeBase Marketing, Experian, or Acxiom often have the Claritas PRIZM NE database in-house. You can send them your customer file, and have them append segmentation data to it. By doing this you can determine which segments have a propensity to buy your product and which ones do not.

As a test, a non-profit mailer that appealed to a certain group of older donors used Claritas' previous segmentation system—PRIZM 62 to generate market research information for a nationwide mail campaign. They applied Claritas cluster coding to a sample of their prospect file and donor base. The results were quite revealing. They discovered that their best donor segments were as shown in Figure 8-6.

The index was created by comparing the percent of the population in the area being mailed with the percent of the donors. An index of 100 meant that the percent of the donors was exactly equal to the percent of the population mailed. The bottom clusters were as shown in Figure 8-7.

---

15. Pools & Patios — Formed during the postwar Baby Boom, Pools & Patios has evolved from a segment of young suburban families to one for mature, empty nesting couples. In these stable neighborhoods, graced with backyard pools and patios — the highest proportion of homes were built in the 1960s—residents work as white-collar managers and professionals, and are now at the top of their careers.

17. Beltway Boomers — The members of the postwar Baby Boom are all grown up. Today these Americans are in their forties and fifties, and one segment of this huge cohort—college educated, upper-middle-class and home-owing—is found in Beltway Boomers. Like many of their peers who married late, these Boomers are still raising children in comfortable suburban subdivisions, and they're pursuing kid centered lifestyles.

18. Kids & Cul-de-Sacs — Upscale, suburban, married couples with children—that's the skinny on Kids & Culde-Sacs, an enviable lifestyle of large families in recently built subdivisions. With a high rate of Hispanic and Asian Americans, this segment is a refuge for college-educated, white-collar professionals with administrative jobs and upper-middle-class incomes. Their nexus of education, affluence and children translates into large outlays for child-centered products and services.

Figure 8-5. PRIZM NE examples.

Cluster	Index
Rustic Elders	159.8
Blue Highways	148.5
New Eco-topia	146.0
Grain Belt	142.9
Back Country Folks	142.8
Hometown Retired	135.7
Shotguns and Pickups	134.1
Agri-Business	133.2
Gray Power	132.4
River City, USA	130.7

Figure 8-6. Best performing clusters.

These were losing clusters for this non profit. Increased profit for them came from mailing only to profitable clusters, and not mailing to unprofitable clusters. They mailed about 70 million pieces per year. To do the cluster selection, they worked with a service bureau that had

Cluster	Index
Young Literati	61.1
Urban Gold Coast	61.1
Latino America	57.9
Hispanic Mix	57.5
Inner Cities	55.8
Norma Rae-Ville	54.5
Southside City	54.1
New Beginnings	47.8
Military Quarters	42.2
Towns and Gowns	32.6

Figure 8-7. Worst performing clusters.

a database of compiled names, which already had the cluster codes appended. They were able to use cluster as a selection criteria. The projected results of using this system were quite remarkable (Figure 8-8).

The previous overall response rate was about five percent with an average gift of $10.00. By mailing only to the top 30 clusters, they increased their response rate to 5.93 percent producing an increase in gross revenue of $6.5 million. From this, they had to subtract the cost of selecting by PRIZM cluster, priced at $20 per thousand names (in addition to the other costs of the names and the costs of the mailing). The net increase in gross revenue was $5 million per year. How were they able to know that the response rate would increase from 5.0 to 5.93 percent? Because in their previous mailings, that was the response rate of the top 30 clusters.

Appending Data to Your Segments

To create a customer segment, you need to know something about the membership of that segment. You will want to keep track of their spending

	Mailed	Response Rate%	Responders	Average Gift	Total Revenue
Previous Mailing Plan	70,000,000	5.00%	3,500,000	$10.00	$35,000,000
Top 30 Clusters Mailing	70,000,000	5.93%	4,149,894	$10.00	$41,498,941
Additional Gross Revenue					$6,498,941
Cluster Selection Cost	70,000,000			$20/M	$1,400,000
Net Incr. Gross Revenue					$5,098,941

Figure 8-8. Revenue gain from mailing to profitable clusters.

with you, of course. But you may want other information: what they are spending with other companies and something about them personally and their lifestyle. By this, I mean their age, income, children, type of home ownership, and other aspects of their lifestyle in addition to their cluster.

There is quite a bit of information that you can get appended to your customer and prospect database. You can use the appended data to create your segments and build relationships with your customers. Let us examine this available data.

Start with the Census

Let us begin with the U.S. census. The last census was in 2000. Every U.S. household was visited, and every sixth house was given the "long form" which was 40 pages long. The remaining five households completed the short form—about one page for each person. To protect privacy, in the reports on the census, the extensive data on the long form was attributed to the other five households which got only the short form. All of this data was made available to the public. Several large data compilers including InfoUSA, KnowledgeBase Marketing, Equifax, and Experian have put this data in a useful form and combined it with information from other sources. KnowledgeBase Marketing, for example, provides AmeriLINK® which is a database of about 236 million U.S. consumers with exact age, income, type of home, and other data. This data is updated monthly from about 20 different sources including the census. If you have a customer database, you can get one of these compilers, or a service bureau, to append this data to your customer records so you will know much more about them.

Digital Neighborhoods

Some compilers have gone beyond providing an e-mail, to categorizing consumers by their attitude or behavior on the Web. Digital Neighborhoods is one example of such a product. It examines consumers where they live—on land and online. To create these groups, KnowledgeBase Marketing and Wunderman combined on-line insight gleaned from a cross-section of the on-line population by Internet market intelligence company comScore Networks®, with demographic, lifestyle, and transaction data from the AmeriLINK® national consumer database. This combination produced a segmentation of consumers—and an interesting set of consumer clusters—based on detailed on-line characteristics and activity.

Digital neighborhoods created three components of consumer's involvement with the Internet:

- *Presence.* The degree to which the consumer is present online over time—how long, how often, and how broadly they surf.
- *Relationship.* Propensity to go to a password-protected site.
- *Transaction.* Likelihood to transact business and make a purchase on the Web.

The higher the consumers scored on each of these three factors, the more involved they were online. The system segmented consumers into 17 clusters using three age groups (younger, mid-life and mature) across three major e-involvement levels (Super Involved, Involved, and Less Involved) (Figure 8-9).

Companies wanting to communicate with their customers over the Web can have the digital neighborhood of each of their customers appended to their database. Knowing which of the 17 segments each customer is in can help target messages more effectively.

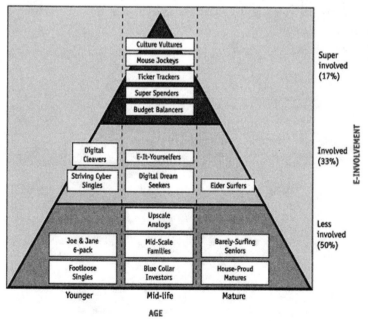

Figure 8-9. Digital neighborhoods.

Quadrant Analysis

One of the most powerful techniques of looking at customers is quadrant analysis. Following is an example from the travel industry. It compares hotel guest spending with guest household income. A sample of such chart is shown in Figure 8-10.

Quadrant analysis can be used for a particular property, or for a segment. It enables a hotel chain to determine a different strategy for each quadrant. In this example, strategy might be to focus marketing efforts in Quadrant 1, who are people with a high income that spend a lot at the hotel. Quadrant 3 might be ignored in marketing because they spend little, and have few resources to spend more. Quadrant 4 is a most interesting quadrant. These lower income guests spend a lot. Why? It could be because their companies are picking up the tab. Marketing messages to this segment should probably be directed to their employer in addition to the member.

How Many Segments Should You Have?

Some marketers create hundreds of segments. That is a mistake. Limit yourself to the ones that you can manage. For most companies, ten segments are plenty.

Q2 High Income, Low Spend		Q1 High Income, High Spend	
Population	18,270	Population	5,337
% Total	36%	% Total	11%
Income	$132,330	Income	$132,713
Marital	80%	Marital	77%
Average Spend	$625	Average Spend	$4,527
Total Spend	$11,418,750	Total Spend	$24,160,599
% Spend	15%	% Spend	33%

Q3 Low Income, Low Spend		Q4 Low Income, High Spend	
Population	21,687	Population	5,368
% Total	43%	% Total	11%
Income	$60,375	Income	$59,296
Marital	55%	Marital	51%
Average Spend	$589	Average Spend	$4,766
Total Spend	$12,773,643	Total Spend	$25,583,888
% Spend	17%	% Spend	35%

Figure 8-10. Quadrant analysis for hotel guests.

Let us conclude this chapter with a few case studies or examples showing how companies have successfully developed and used segmentation.

Case Study: Airline Passenger Segmentation

An international airline decided to develop specialized programs for its frequent flyers with segments based on their travel patterns. The goal was to increase revenue by customized communications. Based on the exploratory work, the airline set up seven major passenger segments (Figure 8-11).

The High Flyers comprised about 15 percent of the file but over 50 percent of the revenue and combined round-trips and trip fragments. Based on the analysis, the airline for the first time had a workable customer segmentation plan which could be used to drive their marketing activities. Since 15 percent of their file represented 50 percent of their revenue, they could concentrate on retaining and expanding this segment. More important, they were able to identify 39 percent of their customer base as having very low revenue potential so that they could be given minimal marketing resources. The airline was able to create a marketing budget that gave them a much higher return on investment than their previous efforts.

Case Study: Life Stage Segmentation

An international resort company wanted to create customer segments based on their life stage. To do this, with the help of KnowledgeBase Marketing, they:

- Used AmeriLINK® demographic data as the basis for segregating the customer base into six pre-defined life stages.

Segment	Size	2 Yr Round-trips + Trip Fragments	Business Round-trips	Comments
High Flyers	15%	6 or more	1+ but not all	Heavy business and leisure
Big Business	6%	6 or more	All	Heavy travel, all business
Leisure Life	10%	6 or more	0	Heavy travel, all leisure
Up and Coming	9%	2 to 5	1 or more	Some use, mostly business
Temporary Tourist	23%	2 to 5	0	Some use, all leisure
One-timers	17%	1	0 or 1	Minimal 2 year flight activity
Lapsed	22%	0	0	Some flights prior to 2 years

Figure 8-11. Airline passenger segments.

■ Compared group differences to guide the creation of marketing messages tailored to each life stage.

The analysis showed that travel patterns, interests, and spending could be predicted based on two key factors: age and presence of children. Combining these factors with number of resort stays, the company created six segments based on analysis of 91,000 customers.

1. *Gold coaster.* 45+ years, not traveling with children 15 years or under.
2. *Family.* All adults traveling with children.
3. *Older independents.* 35–44, not traveling with children.
4. *Younger independents.* 25–34, not traveling with children.
5. *High school students.* 16–18, not traveling with children.
6. *College/University students.* 19–24, not traveling with children.

The top three segments represented 79 percent of all guests. The bottom three segments contained the remaining 21 percent of the guests.

Individual marketing programs were created for each of the six segments, with the marketing budget allocated based on the importance of the segment to the company. The most valuable 10 percent of customers contributed to 43 percent of total revenue. Lodging and activity passes were most strongly associated to the top 20 percent of high revenue customers. Using these segments, the company was able to:

■ develop customized marketing programs for each segment,
■ retain and expand the most profitable segments,
■ produce a higher return on investment from marketing than had prevailed before.

Summary

Segmentation is essential to successful database marketing. If you have a million customers, you cannot have a million marketing strategies, one for each customer. Instead, you divide your customers into eight, nine, or ten segments, and develop a strategy for each of them. The messages to the customers in each segment should be personalized, of course, based on what you have stored about them in your database, but they will be activated by a strategy developed for the segment that the customers are in.

Segments are different from status levels (Gold, Silver, etc.), although they may be combined with them. Status levels are designed for customers. They motivate them to achieve certain buying levels. Segments tend to be created by and for the marketing department as combinations of behavior and demographics.

Creating segments is a work of art. Included in the chapter are many examples of types of segments that should get your creative juices flowing. The segment has to be big enough, be clearly defined, have a behavioral goal, and have someone on your staff who is put in charge of it. There must be a control group to prove that your segment strategy is working with a significant ROI.

Executive Quiz 8

Put the appropriate letter before each term to be defined		
	Definition	**Term to be defined**
a	Families with children	Anecdote
b	Gold, Silver	Automated Communication
c	On line database access	Behavioral Data
d	A strategy that worked elsewhere	Beltway Boomers
e	Aha! This will work for us.	Control Group
f	Age, Income	Demographic Data
g	Mail responsiveness	Gold Coaster
h	Points and Perks	High Flyers
i	First Class	Index of response
j	Happy Birthday	Infrastructure
k	High responding non profit cluster	Insight
l	I think these folks will respond	Length of Residence
m	Don't send them what others get	Long Form
n	Loyalty	Migration
o	Move up or down	Opt In Email Addresses
p	Percent spending in your category	Perk
q	A PRIZM NE Group Name	Quadrant Analysis
r	Response compared to cell population	Retention
s	US Census Data	Rewards
t	Long time no move	Rustic Elders
u	Airline Segment	Segment
v	You can send me commercials	Segment Hypothesis
w	Digital neighborhood cluster	Share of wallet
x	Income versus spending	Status Levels
y	Resort Chain Segment	Upscale Analogs

Figure 8-12. Quiz 8.

9

How Predictive Modeling Boosts Response

Predictive modeling makes it possible for businesses to react to what their customers are going to do rather than what they have already done. It begins by identifying a problem or opportunity—losing too many valuable customers or a need to grow the customer base, for example—and possible actions to address it. It models each customer's likely response to various possible actions and helps the marketer choose the most appropriate action for each of those customers.

MICHAEL J. MCDERMOTT

What if you could predict, in advance, how a large group of prospects or customers would react to an offer from you? If you could separate people likely to respond and buy from those unlikely to respond and buy, you could be much more successful as a marketer. That is what predictive modeling can do for you. With a good predictive model you can determine:

- Which customers and prospects are likely to buy, and which are unlikely to buy.
- Which customers are in danger of leaving you, and which are more likely to stay.
- Which products they are more likely to buy.

The ideas behind database marketing predictive models rest on some simple principles:

■ *Prospects and customers in many segments react in predictable ways.* This predictability is vital. If everyone had unpredictable reactions to your services and marketing efforts, a model could not provide reliable predictions.

■ *Clues to expected customer behavior can sometimes be discerned in their previous behavior and their demographics.* The behavior used in predictions can usually be stored in your database in the form of transactions. The demographics can be appended from an outside source. This does not always work. It is not always possible to predict customer behavior based on the data you can collect in a database.

■ *A predictive model is usually developed from the response to previous promotions.* It is difficult to run a successful predictive model unless you have already sent a promotion to your customers or prospects and got a reaction from them. What this means is that you usually cannot just take a file of names and addresses and do a model to determine which ones will be more interested in your product. For example, what kinds of customers are more likely to want to purchase a recreation vehicle? You can make some assumptions (over 65, lower middle income, perhaps), but without the results of an RV promotion to a number of prospects, you will not be able to build a model that gives you reliable predictions.

Once you have built a model that works, you can improve your response rates. The basic use of a predictive model is to concentrate your attention on those most likely to respond and purchase, and avoid promotions to those least likely to respond. Say that you send a promotion to 100,000 people offering a product. You get a 2 percent response rate.

Using the results of this promotion, you build a statistical model which successfully identifies the characteristics of the responders and the nonresponders. You use that model to score a new batch of 100,000 names. If you mail only to the 50,000 who the model identifies as the most likely responders, you should get a response rate of more than 2 percent— perhaps 3 percent or more. This will be much more profitable for you, and avoid bothering people who are not interested in your product.

How Modeling Works

How does predictive modeling work? There are some simple steps:

1. *Do a promotion, or use a previous promotion as your base.* You will need enough customers in your model to get statistically valid results.

A promotion to a few hundred people is seldom adequate as a base for a model. I use a rule of thumb for an adequate test file size: as a base for a typical model, you need about 500 conversions (sales). If, for example, you typically get a 2 percent response and sale rate, then you need to send your promotion to 25,000 people (500/0.02).

2. *Append demographic and behavioral data* to your responders and non-responders. There are several companies that provide demographic data. AmeriLINK® from KnowledgeBase Marketing is one example. They maintain a file of 236 million U.S. consumers with exact age, estimated income, shopping behavior, and about 200 other pieces of data. For a modest cost, you can get some or all of this information appended to your file of 25,000 consumers. The following chart is taken from AmeriLINK®, but it is typical of the data available from other suppliers (Figure 9-1).

3. *Add geographic data.* Some of the above data is demographic (age, income). Some data is behavioral (Mail Order Buyer, Non-Profit Donor). You can also add geographic data: code people by whether they live in rural areas, suburban areas, or urban areas. You may find differences in people who live in the North, South, East, or West. Those who live near the ocean or a lake may differ in their response

	Millions
Age	236
Income	236
Auto Loan	84
Census Data	236
Dwelling Type	236
Gender	236
Glasses Wearers	19
Height	61
Weight	55
Home Ownership	153
House Value	123
Length of Residence	185
Mail Order Buyer	108
Non Profit Donor	84
Persons in Household	236
Occupation	90
Religion	208
Student Loan	22
Wealth	236

Figure 9-1. Data available for appending.

from those who live inland. Do they have a listed telephone or an unlisted telephone? This phone listing may seem irrelevant, and may be so, but for some products, marketers have found that those with unlisted phones respond differently from others. Besides this appended data, you should add previous purchase history with your company to your mix of data grouped with every customer record that you plan to use in your model.

4. *Divide your data into two parts.* Before you begin to create your model, you will divide your customer data in two parts: a test group of 12,250 non-responders and 250 responders and a validation group of 12,250 non-responders and 250 responders. Both groups should have exactly the same type and variety of people (Figure 9-2). The validation group is set aside for now, and the model development process works with the test group.

5. *Discard the outliers.* The modelers will first discard the "outliers." These are customers whose purchases were so unusual that they will distort the outcome. For example, if the average customer bought one or two items for an average sale of $200, you would consider as an outlier a lone customer who bought 482 items and spent $96,400. You toss out this customer's records in building your model.

6. *Construct your model.* Now that you have a file rich with appended data, you are ready to construct a predictive model. As a first step, you will typically use a multiple regression model. (We will discuss CHAID later in this chapter.) A regression is an equation that describes the

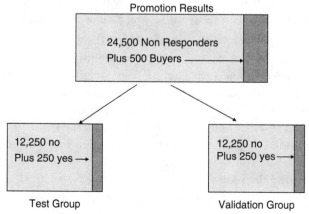

Figure 9-2. Splitting out a validation group.

relationship between a dependent variable and more than one independent variable. The dependent variable is the purchase that the customer made as a result of your promotion (500 bought, and 24,500 did not). The independent variables are the behavior and appended data listed above. Which of the independent variables will be most valuable in predicting who will buy and who will not buy? That is what the model is designed to find out.

The model is typically run on a PC using the software products SAS or SPSS. When the model is run, it applies weights or levels of importance to each of the independent variables. A variable importance is a number that indicates how important (weighty) is each variable in predicting the desired result (they bought the product). Typically a high importance number means that the variable has a significant influence on the possibility that the consumer will take the action. A negative effect means that the variable influenced the purchase process in a negative way (The higher the negative value, the less likely is the person to buy the product.) Higher importance values mean that the factor is more likely to influence the outcome. An effect of minus and an importance of 60 in the case of Family Member 65+ in this example means that households with older people living there are highly unlikely to purchase the product.

This is a sample table of effects and variable importance levels created by a regression model. There were 24 independent variables with levels of importance from minus 60 up to plus 21. Some effects are positive (+) and many are negative (–). If, for example, the customer was age 30-41 he was more likely to respond than if he were 42-49. The chart shows that households with a net worth of $50,000 to $249,000 were more likely to respond than those with incomes above or below this range.

7. *Determine the weights for each variable.* Using the weights determined by the model, you may want to concentrate on using in the model those independent variables that have a high weight in determining the outcome. You can ignore those variables whose weight is very low. So instead of using 30 different variables (age, income, religion, student loan, etc.) you may build your model based on the five or six variables that provide the greatest predictive power. This may save you money later on when you have to append data to a large file so it can be scored using the model.

8. *Develop an algorithm.* The final outcome of the model is an algorithm. An algorithm is a mathematical routine used to perform computations.

Attributes In The Model	Variable Description	Effect	Variable Importance	% Of File
Family Position	Husband	+	21	36.98
	Male Head of Household	+	4	40.21
	Female Head of Household	–	42	22.81
Census Median Age of	41-45	+	13	27.74
Householder	46-79	+	1	62.06
	24-40	–	41	10.19
Age	30-41	+	13	60.84
	42-49	–	20	39.16
Census Percent Households	45-99	+	16	21.04
with Children	33-35	+	8	9.63
	21-29	+	6	19.45
	39-44	+	1	19.39
	30-32	–	10	9.97
	36-38	–	15	10.53
	0-20	–	30	9.97
Net Worth Indicator (000s)	50-249	+	9	59.32
	250+	–	5	26.39
	0-49	–	29	14.29
Census Percent Blue Collar Employed	18-32	+	10	40.53
	13-17	+	5	21.95
	0-12	–	10	28.18
	33-60	–	23	9.33
Family Member 65+	No	+	2	96.36
	Yes	–	60	3.64

Figure 9-3. Weights assigned by a regression model.

In the case of a statistical model in marketing, the algorithm usually includes the computer code that creates a score for each customer or prospect record. The scores may vary from 95 percent certain to buy the product down to 5 percent (unlikely to buy). Here is a sample

Decile #	Mailings #	Responses	Response %	Index
1	15,853	1,085	6.84%	297
2	15,853	640	4.04%	175
3	15,853	564	3.56%	154
4	15,853	390	2.46%	107
5	15,853	286	1.80%	78
6	15,853	279	1.76%	76
7	15,853	193	1.22%	53
8	15,853	142	0.90%	39
9	15,853	69	0.44%	19
10	15,853	9	0.06%	2
Total	158,530	3,657	2.31%	

Figure 9-4. Scoring the test file into deciles.

Decile #	Mailings	Responses	Response %	Index
1	15,984	1,092	6.83%	292
2	16,265	618	3.80%	163
3	15,528	524	3.37%	144
4	15,900	397	2.50%	107
5	16,391	339	2.07%	89
6	15,378	295	1.92%	82
7	15,812	217	1.37%	59
8	15,471	128	0.83%	35
9	18,258	89	0.49%	21
10	13,542	4	0.03%	1
Total	158,529	3,703	2.34%	

Figure 9-5. Validation file scored by the algorithm into deciles.

ranking of deciles from an actual mailing showing the response rates (Figure 9-4).

9. *Score the validation group.* Using the algorithm that emerges from your modeling of the test group, you can "score" the validation group. Now, bear in mind that the validation group has already been promoted. You know the outcome (2 percent bought and 98 percent did not buy). So, if the algorithm developed for the test group is going to be useful in predicting, it should correctly identify most of the people in the validation group who bought (with a high score) and those who did not buy (with a low score). If the algorithm does correctly score the validation group, then you have a successful model which can be used to predict customer response in your next promotion (Figure 9-5).

In the above example, look how closely the validation group response rates came to that of the test group. This was an excellent model which was used to accurately predict response to a large mailing. The break-even response rate was about 2.3 percent. From this chart you can see that deciles 6–10 should probably not be mailed (depending on the profit from the purchased items).

What if It Does not Work?

If the validation process is unsuccessful, of course, you either have to redo your model, or give up the whole process as a bad job. It may be that with the data you have available, a model cannot pick predict the responders. This is very often the case. Modeling does not always work.

Most direct marketing dilemmas cannot be solved by predictive modeling. Why? Because the answer may not lie in the available data. For example, it could be that purchasers of your product cannot be determined by age, income, presence of children, or any standard demographic factors. Why not? Well, suppose you are selling cold remedies, or snow tires, or vacuum cleaners. It is highly possible that these demographic variables will not show a difference between purchasers and non-purchasers. If so, all the modeling in the world will not help. A general rule: if the solution does not seem to make sense to you, then it probably does not make sense. Modeling is not magic. It is only a quantification of intuitive logic.

Many models take weeks to develop. That is because the modelers are constantly tweaking them to get more and more predictive results using different variables.

What You Can Do with Your Model

If you have a model that works, you can use it to generate profits. There are two main uses for predictive models:

- Determine who will buy a product or service, and which product to offer them.
- Determine which customers are most likely to drop your service, and when they are most likely to depart.

Who Will Buy?

To use your model, you could start with your next planned promotion (of the same product). Score the mail file. After scoring a file of prospects or customers, you typically divide the scored file into deciles based on the score. The top decile (10 percent of the file) contains those people most likely to buy. You will be able to arrange your customer or prospect data like this (Figure 9-6).

On this chart deciles 6–10 are your worst performing deciles. You probably should not mail this group. You should, however, mail a few (5 percent) of each of these low performing deciles just to prove to yourself, and to your management, that the model is still working properly and actually does predict the buyers correctly.

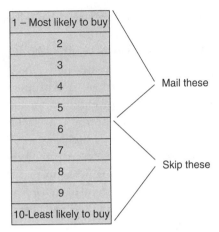

| 1 – Most likely to buy |
| 2 |
| 3 |
| 4 |
| 5 |
| 6 |
| 7 |
| 8 |
| 9 |
| 10-Least likely to buy |

Mail these

Skip these

Figure 9-6. Predictive deciles.

The result of mailing only the higher deciles is that you will get a higher response rate overall. The picture should look something like this (Figure 9-7).

How does this work in practice? An automobile insurance company engaged The Summit Marketing Group to build a model to predict response to their monthly mailings to acquire new customers. Summit prepared a model and used the algorithm to select prospects for each mailing. As a result, the insurance company almost doubled their monthly profits (Figure 9-8).

Doing the Math on Modeling

If you are paying a service bureau to build your model, you may pay between $5,000 and $50,000 for a model, depending on complexity. An additional expense is the appended data necessary for your model to work. You can get appended data from several different sources. You can

	Previous Mailing	Modeled Mailing
Number Mailed	500,000	500,000
Cost @$0.50	$250,000	$250,000
Response Rate	2.0%	3.5%
Sales	10,000	17,500
Sales @$100	$1,000,000	$1,750,000
Gross Profit	$750,000	$1,500,000

Figure 9-7. Profit from use of a predictive model.

	Control Group	Optimized Group	% Change	# Change
Total Mailed	1,264,571	1,264,571	0%	0
Cost of Mailing	$547,559	$547,559	0%	0
Number of Responses	13,366	16,090	20%	2,724
Response Rate	1.06%	1.27%	20%	0.22%
Number of Sales	1,599	2,323	45%	724
Sales Rate	12.00%	14.40%	21%	2.47%
Total Revenue	$2,605,603	$3,158,151	21%	$553,208
Revenue per Sales	$1,630	$1,360	-17%	($270)
Profit	$95,896	$187,851	96%	$91,955
Return on Promotion	18%	34%	96%	16.80%

Figure 9-8. Insurance mailing using a model.

expect to pay between $15 and $35 per thousand records for the appended data. This is an additional cost. For example, if you are going to append data to 1,000,000 records, as in the previous example, at $15 per thousand, the data will cost you an additional $15,000.

But this does not tell the whole story. If you are going to use your model to discard prospects with low scores, you may have to pay for the discarded records. For example, Figure 9-9:

Putting all the costs together you will be paying $0.20 per name ($200 per thousand) for names produced from a model. For companies that are used to paying less than $70 per thousand for rented names, the model will be a tough sell.

There are ways around these additional costs:

You Can Negotiate a "Net Name" Arrangement with Your List Brokers. Net names is an arrangement whereby you have to pay list owners only for the names you actually mail, not for the names that you used in the model and discarded. Net name arrangements are usually granted when the rented name is a duplicate of another name that you already have

	Quantity	Price/M	Cost
Rented Names	1,000,000	$70	$70,000
Model	1	$25,000	$25,000
Appended Data	1,000,000	$20	$20,000
Scoring	1,000,000	$5	$5,000
Total Cost			$120,000
Names Used	600,000		
Cost per Name			$0.20

Figure 9-9. Cost of names using a model.

on your house file, or on another rented list. You will have to do some fast talking to convince the broker that you do not have to pay for names that you used in your modeling process but did not mail.

You Can Purchase Compiled Names Based on the Model. This brings up a whole new marketing technique using your model. Typically, mailers rent prospect names from companies who have proved the worth of the names by actually selling products to them. These lists are called "response lists." They may be subscribers to publications, purchasers from catalogs, direct mail buyers, or retail store buyers. A response list usually produces better results than a "compiled list." A compiled list is typically a list of all the consumers in a city or in the whole country (see Chapter 10 Customer Acquisition). Since only about half of all U.S. households ever buy anything by mail, a response list will usually produce twice the responses per piece mailed as a complied list.

Your model changes the picture. Your model has identified six or a dozen characteristics of buyers of your product that differentiate them from non-buyers. If you run your algorithm on a compiled list that has the necessary data appended, the scoring process will yield a table that divides people by deciles indicating likelihood of purchase. The top deciles will buy your product. People who do not buy goods through the mail will be ranked low.

Some suppliers of complied names have already appended census and other demographic data to their names. They will let you select names from their database using your model. In some cases, they will build your model free if you use it to select their names. The resulting prices can be very rewarding (Figure 9-10).

If you rent a compiled list from a savvy supplier you may pay nothing for the model and nothing for the appended data (since their compiled file already has data appended). You may pay only for scoring and selecting the records based on the model. Seven and a half cents per record is much cheaper than 20 cents per record.

	Quantity	Price/M	Cost
Rented Names	600,000	$70	$42,000
Model	0	$0	$0
Appended Data	600,000	$0	$0
Scoring	600,000	$5	$3,000
Total Cost			$45,000
Names Used	600,000		
Cost per Name			$0.075

Figure 9-10. Reduced costs using a compiled list.

Are these compiled names selected by a model less responsive than rented names selected by the same model? Not necessarily. If your compiler has a large file that includes almost all U.S. consumers, the model should select, in many cases, almost exactly the same names that you would produce using the model on a response list.

Using the Model for Cross Sales

Models can be particularly useful in determining which of your current customers will buy again—and what products they are most likely to buy. The advantage of using a model on your current customers is that you usually have much more relevant data to work with than you do with prospects. In a model, behavioral data typically is more powerful than demographic data. In other words, you can predict better what people are going to do in the future based on what they have already done in the past than by basing your model on who they are (age, income, home value).

Msdbm in Los Angeles (now SourceLink) created a customer purchase behavior model for Isuzu mid-sized commercial trucks. Scores were grouped into three ranges to indicate high, medium, and low purchase likelihood. The model predicted the propensity to purchase based on four variables:

- Employee size of business
- Vocation: e.g. landscaping, electrical contractor, towing, etc.
- Time since last purchase
- Total number of trucks owned

Using the model scores, the customers (companies) were divided into three groups showing the likelihood of their purchasing a new truck:

- High probability
- Medium probability
- Low probability

Isuzu decided to use the models to create a mailing designed to drive selected small business owners to Isuzu dealers. The total quantity mailed was 6,000. In addition, 520 companies were set aside as a control group to monitor the success of the promotion.

This test mailing proved that the scoring methodology developed was highly accurate. As a result Isuzu used the same methodology to score

	Group Totals	Companies Buying	Buying Rate	Trucks Sold
High Score	1,899	97	5.10%	107
Medium Score	1,855	32	1.70%	34
Low Score	1,890	15	0.80%	16
Control Group	520	3	0.60%	3
Total	6,164	144	2.30%	160

Figure 9-11. Trucks sold.

their entire customer file for a follow-up mailing. This gave Isuzu the ability to target key customers and insure a sale of a vehicle with very little cost, compared to normal prospect acquisition costs (Figure 9-11).

Based on their previous experience, Isuzu had expected to sell only 85 trucks to 6,000 prospects. The industry estimates that it costs a manufacturer about $1,000 in marketing and sales effort to sell one mid-sized truck. Using the database, Isuzu was able to sell the trucks for half that amount.

Using a Model for Upgrades

A software manufacturer was interested in identifying the most likely customers to upgrade to a new product version. Using the client's customer database going back three years, KnowledgeBase Marketing built some models which predicted which customers were most likely to purchase the upgrades. Using the model the customer base of 2,452,549 was divided into three groups: high probability, medium probability, and low probability of responding positively to the offer (Figure 9-12).

The response rate of the low probability segment showed that marketing to this segment would not be profitable for the company. A second mailing to the same group produced equally definitive results. At a cost of about $0.40 per piece mailed, the company could save about

	Direct Mail Results			
	Mail Qty	Orders	Response Rate	% of Total Orders
High Probability	1,027,914	13,465	1.31%	64.35%
Medium Probability	1,036,188	6,210	0.60%	29.68%
Low Probability	388,447	1,249	0.32%	5.97%
Total	2,452,549	20,924	0.85%	100.00%

Figure 9-12. Direct mail scoring results.

$155,379 by not mailing the lowest group. The model split the combined second and third mailing into 20 segments, from most probable to least probable. The actual results proved the validity of the model.

What Data Should You Include in Your Database?

The power of prior behavior is one reason why it is important in building a marketing database that you keep in your database as much of the customer transaction and promotion history as possible. Keep track of every communication with them: letters, brochures, e-mails, products, services, phone calls. Keep track of all the transactions: what they bought, when, as a result of what offer, product type, price, quantity, how they bought (Web, mail, phone, retail visit). Be sure you record how they paid for the product or service: check, purchase order, credit card, etc. Almost all of this data can be used in constructing a predictive model.

The Next Best Product

Using a model, you can determine what the next best product for every customer should be. Banks, for example, have a lot of data about their customers. They can use their database to examine customers who have only checking accounts. From the data they can determine whether your next product should be a home equity loan, an auto loan, a savings account, or mutual funds. How do they do this? By using a model to see what thousands of their depositors who have purchased mutual funds look like in terms of behavior and demographics, and how they differ from those depositors who have been offered mutual funds but have not bought them. The model is used to score all their depositors. Those depositors whose scores resemble the mutual fund buyers are likely targets for a mutual fund promotion. Mutual funds are their next best product. The next best product is put into the customer record and called up on the teller's screen when you come in to cash a check or make a deposit. It is also used in mailings to depositors. You do the same thing for savings accounts, auto loans, home equity loans, etc. The product that has the highest score for each customer is that customer's next best product.

Not only banks, but insurance companies, airlines, hotels, and Web sites use next best product models. It is a powerful stuff. You can prove the effectiveness of the next best product by comparing the response to a personalized offer based on a next best product model with an offer based on the "product of the month."

A nationwide insurance company developed a next best product model that was designed to bundle the customer's current premiums with the premium on the next best product. An auto insurance customer, for example was offered a monthly saving of $X on his auto policy if he purchased life insurance. Another customer was offered $X saving on the auto policy if he purchased long-term care insurance. As a result of the model:

■ The top decile of scored households had a sales rate of 68 percent higher than the overall average, and 195 percent higher than the bottom decile. Two thirds of all sales came from the top 50 percent. This meant that focusing attention on this group saved marketing dollars.

■ Households sent the next best product mailings had a sales rate 11 percent higher than those who got the regular "product of the month" mailing.

Using a Model to Predict Churn

Long distance and cell phone companies, credit card companies, banks, insurance companies, retailers and scores of other businesses that provide regular services suffer from churn. In the communications industry, the canceling or reducing usage of a communication service by a customer is called churn. Customers may switch to a different service provider due to a better price, quality of service, quality of customer care, equipment and technology, billing issues, or simply more effective marketing campaigns. The percentage of customers who churn in a particular time period is defined as the churn rate. In the U.S. recently, the churn rate in telecom was 2.9 percent per month, or 35 percent per year.

Modeling Using CHAID Analysis

In addition to regressions (already described) modelers use CHAID, or Chi-square Automatic Interaction Detection. CHAID is a classification tree technique that displays the modeling results in an easy-to-interpret tree diagram going from top down instead of from the bottom up.

SmartDrill in Ashland, MA (www.smartdrill.com) are experts in this technique.

The segments in the tree diagram can be shown in a "gains chart." The gains chart shows how "deep" into a file one must go to select prospects that have the results you are looking for in terms of dollar value or response rate. Financial data or assumptions can also be incorporated into the predictive CHAID model results, to generate return on investment, mail cost savings, etc.

When the outcome we are trying to predict has only two values such as mail responder vs. non-responder, modelers can generate what is called a "nominal" CHAID model. CHAID is useful in picking the best prospects for a direct mail effort. But it may be useful to score the remainder of the file using a regression model, if we wish to identify good prospects beyond about the top 8 percent. Modelers can first generate a CHAID model, and then follow this up with a regression model (Figure 9-13).

Above is a small, simplified example of an ordinal CHAID tree diagram provided by SmartDrill. The diagram begins at the top with a box representing the entire modeling sample of 81,040 households to which a consumer product was marketed via direct mail. Also included in this first box is the average profit per household generated by the initial mailing (75 cents). Household size is identified by CHAID

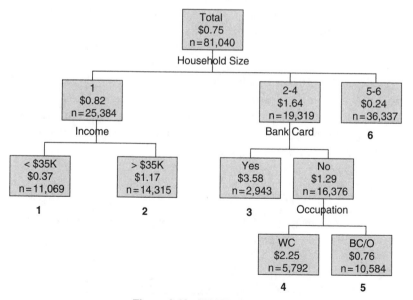

Figure 9-13. CHAID diagram.

as the best predictor around which to begin segmenting the prospect market.

We can see that a household size of two to four persons returns an average profit of $1.64, which is twice the profit generated by a one-person household, and nearly seven times the profit generated by a five-to-six-person household. CHAID then shows us that if a two-to-four-person household has a bank card, the average profit jumps to $3.58. If they do not have a bank card they return an average profit of only $1.29. However, among this non-bank-card group, if the head of household's occupation is White Collar, profitability rises to $2.25.

This diagram is supplemented with a gains chart that shows the gains from each of the segments identified on the CHAID diagram (Figure 9-14).

The fourth column shows the average profit per household for each segment. The fifth column represents this profit number as a relative index, with the average for the entire modeling sample set at 100. Thus, the best segment has an index of 476, which means that it performs at a profit level of 4.76 times the average for the entire modeling sample, and more than 15 times the profitability of the worst segment.

Columns six through nine are cumulative representations of the data from columns two through five: cumulative household count, percent of modeling sample, average profit per household, and profit index. Among other things, the gains chart shows us that the best three segments (segments 3, 4, and 2) represent 28.4 percent of the total sample, have an average profit of $1.75 per household, and are therefore 2.32 times as profitable as the average sample household.

The gains chart is a handy tool for seeing what levels of expected profitability would result from going increasingly deeper into a prospect file. This is useful for planning direct marketing campaigns, since it helps us determine mailing quantities, and gives us information for calculating return on investment.

1 Segment ID	2 Segment Count	3 Percent of Total	4 Average $ Value	5 Segment Index	6 Cum. Count	7 Cum. Percent	8 Cum. $ Value	9 Cum. Index
3	2,943	3.6	$3.58	476	2,943	3.6	$3.58	476
4	5,792	7.1	$2.25	298	8,735	10.8	$2.70	358
2	14,315	17.7	$1.17	155	23,050	28.4	$1.75	232
5	10,584	13.1	$0.76	101	33,634	41.5	$1.44	191
1	11,069	13.7	$0.37	49	44,703	55.2	$1.17	156
6	36,337	44.8	$0.24	31	81,040	100	$0.75	100

Figure 9-14. Gains chart from CHAID.

CHAID helps to create market segments. The tree diagram predicts the performance of each segment. This helps advertising agency personnel and media planners in visualizing and defining market segments. CHAID model algorithms are used to score a master database. As with regressions, new records added to a file can be scored quickly once the basic scoring algorithm is set up.

Descriptive Modeling or Profiling

Even if predictive modeling does not work for you, you should have a profile done of your customer base. This is done by descriptive modeling. It is amazing to note how many companies really know very little about their consumer customers. Any modeler can create useful profiles that look like this (Figure 9-15).

This graph shows the household income of the purchasers of the company's products. They have a much higher percentage of the upper income consumers than the national average.

Using a Model to Determine Catalog Circulation

A major cataloger was looking for a better circulation strategy. They examined three possible mixes of catalogs:

- A few big books and many specialty books with virtually no overlap.

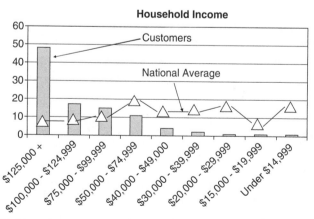

Figure 9-15. Household income of customers compared to the national average.

- A monthly catalog, which changes gradually and seasonally.
- One big and one small book which are re-mailed throughout the season.

The cataloger decided to experiment with modeling, with the help of KnowledgeBase Marketing. The model selected was based on the data in the customer database, augmented by overlay data from AmeriLINK® data including age, income, and home ownership. The model produced an algorithm with this formula:

$$\text{Score} = 1.05 + .04 \times (\text{home ownership} - 0 \text{ or } 1) + .05 \times \text{total orders} + .01 \times \text{income in thousands} - .03 \times \text{age}$$

Should You Outsource Your Modeling?

If you already have an experienced modeler on your staff that does good work and likes it, hang on to her. Good modelers are hard to find. If, however, you do not have such a person, you should not necessarily rush out to recruit one. There are many companies which will do modeling for you for a reasonable price (from $5,000 to $25,000). In addition, some list providers such as Abacus or KnowledgeBase Marketing may include a custom model in the cost of the names that you purchase, so the models are essentially free. In general, I favor outsourcing for two reasons:

- Outsourcing is usually less expensive in the long run
- You will learn what is state of the art in a rapidly changing field

Few mailers can keep an in-house modeler busy all the time, whereas outsourced modelers can be developing models for dozens of clients at once. In-house modelers come to you with the skills they have learned. They will not learn as many new things working only for you as they would if they worked at a service bureau with 20 different clients.

Summary

1. Modeling does not always work. There are many situations in which the variables that go into the customer decision process cannot be captured in a database.
2. Where the model fails to work, experiment with RFM.

3. Where models work, you can increase your profits in acquisition by very significant amounts. For this reason you should experiment with modeling to see if it works for your situation.

4. Modeling to detect propensity for churn can be a highly profitable exercise. You can increase your retention rate if the model is combined with a creative retention strategy.

5. CHAID can help you to create useful customer segments.

6. The modeling function should be outsourced.

Executive Quiz 9

	Put the appropriate letter before each answer	
	Questions	**Answers**
a	Helps to create marketing segments	–0.06
b	Not demographic data	500
c	Factor weight = –0.5. More likely to respond than weight = ?	Addresses
d	Model works well with test, but not with validation. Problem?	Algorithm
e	Why do response rates go up when you use a model?	Behavioral Data
f	A hot line name	CHAID
g	Which predicts response better? RFM or a profile?	Don't mail low deciles
h	If customer income exceeds national average, response = ?	Faster, cheaper
i	Why should you outsource a model?	May not be related
j	NCOA^{LINK} may change some?	Model is bad.
k	A mathematical routine	Models
l	SAS or SPSS are used to run	Much bigger than average
m	Outliers	New Movers
n	Minimum sales for a model	Previous promotion
o	Mail Order Buyer	RFM
p	Needed for predictive model	Zip plus four

Figure 9-16. Quiz 9.

10

Customer Acquisition

The market is always smarter than I am. I rely on it, rather than my own intuition for guidance.

JOSEPH C. KLIGGE, JR.

The tone of a good direct mail letter is as direct and personal as the writer's skill can make it. Even though it may go to millions of people, it never orates to a crowd but rather murmurs into a single ear. It's a message from one letter writer to one letter reader.

HARRY B. WALSH

What is the best way to acquire customers? That is a trick question, because there is no one best way. Mass marketing works for many products. Just having retail branches or distributors all over the country works, but these usually have to be promoted with mass marketing. Credit cards are often promoted by direct mail and TV ads. Home equity loans are very big on TV. How do you know which is best? You try everything, and see what works best.

In this chapter, we are going to discuss various methods for acquiring consumers and business customers, beginning with direct mail.

How Direct Mail Customer Acquisition Works

You begin with a list. There are more than 40,000 different lists of consumers and businesses available for rent for direct mail acquisition. Most of these are lists of people who are customers of some American company. They may be catalog purchasers, subscribers to magazines, people with credit cards, purchasers over the Internet, donors to causes, etc. The owners of these lists are supposed to have asked their customers whether they object to having their names exchanged with other companies. Most people have no objection. Some unethical companies rent their responders names without asking permission. When you rent lists, be sure to ask whether specific permission has been granted.

To negotiate your way through the many lists available, it is best to use a list broker. There are scores of these brokers. Many specialize in particular fields, such as non-profit or financial services lists. A broker will negotiate on your behalf with list owners or managers to get you the names you want. Rented names for acquisition are usually rented for one time use. You are not allowed to keep the name on your computer after the mailing is over. Anyone who responds to your offer, however, becomes your property. You can expect to pay between $50 and $250 per thousand names for a one-time rental.

Types of Lists

In general, there are two kinds of lists: response lists and compiled files. A response list consists of customers who have made a purchase or responded to an offer. You can ask the list owner what these people responded to, and how much they spent. You can also ask for hot line names. These are the names of people who have made a purchase within the past 30 days. They usually respond better than other names (see Chapter 5 on Recency).

The other kind of list consists of compiled names. Some companies, such as Experian, or KnowledgeBase Marketing have compiled the names of almost all the consumers in America complete with income, age, type of home, etc.

About half of the consumers in America never buy anything by mail. For this reason, an offer to a response list of confirmed mail order buyers almost always produces better responses than an offer to a compiled list. Compiled lists are very useful, however. They are rented by newspapers seeking subscribers, Cable TV companies, voter registration drives, and hundreds of other enterprises. Later in this chapter, we will discuss a new use for compiled names in a prospect database.

You can also rent new movers names. These people have not necessarily responded to anything, but because they have recently moved they will need to buy a lot of products and services that non-movers already have. For this reason they are often more responsive than people who have not moved.

A Direct Mail Campaign

To see how direct mail customer acquisition works, let us follow a mail campaign from start to finish. Let us assume we are selling some product or service, such as automobile insurance.

We begin with an offer. In this book, we are not going to cover copy writing, which is discussed in excellent books such as Profitable Direct Marketing, by Jim Kobs, or Direct Mail Copy that Sells, by Herschell Gordon Lewis, or 2,239 Tested Secrets for Direct Marketing Success by Denny Hatch and Don Jackson. In general, every database marketing communication should always be a test, so you will be testing at least two offers.

Choice Kills

In direct mail, you should not give recipients a choice. If you are selling insurance, sell one policy in your mailing piece, not several. If you are inviting people to take a tour, tell them the tour begins on July 26. Period. You may have tours going every week all year. But you will find that your response rate to a specific offer beats your response rate to an offer about which the recipient has to make a decision. Mitch Martin, who has many years of direct marketing experience with the Marriott Vacation Club put it simply: "Choice can kill response."

Selecting Lists

Let us say that you want to mail two million pieces. You find a list broker and get him to determine the best lists for your offer—these will be people who have responded to some offer in your price range, who have the proper age, home ownership, income, etc. You may be renting 200 lists with an average of 10,000 names per list. Because there will be many duplicates among the various lists that you rent, to end up with two million, you will probably have to rent about three million names.

Traditional Merge Purge

To prepare the names for your mailing, you should use a service bureau such as Acxiom, KnowledgeBase Marketing, or Merkle Direct Marketing. There are scores of them. Your broker will arrange for name files from the 200 selected lists to arrive at the service bureau on a date that you select. This date needs to be a couple of weeks before the mail drop to give your service bureau time to receive all the names and reformat them for the mailing. You will also provide the service bureau with your customer house file to be used as a suppression file. You may want to mail your house file as well, in some cases, but first you want to make sure you are not paying to rent names that you already own. In renting the names, your broker will have negotiated a "net name" agreement with each list owner that specifies that you do not pay for a name you already own. In addition, if the same name appears on four rented lists, for example, you pay each list owner 25 percent. Most net name arrangements have a minimum net, such as 75 percent, which means that they get paid for 75 percent of the names that they send you, regardless of how many are actually duplicates.

The service bureau will go through a series of steps now called "traditional merge purge" which are described in detail below. In summary, the steps involve:

- Converting all 200 lists plus your house file to a single format—keeping track of the source of each name.
- Running the file through National Change of Address ($NCOA^{LINK}$).
- De-duping the combined file to consolidate the duplicates and to suppress names on your house file. At this point your three million rented names get reduced to two million unique names that are not already your customers.
- Dividing the file into segments that permit you to test the effectiveness of each of your 200 lists, and of your two offers.
- Running the file through a series of postal software routines to be sure that they are deliverable, and organized to receive the maximum postal service discount.

National Change of Address

This is one of the most useful services ever devised by the US Postal Service. When people move, they usually notify their local post office of their new address. The form that people fill out is sent to a central location where it is put into a USPS database and sent to service bureaus that are authorized to sell the *NCOA^LINK* service to mailers. *NCOA^LINK* contains approximately 108 million permanent change-of-address (COA) records. Approximately 40 million COA forms are filed annually with the USPS. The *NCOA^LINK* database is updated every week with this information.

Service bureaus running *NCOA^LINK* usually charge a few cents per hit. That means that you send them your tape of three million names. They will send the tape back with the new addresses of the folks on the tape who have moved. *NCOA^LINK* changed addresses are kept for four years. About 20 percent of all households move every year, so running your file through *NCOA^LINK* can save you a lot of money. Rented lists often contain obsolete addresses.

Deliverable Software Routines

First class mail has to be delivered by the USPS, or it will be returned to you. Third class mail used for most acquisition mailings gets delivered if it is addressed properly, and the recipients are actually living there. It does not get forwarded. If there is some problem with the address, the USPS just discards undeliverable third class mail—and you will not know about it. Here are some of the routines used by KnowledgeBase Marketing to clean your mail file. Other service bureaus have similar systems:

The Coding Accuracy Support System (CASS) is a USPS certified system that improves the accuracy of delivery point codes, Zip+4 codes, 5-digit Zip Codes, and carrier route codes on mail pieces.

Delivery Point Validation. DPV contains all delivery point addresses serviced by the US Postal Service.

Delivery Sequence File—Second Generation. DSF^2 is an address hygiene tool that provides additional address information about a DPV-verified address to minimize address delivery errors not detected by *NCOA^LINK* or CASS-certified processing.

Address Element Correction. AEC focuses on inaccurate addresses, specifically those addresses that cannot be matched to the national Zip+4 file because of a missing address element.

Locatable Address Conversion System. LACS enables companies to update their mailing lists when addresses have been converted by local authorities from rural to city style address.

Dynamic COA. Over 30 percent of people who move never submit a COA with the USPS. In addition, records on the $NCOA^{LINK}$ file are dropped 48 months after the move effective date. This file retains records of address changes for more than seven years, including multiple moves and forwarding addresses.

Nixies. USPS provides a Nixie Elimination Service as an addition to $NCOA^{LINK}$. This service provides footnotes as to why an address match could not be found. This service is very useful in correcting bad addresses.

Suppression Services. For acquisition you will want to eliminate your existing customers plus people who do not want to receive mail, or should not receive it. This includes the DMA Mail and telephone preference files, state "do not call" lists, people in prison, and people who have died.

Why These Software Routines Are Important

Running these routines increases the cost of a mailing. But they also can save you a lot of money. KnowledgeBase Marketing analyzed an acquisition mailing of 3.5 million names that had been done by a non-profit mailer and processed by an independent service bureau (not KnowledgeBase Marketing). The goal was to see how deliverable the mail was. This is what they found (Figure 10-1). 319,662 of the pieces actually mailed were either duplicates or undeliverable. At about $0.50 per piece, the non-profit had wasted $159,831 on the mailing. The mailing produced a net loss. If they had run the proper software routines before they mailed, they could have turned a $50,000 loss into a $109,000 profit.

Looking at the Type of Address

The DSF^2 software produces some interesting reports concerning the type of address. Here is the result of the analysis of a third class mailing (Figure 10-2).

Looking closely at the response numbers in the last column, you will see that mail sent to a business address in this consumer mailing had half the response rate of the same mail sent to a residence address. Mail sent to a "drop" had a 30 percent lower response rate than mail sent to non-drop addresses. A "drop" is usually an apartment building where

	Quantity	Percent
Input Quantity:	**3,588,006**	**100.00%**
2 Line Street Address Omits	88	0.00%
Input To AEC Processing (Non-Zip+4 only):	67,659	**1.89%**
Records Matched, Changed (Zip+4 appended)	13,189	0.37%
Input To NCOA/DCOA/DSF Processing:	**3,587,918**	**100.00%**
Nixie Omits	48,397	1.35%
NCOA No Forwarding Address Omits	4,848	0.14%
DCOA No Forwarding Address Omits	26,036	0.73%
Unconfirmed or Invalid Zip code Omits	650	0.02%
NCOA Moved with Forwarding Addresses (not omitted)	79,979	2.23%
DCOA Moved with Forwarding Addresses (not omitted)	86,430	2.41%
Post NCOA Processing:	**3,507,987**	**97.77%**
APO/FPO Omits	1,076	0.03%
South Pacific Omits	397	0.01%
Prison Omits	294	0.01%
Vulgar Omits	636	0.02%
No Address Omits	88	0.00%
DSF Vacant Address Omits	10,994	0.31%
Input To Merge/Purge Processing:	**3,494,502**	**97.39%**
Internal Duplicate Omits	52,458	1.46%
Mail Preference File Omits	107,953	3.01%
Deceased File Omit	65,747	1.83%
Net Output from Merge/Purge:	**3,268,344**	**91.09%**
Unmailable Addresses Removed	**319,662**	**8.91%**

Figure 10-1. Deliverable mail report.

third class mail is dropped in a bundle, rather than put into each person's mail box. In the above situation, suppose that your breakeven rate is 3.09 percent. You could have saved more than $100,000 in this mailing by not mailing to cells whose response rates were shown in previous mailings to be lower than the breakeven rate.

Creating the Mailing Campaign

While the service bureau is running the traditional merge purge, your marketing staff will be busy creating the campaign. A direct mail campaign often consists of hundreds of different mailing cells, each designed to test something. You typically want to test each list that you rented. You may also be simultaneously testing various offers or packages or copy. Let us say that you have two offers: a standard offer and a deluxe offer. If you have 200 rented lists of about 10,000 each, you might split each one in half (called an A/B split) and send half the deluxe offer and half the standard offer. That means that you will have 400 mail segments (200 × 2). You may

DSF² Summary Report						
ABC Co. - Holiday Initiative						
Total Mailing		**Mail File**		**Response File**		**Response**
ABC Co. - Holiday Initiative		3,126,612		98,288		3.14%
Delivery Type		**Mail File**		**Response File**		**Response**
1 - Curb delivery		1,325,605	42.4%	40,995	41.7%	3.09%
2 - NDCBU (Delivery Boxes in Neighborhood)		337,515	10.8%	10,730	10.9%	3.18%
3 - Central Delivery		255,539	8.2%	7,829	8.0%	3.06%
4 - Door Slot		1,140,432	36.5%	36,970	37.6%	3.24%
U - Unknown		67,521	2.2%	1,764	1.8%	2.61%
Address Type		**Mail File**		**Response File**		**Response**
B - Business Address		120,677	3.9%	1,983	2.0%	1.64%
R - Residence Address		2,938,414	94.0%	94,541	96.2%	3.22%
U - Unknown		67,521	2.2%	1,764	1.8%	2.61%
LACS Converted Address		**Mail File**		**Response File**		**Response**
Y - Address Has Been Converted to a New Address		361	0.0%	18	0.0%	5.03%
N - Address Has Not Been LACS Converted		3,126,251	100.0%	98,270	100.0%	3.14%
Seasonal Indicator		**Mail File**		**Response File**		**Response**
Y - Seasonal Address		2,955	0.1%	70	0.1%	2.37%
N - Permanent Address		3,056,136	97.7%	96,454	98.1%	3.16%
U - Unknown		67,521	2.2%	1,764	1.8%	2.61%
Vacant Indicator		**Mail File**		**Response File**		**Response**
Y - Vacant Address		13,185	0.4%	278	0.3%	2.11%
N - Occupied Address		3,045,906	97.4%	96,246	97.9%	3.16%
U - Unknown		67,521	2.2%	1,764	1.8%	2.61%
Throwback Indicator		**Mail File**		**Response File**		**Response**
Y - Throwback		4,000	0.1%	91	0.1%	2.28%
N - Not a Throwback		3,055,091	97.7%	96,433	98.1%	3.16%
U - Unknown		67,521	2.2%	1,764	1.8%	2.61%
Drop Indicator		**Mail File**		**Response File**		**Response**
Y - Drop		22,250	0.7%	482	0.5%	2.17%
N - Not a Drop		3,036,841	97.1%	96,042	97.7%	3.16%
U - Unknown		67,521	2.2%	1,764	1.8%	2.61%

Figure 10-2. DSF results of a mailing.

also be testing other things: teaser copy on the envelope, different paper, fonts, etc. These additional tests will multiply your segments.

Caution: Do not create too many segments. The cell size will be too small to give valid results, and you probably cannot use all the information generated from the test. A single-variable test is the best policy.

For each test cell you create a mail code: HA322, HA323, HA324, etc. These codes correspond to the list and the offer being tested. Your mail shop will print these codes on the mail piece that you send out. When the customers respond by phone or through the Internet, you attempt to capture this code from them so that you can see which list and which offer gets the credit for the response. If the mailing is to your existing customers you may also create a customer number which is printed on the mail piece.

The resulting final mail file will be sent to a mail shop that prints your mail pieces, together with the mail codes. Their first step will be to run postal presort routines designed to get the maximum postal discount.

Postal discounts come from arranging the mail in USPS required order with USPS codes that help in the sorting of mail and delivering it in trays or bags directly to the post office, or the mail man, who will actually deliver each piece.

Spam Is Out

Not listed above is customer acquisition by e-mail. Anyone who has had an e-mail account for any length of time knows that there are billions of e-mails sent daily trying to acquire customers. This mail to people with no previous connection to the sender is called SPAM. Spam is illegal in some states. It is annoying everywhere. Nothing in this book should be used to suggest that Spam is a valid way to acquire customers.

That does not mean that the Internet is out as a customer acquisition medium. If you sign up as a frequent flyer member of an airline, the application form might ask if you are willing to receive solicitations from partners of the airline. If you do not say no to that question, you might subsequently get an e-mail from a hotel or car rental company or credit card issuer which provides miles on the airline program. That is not spam. If you want to acquire customers in this way, there are some rules that you should follow:

- Always identify yourself clearly in the address line.
- In your e-mail provide a physical address, a Web site address and a phone number.
- Explain in your message how you got the person's name and address.
- Provide a simple one-click opportunity to have the person's name dropped from your mailing list.

Of course, e-mails to your existing and previous customers are not spam, unless they have asked you to drop them from your mailing list. To avoid the accusation keep a suppression file of everyone who has asked you not to send them e-mails. Be sure your service bureau uses this suppression file on every single e-mail blast.

How Junk Mail and Spam Are Different

The phrase "junk mail" is often used to describe the promotional mail you find in your mailbox every day. Another way of describing it is "direct mail advertising." Some people object to junk mail. I love it. It works. It gets results. It is part of why America leads the world in marketing, mass production, productivity growth, and affluence.

Where direct mail and spam differ is in the cost of production. In general, it costs about $0.40 to $0.50 to put a direct mail piece in the mail. Spam e-mails can be sent by the billions for less than one cent each. Cost is no restraint. So unscrupulous enterprises fill up your e-mail boxes with worthless advertisements for pornography, pharmaceuticals and get rich quick schemes. When you get a direct mail piece, you know that the sender had to earn enough in sales to pay the $0.40 to $0.50 it cost to get it to you. Direct mail, because of the cost, is almost always legitimate. Worthless enterprises cannot afford direct mail.

What Kind of Response Rates Will You Get?

Direct mail response rates are seldom very high. For most third class mailings, a 2 percent response rate is normal, and if well designed, profitable. Some mailings have achieved response rates of 10 percent or 20 percent but that is very rare. Some mailers get a response rate of 1/4 of 1 percent and still make a profit. The Direct Marketing Association (www.the-DMA.org) provides a report on average response rates in various industries. Before you do your mailing, determine the normal response rates for your type of offer. The response rates you get will depend on a number of factors: the offer, the copy, the package, and the competition. But the most important single factor in response is the list. If your list is poor, excellence in the other factors will not save your mailing.

Back End Analysis

When the mailing is over, it is important to study how you did: what worked and what did not work. Back end analysis is done to check the response and sales by product, cell code, list, offer, package, and zip code. If there was no cutoff date on your offer, you may get responses over a period of time. This is particularly true of catalogs. You may want to try half-life analysis (see Chapter 11 on Tests and Controls). If you have appended demographic data to your mailing file (see prospect databases later in this chapter), you will want to see how your offer did by income, age, education, type of home, length of residence, and many other factors. Back end analysis is vital to successful database marketing. You should get better and better at customer acquisition as a result.

Acquiring Retail Customer Names

If you have a retail operation, you probably have thousands or millions of customers. They may be regular customers, but how would you know it? You want to add them to your database so you can communicate with them. There are several ways of doing this. Here are three:

- Creating an in-house credit or frequent buyer card
- Registering customer credit cards
- Reverse phone append

Reverse Telephone Number Append

The credit card idea fails to catch one large group of customers: cash or check customers. Here we can use reverse append. Many retail outlets have made it a practice to collect the customer's home phone when they make any kind of a purchase—cash, check, or credit card. Armed with this number it is possible to have a service bureau look up the name and address of the owner of the phone by a reverse append process. The Sports Authority has been using this for years. Using this process, they were able to send a postcard to cash customers who visited their stores in November, encouraging them to come back to the chain before Christmas. The result: 11 percent came back, using the card. This is an almost unheard of success rate, and all due to reverse append.

Prospect Databases

The standard direct mail list system described in this chapter is about to change.

What is about to disrupt this industry is the concept of prospect databases. Right now, most mailers learn only two things from their acquisition mailings: which lists work best, and which offers work best. After the mailing, they are required to wipe their systems clean of the mailed addresses. They get to keep only the responders.

A prospect database works this way: A mailer negotiates with list suppliers to let him have their names on his file for an entire year (or a quarter). He pays the list owner whenever one of their names is used. Since he has the names for a year, he can afford to append demographics to the names to learn the age, income, presence of children, home value, dwelling type, own vs. rent, length of residence, mail responsiveness, cluster coding, and about 20 other important facts. He could never afford to append this information to a list that he rents for a single use. Armed with this information, after the first mailing he can use back end analysis to see which clusters, age groups, income groups, etc., respond to his offer. His subsequent mailing selections can be made not only by list, but by demographics and behavior. Those who have done this find that they get much better response rates than they did when selecting by list alone.

The next step, of course, is to develop models that predict the type of person that will respond to each offer (see Chapter 9 on Modeling). Selecting mailed names using a model enables response rates to go way up. But that is not the end of it.

Compiled Lists

Until recently, most mass mailers used compiled lists only as a supplement to response lists. But with your model, a compiled list becomes more valuable. Using the prospect database, the model that is used to select potential buyers from response lists can also be used to select consumers from a compiled list. Since a good compiled list consists of almost every consumer in the country, a good model will select almost exactly the same people from a compiled list that it would from a large group of rented response lists. Compiled lists are cheaper. Here are some examples of the costs of various types of lists (Figure 10-3).

As you can see from this chart, compiled lists can be rented for about half the cost of response lists. A mailer that has been paying between $75 and $120 per thousand names from response lists finds that he can get compiled lists for $45 to $55 per thousand. With the model, he can pick the responders from the compiled list. But that is not all: many compiled lists are already coded with all the appended data that are needed for a model. You can buy a compiled list based on an algorithm resulting from a model. There is no need to rent names that your model says are not likely to respond.

Category of List	Price/M
Attendees	$116.00
Books and CDs	$119.00
Business Magazines	$140.00
Consumer Magazines	$108.00
Donors	$75.00
Newsletters	$170.00
Permission Based Email Consumers	$170.00
Permission Based Email B2B	$283.00
Compiled Lists	$55.00

Figure 10-3. List costs per thousand records.

In the previous chapter on Modeling, we provided a case study from Summit Marketing. We repeat the results here because we are going to use these results to show the benefit of a prospect database (Figure 10-4).

As you can see, the monthly profits doubled by using the model. This example does not use compiled lists to reduce costs. The cost of the mailing was identical before and after. Let us take this example one step further. When you factor in the reduced cost of the names from using a compiled list, the profit takes another jump (Figure 10-5).

That is not the end of it. One big cost of monthly mailings is the merge purge process. In a typical situation that I have already described, 200–300 tapes arrive which have to be reformatted, run through $NCOA^{LINK}$, have address hygiene applied, and are de-duped to produce a mailable output file. Few merge purge processes can be run for much less than $12 per thousand. With a prospect database, the monthly merge purge is unnecessary. The file is already de-duped, has been run through $NCOA^{LINK}$ and data hygiene. This needs to be done only once a quarter. The only monthly cost will be the cost of renting and adding

	Control Group	Optimized Group	% Change	# Change
Total Mailed	1,264,571	1,264,571	0%	0
Cost of Mailing	$547,559	$547,559	0%	0
Number of Responses	13,366	16,090	20%	2,724
Response Rate	1.06%	1.27%	20%	0.22%
Number of Sales	1,599	2,323	45%	724
Sales Rate	12.00%	14.40%	21%	2.47%
Total Revenue	$2,605,603	$3,158,151	21%	$553,208
Profit	$95,896	$187,851	96%	$91,955

Figure 10-4. Prospect database optimization.

	Response List	Complied List
Names	1,264,571	1,264,571
CPM	$105	$55
Name Cost	$132,780	$69,551

Figure 10-5. Compiled list costs.

hot line names, plus postal presort. The annual savings therefore are substantial (Figure 10-6).

Knowledge Base Marketing built a prospect database for a major mailer. This mailer sent several products in more than 30 campaigns annually. The idea was to reduce list acquisition costs by building a prospect database which would permit more efficient targeting of prospects.

To build the prospect database, KnowledgeBase Marketing had to combine the rented names with the AmeriLINK® database of 236 million U.S. consumers and the mailer's customer database which included solicitation and response history. Altogether, the process involved more than one billion records. The mailer negotiated a fixed price for the AmeriLINK® core consumer list which allowed unlimited use of the data. Then the two companies contacted a list broker to renegotiate usage arrangements for their rented lists.

Under the new arrangements, AmeriLINK® became the high-order priority list because of its cost advantage. Priority dictates the name that gets the credit when there is a duplicate record. In total the overall list cost reduction was significant.

The model developed for the mailer analyzed both the responders and the people who were very unlikely to respond. Avoiding these non-responders reduced the mail universe by 5 percent. What was the overall result? In the first year, the prospect database produced cost savings for the mailer of more than $1 million, while at the same time boosting response rates per piece mailed.

Building a prospect database will work for you if you are a high volume mailer marketing to consumers. You can use a prospect database if you are renting a wide variety of lists with multiple campaigns each year,

	Response Lists	Prospect DB
Annual Names	15,174,852	15,174,852
Processing	$12/M per month	$12/M per Q
Annual Cost	$2,185,179	$728,393
Monthly	$182,098	$60,699

Figure 10-6. Savings from reduced processing costs.

and if you are willing to negotiate with list managers and owners. One by one these high volume mailers are shifting to building prospect databases. The list industry will never be the same.

Use of a Prospect Database in Insurance

A major insurance company had been getting one qualified lead in 20 cold calls. With the help of a service bureau, they built a prospect database. Using this database, they were able to pre-qualify leads using customer profiles developed from transaction history and demographic enhancement data. By matching their prospect database against the profiles, the company was able to determine the customers most likely to buy a life, auto, or homeowner product. Using the new system, they were able to get one or two qualified leads from 10 cold calls—more than double their previous rate. The prospect database plus behind-the scenes work eliminated $3 to $4 million dollars per year in data costs.

Business-to-Business Customer Acquisition

To be successful in customer acquisition through direct mail to businesses, you need to know what type of business buys your product. A first step is to code your customer database by SIC or NAICS codes. These codes indicate what type of business your customers are: restaurants, law firms, plastic manufacturers, or farmers. Dun and Bradstreet or a service bureau can do the code appending process for you. You can learn a lot from this process. One molded wood manufacturer had been mailing to companies with certain SIC codes for years. When they applied the D&B process to their database, they discovered a whole new industry that had been buying their products without their having recognized it. A mailing to companies with this SIC code produced outstanding response rates. Here is a chart of U.S. enterprises by SIC code (Figure 10-7).

This chart is taken from Dun and Bradstreet listings. You will note that most businesses are classified as services.

A further breakdown of business types can be by number of employees or annual sales. This information is also available from Dun & Bradstreet and their competitors. You can also often obtain the names and titles of the executives in the companies who make or influence the purchasing decisions for your products.

	SIC Range	Number of Businesses	Percent
Agriculture/Forestry/Fishing	01-09	750,070	3.97%
Mining	10-14	43,635	0.23%
Construction	15-17	1,475,050	7.80%
Manufacturing	20-39	815,949	4.31%
Transportation/Communications	40-49	723,649	3.83%
Wholesale	50-51	844,136	4.46%
Retail	52-59	3,046,430	16.11%
Finance/Insurance/Real Estate	60-67	1,566,304	8.28%
Services	70-89	7,355,026	38.89%
Public Administration	90-97	241,448	1.28%
Non Classified		2,051,173	10.85%
Total		18,912,870	100.00%

Figure 10-7. SIC codes.

In trying to acquire business customers, therefore, your primary interest is SIC code, annual sales (of the company involved) and their number of each company's employees. Using D&B or other data, you often can know much more about business prospect purchasing plans and needs than you can learn about consumer prospects.

Using a Database to Acquire New Business Customers

Besides their famous earth moving equipment, Caterpillar sold $2 billion per year of large truck engines. These trucks are custom built by truck assemblers, such as Peterbilt, Kenworth, or Mack. For this reason, until they built their database, Caterpillar and the other truck engine manufacturers never knew who was using their engines. The Caterpillar sales force, therefore, did not really sell engines. They just tried to influence the choice of engine.

To improve their business, Caterpillar engaged two very experienced database marketers: Alan Weber, who is now President of Marketing Analytics Group in Cleveland, MO and Frank Weyforth, Chairman of the Board at Weyforth-Haas Marketing in Overland, KS.

In the beginning, Caterpillar had no database, and no one really saw the need for one. Instead, their executives had a lot of questions: "What truck fleets are we not calling on? What fleets should test our two new engines? How can we get a marketing strategy that can be measured? How do we adjust to the coming downturn in sales?"

To try to answer these questions, Weber and Weyforth got each of the six groups in the company involved in Caterpillar truck marketing to chip in money for a project designed to get the needed answers. They used part of the money to give laptops to the 260 Caterpillar salesmen with this proviso: "You get paid for sales, but only if the customer name and other data is entered into the laptop database." It worked.

The consultants' goal was to determine the potential universe for truck engine sales. There were four internal databases in Caterpillar that were not compatible with each other. To get the data, the team combined the internal databases, appended data from the National Motor Carriers directory, D&B and TRW data, and trade publication lists. After two years of work, they had a file of 110,000 customers, 8,000 mid-range fleets, and 34,000 heavy duty fleets—the universe of all heavy truck fleets in America.

Using the data they assembled on SIC code, truck owner vocations, engine models, number of trucks and trucking category, they were able to predict using CHAID which non-customers were most likely to buy. They used regressions to predict how many miles would be driven per year for each truck on the road, and the trade cycle (how many years before the engine would be traded in). They grouped their customers and prospects into 83 Heavy Duty Groups and 34 Mid-Range Groups.

With the data available, they estimated customer lifetime value. When they got through all the analysis, they were able to develop a score for each fleet: a real score based on that they were buying now from Caterpillar, and a potential score based on what they could buy with the type of trucking business that they did.

With these scores, the consultants developed different messages that could be sent to each customer and prospect. Messages that stressed retention were different from messages that were designed for conquest.

They developed a new incentive plan for the sales force. It worked this way:

- You get $X for each engine sold in your assigned territory
- You get $2X for each engine sold to a retention customer on your list
- You get $3X for each engine sold to a conquest customer on your list

That got the sales force attention. For the first time, the sales force focused on the most profitable targets, and they targeted every profitable target in the whole country.

What was the result of three and a half years work? During the first year with the new database Caterpillar was able to sign up 500 conquest fleets. They sold an average of 50–100 engines per fleet at about $15,000 per engine. The total increased sales that could be attributed to the new database system were approximately 500 million dollars. Caterpillar market share went up by 5 percent in a period in which all truck engine sales nationwide were down.

This is real database marketing. Few companies today have done what Weber and Weyforth did for Caterpillar. Most companies do not know how to do it, and do not have the initiative to put their resources into such a project.

Trade Show Attendees

An innovative direct response agency created a prospect mailing for a national company that achieved an almost unheard of 19 percent response rate. Here is how they did it.

The National Association of Broadcasters is a huge convention. Every year there are more than 5,000 attendees. It is tough to get noticed at a show of this size, no matter how lavish your booth. How do you get people to visit you, and how do you get vital information so that you can get an informed telemarketer and sales force follow-up?

The direct response agency began with the list of 5,000 attendees at the previous year's conference. They wrote 5,000 personalized letters, each including a free phone card. When the recipients activated the card, they were routed to the agency's interactive voice response (IVR) system. The callers responded to a survey by pushing buttons on their phones. The survey asked if they were planning to attend the conference, and 13 questions about their planned purchases for the next year. While it was not necessary to answer all the questions to activate the card, most respondents did, in fact, answer all the questions (Figure 10-8).

There were 950 respondents to the survey in all. The agency appended business data to the file to learn the SIC code, annual sales, and number of employees. The respondents were then broken into the top five SIC codes. Summary data was compiled of their responses to the questions.

In the case of this innovative phone card, a way was found for the prospect to benefit by the survey. Some mailers include a dollar bill—and

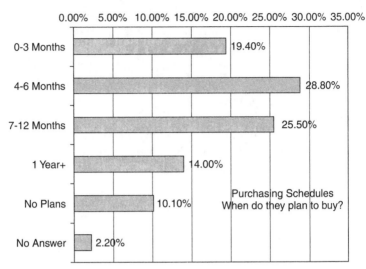

Figure 10-8. Results of a phone card survey: purchasing schedules.

that works. The phone card may have worked even better. It got a high response rate—and it was much faster than a mail response survey. Most people called right away. As soon as they called, the survey data was in the system—there was no need for data entry. In addition, it was comparatively inexpensive. Putting a dollar bill in with every survey costs a lot of money. You are sending a dollar to thousands of people who do not respond. Phone cards in letters sent to people who did not use them cost the agency less than 50 cents apiece.

Other companies have extended this business-to-business prospect mailing concept beyond phone cards. Hewlett Packard had success with $15 Pizza Hut coupons. HP and others use the Internet for the responders rather than a touch-tone phone. There are many variations on this same theme.

Acquiring the Wrong Kind of Customer

A continuity club faced a difficult problem: direct mail solicitations were attracting the wrong kind of customer. Direct mail solicitations offered a number of "free" products for shipping and handling costs plus the promise to purchase additional products at "full price."

The solicitations attracted many customers who had little loyalty and frequently refused to pay even the shipping and handling costs.

- A high percentage of individuals who responded to these solicitations would obtain the "free" products and never pay.

- Those who paid for their initial selections often failed to meet their full commitment, or terminated shortly after meeting their commitment.

- The Web was no solution: online signups yielded payment rates even lower than direct mail.

- This led to a default rate that was unacceptable. There was a high degree of customer defection.

To solve these problems, the continuity club created a number of in-house response models which inadvertently targeted likely responders who were unlikely to pay and remain loyal. See the bottom group on Figure 10-9. The in-house models which focused on likely payers produced mailings with response rates which were too low to be profitable. See the top group on Figure 10-9. The challenge was to find prospects with balanced probabilities of responding and paying. See the middle group.

The continuity club asked KnowledgeBase Marketing to create a two model chain. One model focused on response and one focused on payment after response. The analysis showed that creative use of all available information provided good predictive power. Some of the most important variables were:

- Wealth
- Urban/suburban/rural
- Occupation concentration

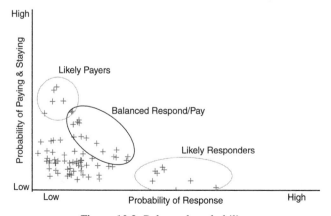

Figure 10-9. Balanced probability.

- Zip Code or Zip + 4
- Percentage defaulted
- Number of applicants divided by number of club members

As a result of using the models to direct the acquisition program:

- No-payment rates were reduced by 20 percent when mailing to the top three deciles.
- Overall, the mailings shifted from negative returns to a cumulative profit of 5 cents per piece when mailing the top three deciles.
- In-market tests demonstrated the strength of the approach, and replaced the previous models as the "gold standard."

Executive Quiz 10

	Put the appropriate letter before each definition		
	Term to be defined		**Definition**
a	CASS		Classifies an address as a business
b	DPV		Confirms that an address exists
c	DSF^2		Corrects for missing address elements
d	AEC		Don't mail these
e	LACS		Don't pay for duplicates
f	NCOA		Finds addresses of those who move
g	Nixie		Forecast results in a couple of weeks
h	Throwback		How did you do?
i	Drop		Improves Accuracy of Delivery Point Codes
j	Half Life Reports		Inaccurately Cased Mail
k	Back End Analysis		Mail delivered by in house staff
l	Third Class Mail		Undelivered mail is not returned
m	Net Names		Updates rural addresses

Figure 10-10. Quiz 10.

11

Strategy Verification: Testing and Control Groups

The Holy Grail of direct marketing is the single-variable test. You want only one thing to change in each test. If you're going to test price, then you test two packages that are the same in all respects except for price...The goal is to make sure that when something wins or loses on a package or panel, you know the cause of the difference so you can repeat it if it wins...Don Nicholas in 2,239 Tested Secrets for Direct Marketing Success (Hatch and Jackson)

Don't test stuff your competition has already tested, especially the big competitors. If they tried a certain approach and dropped it, assume it didn't work. And if they are using something over and over, assume it does work. No need to retest and reinvent until your model proves itself. Anver Suleiman (ibid).

*To this day, I believe that the most important tool available to the direct marketer is the ability to test, a form of pragmatic research that doesn't just tell you how a customer **might** react to an ad but how consumers really do react. Direct marketing makes advertising totally measurable and accountable.*

LESTER WUNDERMAN
Being Direct

Why Testing Is Essential

The market is constantly changing. What worked last year, does not work as well this year, and may not work at all next year. Capital One pioneered the "teaser rate" for credit cards. They were the first to make an introductory offer of 3.9 percent annual percentage rate to get people to switch to their credit cards. They were wildly successful. Their card memberships and profits grew at a phenomenal rate. Of course, after a few months, the teaser rate expired. The card interest rates for each new member went up to 18.9 percent. They lost some customers, but kept most of them. Soon, everyone was offering teaser rates. In a couple of years, the idea lost its luster. People were no longer fooled. Capital One, again ahead of the market, shifted to offering a firm 9.9 percent permanent rate, while the rest of the world was still offering teasers.

The object of testing is to learn how well you are doing, so you can modify your marketing strategy. The goal: to constantly get better and better at what you are doing.

Why Management Resists Testing

You have 400,000 customers to whom you can make an offer. You are pretty sure of what that offer should be and which customers should get the offer. But, you want to test your theory before you blow your whole budget on a hunch. You want to send two different offers to 25,000 each, and then roll out the best offer to the remaining 350,000. Management will resist the idea. "Our goal is to increase sales this quarter. Your tests will delay the results until next quarter. Forget the test, take your best offer, and roll it out. You can test later."

It might seem best not to argue with your managers. But postponing testing could cost you your job. Without tests, you cannot learn anything. If you cannot learn, you cannot improve, while your competition may be learning a great deal. There is real danger in not testing. If you are not really on top of things, you may not be around next year after company profits take a nosedive, and management looks around for something to cut.

Fortunately, database marketing is in a much better position to test and prove their contribution to profits than advertising, customer relations, corporate planning, R&D or most other staff functions. We just have to go about it in an organized way.

Marketing Objectives

The first step in any testing program is to determine what you are trying to accomplish. The goal of database marketing programs is usually to:

- increase sales to existing customers,
- reduce attrition, or
- gain new customers.

The best method is to define your customer lifetime value, and test the effectiveness of various alternate ways of increasing lifetime value. Lifetime value includes all the marketing and other costs, so any increase builds the company bottom line. Building lifetime value thus becomes a solid, measurable goal.

Let us begin by devising a test for a department store. Many of the concepts in this chapter were developed by Annette Champion of Arthur D. Little, Inc. the international management and technology consulting firm.

Creating a Controlled Test

Let us assume that your department store has a house credit card which is tied in to a customer database. This house card permits you to capture data about purchases. You are planning a new offer to increase sales. The question: how much does the offer actually increase sales, and what is its effect on lifetime value?

To set up a test you need two groups of customers: a test group (which gets the offer) and a control group (which does not get the offer). Without the control group, you will learn very little.

Assume that your department store has 400,000 customers who use the store credit card. You have brought in a new line of high fashion clothes for women. This is being promoted through print advertisements. You want to test, in addition, the effectiveness of a direct mail offer to female customers. For the purpose of the test, you have decided to mail your offer to 20,000 women.

As a first step, you query your database to see how many women have credit cards in their name. There are 200,000. You must select two groups: a test group of 20,000 who will get the mailing and a control group of 20,000 who will not get the mailing. Control groups do not have to be the same size as test groups. They could be larger or smaller. They have to be big enough to give valid results, and they have to be exactly the same type of people as the test group in demographics and purchase behavior. To create these two groups, you use a procedure called an Nth described in Chapter 5.

Separate the 40,000 into two groups of 20,000: a test group and a control group. Do this, as well, using an Nth. You will have to come up with an organized coding system so that you can remember who was in which group. You must keep other marketers in the organization from ruining the validity of your test by sending some other promotion to your test or control group during the test period.

When the groups are set up, a promotional offer is made to the test group. The control group is treated like everyone else, and does not receive the promotion or other related communications. They do, of course, get all other normal communications that customers get. In the example we are using here, both groups are on the database and use the store's credit card. Their purchase behavior is registered in the marketing database. A month later, the purchases of the two groups are compared. The effectiveness of the promotion is measured by the difference in purchases by the test group from purchases by the control group.

Let us assume that we are promoting a woman's suit that costs $150.00. Let us assume that 1,000 of the 20,000 test households (5 percent) took advantage of the offer, buying a net average of $150 of promoted items (the suit) plus $80 non-promoted items during the month. The remainder of the test group (19,000 households) bought an average of $30 of non-promoted items during the same month. Let us assume that during the same month, the controls bought an average of $2 of the promoted items (the suits—even though they were not promoted to them) and $22 of non-promoted items during the same month (Figure 11-1). How successful was the test?

Overall, sales due to the test increased by $320,000 and profits increased by $118,000.

- Why did sales of non-promoted items increase in responding households? Because, when the customers went into the store to look at the suit, they saw other items and bought them too.

- Why did sales of non-promoted items to non-responding test households increase over sales to control households? Because some of the non-responding customers went to the store because of the promotion, did not buy the suit, but bought something else anyway.

The return on investment from this promotion was 11.8 ($118,000/ $10,000). Since the test generated a clear $118,000 profit over the cost

Group	Number of Customers	Average Sale of: Promoted Items	Average Sale of: Non-Promoted Items	Combined Sales	Total Amount
	Sales to control and test groups in first month after a promotion				
Responders	1,000	$150.00	$80.00	$230.00	$230,000
Non-Responders	19,000	$0.00	$30.00	$30.00	$570,000
Controls	20,000	$2.00	$22.00	$24.00	$480,000
Total	40,000				$1,280,000
Total Sales to Test Group					$800,000
Total Sales to Control Group					$480,000
Increased sales due to the promotion					$320,000
Gross profit from sales @40%					$128,000
Cost of promotion to test group @ $500/M					$10,000
Net Profit					$118,000
Return on investment $118,000/ $10,000					11.8

Figure 11-1. Measuring results of the test promotion.

of the promotion itself, the promotion can now be repeated to the other customers with, presumably, equal success. So far, however, what we have done is straight direct marketing using a database. What follows is real database marketing.

In database marketing we consider the long-term effect on the customers of every customer contact. This promotion was a success in that it increased profits by more than the cost of the test. That is not the end of the impact on the customers, however. We must look at the results on the test group in the following months. After all, the test resulted in bringing many more than 1,000 women into the store: the 1,000 respondents plus an unknown number of non-respondents. Many of these women might not otherwise have come in to the store that month. How do we know that? Because most of the women in the control group stayed at home. As a result of this promotion, these women who did respond moved to higher RFM cells. They all became recent buyers, they probably became more frequent buyers, and their monetary scores probably advanced. A woman responder whose RFM cell was 423 before the promotion, could have become 534 because of her purchase of the suit. The same type of thing probably happened to almost all of the 1000+ respondents. In addition, the lifetime value of the respondents probably went up as well. We can see this from their subsequent behavior.

The following months, some of those in the test group who moved to higher RFM cells will probably visit the store again. Why? Because of increased Recency, Frequency, and Monetary scores. These responders (and some of the others) have become recent buyers because of the promotion. Recent buyers (we remember from Chapter 5) are the most likely customers to buy again soon. This is normal behavior. This subsequent behavior can also be measured (Figure 11-2).

Sales to All Groups in Second Month after Promotion			
Group Name	Number	Sales Per Customer	Total Sales
Test-Resp	1,000	$30	$30,000
Test Non-Resp	19,000	$21	$399,000
Controls	20,000	$20	$400,000
Total	40,000	$20.73	$829,000
Increased Sales from Last Month's Promotion			$29,000
Cost of promotion (this month)			$0

Figure 11-2. Sales in the second month.

Total sales this month are down. Why were sales to controls only $400,000 during the second month? Who knows? This was a slower month, for reasons unrelated to the test. If the controls had not been followed, however, and only the test group measured, one could have concluded that the test promotion depressed sales in the following month, which, of course, was not true. The testing shows that even in a slow month, the test in the previous month helped overall sales this month.

■ Why did the respondents buy more than the controls in the second month? They received no promotion. The reason: Recency (and possibly Frequency and Monetary). They had moved to higher RFM cells. This is the long-term effect of any promotion, and shows the difference between direct marketing and database marketing.

■ Why did the non-respondents buy more than the controls in the second month? For the same reasons. Some of them had become recent buyers because of the promotion, even though they did not buy the suit. Database marketing works!

Good testing programs will follow the test and control groups for the following 12 months to determine the residual effects of the test. In some situations, the residual effects can be even more important than the initial response to the promotion, and can, in themselves, make them the justification for the marketing effort itself. The next step, of course, will be to determine the effect on the lifetime customer value from the promotion. Lifetime value, rather than the immediate short-term payoff, should be the real goal of marketing database strategy.

Control Group Problems

A major retailer set up a special program designed for the top 10 percent of their customer base—about a half a million customers in all. To measure their success, they needed a small control group. Here is how they went about constructing a control group, as described by the master marketer who created it:

> "To prove that the money spent on the program was paying off, we had a control group. The company had never had one before. It is difficult to measure a program unless you have a control group. When we set up the control group, we made sure that no store executives were in it, no board members, no employees, but we did not have a smart enough database to tell us who was the next door neighbor and best friend of the President's wife. She was in the control group. We got some angry calls from people who were in the control group. We didn't tell them that they were in a control group, of course. We just told them that there had been "a terrible mistake," and shifted them to the test group. These people were tagged as the "out of control group." Others called to complain about being left out who were not qualified for the program. We explained that you have to spend so much to qualify. Most said OK, but for those who were adamant we made exceptions."

Control Group Size

How big should a test or a control file be? Cost considerations say, make them small. Statistical accuracy says, make them big. As a good rule to thumb, each group must be big enough so that you can anticipate a minimum of 500 responses from the promoted group.

$$\text{Control Group Size} = 500 \text{ / Anticipated Response Rate}$$
$$= 500 \text{ / } 0.02 = 25,000$$

If you anticipate a two percent response rate, then your test group must have at least 25,000 people in it. If you have too few respondents, the test may give you invalid results for future predictions. The control group can be smaller than the test group, but still must be large enough for statistical accuracy.

Control Group Substitutes

Sometimes it is not possible to set up a control group. One example is the Travelers Property and Casualty study reported in Chapter 6. In this case, a series of communications were sent to customers of participating independent agents. The control group was designed to answer this question: "Will these communications improve the retention rate of these customers?" The perfect control group would be to select 20 percent of each participating agent's customers and not send them the messages. Independent agents, paying for the programs with their own money, would not willingly participate in such a test. Alison Bond, who ran the original Travelers program, used the retention rate of non-participating agent customers as the control group. Using the customer data from these agents, she was able to show that her program increased the retention rates by about 5 percent. A statistician might object to this control group. Perhaps, the participating agents were more customer friendly than the non-participating agents. If this were to be so, their higher retention rates were due to the agent's effectiveness, not the communications. Control groups are almost always a compromise, but that does not mean that you can do without them.

Control Group Failure

I worked with a large financial services company that was persuaded by their direct agency to issue plastic "Preferred Member" cards to their customers who had used their services three times or more. The cards gave their holders check cashing privileges and other benefits. There seemed to be a definite spike in sales to holders of the cards, so the company was happy with the results. A couple of years later, the marketing staff of the company was changed and the new managers asked the direct agency to show them evidence that the results from the preferred member cards was worth the money spent on them. The agency came to our company for help, since we were maintaining the database. "We know that the cards are valuable, but how can we prove it?" They asked.

"By comparing the performance of the card holders with the performance of your control group that did not get the cards," I explained.

"What is a control group?"

"It is those people who used the service three times or more, but were not issued cards to measure the performance of those who got the cards."

"There is no such group. We gave the cards to everyone who deserved them."

"Then you are out of luck. You can't prove that the cards have done any good."

The agency lost the account.

Let that be a lesson to you. Using test and control groups can mean the difference between keeping your job and losing it. You must have a control group every time you do anything new that involves the expenditure of money.

Using Half Life in Tests

One difficulty in testing is the length of time that it takes to learn the results of your test. If you sent out a promotion, it may take many weeks before all the responses have come in. That is why half-life analysis is so useful in testing.

As soon as you launch any test, you should record every day how many responses have come in that day—both the number of responses, the quantity sold, and the amount of money received. Let us say that you send out a catalog. If you do not have a definite cut-off date, the catalog may result in sales coming in over a period of many months. Let us say that you get 2,000 orders from the catalog over a period of five months. If you have recorded your daily sales, you will find that there is one day on which the 1,000th response was received—exactly half of your total. That is your half-life day. Typically, the half-life day comes within the first 30 days after any promotion. On your next promotion, you will find that the half-life occurs on approximately the same day. Sears Canada, for example, mails out 13 different catalogs every year. They have discovered that their half-life day is Day 20. That is the day on which they have received half of the dollars that they will eventually receive on each catalog. All they have to do is to multiply the amount that they take on by Day 20 by two, and they know the results of the catalog—several months early.

In the chart (Figure 11-3), the days since the first response are plotted across the bottom. The revenue received is on the left. It took 197 days before the full revenue of $133,986.00 from the promotion was received from all purchasers. The details are shown in Figure 11-4.

On the 35th day, in this example, you have taken in $67,000 that is exactly half of what you will receive from the entire catalog, after waiting for some 197 days.

The beauty of half-life analysis is that you can conduct many more tests, and learn the results of your tests much faster. If you are doing tests—and you must, if you are going to be successful at database marketing—you must learn to do half-life analysis. Free software available from The Database Marketing Institute (RFM for Windows) enables you to do half-life analysis (www.dbmarketing.com).

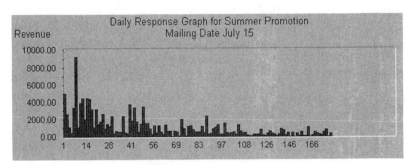

Figure 11-3. Daily response of typical promotion.

	Days	Revenue
Total	197	$133,986.00
Half Life	35	$67,007.17
Third	15	$45,643.97
Quarter	12	$33,557.45

Figure 11-4. Details of the half-day analysis.

Outboard Motor Sales Test

In Chapter 19, we describe a nationwide launch of a new outboard motor. In this launch, of the 250,000 selected for the first mailing, 20,000 were set aside as a control group. This group received no mailing, but was tracked in their purchases. It was this group that permitted the marketers to learn the effectiveness of their entire program.

Once they began their rollout, the marketers, David Christensen and Stanton Lewin, did 32 mailings a year, setting aside 32 control groups to validate their results. They used it not only to sell the new motors but also parts and accessories. The result: they learned that parts sold 24 percent more to the test groups than to the controls.

They mailed two million pieces a year for the next three years, using the controls to validate their results. Some boat dealers experienced an 8 percent response to the mailings. The average response rate was 2.83 percent.

Failure in Testing to Existing Bank Customers

Several years ago, I took out a home equity loan with the Chevy Chase Bank in Maryland. The program was widely advertised; the rates were low. I used the loan to finance the building of a barn, a swimming pool, and an addition to my house.

Some time after I took out the loan, Chevy Chase sent me a pre-approved invitation for a Master Card at low interest rates. I have received dozens of others over the years, which I routinely toss in the trash. I responded to Chevy Chase because I had formed a favorable opinion of the bank from the home equity experience. I canceled my American Express Card. American Express, by the way, did an excellent job of trying to keep me. They just could not accept the idea that anyone would voluntarily drop the card. I got three different telephone calls and more than four letters on the subject before they finally gave up.

A couple of years later, I noticed that my broker was handling Chevy Chase Bonds. They were selling at about 40 percent of par, due to the national savings and loan problem. I asked the broker to buy some for me, because I had such good feelings about the bank. In a couple of years the bonds came up to 104 percent of par value, besides paying a 13 percent rate of interest. I became a loyal Chevy Chase customer.

The point of this personal story is to illustrate the way in which customer lifetime value builds up based on the way that the customer is treated by the institution in more than the specific situation under review. Chevy Chase, if they calculated lifetime value at all, could see me as a cardholder, home equity customer, and bondholder, each one of which contributes to overall bank profits.

In fact, Chevy Chase was not doing much of a job in profiling their customer base. A very persistent Chevy Chase telemarketer called me at dinnertime one night telling me that "as a long time card holder with an excellent record" I was being awarded two months free life insurance, with no preconditions. After the two months, the policy would be charged to my credit card at the rate of $14.40 per month unless can-celed by me. I asked how much the policy paid, and was told $2,000—a ridiculously small amount of life insurance. The worst part of the call was that Chevy Chase knew that I had $300,000 worth of insurance for which I was paying about $180 per month. How did they know? Because I had to tell them in my credit application for the home equity loan. I left the phone angry with Chevy Chase for bothering me with a totally irrelevant offer. They saw me as a name on a list, not as the valuable customer that I thought I was. After a few months, I left Chevy Chase and have never gone back.

Most companies, like Chevy Chase, have data about their customers buried in their files somewhere. Digging that data out and putting it into their database to use in customer profiling and testing would be an inex-pensive and profitable strategy before they ruin their customer base with worthless outbound telemarketing calls.

Summary

To know if a marketing program is successful, you must test it properly. The steps are:

- Determine the objectives of the marketing program, and be sure that it will result in a positive return on investment.

- Test one thing at a time. Create a test group big enough that should result in a minimum of 500 responders. You will need a control group of roughly the same minimum size.

- Develop a method to measure sales. This may be easy, or may be the most difficult part of the whole effort.

- Carry out your marketing program to the test groups. Treat the control groups normally, except do not promote them.

- Measure the incremental sales by comparing sales in the test groups with those in the control groups.

- Calculate the direct costs of your program.

- Figure the short-term net profitability of your program, and the return on your investment.

- Figure the long-term net profitability of your program based on change in lifetime value of your customers.

Executive Quiz 11

Answers to quiz questions (Figure 11-5) can be found in Appendix B.

Put the appropriate letter before each definition	
Term	**Definition**
a	Early Promotion of Teaser Rates	35,714
b	Select a sample file just like main file	Attendance increase of 3%
c	What determines test group size	Capital One
d	Non Responders	Could lose your job
e	Sears Canada Catalog Half Life	Day 20
f	Dynamic emails before a race	Eight percent
g	Holy Grail of Direct Marketing	Five percent
h	How Travelers faked a control group	Home Equity Loan application
i	How high did boat dealer response rates go?	May buy more anyway
j	How did Chevy Chase know insurance levels	Minimum of 500 responders
k	Danger in not testing	Single Variable Test
l	Assumed Response Rate 1.4%. Test size?	Use an Nth
m	Travelers increased retention rate was:	Used non participating agents

Figure 11-5. Quiz 11.

12

Internet Marketing

*Most companies understand Web business very poorly.
Everybody involved in Web design or Web strategy
should do as much of their personal business on the
Web as possible to get direct experience with the "Web
lifestyle." Following this philosophy, I recently bought a
present for my nephew from the Web site of a famous
toy store. After completing the order, I received a confirmation email that listed the name of the toy and its
price. So far, so good. The email then went on to say,
"if we have the toy in stock, you will receive it in about
one week; if it is not in stock, you will receive it in
three to four weeks." Have these guys never heard of
integrating order processing with inventory management? Don't send an IF-THEN-ELSE statement to
your customers: that's what computers are good for.*

*In the physical world, sales clerks may have to tell
customers that they don't know when an order will ship.
But the Web should be better than reality: check inventory and shipping schedules in the background and
hold the email confirmation until you know the ship
date. If you can't find out within a few hours, then
send a preliminary confirmation followed by more
precise information the minute you know. Again we
can go beyond the real world: sending an extra message
when a condition is triggered is virtually free on the
Internet. Also, since the message doesn't go by snail
mail, it will reach the customer in time to do some good.*

JAKOB NIELSEN
(www.useit.com)

233

"To use the Internet to generate leads for agents, your data strategies must focus on qualifying the leads generated so that agents can handle the increased volumes. If you can improve conversion rates with demographics, It's worth any amount of money,"

JANET PARKS
President of Frontier Marketing in Woburn, MA

Every company today must participate in electronic marketing. It is no longer a novelty. It is not something to leave to the IT department or some technical staff. Electronic marketing today is mainstream marketing.

That does not mean that electronic sales were anything to write home about. Online retail sales (not counting travel) were predicted when this book was written to rise to 2.9% of all retail sales within two years. Include travel and the total is 4.4%. Online sales were growing at about the rate of 26% per year for several years, but they started from nothing. Web sales differed significantly by industry. Some catalogers have reached numbers like 35% of sales through the web. Amazon showed what could be done in selling books, music, and videos. But, on the whole the aggregate web sales numbers were small.

So why is the Web important as a marketing channel?

Affluent People. Studies continually show that Web shopping people have higher incomes than non-Web shopping people. In addition, multi-channel people spend more than single-channel people. An online study conducted by washingtonpost.com and Nielsen//NetRatings found that affluent adults access the Web nearly every day, and use it far more than any other media during the day. The study defined affluent adults as Web users with a household income of $100,000 or more. They found that the fastest growing online shopping group makes between $100,000 and $149,000.

Purchasing Research. Many Web users do their purchasing research on the Web before they go out and buy. Helena and I bought a new Chrysler Town and Country, a wonderful car. I wanted a Honda Odyssey, but Helena wanted an American seven-passenger car. I searched the Web for one and found the Town and Country. Then we went to a dealer to take a test drive and buy. This same sequence is true of refrigerators, washing machines, cameras, new homes, and almost all major purchases. These are not Web sales. Therefore, none of this activity shows up in the Web statistics listed above. But, clearly, the research is promoting sales. The Washington Post study showed that virtually all affluent adult shoppers use the Web to research their purchases. For automobile, computer, and travel purchases, use of the Web was extraordinarily high (over 90 percent of those surveyed).

Reviews. Helena and I never go to the movies today without first consulting the Fort Lauderdale Movie Times, which tells us what is available and where, and has a link to the Chicago Sun Times Web site—the best movie reviews available. We have found a dozen new restaurants in Fort Lauderdale using the Fort Lauderdale DiningGuide which has user menus, prices, maps, and user reviews. It is probably impossible to keep track of the impact of these Web reviews on total sales, but their overall influence is certainly growing. Once people start making a habit of looking up local retailers before they venture forth, the reviews will become a part of their lives and therefore, must be part of retailers' marketing programs.

An Information Medium

For most companies the Web is not really a sales medium, like a catalog or a retail store. It is an information and research medium. What used to take hours tramping through malls or department stores (finding out what is available) now takes a few minutes. Armed with information from the Web and a map, you telephone or go somewhere to buy the product or service.

Helena has taken up knitting. She knits ponchos, capelets, shawls, and throws. A posh store on Las Olas Boulevard here in Fort Lauderdale buys her products. She buys her exotic yarns through the Internet. Every couple of weeks she places orders for colorful yarns like Velvet Touch, Allure, Micro Fiber, Fun Fur, Simply Soft, Chenille, Cotton Twist, or TLC. She used to spend hours driving to and tramping through yarn stores in Miami. No longer. The Web does it all.

"The bottom line is that retailers and manufacturers need to advertise on the Web if they want to influence Americans with high purchasing power," says Christopher M. Schroeder, CEO and publisher of Washingtonpost.Newsweek Interactive. "The messages that affluent Americans see on the Web are having a very real impact on their purchasing decisions… messages being delivered on the Web are heavily influencing both online and offline sales."

I am not sure that I agree with Chris Schroeder's conclusion. From what I can see, most people who use the Web a lot, like Helena and me, rarely look at the ads. We are looking for something that we already have in mind. We use Google to find Web sites that have what we want. Do not put all your money on Web advertisements just yet.

How Does This Apply to Database Marketing?

Search Box. If you want an excellent customer friendly Web site, the site has to be filled with useful information. To start with, the site has to have a search box right at the top of the home page. Spend a lot of effort to make the search box responsive to what people want. To do this, your software has to keep track of what customers are entering in this box. All Web users have had the experience of looking for something and not finding a search box, or finding one that does not have what you are looking for. The Web site should build a file that stores what people put in the search box.

Search Engine. www.google.com, and its competitors have become essential to any successful Web site. There is no point in having a Web site if few people can find it. Google does a wonderful job. You do not have to pay Google to get noticed, although thousands are spending money to do this. For example: I have had a Web site for the past ten years: www.dbmarketing.com. It is the Web site of the Database Marketing Institute which Helena and I founded in 1993. It has more than 150 published articles on database marketing, in addition to RFM for Windows software, slides from speeches, etc. We do not pay anyone for placement in Google or anywhere else. Yet, when you enter "Database Marketing" in Google, here is what you get:

> Education and Software for Relationship Database Marketing
> …Database Marketing. Click here to read them. DMI Features…Speech: Arthur Hughes talks about what works (and what does not work) in Database Marketing. www.dbmarketing.com/ - 18K Cached - Similar pages.

This was the first or second entry on the Google list when this book was written and had been for several years. What got this site top billing? I am not sure. I think it is because there are so many free published articles.

You can also get top billing for your site. Put a lot of information there: case studies, white papers, product descriptions, magazine articles, and statistics. Every company has interesting information that customers want to know about. Give it to them. Make it free, if possible, and add to it often—at least once a week. Do not delete anything unless you have to. Be sure that your site contains a lot of copy that is relevant to your business. Content is more important than meta tags. Some Internet advisors will tell you to put a chain of meta tags (key words) scattered throughout your site. That may work, but Google, I think, is too smart for that. Your customers are also smart. If you attract them with meta tags, but have lousy content, you will not sell very much.

I use Google about ten times a day, every day. I use it to look up movies, books, restaurants, car repair, a dentist, porch furniture, and company information of all kinds. Google can find anything. How do they do it? Crawler-based search engines, such as Google, create their listings automatically.

How Google Does It

There are three parts to an Internet search engine. First is the spider. The spider visits a Web page, reads it, and then follows links to other pages within the site. Everything the spider finds goes into the second part of the search engine, the index. The index contains a copy of every Web page that the spider finds. The search engine software is the third part of a search engine. The engine sifts through the millions of pages recorded in the index to find matches to a search and rank them in the order of what it believes is most relevant.

Offer What the Customers Want

In designing your site, think like a customer. Do not think what you want to sell. Think what you as a customer would be looking for on your site. To do that, you may have to offer things that you do not normally sell. A couple of years ago, when the toner ran low on my Hewlett Packard LaserJet 4, I went to the HP site to order more. Amazingly, the site did not sell toner, nor provide any advice or help on where to buy it. I had to figure out on my own that I had to go to Office Depot to buy the toner. It turned me off. Today, since the reorganization, HP now sells toner and parts for any HP product right on the site. They have learned a lot, and their sales show it.

Let Customers Register without Hassle

At first it was only the New York Times. Now scores of Web sites require visitors to register before they can read articles or get information. What was a good idea has become a major annoyance. Each of these sites requires that you have an ID and password that meet their special requirements (case sensitive, containing both letters and numbers, etc. Why?). Since the specifics differ, you cannot have one universal password that works everywhere. When this book was written you could not read an article in the Los Angeles Times, the Washington Post, the Miami Herald or the New York Times without first registering. No problem, you say. Registration is free. But the money is not the problem. If you have already registered, they want your password before you can come back. If you have forgotten the password, they make you wait a few hours for an e-mail with the required information. If you try to register again (because you do not want to wait for the e-mail) the site tells you that you have already registered, and you cannot do this again. It is a damned nuisance. These sites are not user friendly. Rule: visit your Web site often and do what you want the customers to do. Make sure that your site conveys the public image that you are looking for. Make it easy for your visitors.

Provide Live Help

What was once a novelty is now an essential. If you are selling something, you should have a "Live Help" box on your Web site. AOL now has such a system, and it works wonderfully. I had a problem. For some reason I was unable to send e-mails with attachments. I was so frustrated that I had decided to cancel my AOL service. Finally, I found two buttons on the site: Live Billing Help and Live Technical Help – 24 hours a day, 7 days a week. Clicking on the technical help I was connected by a text chat with a technician (who was probably handling several other customers simultaneously) who typed a welcome to me. I typed in my problem, and he solved it within a minute.

There are many services today, such as Live Person (www.liveperson.com) who can help you to install a link backed up by live agents who will respond to typed queries from your customers. As another option, you can have your agents talk to the customers by phone. Surveys have shown that a high percentage of electronic shopping carts are abandoned at checkout. Putting a live chat box at that point can save some of these sales. Intuit installed this system. The LivePerson Service equipped four Intuit support engineers each with the power to assist simultaneously more than one customer, significantly raising each engineer's productivity level. The live chat service also empowered the Intuit sales advisors managing online queries to cross-sell and up-sell Intuit's products and services.

Live help can be important in establishing a link between you and your prospects or customers. Think about any large company: Microsoft, IBM, HP, or Chrysler. Suppose that you need to contact one of these companies about a problem with one of their products. What happens when you go on their Web sites looking for help? (Answer, IBM had live help, the others, at this writing, did not.)

Shopping Cart. Web shopping carts are everywhere today. Many sites have one. They take credit cards. Even if you are not selling something direct, you can use a shopping cart to provide samples, white papers, reports, or materials to your interested site visitors. You have the cart not just to make the sales but also to establish that you have a modern Web site. The software for a shopping cart is inexpensive. Needed beyond the shopping cart are a series of transaction messages. When a customer has made a purchase online, a screen says, "Thank you for your order. Print this page out..." While they are reading this, they hear "You've got mail" and an e-mail arrives saying that the order has been placed and when it will be shipped. When it is shipped, an e-mail goes out saying just that. After it has arrived, an e-mail should go out saying "Did it arrive OK? What was your reaction to the shopping experience?"

These are the kind of things that the old corner grocer used to say, and that cannot be said with direct mail (too slow) or phone (too expensive). With e-mail they are basically free. Once you have written the software to do them, the messages go out automatically from then on without anyone having to lift a finger.

The software should also store in the customer record not only the transaction but also all the outgoing and incoming messages. If you are wondering if all these messages are useful and helping sales, you can do an inexpensive experiment. Code some of your customers as a control group, and do not send them any of these messages. Just fulfill the orders. After a few months, see if there is a difference in the behavior of those who got the messages and those who did not.

The Goals of Transaction Messages

Jakob Nielson (www.useit.com) is one of the world's experts in Web marketing. Nielsen conducted a study of customer reactions to e-mail. It showed that processing e-mail is a stressful burden on people. Users were usually so busy that they consider any fluff in messages a waste of time. People just want to be done with most e-mail, and quickly move past anything that is not absolutely essential. E-mail writers must be brief.

Nielsen points out that transactional e-mail has three goals:

1. *Avoid being mistaken for spam.* E-mail must survive users' ruthless pruning of inbox messages.

2. *Be a customer service representative.* E-mail should enhance a company's reputation for customer service and increase users' confidence in their dealings with the company.

3. *Prevent customers from calling in.* Telephone call centers are expensive. Rather than simply eliminating contact information (which undermines goal number two), ensure that your e-mail answers all common questions in easily understandable terms.

All three goals are important, but if an e-mail message fails the first goal, it automatically fails the other two as well because it will not even be read.

Making Sure Your Messages Are Read

To avoid having messages summarily deleted from the inbox, Nielsen points out, e-mail designers are restricted to working with two design elements: the "from" field and the subject line. The "from" field should clearly show two things: a recognizable brand name and a wording that shows that the message is not just an advertisement. Tickets@amtrack.com and ship-confirm@amazon work. Most e-mail listings truncate the "from" field to no more than 20 characters. Make those characters count to convince users that you are legitimate.

For subject lines to work they have to be clearly related to a customer-initiated transaction. Subject lines that seem too much like spam (e.g., "Important information") are often deleted. A good subject line is gold. Spend a lot of effort to get it right.

The Content of a Customer E-Mail

Nielsen recommends that you start with the information that matters most to users. Almost everyone looks for tracking numbers, even if they never track packages. The tracking number serves as comforting evidence that there is an actual package and that it is on its way. Tell them exactly what was ordered.

E-mail that begins with marketing messages or other seemingly irrelevant information runs a major risk of being deleted, because people might never scroll down to see the information they need.

Good e-mail should respect users' time and quickly tell them what they need to know. Good e-mail can do wonders for your customer service reputation. Users are often busy and stressed when reading e-mail. Wasting their time makes them feel like you do not care. Worse, you become part of the problem, not the solution.

E-Mail Newsletters

E-mail newsletters build relationships with users, and also permit users to forward relevant newsletters to friends and colleagues. Users are highly critical of newsletters that waste their time, and will delete newsletters that are not useful to them. The Nielsen study showed that users' most frequent complaint about newsletters was that they arrive too often.

Personalization

Just having a Web site or an electronic newsletter is not good enough today. Both need to be personalized. That means having a customer-marketing database, and using that database plus cookies to modify the content of your site and your newsletters. Hewlett Packard has begun to do this. HP uses their database to personalize their monthly e-newsletters, Web portals, and e-mails.

The 4.5 million e-newsletters they send out every month are personalized based on the recipient's profile, choosing from hundreds of possible white papers, tech support alerts, and industry analyst reports, covering the 87 different HP product lines. On their Web sites, customers complete a profile at www.hp.com where they get a login and password. For e-mails, HP has four marketing teams for: consumer, small business, public sector, and enterprise. Each month they match the news and offers available with customer profiles.

To be sure that the information is up to date, customers are prompted to update their profiles in each newsletter, Web portal visit, or e-mail. HP believes that they get three to ten times better response rates with personalized content than with a general campaign. I updated my HP profile on their site and asked for info about my HP printer. When I went back to the HP Web site, it was clear that they were using cookies. The entry page was all about printers! This was behind the scenes personalization, however. The HP site did not say "Welcome back Arthur," as Amazon and Office Depot do.

Replacing Your Call Center

Billions of dollars are spent every year on call centers both here and in offshore locations. People like to talk to live operators. Many of these calls, however, can be handled just as well, or better, by a good Web site. That is why catalogers get a good response by putting their Web site on the bottom of each page along with their toll-free number. Every call to the Web site saves them $2 or more.

I worked with a company that had a 500-person call center used by members who called to reserve spaces at vacation resorts. They had a Web site that could be used for the reservations, but only a small percentage used this route. The live calls were costing them $6.50 each. When we studied the situation it was clear that some members would prefer to make their reservations over the Web because they never got put on hold and could make the calls at any hour of the day or night. Members who tried to do this, however, found that the Web site was not as informative as a live operator. Members would ask, "What is it like in Playa del Carmen?" The live operator (who had never been there) would read from literature on her screen to respond to the question. She had up to date information on what was available on a particular week desired by the members. That information was not on the Web site. It was clear to us that a revision of the Web site could make it as helpful, or more helpful, than a live operator. After all, the Web site could have a modern search engine that would show each site availability, plus a dozen pictures of each resort which the operator was trying to describe in words.

Modifying the Web site to make it more member-friendly involved spending as much as $1,000,000. With these changes, a modified Web site could shift many calls to the Web and save the company as much as $17 million per year.

So, why did the company not make the change? For a reason that is common to many companies. The Web site was run by the Information Technology department which did not have the needed $1,000,000. The call center was run by the Customer Support department with an annual budget of $48 million per year. They would gladly have spent the money to fix the Web site, but they were not allowed to touch it. It was off limits, since it belonged to IT.

Catalog Sales

Miles Kimball has been sending out catalogs since 1935. They asked a service bureau to construct a new customer-marketing database for them that included phone, mail, and Web orders. They used the database to create an e-mail test with their catalog mailings. Vicki Updike, VP of Marketing selected 40,000 customers who had used their Web site to order items from their paper catalog. She divided them into two exactly identical groups: 20,000 got e-mails in conjunction with three different catalogs over a two-month period. The other 20,000 got only the three catalogs. Those who got the e-mails bought 18 percent more than those who got only the catalogs. This is exciting stuff. It is going to change database marketing forever.

Annual Reminders

Some retailers are very good at this. As we were packing to go to Chile for Christmas, Helena received a colorful e-mail from Honeybaked that said: "Dear Helena Hughes: To make your gift giving easier we have attached a recap of your last year's Christmas and Thanksgiving orders. To reorder simply click the *Shop Now* button, enter your gift list pass code, make any changes to your gift list and with a few clicks you are done." Reviewing the list they provided, Helena saw someone she had forgotten to send a gift to. She clicked and sent an 8 lb ham, and while she was at it, sent hams to two other friends who had just e-mailed her Christmas greetings. Is this great Internet marketing, or what?

Last Minute E-Mails

In the past few years, airlines have been sending weekly personalized last minute e-mails designed to sell empty seats. These have been working.

Such messages were impossible before the advent of e-mail. Why? Because direct mail is too slow. These e-mails can be sent out on Thursday to sell seats on Saturday flights. Direct mail could not possibly work. But even more important, these e-mails to air miles members help to maintain the relationship, retention, and loyalty of members, even if they do not grab at the last minute specials.

Unfortunately, the weekly e-mails that I got from American Airlines usually featured last minute deals involving flights from Dallas to Los Angeles or Chicago to San Francisco and other similar opportunities. For me, the problem was that I was in Fort Lauderdale, not in any of the featured cities. Reading most of these messages was really a waste of my time. I deleted them without reading. I really would like AA to write to me about low-cost flights from Fort Lauderdale.

Low-Cost Items

Everyone in the direct mail business knows that you cannot successfully promote low-cost items using direct mail. If the product costs less than $30, and your response rate is 2 percent, you will go broke. E-mails change the equation. Universal Music (UMG) had great success using e-mails to promote their CDs which sell at retail for less than $20. On the case of each CD sold, UMG puts the URL of a Web site for the artist (such as www.sherylcrow.com). Arriving there, fans get a chance to listen to some of Sheryl's music, and to register as a fan. Those registered go into a database from which they will receive e-mails about Sheryl's concert tours and new CD releases. In one promotion, UMG used e-mail to reach 1.4 million fans achieving an 11.2 percent response rate. Fans went to the Web site, registered, and downloaded. 50 percent of these reported that they bought a CD at retail as a result.

Linking Your Web Site to Your Database

For the first 20 years since its invention, database marketing was hampered by one key difficulty: most databases could be updated only once a month. There were good reasons for this: many databases include several million customer records. Each customer might have as many as a hundred transaction records (including sales, responses, survey results, appended data, computed fields, and promotion history).

Do the math: we are talking 100 million or more individual records to update. Even with modern servers, this takes time. Some databases are so big that it takes several days of processing to complete the update.

The result of monthly updates is that the data in the database is rarely fresh. Instead of daily or weekly communications, marketers have to use the main database for monthly or less frequent personalized mass marketing campaigns aimed at segments. While people talked about one-to-one marketing, they really meant periodic segment marketing with the data in the message personalized for each customer. What that means in practice is that you divide your customer base into five to ten segments. You devise a marketing message for each segment (business travelers, retired couples, college students, lapsed customers, etc.) and craft a message that has personal references, "Since you have been a member since 1992, Mr. Hughes, and have rented automobiles from us on 84 occasions, we would like to upgrade you to..."

This is great marketing, and it produces much better results than mass marketing or mass mailings of identical messages customized for each segment. But, let us face it: it is not one-to-one marketing. It is not what the old corner grocer used to do. If you bought a large salmon yesterday, when you come in today, he will ask, "How did your folks like the salmon?" You cannot do that with a database updated monthly. If you wrote such a letter or sent an e-mail based on a monthly updated database, by the time it arrives, most customers would have completely forgotten the salmon meal, and not have the slightest idea what you were talking about.

We can use the Internet for these communications, but we need to support the Internet with a constantly updated database, or it will not be convincing to the customers.

Recently, some database marketing service bureaus, such as Knowledge Base Marketing, have found a way to update a marketing database several times a day. Once this technique comes into general use it will change the way database marketing is done. It permits automated communications. Here is how they do it (Figure 12-1).

Incoming records from the Web site, telesales, or direct mail are processed by business rules that determine whether the records coming from a client are recognizable as names and addresses, or transactions (sales, survey results, preferences, responses, etc.). The name and address records are processed using traditional list processing routines (Figure 12-2):

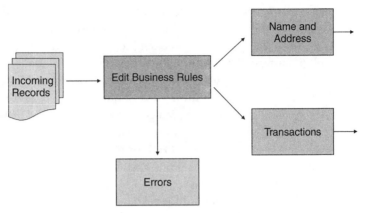

Figure 12-1. Processing incoming records.

Meanwhile, the transaction records are processed using business rules: For example:

- Is this a transaction? Do we have the product code, quantity, price, date, customer number, etc?
- Is this a survey? Does it fit one of the survey templates already established?
- Is this a customer preference response? Does it fit one of the templates?
- Does the customer number match a lookup table in the database?

While this has been going on, the customer database has been spinning around on disk in a server, being accessed and used by marketers throughout the company. An exact copy of the database is on another server being updated (Figure 12-3).

When the update is completed, the two databases are switched (several times a day) in a routine that does not interrupt the analysis and campaigns being conducted by the marketers.

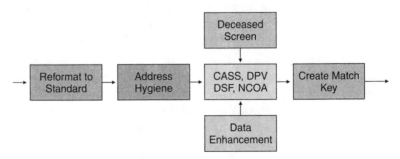

Figure 12-2. Reformatting incoming records.

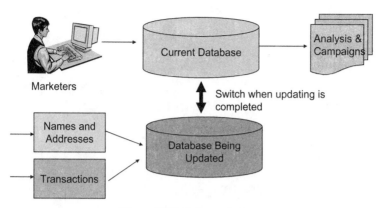

Figure 12-3. Daily updating.

Why This Is a Breakthrough

If you consider a traditional monthly database update, you may have 100 million records (addresses and transactions) in the database. You may have five million input records needed for the monthly update. The update process may take a day or more. If, however, you are updating this same database five times a day (150 times per month), each update will involve only about 35,000 records. This update is so small that it can be done in five or ten minutes. The switching between the two databases will take only a few seconds. With incremental updates, marketers will be working with new data that is on the average about 3 hours old (Figure 12-4).

Some of the data will be only 15 minutes old. We are now getting closer and closer to the processes that went on in the Corner Grocer's head. He dealt with only a couple of 100 customers. We are managing the data for millions of customers. We can now, if we wanted to, ask our customers how the family liked the salmon dinner yesterday. We can develop automated communications.

The effect of incremental updates on automated communications is dramatic. Let us review this diagram in detail.

Activities

All day long the results of activities are streaming in to the database. These activities include transactions and sales, survey results, changes of address, etc. All these activities can be received and reformatted to fit the business rules of the database. Five times a day, the activities can be

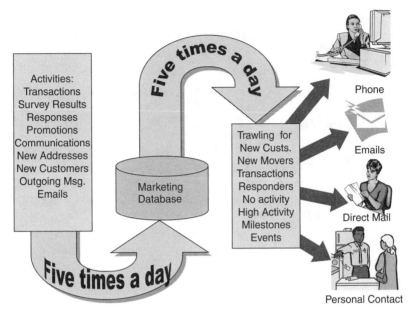

Figure 12-4. Five times a day.

used to update the database. The information can be used to create automated communications.

Trawling

Now that you have all the information about customers and their transactions stored in the customer-marketing database updated several times a day, a set of special programs which carry out a function called "trawling" can begin. Trawling implements a large number of marketing business rules. Trawling software looks at every record in the database which has been changed since the last update and applies business rules to the data it finds. For example, trawling will determine if the customer:

■ Is about to have a birthday or anniversary.

■ Had an unusually large transaction.

■ Reached a milestone with the company in terms of total sales, years with the company, etc.

Each hit during trawling has a programmed marketing response. Depending on the situation and the customer's preferences, the customer may be sent an e-mail or a direct mail message, she may be called by customer service, a sales person may visit her, or the Web site may have a special message for her if and when she logs on. These are automated communications. Once set up and programmed, they will take place automatically.

The National Australia Bank (NAB) served more than 4.5 million customers. The bank's database was maintained on an NCR Teradata computer using Teradata CRM analytical software. Their National Leads system prioritized events and alerted the appropriate bankers each morning so that they could take appropriate action. The goal was to insure that customers were contacted with meaningful opportunities at the right times through the right channels. The system worked this way:

- The Teradata warehouse was updated with an average of 2.2 million transactions per day.

- Every night, queries "trawled" the warehouse to search for any unusual changes in customer behavior.

- Once a month, each customer was scored using a model, which predicted the customer's propensity to purchase various products, and propensity to respond to product offers. The best leads were selected and sent to the bankers.

- Every night 250 communication vectors were run combining the events detected plus the propensity predictions. The software recommended the action to be taken via ATM, e-mail, mail, or leads to call centers, branches or package business bankers who followed up with a phone call or personal mail.

- The system captured all feedback and responses, measuring them against the opportunities developed. Each offer was placed in a location in a three-dimensional "cube" with the three axes being the Segment, the Channel, and the Offer. The system moved customers from one location in the cube to another based on their response to offers.

Trawling Results

- During the first year, more than 1 million leads and $4 billion in growth opportunities were sent to NAB bankers for action.

- During the next six months, 570,000 new leads were sent which resulted in the closing of $4.4 billion worth of new loans.

- During the second year of the system, premium sales of banking products increased by 25 percent over the previous year while sales of wealth management products increased by 40 percent.

- The close rate for leads increased by five times over the close rate before the new system began.

- The bank achieved a $391 million return on investment on one campaign.

In addition to direct mail, e-mails and live phone calls, automated retention building messages can be delivered by automated telephone messages to cell phones and land lines. United Airlines, for example, uses automated CenterPost technology to call customers with Mileage Plus information and flight changes. These are recorded telephone messages personalized for those receiving the call. United uses Microsoft.NET Alerts to enable their customers to stay informed of unexpected flight changes whenever they are online or wherever their mobile device is active. Customers select the notifications they want to receive and where they want to receive them. Intelligent routing rules allow customers to request that alerts be sent as instant messaging (IM) notifications on their computer and on their cell phone or wireless PDA when they are away from their desktop.

How to Respond to Communications

Once you are set up to send automated communications, you also have to be prepared to respond to them. A large company may get thousands of e-mails. Some of them are important. Your response to them reflects on your company's image. What can you do? There are two things that you can, and should do to prepare for customer response:

- Use a micro site
- Install an e-mail response system

MicroSite. Set up your outgoing message with a micro site so that the responses are in a format that is easy for you to handle (Figure 12-5).

Here is an example of an e-mail with a micro-site. When the customer receives the e-mail, it opens up into this page which contains links to many other pages. The customer can download information, read text, buy products (if that is the intent) and contact you for further discussion.

A micro-site like this is relatively easy to set up. This one was done by an in-house staff member in about 4 hours of work. One important feature of a micro-site like this is that there are automatic reports which

UCEA Conference Follow Up - Arthur Hughes

At the UCEA Conference in San Francisco that we attended together last week, a number of people asked me about the various email and Internet techniques that I recommended in my two talks. Since there was such interest, I thought that I would pass on some ideas that you might use in implementing some of these techniques.

Where to find the speeches/slide. If you are interested in the presentation slide shows, click on the links below:

UCEA Mini-Workshop on Database Marketing (2.1 MB)

Building Bridges: Reach Your Customers and Keep Them Coming Back (1.9 MB)

If you are interested in buying any of my books or downloading the free RFM software that I mentioned in the talk, please click here. You can also download Lifetime Value Tables.

Figure 12-5. MicroSite message.

you get as customers respond. Here is an example of the reports on this micro-site after three days (Figure 12-6):

E-mail Response. If you receive e-mails that are not in any particular format, you can get help from companies like www.emailtopia.com. This company provides automated e-mail response software that deals with unexpected e-mail replies. Here is how their system works. An incoming e-mail goes to "Response Manager" software that uses key words to separate the mail into categories. The Response manager sends an automatic reply saying that the message was received and will be answered soon. Meanwhile, the sorted mail is sent to a group of customer service representatives who respond to the mail using scores of standard replies, plus their own ingenuity.

Speech Email Follow Up Results on 3rd Day			
Delivered	Viewed	Clicked	Do Not Mail
168	131	75	0
Download	% Viewed	% Clicked	% Download
68	78%	45%	40%

Figure 12-6. Results after three days.

Summary

Electronic marketing is not a novelty. It is mainstream marketing. Your company must become proficient at it. Keep in mind, however, that:

- Actual Web sales will be a small percentage of your total sales.
- Your Web site will be a starting point for customer research leading to sales through other channels: phone or retail visit.
- You will need:
  - ☐ A comprehensive search box.
  - ☐ Lots of interesting content for the visitors and for Google.
  - ☐ A live agent.
  - ☐ Personalization using cookies.
- The Web site must be managed by Marketing, not by IT, since it is a marketing vehicle.
- One goal should be to use the Web site to replace live phone operators if possible.

Executive Quiz 12

Put the appropriate letter before each definition	
Term	**Definition**
a Micro Site	Every night look for database changes
b Viral Marketing	Find things inside a web site
c Google	Find things rapidly on the web
d Search Box	Five times a day
e Search Engine	Get customers to refer others
f Spider	Get help while on a website
g Shopping Cart	Nuisance when visiting a newspaper website
h Registration	Quicker to set up and change than a company website
i LivePerson	Spend more than other customers
j SPAM	Takes orders and credit cards
k Personalization	Unexpected and unwelcome
l Multi Channel Customers	Used by search engines to visit web sites
m Incremental Updates	Welcome back, Arthur
n URL	What to offer customers
o Trawling	www.yoursite.com
p Next Best Product	Yahoo and Google

Figure 12-7. Quiz 12.

Profiting by Experience

13

Retailing and Packaged Goods

For years, retailers have argued that having regularly advertised, deeply discounted prices brings price-oriented customers into their stores but that, over time, these customers convert to regular, profitable customers. Research done by the Retail Strategy Center Inc. based in Greenville, South Carolina, shows that this widely held belief is a myth. A handful of these customers do convert into "good" regular customers, but the majority actually defect within twelve months of their first shopping visit. I have yet to find a retailer anywhere in the world whose investment in this type of shopper has yielded an attractive return on investment.

BRIAN WOOLF
Customer-Specific Marketing

Retailing went through a series of shocks. Forced out of central cities by the flight to the suburbs, many central hub stores were closed.

Stationed as "anchors" in large suburban malls, they saw many of their customers spending their time in the small specialty shops rather than in their departments. These shops, collectively, offered more personal services and non-homogeneous products than the department stores could afford.

With "on sale" as a draw, they found themselves trumped in this area by Wal-Marts and factory outlets that offered increasingly attractive merchandise at rock bottom prices.

The growth of the specialty catalog industry hit them especially hard. Affluent, fashion conscious, busy, working women spent their few moments at home scanning high fashion catalogs and ordering high-priced merchandise, rather than visiting department stores.

To top it off, the Internet arrived, poised to steal away another group of affluent shoppers.

How to Compete?

Retailers at last fell back on the one group that was right under their nose all along, but which they were neglecting: their customers. Instead of concentrating on the products, and how to move them, they began to look at their customers and figuring out how to motivate them. They learned how to build loyalty and repeat sales by appealing to the hearts and minds of their customers.

Their solutions began to focus on a number of neglected areas:

- Creating interactive Web sites, which recognized customers.

- Increasing the number of people who held and used the store credit card, and getting customers who use Visa, and Master Card to register their cards with the store so that they could build a customer database. People who paid by check or cash were often asked for their phone number which, in many cases, permitted learning the name and address by reverse appending.

- Learning more about their customers through surveys and appended data, so that they could market better to them.

- Teaming up with external specialists to make targeted solo mailing offers to their customer base drawing on their name and reputation to get the envelope opened, and the sale made.

- Following up customer purchases with special personal services: thank you letters, follow-up surveys and telephone calls; becoming specialists in customer service.

- Keeping track of birthdays, anniversaries, and other key personal events in their customer's lives and communicating one-on-one when they occur, so that they can become a family friend, not just another store.

- Understanding the geo-demographics of their store trading areas so that they could do a better job of locating branches, and bringing customers into their stores.

- Profiling their customers into profit groups and marketing differently to each group.

- Experimenting with cataloging themselves as a way of reaching the busy workingwoman, and luring her into the stores.

Building the Cardholder Base

Where does your business come from? Who is buying your products? Strangely enough, many retailers did not really know. The only thing that they could tell for sure was the percentage of their sales that came from store cardholders, as opposed to those who paid by other means.

Once a person used their store credit or frequent shopper card, it was possible to keep track of them, find out what they bought, learn about their interests, and market to them. The effectiveness of these marketing efforts could be measured. Customer lifetime value could be calculated with precision. But all of this could happen only if customers applied for and used a store credit card or a frequent shopper card (or registered their credit card with the store).

Determining Lifetime Value

Once you have a customer database constructed, you can learn wonderful things about your customers. Here is the way supermarkets segment their customers into five groups (Figure 13-1) based on annual spending, based on the systems suggested in Brian Woolf's excellent book, *Customer Specific Marketing.*

A typical chain store had 15,000 customers. The top quintile brought in almost 75 percent of the sales, while the bottom two quintiles, together, produced a little over 1 percent. The annual retention rate varied from 96 percent in the top group to 36 percent in the bottom group. Let us use this data to compile a lifetime value table for two groups: the Gold

Segment	Customers	Visits/ Week	Average Basket	Annual $ Dollars	Percent Dollars	Retention Rate
Gold	3,000	1.48	$96.02	$22,169,098	74.91%	96.00%
Silver	3,000	0.74	$47.23	$5,452,231	18.42%	90.00%
Bronze	3,000	0.43	$21.90	$1,469,052	4.96%	76.00%
Nickel	3,000	0.21	$11.04	$361,670	1.22%	56.00%
Occasional	3,000	0.14	$6.55	$143,052	0.48%	36.00%
Total	15,000	0.60	$36.55	$29,595,103	100.00%	70.80%

Figure 13-1. Supermarket Shoppers at a single store broken into five segments.

customers at the top, and the worthless occasional shoppers at the bottom (Figure 13-2).

The typical Gold customer had a spending rate in his acquisition year of $86 per visit. In this example, there were 4,525 of them who cost $181,000 to acquire, as a result of TV, Radio, and print advertising. They made about one visit per week. Twenty two percent of them dropped out in the first year. By the third year, there were 3,000 left. Their retention rate moved rapidly up from 78 percent to 96 percent in the three years. Their lifetime value today is $883.

Now let us look at the losers, the occasional shoppers at the bottom (Figure 13-3).

Because of their very low retention rate, there was a constant churn in the membership of this group. Out of a total of 33,480 customers who were acquired, only 3,000 were still around in the third year after acquisition. They visited only an average of five or six times a year, spending very little each time. Of course, they were given royal treatment with

Gold Customers	Acquisition Year	Second Year	Third Year
Customers	4,525	3,530	3,000
Retention Rate	78.00%	85.00%	96.00%
Visits/Week	0.98	1.37	1.48
Average Basket	$86.33	$88.79	$96.02
Total Sales	$19,907,180	$22,328,661	$22,169,098
Cost Percent	81.00%	79.00%	78.00%
Direct Costs	$16,124,816	$17,639,642	$17,291,896
Labor + Benefits 11%	$2,189,790	$2,456,153	$2,438,601
Card program $16, $8	$72,400	$28,240	$24,000
Acquisition Cost $40	$181,000		
Advertising 2%	$398,144	$446,573	$443,382
Total Costs	$18,966,149	$20,570,608	$20,197,879
Gross Profit	$941,031	$1,758,053	$1,971,219
Discount Rate	1	1.14	1.3
NPV Profit	$941,031	$1,542,152	$1,516,322
Cum. NPV Profit	$941,031	$2,483,182	$3,999,505
Lifetime Value	$207.96	$548.77	$883.87

Figure 13-2. LTV of Gold supermarket shoppers.

Occasional Shoppers	Acquisition Year	Second Year	Third Year
Customers	33,480	9,374	3,000
Retention Rate	28.00%	32.00%	36.00%
Visits/Week	0.1	0.13	0.14
Average Basket	$6.55	$7.30	$8.01
Total Sales	$1,140,329	$462,608	$174,927
Cost Percent	81.00%	79.00%	78.00%
Direct Costs	$923,666	$365,460	$136,443
Labor + Benefits 11%	$125,436	$50,887	$19,242
Card program $16, $8	$535,680	$74,995	$23,998
Acquisition Cost $40	$1,339,200		
Advertising 2%	$22,807	$9,252	$3,499
Total Costs	$2,946,789	$500,594	$183,182
Gross Profit	($1,806,460)	($37,987)	($8,255)
Discount Rate	1	1.14	1.3
NPV Profit	($1,806,460)	($33,322)	($6,350)
Cum. NPV Profit	($1,806,460)	($1,839,782)	($1,846,131)
Lifetime Value	($53.96)	($54.95)	($55.14)

Figure 13-3. LTV of occasional supermarket shoppers.

special express lanes for them whenever they showed up, while more profitable customers had to wait in long queues to get their heavy baskets rung up.

What were these people worth to the company? As you can see, their value was a minus $55. They cost the supermarket more in expenses than the profits from the meager sales to these folks paid for. They were being subsidized by the more loyal customers.

These were not necessarily worthless people. The chances are that they did the bulk of their shopping elsewhere and just dropped into this supermarket occasionally to use the express lanes, and waste the company's time and money.

Now that you know about these people, what can you do about it? The answer, clearly, is to develop some simple policy that will nudge these losers into the profitable column. That is where customer-specific marketing comes in. Once you know who these people are, you should find a way to charge them more, and at the same time to reward the loyal customers.

Migrating the Silver Customers

A third group to look at are the Silver customers, those just below Gold. Research in Safeway, for example, shows that this group has the greatest potential for an improvement in lifetime value. The Gold customers are probably maxed out. They are loyal and are spending all their food money in this store. The Silver customers, on the other hand, are probably splitting their patronage among more than one store. This is something that we can change. Let us look at their lifetime value today, and then what we could do to modify it (Figure 13-4).

Here we have a solid lifetime value of $87 based on about 38 trips per year, spending an average of $47.23. Let us do a little database marketing with this group. Let us really go all out on Customer-Specific Marketing. We will use straddle pricing, with the average prices in the store a few percent higher than the competition, but the prices for

Silver Before Migration	Acquisition Year	Second Year	Third Year
Customers	4,412	3,530	3,000
Retention Rate	80.00%	85.00%	90.00%
Visits/Week	0.65	0.7	0.74
Average Basket	$42.97	$45.89	$47.23
Total Sales	$6,407,927	$5,896,498	$5,452,231
Cost Percent	81.00%	79.00%	78.00%
Direct Costs	$5,190,421	$4,658,233	$4,252,740
Labor + Benefits 11%	$704,872	$648,615	$599,745
Card program $16, $8	$70,592	$28,237	$24,001
Acquisition Cost $40	$176,480		
Advertising 2%	$128,159	$117,930	$109,045
Total Costs	$6,270,523	$5,453,015	$4,985,531
Gross Profit	$137,404	$143,409	$157,165
Discount Rate	1	1.14	1.3
NPV Profit	$137,404	$125,797	$120,896
Cum. NPV Profit	$137,404	$263,201	$384,097
Lifetime Value	$31.14	$59.66	$87.06

Figure 13-4. Lifetime value of supermarket Silver customers before migration programs.

cardholders a few percent lower than the competition. We will cut our advertising budget in half, using the resulting money to reward our Silver (and other loyal) customers with specials throughout the store. We will give free ice cream on frequent cardholder's birthdays, and reward them with occasional thank you letters and certificates. Finally, we will admit heavy buyers into a special club that rewards them with points—points that they would lose if they shopped elsewhere. Let us see the impact of all of these changes on this Silver group (Figure 13-5).

Several things have happened to the Silver group as a result of these programs. In the first place, their retention rate has gone up, in the third year, from 90 percent to 92 percent. There are 3,148 of them instead of 3,000. Their visits per week have gone up from 0.74 to 0.78. Their average basket has also grown from $47.23 to $49.03. The lifetime value has grown from $87 to $220. What does this improvement in LTV mean for the chain as a whole? Assume that the chain has 100,000 customers

Silver with Rewards	Acquisition Year	Second Year	Third Year
Customers	4,412	3,618	3,148
Retention Rate	82.00%	87.00%	92.00%
Visits/Week	0.68	0.74	0.78
Average Basket	$44.06	$47.10	$49.03
Total Sales	$6,873,727	$6,557,002	$6,259,339
Cost Percent	81.00%	79.00%	78.00%
Direct Costs	$5,567,719	$5,180,032	$4,882,284
Labor + Benefits 11%	$756,110	$721,270	$688,527
Card program $16, $8	$70,592	$28,237	$24,848
Acquisition Cost $40	$176,480		
Migration Programs $13	$57,356	$45,885	$40,379
Advertising 1.5%	$103,106	$98,355	$93,890
Total Costs	$6,731,362	$6,073,779	$5,729,928
Gross Profit	$142,364	$483,223	$529,410
Discount Rate	1	1.14	1.3
NPV Profit	$142,364	$423,880	$407,239
Cum. NPV Profit	$142,364	$566,244	$973,483
Lifetime Value	$32.27	$128.34	$220.64

Figure 13-5. LTV of Silver customers after migration programs.

who are in the Silver group. The annual profit from this group has increased from $8.7 million to $22 million, an increase of more than $13 million. These are real profit increases, because LTV takes into account all costs, including the costs of getting the customers to change their behavior.

What did we have to do to create this $13 million increase in profits? We had to develop creative migration programs that cost us $13 per customer per year. We paid for much of these costs by cutting the advertising budget by 25 percent from 2 percent to 1.5 percent.

Sears Canada Experience

Sears Roebuck terminated their big catalog in the U.S. several years ago, but the catalog was still going strong in Canada. It was the largest mail-order catalog in the country. Sears was also a big retailing presence in Canada with 110 retail stores and 1,800 catalog agents. What is more, you could order any Sears Canada product directly off the Web.

The Sears database had been maintained on a mainframe, using 30-year-old software. It took 120 people to do the manual file maintenance. The file was loaded with duplicates. The file was not on line. It could be accessed only through hard copy reports that took a week to produce. Fred Hagerman, list manager for catalog marketing, decided to make a business case for a new database system with modern software, and on-line access to do counts, reports, and selects. He showed that he could pay for the system by just finding and eliminating the estimated 10 percent duplicate names on the system. Saving the cost of 10 percent of the catalog mailings to an 11 million name database amounted to a lot of money.

He set up a system whereby the data from the mainframe could be viewed by a client server through a simple spreadsheet. The new system permitted looking at circulation, media, performance analysis, growth and response rates, and tracking of promotions. The 11 million-name database was updated weekly in about 2 hours, producing all sorts of reports.

Building Active Customers

Before Fred arrived, active customers were defined as people who had shopped with Sears in the last 12 months. During the previous decade, the active file had been going down by 3 percent per year. Fred stopped the practice of dropping people who had not bought in 12 months.

Each year, Sears was losing valuable data on people who had not purchased in a year. It was very difficult to maintain or build any kind of relationship, or any kind of long-term learning with customers when you dump their data after a year.

Six Capabilities

The new database system was able to do six new things:

- *Planning* was aimed at knowing how many customers Sears had, and what they were doing. They developed an RFM model, based on the customer's lifetime value, showing what they spent on catalog items. They created 189 RFM segments. The segments tracked response rate, average order, and dollar per book across all 189 segments for every one of Sears 13 catalogs. All the variable costs of each promotion, whether it was a catalog or a direct mail promotion, could be applied to each of the 189 segments to forecast segment profitability. This told Sears whether it would be profitable or not to mail to each segment. They could understand the ramifications of what they are doing for each major promotion. They could accurately forecast what sales they were going to have at the end of the year.

- *Migration analysis* enabled Sears marketers to track customer migrations through all the 189 segments on a weekly basis. They were able to learn the level at which the customers came in, how they were moving around in the file, and what their performance was. They were able to forecast an annual file growth projection on a weekly basis. They were able to know whether they were growing or shrinking, and where they needed to worry and re-plan.

- *Tracking customers.* If a Sears customer had a lifetime value of $2,500 and had made a purchase in the past three months, the customer would be in a specific segment. If there were no purchases in the next three months, the customer would move to a lower segment. Using the new system, it was possible to do stimulation activities. They could identify Sears customers who left so as to start reactivation programs. In addition to the RFM analysis, they also developed a predictive model.

- *Early warning system.* If business is starting off below the marketing plan, with the new system, Sears could re-adjust and re-allocate marketing expenses to deal with it. Customers were compared not just by RFM segment, but also by media. Do people perform better in a wish book, a sale book or a spring and summer book? What kind of merchandise do they buy? Do they buy just men's clothing or women's or children's? Do they buy appliances through the catalog?

- *Payment methods.* With the new system, Sears could also look at segment payment methods: Sears credit card, third party card, cash and how performance differs among them. They can also look at performance by catalog distribution method; there were eight different methods.

- *Half-life analysis.* By tracking sales in the past, Sears learned that their half-life was 20 days after a catalog was mailed. They were able to track the entire success of a book by sales made during the first 20 days.

What Was the Payoff for the Investment in the Sears Database?

- Customer activity and sales turned up, not down as it had for the previous decade.
- Every single media but one, after the database kicked in, was up.
- The fall and winter catalog had a 10-percent increase in sales.
- The Fall Values catalog had a 7-percent increase.
- The Super Sale catalog sales were up 10 percent.
- The Christmas Wish Book sales increased by 26 percent.
- The Winter Celebration catalog dropped 2 percent but space in the book dropped by 30 percent.
- The Lowest Price catalog sales were up 37 percent.
- The first reactivation book went out to people who did not receive the regular catalog. The break-even response rate was 3.5 percent. The actual response rate was 4.5 percent. Sears reactivated 12,000 customers, and made a profit while doing it.

Later, Sears used the information developed in this database to make a major reorganization of the entire chain combining catalog and retail in a single system (see details in Chapter 16).

Supermarket Frequent Shopper Cards

Several years ago, retailers began to issue proprietary cards to frequent shoppers. When these cards were presented at the checkout counter, point of sale equipment permitted the retailer to know what every household was buying and when. Retailers used this data to build databases to study their customer's shopping habits. They discovered, as we have illustrated above, that the top 20 percent of their customers over the course of a year spent about 50 times the amount of their bottom 20 percent. Combining this knowledge with modern POS technology, and it became possible for any retailer, according to Brian Woolf, President of the Retail Strategy Center, to "make one offer to a frequent, high spending customer, a completely different offer to a low spending customer, and yet a third offer to a new customer with moderate spending habits."

The Evil of Average Pricing

Trapped in mass marketing, retailers had always had to charge the same price to everyone. When they announced a sale, everyone got the sale price—loyal customers and occasional transaction buyers. Using customer-specific marketing, retail stores could use their proprietary shopping cards to identify who was shopping. They could reward the best customers while they were in the store. The cards then became the basis of the store's customer database. With such a database set up, the stores could adopt two basic principles, as defined by Brian. The principles are:

- Customers are not equal.
- Behavior follows rewards.

To put these principles to work, retailers had to see that different customers received different offers. Occasional, unknown customers paid full price. Loyal, regular customers paid a lower price—on certain merchandise, or on all merchandise. Furthermore, the loyalists were made aware that they were the favored ones. They were treated as gold card customers—as long as their behavior warranted it. What retailers discovered, is that they could modify customer behavior by the appropriate application of rewards.

Brian Woolf cites some interesting examples of customer-specific marketing:

- A retailer offered a free turkey to those customers who spent an average of at least $50 a week in the two months prior to Thanksgiving.

The number of households spending over $50 per week increased 20 percent over the preceding year.

■ A retailer told customers that 1 percent of their spending would be donated to the church of their choice. Result: participating cardholders increased their annual spending by more than 5 percent.

■ Senior citizens were given a 10 percent reduction at one chain if they purchased on Mondays. As a result, 67 percent of the seniors' shopping took place on Monday. That was five times the spending level of all other customers on Monday.

New Marketing Focus

"We are no longer trying to take customers away from our major competitor. Our focus is to make money on the customers who are already shopping with us," reported one retail chain executive who used the new system. These customer-specific marketers reduced their advertising costs because through analysis of their databases, they learned the low profitability and low loyalty of the promiscuous shoppers who were attracted to their stores mainly by heavy advertising. The new customer-specific marketing had three approaches:

■ Withdraw low margin offers to unprofitable customers.

■ Offer the best customers aggressive pricing and special benefits.

■ Switch from item pricing to total pricing.

This was accomplished by

■ Increased prices for customers with low profitability.

■ Decreased prices for high margin customers.

How could this be done? One retailer's program illustrates the method. He:

■ Took a quarter of the items featured in newspaper advertisements and aggressively priced them but only for cardholders.

■ Converted 1,000 of their 3,000 temporary price reductions to cardholder-only specials.

The result was a jump of 6 percent in sales in some of his stores. Overall, his gross profits were 1 percent higher due to the new system.

Sweepstakes Can Be Fun

Big Y, a supermarket in Western Massachusetts spiced up their Express Savings Club with a grand prize sweepstakes of $1 million, plus numerous weekly prizes of $1,000 in cash and $50 gift certificates and state lottery tickets. A cardholder did not know whether she had won one of the fifteen $1,000 weekly cash prizes until she shopped the following week when her card was swiped. If the card carried a winning number, a red light started flashing in the ceiling and alarm bells sounded in the store. Everyone in the store stopped to see who the lucky winner was.

Non-Cash Benefits

Neiman-Marcus offered their best customers lunch with the store manager, along with two of the customer's friends, followed by a private fashion show. Caesar's Palace penthouse was available only to those who had at least a $1 million line of credit for gambling at the hotel. Paw Paw Shopping Center in Michigan sent customers prior to their birthday, a gift certificate for a free decorated birthday cake. As a result, total cake sales increased tenfold in one year. Safeway offered free ice cream on a cardholder's birthday. Tracking showed an average of $10 increased sales when birthday certificates were redeemed.

At Lees Supermarket in Westport, MA, when the customer cards were swiped, the computer flashed information to the store clerk that he could use in conversation with the customer: how long had she been a customer? Is she one of the best store customers? How big a check is she authorized to cash without the manager's approval? Mark Dodge of Easy Access in Wisconsin set up a program to activate a store manager's beeper whenever any particularly good customer or group of customers used their card in the store. Albert Lees of Lees Supermarkets thought he knew the identity of his best customers until he set up his database. He was amazed to find that he did not even recognize his top customer who was spending over $10,000 per year in his store.

Customer Category Management

The cardholder database permitted retailers to group customers not by where they lived, but by how much they spent per week. Research at the Retail Strategy center showed that demographics were not particularly useful as a primary segmentation basis for retailers because there was little correlation to profitability. Instead, by classifying customers by spending, it was possible to determine the Lifetime Value of retail customers.

How else was this card-based customer data used? One retailer had a 40-ft aisle devoted to candy. Candy was profitable, but was that the best use of his space? Looking at his customer database, he found that his top customers (top 30 percent who provide 75 percent of the sales) did not buy much candy. What did they buy? Baby products. So he cut his candy counter to 20 ft, and added 20 ft of baby products. The reasoning? "We are concentrating on our *top customers* not our *top merchandise*. It is more profitable that way."

Reasons for Failure

Not all attempts at customer-specific marketing have achieved success. There are a number of reasons for the failure. They include:

Timidity—In some cases top management is not committed and does not push the system sufficiently. If you have only 30 percent of your transactions recorded on your cards, there is no obvious profit gain from the system.

Puny rewards—In some stores, the electronic discounts were not meaningful. If the savings are minuscule, the customers will leave their cards at home.

Over reliance on vendors—In some cases, retailers tried to transfer all the costs of markdowns to the vendors. What happened is that the program featured mainly slow moving items that the vendors want to push, instead of those items the customers wanted to buy. These programs tended to fail.

Information starvation—To reduce costs, some companies used their system as a shelf electronic discount without capturing customer purchases. Such practices lose the real value of customer-specific marketing, which lies in the information it can provide.

Failure to differentiate—Where there was insufficient differentiation between the best and the worst customers, the systems did not reward profitable behavior sufficiently to improve the bottom line.

Customer-specific marketing was not the core strategy—If customer-specific marketing did not become the core marketing strategy, the programs usually failed. When the stores continued existing marketing practices unchanged, the new initiatives simply became another promotional program.

Internal political problems—The bigger the chain, the greater the resistance to change. Unless top management was behind it, internal squabbles tended to kill customer-specific marketing before its potential could be realized.

But Does It Pay off?

What is the payoff from customer-specific marketing when it works?

Daniel Lescoe, VP of Sales and Marketing of Big Y Foods in Springfield, MA said, "Before we adopted this program, our sales in Western Massachusetts were $272,400,000 which represented about 25 percent of the market. Two years after adopting the system we moved into the number one position with sales of $364,662,474 and a market share of almost 29 percent. Every marketing program we develop has one mission: to promote our Express Savings Club. It is a religion for us, not just another promotion."

Roger Morgan, Managing Director of Morgan's Tuckerbag Supermarkets in Melbourne, Australia reported on his first full year of customer-specific marketing: "In an industry that has seen average customer transaction values dropping, and customer visits increasing, our stores with this program in place radically went against this trend. We experienced increased customer transaction values with increased customer traffic as well. Some identical weeks experienced 40 percent sales increases over the previous year. Overall, our annual increase over the previous year was in the 20 percent + range."

Adding the Non-Cardholders to Your Database

Once you begin to experiment with building a retail marketing database it will become obvious that there is a definite cash value for every name retained on the database. Profits (from a well managed database strategy) will be a function of the number of customers (not necessarily credit cardholders) on the database. How can you get at the anonymous majority who pay with cash, check, or non-house credit card?

One method, of course, is to provide applicants with a non-credit "check cashing card" which speeds up the acceptance of checks. Supermarkets use such cards routinely. Department stores can do the same.

Jennifer MacLean reported how one retailer added thousands of customer names to his database in a short space of time. All cash and non-house credit card customers were asked to supply their telephone numbers as a part of the transaction. The numbers were keyed into the POS device. Capturing the information on 304,427 transactions, they discovered that 28 percent were repeat buyers. The unique telephone numbers were sent to a service bureau where the numbers were looked up through an electronic reverse telephone directory system. The names and addresses of 129,623 customers were identified through this process.

The resulting file was checked against the house credit card file. It turned out that 36 percent of these customers were house credit card-holders: two thirds were active, and one third was inactive. The remaining 82,869, of course, were new names that were added to the store's marketing database. The fact that many cardholders, previously thought inactive, were actually making purchases at the store came as a pleasant surprise, and added to the store's knowledge about their customer base.

Of course, today, one of the best ways to add names is to ask for them on the Web.

Profits from Promoters

What is your name worth? A retailer name carries an image that sends a message: Sears, JC Penney, Bloomingdale's, Nordstrom, LL Bean, Land's End. As you read each of these names, an image is formed in your mind of the store, what it stands for, and what a message from that store is likely to mean to you.

American Express spent years cultivating their brand name ("Membership has its privileges"). An envelope from American Express, or Bloomingdale's, is more likely to be opened than one from an unknown retailer. The name alone, in other words, is worth money. Some retailers have put their name to effective use by working with small promoters to make special offerings to their cardholders. The way it works is this:

- The promoter comes to the retailer with a product and an idea. Let us say that it is a cellular phone, which fits into a woman's pocketbook.

- Together, they figure out the demographics and purchase behavior of the store customers most likely to respond to such a product.

- The retailer does an advertisement hoc search of his cardholder database to identify the likely prospects.

- The promoter prepares direct mail materials describing the offer. A contract is signed with the retailer indicating the percentage of sales going to the retailer and the percentage to the promoter.

- The promoter carries out the mailing using a list provided by the store, letterhead and envelopes from the store, and his own resources. The store pays nothing for the mailing. Alternative: the offer can be included in the store's monthly statement mailing. Advantage: less costly. Disadvantage: much lower response.

- Fulfillment is carried out by the store's fulfillment department. Payment is made to the store's accounting department. Once a month, the promoter is reimbursed for his share in the venture.

What are the advantages in such an arrangement?

Knowledge. The retailer gets to experiment with direct marketing with very little cost. Valuable knowledge is learned about the customers, their responses, and their propensity to buy certain products.

Profits. The profits from such an arrangement can be far greater than any similar retail venture. With virtually no investment, some retailers have made more total profits from such a system than from their entire retailing operation.

Is there a downside? Will customers feel "exploited" by having their names "used" in this way?

The answer involves the entire philosophy of marketing. In the first place, the retailer must scan each of these offers carefully to be sure that the products and the way that they are presented fully reflect the standards which customers have come to expect from the store. The promotion of trash in the name of the store will cheapen the store in many ways.

Second, the retailer must do a good job of targeting its mail to the right customers. Picking your targets is not only good economics but is also a favor to the customer. If every letter from their department store is loaded with merchandise in which the customer has no interest, she will soon lose interest in the store and in opening envelopes from the store.

Assuming that it is a quality product, well targeted to the right customers, retailers can only gain from such a system. If the customer is buying, she must be happy: she has made a profit from the transaction. Making customers aware of profitable opportunities that they take advantage of is doing them a favor.

Database Marketing and the Web with Packaged Goods

Does database marketing or the Web work for packaged goods? There is no clear-cut answer to this question. Many manufacturers have tried it. Some have succeeded, but most of them have failed. Does that mean that it cannot be done, or does it mean that they did not go about it correctly? That is the key question. Strategy is very important here. If you do not have a really good idea, and execute it well, you will lose your money trying to do database marketing or Web branding with packaged goods.

There are several reasons why packaged goods database projects seldom work out. They are:

- *There is not enough margin to do database marketing.* The margin on packaged goods is pathetically thin. The last time I looked, Ivory soap was selling for $1.29 for four bars. There is very little margin in such sales. In database marketing, you are trying to modify customer's behavior in some way that will be profitable for you, and satisfying to the customer. To modify behavior, you have to provide some benefit for the customers who are on your database. There has to be some margin to pay for the communications, and for the benefit.

- *You cannot find out what the customer is doing.* To do database marketing, there has to be a feedback loop. You have to have purchase history in the database. You have to know whether the specific promoted people listed are buying the product: when, in what quantities, and in response to what promotions? You cannot do that with packaged goods. You cannot afford to provide and redeem a coupon with every case of beer, OTC medicine, or box of cereal. Most customers just will not bother to send in such coupons, even if you could afford to pay for them. Stores that have frequent buyer cards know exactly who is buying your product and when, but few stores will sell this information to manufacturers. Selling the data was the premise for the Reward America program started by Citicorp and reported in Chapter 16. It failed. Since then most retail stores are worried that privacy concerns would ruin their profitable frequent buyer programs if they were to sell the data to manufacturers.

- *Coupons have seriously eroded brand loyalty.* Billions of coupons are available from every conceivable source: Carol Wright, local coop programs, Sunday newspapers, in-store coupons, etc. There are millions of people who plan their shopping trips around the coupons they collect. Coupons can be placed in a Sunday newspaper for $6 per thousand. Coupons sent directly to targeted homes by mail cost a minimum of $300 per thousand. Your package, offer, and concept will have to be outstanding to permit your targeted offer to overcome this cost differential. Few companies know how to do it. Database marketing is almost impossible in these circumstances.

So what can you do?

You Can Work with Retailers. Many retailers maintain customer databases that keep track of customer purchases in very great detail. From these databases, you can learn shopping habits and the response to various promotions by different categories of consumers. Store chains may help with statistical reports. They will not let you correspond directly with these consumers, in most cases, but that does not matter. Direct communications are too expensive for packaged goods anyway.

You Can Build a Web Site. Several packaged goods retailers have built customer Web sites. They put the Web address on their packages and ads. Some of the Web sites are quite creative, like the site for "I can't believe it's not butter" (www.tasteyoulove.com) Doing the second edition of this book, I went to this site and registered. I received a coupon for 50 cents off on butter spray that I buy all the time. Can they make money doing this? I doubt it. Can they influence more than a tiny fraction of their customers through such creative Web sites? I doubt it. They obviously realized this, because today the Web site does not offer a coupon. Such Web sites are relatively inexpensive, however. You can build and maintain a very satisfactory Web site for what a single annual direct promotion to 200,000 households would cost. They are part of building the brand. They may do more for the brand than a full page in Better Homes, but I doubt it. Such Web sites do not permit database marketing which is really not possible for packaged goods, except for baby and highly specialized products.

You Can Set up a Club. Wacky Warehouse increased Kool-Aid sales over several years to 83 percent of the powdered drink market and, at the same time, reversed the preference by youngsters for Pepsi and Coke over Kool-Aid.

Kraft General Foods pioneered with user clubs for packaged goods. Clubs for gardening, sports, gourmet cooks, automobiles, children, computers, dieting, travel, nature have been created, using the Web. The idea in such clubs is to provide customers with something unusual, which does not involve price, but involves the use of the product.

In such a club, the idea is to build the interest in the activity, not your product. The product, instead of being the central feature, is an assumed fact. The idea is that "Everyone uses Buitoni Italian products when serving a meal. Look at these great Italian recipes you can get. Look at Italy, the home of wonderful food."

If your club is good enough, and provides enough benefits for members, it can eventually become self-supporting through sales of services and merchandise (other than your immediate product), or paid advertisements in the club magazine.

A few years ago the *Nintendo Power* magazine built up a readership of two million customers eager to learn more about how to use the product. A 900 telephone number (paid by the customer) was used by 10,000 kids a week. Up to 40,000 letters were received every month by readers all of whom were answered. Such a club, once established, is ideal for launch of a new product. When Nintendo introduced *Game Boys* they sold five million in the first year, and 20 million cartridges in follow-up sales. The clubs were reached through their Web site.

Can you copy Nintendo, and build a club? It is a strategy that, if done well, will never go out of style. Done poorly, or half-heartedly, it will just drain your treasury.

Affinity Groups

A little less demanding than a club is an identified affinity group to which you can mail a newsletter and invitations to purchase the product.

The average baby uses over $1,400 worth of disposable diapers per year. Kimberly Clark spent over $10 million to set up a database system for Huggies diapers, which covered 75 percent of the expectant mothers in the United States. The names were obtained from doctors, hospitals, and childbirth trainers. During the time that they were pregnant, the expectant mothers received personalized magazines and letters with ideas on baby care. When the baby was born, the mother got a coded coupon for diapers.

Every other manufacturer who provides consumable baby products has copied this idea and maintains a profitable baby product database. In this case, database marketing works.

Referral Programs

There is a progression that most customers go through: Awareness, Trial, User, Advocate, Regular user. Once some people become hooked on your product, they want to tell their friends about it. They become advocates.

In most cases, there is little that advocates can do, except to tell a couple of friends at the office, or a neighbor. Why not capitalize on this brief phase of infatuation, before they become blasé regular users, by giving the advocate something positive that she can do to promote the success of this wonderful product; to spread to others the joy and satisfaction that she feels every time she uses it?

This is where referral programs come in. If you can use your database to encourage advocates to spread the word in a positive way, you can boost your own sales, and make your customers happy.

The Perform program did this. Members were encouraged to recommend friends and neighbors who might want the product. When these friends and neighbors purchased, the recommender received a thank you letter together with a $2 reduction on her next pet food bill. MCI did this with their Friends and Family Program. MCI, of course, was not a packaged good, but the concept still applies.

Packaged goods programs can do the same by on-pack referral programs, inviting people to send in names. You build a database of the recommender and the recommendee, with benefits accruing to the recommender when the recommendee takes some recorded action (proof of purchase, enrollment in a club, etc.)

Such a program can be quite inexpensive. On-pack offers have a delivery cost that is almost zero (compared to direct mail or advertising). The customer pays the postage. You pay only when you receive a response. Better than direct mail is to develop a method whereby the on-pack coupon can be redeemed over the Internet by having the customer enter a unique number from the coupon plus her name, address, and e-mail. The check can be sent to the address, once the e-mail and opt-in status is confirmed. The problem is, however, what to do with the name once your have captured it.

Recapitulation

If you feel that I am warning you to go slowly and carefully before you rush into database marketing for packaged goods, you have gotten the message. A really creative idea can build a package goods database. Nintendo did it. Could Lipton? Kool Aid did it. Could Del Monte?

My feeling is that, with the exception of baby products, it is tough to surmount the economics of packaged goods. The database, in almost all cases, will make only a modest incremental increase in sales. Will that increment be sufficient to provide enough benefits to the members of the database that they will want to be members of whatever affinity group you establish, and will develop a loyalty to your product and company? Will the modest increment be sufficient not only to pay the benefits to the customer but also to pay all the expenses of the database? Will the fact that you will never really know in detail whether your efforts are paying off, ruin your chances for approval by management, and reduce your self-respect as a database marketer?

Increasing Store Traffic

A national fashion retailer was interested in identifying the best prospects to drive store traffic. The goals of the analysis were to:

■ Profile current customers based on demographics, psychographics, and geographical indicators.

■ Account for different purchasing trends of seasonal influences.

■ Identify prospects most likely to visit and purchase from a specific store location.

The retailer asked KnowledgeBase Marketing to do the analysis. KnowledgeBase Marketing used TrafficMax® a proprietary modeling technique that identified prospects that had a propensity to behave like the retailer's best customers. They obtained their prospect names from the AmeriLINK® national consumer list. This provided them with prospective customers with the proximity to the store locations.

The first step was to analyze the fashion retailer's customer purchases over the past two years. The analysts:

■ Performed a comprehensive data integrity and hygiene analysis of the retailer's customer information.

■ Created a demographic and psychographic profile of the retailer's customer base and best customers.

■ Plotted the precise location of the retailer's stores and determined appropriate trading areas for each store.

■ Identified prospective customers, within the trading areas of the retailer's store locations (proximity) who had the profile of the retailer's best customers (propensity).

CHAID Level	Variable	Value	Importance
1	Age and Home Value	19 to 20 > $164K	187
2	Age	16 to 18	174
3	Age And % Divorced	24 to 39 0 to 5%	149
4	Age and Home Value	19 to 20 $98K to $133K	149
5	Age And % Divorced	51 to 55 8% to 9%	131
6	Age And Affluence Index And Income	21 6 to 10 $55K to $100K	130
7	Age and Home Value and Early Card Adop. and Nielson County Rank	24 to 39 $78K to $189K 1,2 2 to 4	130
8	Age And % Divorced and Nielson County Rank And % Employed PTM	40 to 50 9% to 14% B, C, D 26% to 99%	126

Figure 13-6. CHAID analysis of retail store customers.

Using the data collected, KnowledgeBase Marketing did CHAID analysis of the retailer's customers to determine the characteristics of the retailer's best customers. A portion of the CHAID analysis looked like this (Figure 13-6):

This chart is just the top of a long list of CHAID identified segments. The last column, importance, was based on the annual sales per customer from this segment. The retailer used the analysis to select prospects for mailing in the areas surrounding its stores. As a result:

■ Over a 2-year period, the new system pulled response rates as high as 8.9 percent for prospect mailings.

■ Seasonality adjusted prospect models were tracked separately, with the highest response rate being 9.5 percent.

Summary

1. Retailing is tough. Database marketing and the Web today, however, offer a new solution to the retailing problem.

2. The first step is usually to boost the number and percentage of customers who use the store's credit card or are registered on the Web. This forms the basis for the database.

3. Retail database files can be very large. The solution to the size problem can be found in: keeping detailed data for a short time only, rolling up older data by department, using modern marketing software which provides access to customer files to do advertisement hoc counts and selects.

4. Retailers can combine with external promoters to market directly to retail customers. The result can be very profitable for the retailer.

5. Database marketing for packaged goods is particularly difficult because margins and loyalty have been seriously eroded by billions of coupons issued yearly. Many companies who have entered this field have failed to build a satisfactory long-term database system.

6. Coupons in a newspaper cost $6 per thousand. Any type of direct mail costs a minimum of $300 per thousand. You have to prove that direct mail is better, or give up the project.

Executive Quiz 13

Answers to quiz questions (Figure 13-7) can be found in Appendix B.

Put the appropriate letter before each answer	
Questions	**Answers**
a Occasional Shoppers	189 Segments for all 13 catalogs
b Silver Customers according to Safeway	A top retail store customer CHAID segment
c Sears Canada RFM system	Best customers buy baby products
d Free Turkey for Thanksgiving	Can't find out whether the customers are buying
e Why 40 foot aisle of candies was changed	Capture thousands of customer names
f Telephone numbers in POS	Card Holders pay less than occasional shoppers
g Why packaged goods DB fail	Elimination of 10% duplicate names
h Age 19 to 20 and >$164K Home Value	Fifty times as much
i Promoters use your brand name	From two weeks to thirty seconds.
j Why Customer Specific Marketing Fails	Increased sales 20% over the previous year
k Sears Canada Half Life Day	Market share for went up from 25% to 29%
l Straddle Pricing	Maxed out. Doing all their spending with you.
m The effect of coupons on brand loyalty	Often have a negative lifetime value
n How customer specific marketing helped Big Y	Register their credit cards with you
o Spending difference top 20% vs bottom 20%	Send them birthday cards
p How Sears Canada paid for their new database	The greatest potential for increased sales
q Why Gold Customers should not be marketed	The majority defect within twelve months
r Outsourcing cut selection time for 60,000 custs.	The twentieth day after the first order comes in.
s Customers earned by deeply discounted prices	There are puny rewards
t How to track customer sales	There has been serious erosion
u How to build retention	Valuable profit & customer knowledge at no cost

Figure 13-7. Quiz 13.

14

Building Retention and Loyalty in Business Customers

It's a familiar saying that business would be great if we didn't have to deal with customers. But have you ever stopped to consider that your business might be more profitable without customers–without some of them, at least? ...Cooper and Kaplan reported the astonishing case of a heating wire company which analyzed its customer profitability and discovered that the famous 20–80 rule, which would suggest that 80% of profits came from 20% of customers, had to be revised:

"A 20–225 rule was actually operating: 20% of the customers were generating 225% of profits. The middle 70% of customers were hovering around the break-even point, and 10% of customers were losing 125% of profits" Even more amazing: it was the largest customers who were producing the biggest losses.

LYNETTE RYALS
Cranfield University, UK

There are many products and services where database marketing has limited value. In business-to-business marketing, however, relationship-building activities *always* pay off. Why is the business-to-business area so productive? There are several reasons:

■ The sales amounts are usually large. Sales are large enough that there is a significant margin available for relationship-building activities.

- The data on customer purchases is almost always available, since so much of the business is on open accounts. Getting the names of the decision makers, influencers, and ultimate users is often a challenge, however.

- The number of customers is usually quite small. In many cases we are dealing with 50,000 customers or less. We can concentrate on these companies and build a complete database of contact history, purchases, and preferences, and use this data to support our relationship-building activities.

- Each business customer has problems of their own to solve, including channel conflicts, inventory maintenance, customer acquisition, and retention. The supplier is often in a position to help his customers to solve their problems.

Professor Paul Wang divides business customers into four basic categories (Figure 14-1):

There are two axes of the chart shown in Figure 14-1: price and service. Some business customers pay a high price and get little service. On the other end, some pay very low prices but get the best service. Let us see why that is.

Bargain Hunters are customers who have tremendous market power. Wal-Mart is an example. Here is a customer who demands —and gets—the absolutely lowest prices in the market. Wal-Mart is in a position to make massive purchases at rock bottom prices. At the same time, they can demand—and get—a very high level of service from their suppliers. Wal-Mart often makes their suppliers provide daily shelf restocking. Some goods are placed on Wal-Mart shelves on consignment so Wal-Mart has little investment. In some cases, the suppliers must clean up the sales areas each day. Few other retailers can get such services from their suppliers. For bargain hunters, the supplier has to meet

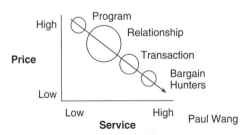

Figure 14-1. Types of business customers.

specified requirements in order to sell massive amounts at very low prices. There are many such bargain hunters around. Anyone who sells to Home Depot or Staples knows that it is like holding a tiger by its tail.

Program Buyers are at the other end of the scale. Small purchasers of office supplies, for example, do not have the time or the economic incentive to shop around for the best deal. They do not have the market power that comes from volume purchases. Typically, they will buy from a nearby source one month, and shift to another source the next month, without any really well thought out plan. Many governments, including the Federal Government, are program buyers. They issue purchasing manuals to their employees which restrict how, what, where, and when purchases can be made. These program buyers have the worst of both worlds. They pay the highest prices and get the lowest level of service. The famous Defense Department purchase of expensive toilet seats is a well-known example. Their purchases are either so small or so specialized that few suppliers find it profitable to do much to attract them. Relationship building may not work here.

Transaction Buyers, on the other hand, represent a major segment of any market. These customers try to engage in comparison-shopping for every transaction. They read the advertisements, consult the Internet, make phone calls, and get comparative bids. For them, the past has no meaning. They have absolutely no loyalty. Never mind what the supplier did for you in the past, the question is what is your price today? They will shift suppliers of any product for a few pennies difference in price.

Transaction buyers usually get little service. Service is not important to them. Price is everything. There is not much point in trying to win their loyalty, since they have none to win. Database marketing may be ineffective here—only discounting. They are seldom profitable customers, even though they may buy a lot of product, and represent an important segment of any market. The best thing that could happen to these transaction buyers would be for them to shift over to buying from your competition. Give them the competition's catalogs and phone numbers and hope they take the hint. Paul Wang suggests that the only way to make money with transaction buyers is to negotiate annual volume purchase agreements. The buyers get a good deal on price, and you get the volume without having to spend valuable marketing and customer service dollars.

Relationship Buyers are the customers for whom database marketing was invented. They are looking for a dependable supplier:

■ Someone who cares about their needs, and who looks out for them.

- Someone who remembers what they bought in the past, and gives them special services as a reward.

- Someone who takes an interest in their business, and treats them as individuals.

Relationship buyers know that they could save a few dollars by shopping around. But they also recognize that if they do switch suppliers, they would lose something that they value very highly: the relationship that they have built up with a dependable supplier that recognizes them and takes good care of them. Many of them also realize that there is an emotional and monetary cost to shopping around for every purchase. They want to concentrate on their business success, not on their purchasing prowess.

By classifying your customers into these four segments, you can focus your marketing efforts on the one segment that is really profitable: relationship buyers. Your database is used to record the purchases of these buyers, and to give them personal recognition and special services. You recognize your Gold customers. You communicate with them. You partner with them.

Classifying Customers by Segment

How can you classify customers by these four segments? Part of it is easy. You already know who the bargain hunters are. No one who deals with Wal-Mart or Sears or other giant retailers has to be told who they are. Program buyers can almost be ignored. They make small purchases on an occasional basis. They pay full price, and seldom respond to sales offers. They, too, are easy to classify.

Your big problem lies in distinguishing transaction buyers from relationship buyers. Here is how one retailer does it. New customers are given a survey form. One question asks: "How important are the following in making your decision about where to buy this product? Rank from 1—most important—to 5—least important:

a. Price

b. Service

c. Reputation of manufacturer

d. Recommendation of a friend

e. Company policy

f. Previous experience

g. Customer service

Those who code *Price* as most important are probably transaction buyers. The others may well be relationship buyers. This can be tested later in other ways (Figure 14-2).

Your management may insist that most of your customers are transaction buyers. They will point out that when you are on sale, you get more sales. When you are not, the sales decrease. What may be happening, however, is shown on this chart. Each of the four companies, A, B, C, and D have a stable base of relationship buyers that stay with them. There is a floating group of transaction buyers that jumps from company to company taking advantage of the sales. They never pay full price for anything. No one makes much money from them. Each company assumes that all of their customers are price sensitive, when, in reality, few of their loyal customers are price sensitive at all.

Training Your Customers

How do customers become transaction buyers? They are not necessarily born that way. They become transaction buyers through exposure to their environment and their management. As suppliers, we may feel that we have to take the world as we find it, but that is not necessarily true. We can take a group of customers who are quite prepared to develop a relationship with us, and *ruin* them by converting them into transaction buyers. How do we do this? By talking price to them all

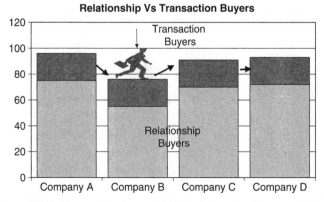

Figure 14-2. Transaction buyers shifting from supplier to supplier.

the time, instead of talking services and relationships. Look at how we do it:

You attract customers by offering discounts. Once you have acquired the customer, you hold periodic sales, and send out literature extolling your low prices. What a mistake! You are training your customers to think of your product or service as a commodity whose value can be measured only by price. Once you have implanted this idea in their minds, they will learn to shop around. Soon they will find someone who sells something cheaper. Of course, if you are truly an everyday low-price dealer like Staples, the focus on price is a valid tactic. But most business-to-business suppliers do not want to be in that league.

What should you do for relationship buyers?

- Describe what your products do, how various businesses are using them, how they are made, and new developments in your field.

- Divide your customers into groups, based on their SIC code: Surveyors, Architects, Builders, Contractors, and send them different messages.

- Create an advisory panel for each group, putting key executives from among your Gold customers in each group on the panel.

- Create a newsletter for each group, with the advisory panel on the masthead.

- Sponsor contests in trade associations for the most creative use of your products.

- Learn the birthdays of key people in your customer's companies and send them a card.

- Write thank you letters periodically for their purchases—not combined with a pitch for more sales—but just a genuine thank you.

Integrated Account Management

At a business-to-business conference, I was asked "How big a customer base do you have to have so that you can profit from database marketing." It was an interesting question. The answer, it seems to me, is to divide customers into three categories (Figure 14-3):

The top group, in most business-to-business situations, is visited directly by the sales force. The sales people know these customers by sight and name. You can build a database of these customers, but it

Sales force calls on all of these	Gold Customers	10% of customers; 70% of sales
Sales force won't call them	Profitable Customers	40% of customers; 25% of sales
Don't bother with them	Lower Value Customers	50% of customers; 5% of sales

Figure 14-3. Typical business-to-business customer grouping.

may not help the sales force much. If you only have 300 customers in this group, and all of them are large enough to justify a sales visit, you do not need a database there. Relationship marketing really works with the middle group. These are profitable customers whose sales do not justify a sales visit. Here, you can organize effective teams to reach these customers by a combination of techniques using the database.

Hunter Business Direct developed a method for doing this, described in Mark Peck's book *Integrated Account Management*. The idea, IAM, developed first by Hunter for Amoco and Shell, was outlined in my book, *The Complete Database Marketer* (pp. 461–471). IAM works this way:

The existing sales force is replaced by regional marketing teams each headed by a regional marketing chief (RMC) who talks to customers on the phone, or by e-mail. The RMC schedules the visits of the field representatives. The field representatives no longer sell. Instead, they become business consultants that help the customers to solve their business problems. They help them with their own sales, customer support, accounting, hiring and training employees, etc. The RMC works from a database that includes all contacts with each customer. Typically, the RMC negotiates an annual contract with each customer with prices based on volume. All sales are taken by phone, or e-mail, or from a Web site, under the control of the RMC.

Under integrated account management, customer service is empowered to solve problems. When a customer calls with a problem, the customer service representative (CSR) must stay with the case until it is solved. Cases are not handed over to someone else. The field representatives do not sell and do not get bogged down in solving product delivery problems.

Integrated account management is usually highly efficient as compared to more traditional methods of dealing with business-to-business customers. Customers like it better, and respond well to the new setup.

Business-to-Business Lifetime Value

Lifetime value tables for business-to-business customers are easy to develop, and highly useful for evaluating strategy. Let us develop the lifetime value of customers of an artificial construct: the Weldon Scientific Company that sells high-tech equipment to factories and laboratories (Figure 14-4).

The table shown in Figure 14-4 is similar to those explained in Chapter 3, with some exceptions. Weldon has about 20,000 business customers including 1,800 independent distributors. The average customer placed an average of 1.8 orders in their year of acquisition, with an average order value of $2,980. Weldon retained 70 percent of their first year customers into the next year. As customers became more loyal, they placed more orders per year, of increasing size, and the retention rate of the remaining customers also increased.

The acquisition cost was $630 per customer. The cost of servicing customers came down substantially after the first year. Most interesting in this chart is the discount rate, which is developed in a separate table (Figure 14-5):

The formula for the discount rate is this:

$$\text{Discount rate} = ((1 + \text{interest rate}) \times (\text{risk factor}))^{\text{Year} + \text{AR}/365}$$

	Acquisition Year	Second Year	Third Year
Retained Customers	20,000	12,000	7,800
Retention Rate	60.00%	65.00%	70.00%
Orders/year	1.8	2.6	3.6
Avg. Order Size	$2,980	$5,589	$9,016
Total Revenue	$107,280,000	$174,376,800	$253,169,280
Direct Cost %	70.00%	65.00%	63.00%
Direct Costs	$75,096,000	$113,344,920	$159,496,646
Acquisition Cost $630	$12,600,000	$0	$0
Total Costs	$87,696,000	$113,344,920	$159,496,646
Gross Profit	$19,584,000	$61,031,880	$93,672,634
Discount Rate	1.18	1.36	1.49
Net Present Value Profit	$16,596,610	$44,876,382	$62,867,539
Cumulative NPV Profit	$16,596,610	$61,472,993	$124,340,532
Customer Lifetime Value	$830	$3,074	$6,217

Figure 14-4. LTV of Weldon Scientific Company.

	Year 1	Year 2	Year 3
Year	0	1	2
Risk Factor	1.8	1.5	1.4
Interest Rate	0.08	0.08	0.08
Acc/Rev. Days	65	85	90
Discount Rate	1.18	1.36	1.49

Figure 14-5. Computation of the discount rate.

In the first year, Weldon tries to get new customers to pay up front, relaxing to a 60-day policy with subsequent orders. For established customers, 90-days payment is customary. The risk factor drops substantially with long-term customers. The combination of all of these factors gives Weldon a sophisticated discount rate that is responsive to the business situation that they face.

Relationship-Building Initiatives

Let us suppose that Weldon has decided to experiment with database marketing. They will take the following steps:

- Build a Web site with distributor and direct customer access by means of a PIN number. The site will include all of their products, with prices shown based on the customer's volume situation.

- Set up an integrated account management team that contacts all medium sized and large customers at least six times per year, learning the names of the decision makers, influencers, and actual users of Weldon's products. Annual sales agreements are negotiated with volume discounts.

- Create an advisory council for each of their six major customer groups, complete with a newsletter which is published on the Web, and prizes given at professional trade shows for the best use of Weldon's products.

- Design a series of communications to each identified Weldon contact in customer firms. Each new customer receives a welcome letter and a request to go to the Weldon Web site to take a survey. There are thank you letters for large orders.

What the Web Site Does

The savings cost from the Web site is larger than that the time saved would indicate. Because orders are processed so much faster, and without human intervention, personnel are saved in the order-process-ing department (Figure 14-6). In addition, by cutting more than a day from each order processing time, customers get their products faster which gives Weldon an edge over its competitors. Finally, by getting bills out one day earlier, Weldon's cash flow is improved by a measura-ble amount. In all, use of the Web site ordering system can cut costs by 3 percent per order. The problem is that in the beginning, only about 10 percent of Weldon's customers would use the Web site to place their orders. To change this, Weldon could give a discount of 1/2 of one percent for all orders placed on the Web site. By the second year, the percentage of customers using the Web site could grow to 60 percent and by the third year it could be close to 90 percent. The cost savings could look like Figure 14-7.

Let us assume the cost of the first three initiatives is as shown in Figure 14-8.

The relationship-building communications to customers, based on their preferences as shown on the survey have an average annual cost per person of $40 each. The average customer has about 2.4 people that Weldon needs to contact, so the average cost per company of the relationship-building program is about $96. For each customer that recommends a new customer who becomes a Weldon customer, Weldon provides a reward worth $200.

The result of the initiatives could be a major change in customer life-time value, as shown in Figure 14-9.

	Order Processing Time*	Cost Per Order
Phone	28hrs	$27.00
Fax, Email, Mail	42hrs	$18.00
Website	1.6 minutes	$1.62
*From order receipt until paperwork arrives at factory		

Figure 14-6. Order processing times and cost of various ordering systems.

	Year 1	Year 2	Year 3
Old Costs	70.00%	65.00%	63.00%
% Using Website	10.00%	60.00%	90.00%
Net Saving per Order 2.5%	0.25%	1.50%	2.25%
New Costs	69.75%	63.50%	60.75%

Figure 14-7. Cost reduction from use of Web site for orders.

	First Year	Annual Incremental Cost
Web Site	$1,600,000	$300,000
IAM	$600,000	($100,000)
Advisory Councils	$200,000	$150,000
Total	$2,400,000	$350,000

Figure 14-8. Cost of relationship-building initiatives.

	Acquisition Year	Second Year	Third Year
Referral Rate	4.00%	6.00%	8.00%
Referred Customers	0	800	828
Retained Customers	20,000	13,000	9,660
Retention Rate	65.00%	70.00%	75.00%
Total Customers	20,000	13,800	10,488
Orders/year	1.9	3.4	4.8
Avg. Order Size	$3,078	$6,170	$11,005
Total Revenue	$116,964,000	$289,496,400	$554,018,112
Direct Cost %	69.75%	63.50%	60.75%
Direct Costs	$81,582,390	$183,830,214	$336,566,003
Acquisition Cost $630	$12,600,000	$0	$0
New Initiatives	$2,400,000	$350,000	$350,000
Relationship Building $96	$1,920,000	$1,324,800	$1,006,848
Referral Incentives $200	$0	$160,000	$165,600
Total Costs	$98,502,390	$185,665,014	$338,088,451
Gross Profit	$18,461,610	$103,831,386	$215,929,661
Discount Rate	1.18	1.36	1,49
Net Present Value Profit	$15,645,432	$76,346,607	$144.919.236
Cumulative NPV Profit	$15,645,432	$91,992,040	$236,911,275
Customer Lifetime Value	$782	$4,600	$11,846

Figure 14-9. LTV of Weldon Customers after new initiatives are in place.

The effect of these new initiatives would be to increase the average customer lifetime value in the third year from about $6,217 to $11,846. What does this mean for Weldon? Assuming that their acquisition program continues to replace the lost customers and that Weldon has a steady customer base of 20,000, the program has increased Weldon's profits by $112 million (Figure 14-10).

	Acquisition Year	Second Year	Third Year
New LTV	$782	$4,600	$11,846
Old LTV	$830	$3,074	$6,217
Difference	($48)	$1,626	$5,629
With 20,000 Customers	($951,178)	$30,519,047	$112,570,743

Figure 14-10. Effect of new initiatives on Weldon Profits.

The first year is costly. Introducing these changes reduces Weldon profits by $1 million. These figures show, however, that if Weldon were to institute the relationship-building programs described here, their profits in the third year would increase by over $112 million. Business-to-business relationship building works—and can be shown to work by careful and controlled tests. Where do these figures come from? How do we know that we can increase the orders in the third year from 3.6 to 4.8, and the average order size from $9,106 to $11,005? By careful testing using control groups, as described in Chapter 11.

Of course, Weldon would probably not apply this program to their entire customer base. Weldon, like all other companies, has some highly profitable customers, and some highly unprofitable customers. The relationship-building program will probably work best with the middle group. The top group—Weldon's Gold customers—are probably maxed out. They are loyal customers. Many companies have found that they cannot profitably cross-sell or up sell their best customers. In the same way, Weldon probably cannot have this kind of success with its unprofitable customers. Building a relationship with losers is not a recipe for success. The most profitable group for Weldon's program are the relationship buyers just below the top—people who are profitable, but probably dividing their spending for Weldon type products amongst a number of different suppliers (Figure 14-11).

Weldon Instruments Corporation Customer Segments						
	Customers	Average Sales	Total Sales	Sales Ranking	Lifetime Value	LTV Ranking
Metal Production	254	$339,736	$86,292,944	4	$145,067	2
Light Manufacturing	15,442	$13,851	$213,887,142	1	$5,914	4
Heavy Manufacturing	44	$2,314.189	$101,824,316	3	$988,146	1
High Technology	612	$299,007	$182,992,284	2	$127,676	3
Others	3,613	$2,176	$7,861,888	5	$929	5
Total	19,965	$29,695	$592,858,574		$12,679	

Figure 14-11. Weldon Customers divided by type of industry.

Once Weldon has been able to determine their average customer lifetime value, they can compute it for various segments. The results are often interesting. If you look at Weldon sales, the big money is clearly in Light Manufacturing, with $213 million in annual sales. But if you look at lifetime value, the 44 Heavy Manufacturing customers account for almost $1 million apiece. Clearly, any retention strategy should start with Heavy Manufacturers. You are going to get much more bang for a marketing buck. Next would be metal production which is low in overall sales, but clearly high in average customer lifetime value.

The chart shown in Figure 14-11 represents the ultimate users of Weldon products. Most of the 15,442 light manufacturing firms and laboratories are served through Weldon's 1,800 independent distributors. That does not mean that Weldon should not cultivate them, but should not try to sell directly to them. By keeping their distribution channel on their database, their efforts can be directed at driving them to visit or call their authorized distributor.

Finally, let us look at the distribution of Weldon customers by total lifetime value (Figure 14-12). In this chart, we have divided Weldon customers into five status groups of approximately equal numbers based on their lifetime value.

The top status level, the Platinum, has an average lifetime value of $50,410 and represents about 79 percent of the total customer lifetime value. The bottom group of 3,903 customers includes the true losers, being responsible for a net lifetime value of minus $309. What can we do with this chart? It probably should be combined with the previous chart to determine the direction of Weldon's retention efforts. Why spend money trying to retain customers with a negative lifetime value? Even if they are in a favored group, such as Heavy Manufacturing or Metal Production,

	Number of Customers	Lifetime Value	Firm Value Total	Percent LTV
Platinum	3,967	$50,410	$199,976,470	79.0%
Gold	4,004	$9,603	$38,450,412	15.2%
Silver	3,881	$2,903	$11,266,543	4.5%
Bronze	4,210	$1,108	$4,664,680	1.8%
Lead	3,903	($309)	($1,206,027)	−0.5%
Total	19,965	$12,679	$253,152,078	100.00%

Figure 14-12. Weldon Customers organized by Lifetime Value.

if they persistently result in a loss of value to Weldon, the retention effort should be reconsidered. This chart reflects the situation in many companies as illustrated in the quote that begins this chapter.

Business to Business on the Internet

Customer service is expensive. At a cost of $3 to $8 per call, with thousands of calls per day, companies have seen a significant drain on the bottom line. Customer lifetime value analysis must be used to determine whether the helpfulness and relationship building is worth the cost. In some cases, companies found that it was not paying its way. Most banks that have done profitability analysis have discovered that about half of their customers are unprofitable. A good part of the lack of profits can be traced to the expense of customer service. Federal Express provided a shining example of customer support by having customer representatives that could field questions on the exact status of every package shipped at any time. A couple of years later, UPS set up a similar system. But these shining examples came at a significant cost. If every customer called by phone to learn the status of their shipments, all shipments would cost at least $3 more than they do.

Customer Service on the Web

The big savings come from inviting customers to come into our Web sites to read the same screens that our employees read. Customers become part of our company family. This is real relationship marketing. It is particularly useful in business to business.

Picture the situation of a company meeting planner setting up a two-day seminar for about 50 customers. The planner was looking for a suitable hotel near Fort Lauderdale that had the facilities she wanted at a cost that was within her budget. Let us see what could be done by clicking on the marriott.com Web site.

The Web site asks meeting planners to specify the number of guests and the features and amenities (golf, swimming, beach, boating, etc.) that they want nearby. The screen showed the planner that there were seven Marriott hotels that match the specifications exactly. Clicking on the Fort Lauderdale Marriott North Hotel, the planner saw the available meeting rooms and specifications. Another click brings up a picture of the hotel, and another a map of how to get there.

This is great marketing. The Marriott Web site provided information on 1,500 hotels whose annual revenue exceeded $10 billion. Think back to how you would have planned a meeting before all of this was available. You had to call Marriott or another hotel chain on the phone. A CSR, looking at information on her computer screen would attempt to describe to you what she saw. She would offer to send you an expensive packet of information on hotels in the Fort Lauderdale area that would arrive a few days later. In the meantime you would probably have booked a hotel somewhere else. Your call would have cost Marriott at least $10, plus the cost of the fulfillment.

Since this case study appeared in the second edition of this book, many of Marriott's competitors have worked very hard to catch up. This example is not just about hotels. Every business-to-business company in America (or the world, for that matter) can profit by opening up their internal company data and making it available to customers on the Web. There are three reasons:

- The Web site will probably pay for itself in the saving of toll-free calls and operator time.

- It may increase sales to new prospects (although that is not a sure thing).

- It provides a way to recognize and build relationships with customers that will improve loyalty and retention.

Who is doing this? Customers used Dell Computer's Web site to check their order status 50,000 times per week. The same calls to Dell's CSRs cost Dell $200,000 per week. Dell also saved several million dollars per year by encouraging 200,000 customers per week to make their troubleshooting inquiries through the Web.

But Dell did something else. They created more than 40,000 premier pages for individual companies. Each page displayed standard machine configurations and prices that were negotiated in advance with the company management. A secure page linked to the premier page with a password provided account information for senior purchasing managers of the company so that they could track their company's acquisition of computers.

Hundreds of companies are *saving money* and *building customer relationships* on the Web. In the long run, these two functions will probably be more important than the total amount of direct sales to new people.

Commercial Messages Using E-mail

Business to business web communications can be outsourced. Cyfun Media uses ExactTarget's email service to develop communications for commercial clients. For one client, the Consumer Credit Counseling Service (CCCS), they developed 64 unique, operational e-mails that CCCS could deliver to their Debt Management Plan clients. The messages included reminders of payments, account status updates and help with re-establishing credit. They used the system to send up to 16 different variations of the many e-mails sent per day.

Each letter had upwards of 10 fields with information from the database. The goal was to make each email as personalized and relevant as possible. Each daily process began with CCCS pulling a list of e-mail recipients with the relevant information from their database. The file was automatically sent over the web to Cyfun which created and sent the emails. Open rates, and click-throughs were captured and reported to CCCS. At a saving of $0.40 per message, the new system provided by ExactTarget saved CCCS nearly $3,000 per month in mailing costs. To CCCS the system was a money saver. The real benefit, however, was that it built a closer personal relationship with their customers that improved their retention rate. This would not have been possible prior to the web.

Alliances

Amazon.com has had great success with their business partner program. They had 30,000 Web sites as partners. The Database Marketing Institute was one of those partners. The DMI Web site featured about 15 books that we thought were great reading for people in our industry. At first we kept a stock of these books in our warehouse. It was a nuisance. We had to order the books from the publishers in bulk, paying for the shipping. We had to take the orders, process the credit cards, and wrap and ship each book ordered. We made very little money from this business. Then we discovered Amazon. We became an amazon.com business partner. Our Web master linked on each book in the amazon.com bookstore that we wanted to feature on our Web site www.dbmarketing. com. A visitor to our Web site sees the covers of these books in living color with a few lines of text about why we recommend the books. When a visitor clicks on the picture of the book, he is transported electronically to amazon.com where he orders the book. Amazon takes the money and fulfills the order. They send us about $1 per book in a quarterly check. We have no inventory, no cards to process, no wrapping and packing, and no employees, and it makes our Web site more useful for the visitors. It is wonderful.

Segmenting a Paging Company's Customers

A business-to-business paging services company with more than 22,000 customers and annual revenue of more than $109 million needed help in reducing the attrition of their customer base and in increasing the revenue per account.

Knowledge Base Marketing divided the client's customers into nine segments organized into three major groups based on customer monthly revenue. They developed a model that predicted attrition based on prior history and company information (SIC code, annual sales, and number of employees). They developed a (by now familiar) risk revenue matrix (Figure 14-13).

Looked at from a monthly revenue standpoint, the numbers were as shown in Figure 14-14.

A breakdown of the customers in each segment is shown in Figure 14-15.

What this showed was that to maintain their business in the most effective way, the paging company had to concentrate on the 84,521 customers (38 percent) in Priorities A and B, instead of using up valuable

Attrition Likelihood	Monthly Revenue		
	High	Medium	Low
High	Priority A	Priority B	Priority C
Medium	Priority B	Priority B	Priority C
Low	Priority C	Priority C	Priority C

Figure 14-13. Risk revenue matrix.

Attrition Likelihood	Monthly Revenue		
	High	Medium	Low
High	$477,273	$271,708	$96,161
Medium	$1,583,693	$1,923,731	$285,112
Low	$2,233,553	$1,820,940	$418,557

Figure 14-14. Revenue by segment.

Attrition	Monthly Revenue		
Likelihood	High	Medium	Low
High	6,011	7,504	12,709
Medium	19,376	51,630	18,996
Low	27,370	51,774	27,242

Figure 14-15. Customers in each segment.

resources trying to retain the 138,091 (62 percent) who had either a very low likelihood of defection, or low monthly revenue.

Methods of Retention Used

All customers received the basic retention package: a welcome kit and a contract anniversary package. In addition, they all received the monthly company newsletter and a product and services communication mailing.

The 84,521 customers in Priorities A and B were given special personalized attention. They were called periodically to check on how they were doing, and received a customer satisfaction questionnaire. Proactive calls were made to these customers, plus a customized revenue optimization review designed to show them how they could improve their revenue while, in some cases, reducing the number of calls made. The responses to the customer satisfaction questionnaires were then put through a process designed to identify and resolve any customer problems. Those 84,521 customers in the personal attention group were divided into a test group that received all the communications, plus a control group that received only the basic retention package.

The monthly attrition rate of those customers in Priorities A and B who received the special personalized attention was 2.2 percent per month, whereas the controls in those two priorities had an attrition rate of 3.5 percent per month. The program thus reduced the overall attrition rate of these customers by 37 percent, yielding an overall reduction in annual attrition of $7.9 million dollars in these high priority groups.

Summary

Business customers can be divided into Bargain Hunters, Program Buyers, Transaction Buyers and Relationship Buyers. There is profit in all types, but relationship buyers respond better to database marketing than do other types.

Once you have identified your relationship buyers, you can increase their loyalty and sales by a number of techniques, including:

- Special communications
  - □ A Web page with PIN numbers for each customer.
  - □ Advisory panels.
  - □ Newsletters.
  - □ Professional contests.
  - □ Thank you letters.
  - □ Set up test and control groups to prove that what you are doing is paying off.
  - □ Shift from the sales force full court press model, to an integrated account model with the field representatives becoming business consultants, and orders taken by phone, fax, e-mail or the Web site.

- Use measurement of the lifetime value of your customers to determine the value of a strategy before you have spent serious money on it.

  The formula for the discount rate in business to business is:

  $$\text{Discount rate} = ((1 + \text{interest rate}) \times (\text{risk factor}))^{\text{Year} + \text{AR}/365}$$

- Web sites can reduce processing time, improve accuracy, save processing costs, and improve cash flow. On the other hand, they are expensive to set up, and require regular maintenance. Their effect on costs should be estimated in advance.
  - □ The old-fashioned method of looking at sales by industry has been replaced by looking at lifetime value by industry. It helps to focus your attention on the most important companies.
  - □ Customers can also be ranked by lifetime value, with retention activities focussed on the more valuable customers.
  - □ Businesses now serve their customers over toll-free lines with agents reading company data off a computer screen. The Web will permit customers to access that data directly, saving the cost of the agent and the telephone call.

Executive Quiz 14

Answers to quiz questions (Figure 14-16) can be found in Appendix B.

	Put the appropriate letter before each answer	
	Questions	**Answers**
a	Least service pays highest price	5.82
b	Risk rate 1.6, Interest 8%, payment 80 days, 3 yr disc. Rate=?	Advisory council
c	Builds customer loyalty	Bargain Hunters
d	Not prime candidates for b 2 b database marketing	Gold Customers
e	Shift from supplier to supplier	Price
f	Most service pays lowest price	Program Buyer
g	Most important to transaction buyers	Relationship buyers
h	Most important segment for any business	Talk price
i	How to ruin relationship buyers	Transaction Buyers

Figure 14-16. Quiz 14.

15

Financial Services

Over the past three years, research has taught us several lessons: Nearly half of our customers are unprofitable; almost 20% are very unprofitable. Balances are only loosely correlated with profitability. Demographics are even more poorly correlated with profitability. As a result, every day, over half the new accounts sold will never be profitable. Every day our staff work very hard to retain customers who destroy customer value... We have also learned that it is hard, if not impossible, to profitably cross sell our most profitable customers. Most sales to them cannibalize profitable usage. Sales efforts to these good customers should be restricted to retention-aiding devices.

RANDALL GROSSMAN
Former SVP Fleet Bank.

"The need for insurance is usually tied closely to life stage events. Insurance companies should make sustained efforts to gather descriptive family information from their own policyholders through questionnaires, agents, or customer service contacts. Companies can also append purchased data to their policyholder records... The objective is to make offers that are relevant to each life stage, rather than offering the same type of coverage to all individuals and families... This is an approach that successful agents follow intuitively. Database managers at company headquarters can assist in the process by appending and updating information in their central marketing database

so that it is available to agents and marketers through-
out the company. "

PIERRE PASSAVANT
President of Kobs Gregory Passavant

Financial services offer one of the most profitable applications for database marketing. This is so because financial institutions:

- usually have a lot of useful information about their customer's demographics and purchase history;
- can accurately determine the profitability of each customer;
- are usually important to their customers' lives;
- have many opportunities to interact with their customers during the average month.

Despite these advantages, banks and other financial institutions have been slow in taking advantage of their database marketing opportunities. To build a marketing database, most banks had to start by attempting to consolidate all their customer's accounts into a single Marketing Customer Information File (MCIF) so that they could understand each household's financial situation. This was not easy. Most banks had their mortgage loans on one computer, checking accounts on another, credit cards on a third. The records were created by different people in different formats, based on accounts, not on customers. It took most banks several years to realize the importance of an MCIF and muster the resources to create one. This all came at a time of great turmoil in the banking industry in the 1990s during which almost half of the U.S. banks were acquired and consolidated with other banks—thus further complicating the MCIF creation problem.

Once the MCIFs were created, however, there was no great rush among banks to do any relationship marketing. Why not? Mainly because banks were then and still are organized along product lines. There were separate vice presidents for credit cards, retail banking, home mortgages, automobile loans, trust accounts, etc. Each VP was expected to improve sales and profits in his department. The manager of credit cards was not compensated for the number of credit card customers who signed up for a checking account or an auto loan. Nor did the other VPs care much about credit card operations. People do what is in their own economic self-interest.

I was approached at a recent conference by an assistant vice president of a bank who was in charge of selling insurance. He asked me what he could do to sell more insurance to his customers and improve the retention rate of those that he already had. He explained that he had been sending letters to existing insurance customers trying to build a relationship with them, but it was not paying off.

"The best way to sell insurance to bank customers," I told him, "is to examine the MCIF to determine which customers are most likely to buy insurance, and market to them. If they don't have insurance now, but since they already have another account with the bank, they should be responsive. For those who now have insurance, the best way to retain them is to sell them another non-insurance bank product. Once they have two or more bank products, their retention rate for insurance should be higher."

"Oh, I couldn't do that. They won't let me have access to the names of other bank customers."

This is the problem.

Many banks today have gotten religion. They understand that customers look at their bank as a single institution, not as a bunch of unrelated products. They understand that to improve sales and retention, they have to become a total financial solution, looking at customers and households, instead of individual product owners. Banks have discovered that there is a clear relationship between the number of bank products owned by a customer and the customer's retention rate. It looks something like Figure 15-1.

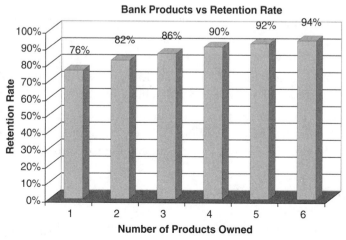

Figure 15-1. Increasing retention rate based on number of bank products owned.

Why is this so? Because if you have a credit card only at a bank, you obviously have your checking account somewhere else. You do not think of this card issuer as your bank. If you get an offer for a cheaper card, you might well take it. But if you have your checking account and savings account at a bank plus the credit card, you will most likely tend to think of the credit card as a part of your total banking experience. You may know the branch personnel. Will they not wonder why you dropped their card?

Unintended Consequences

I had breakfast one day at the National Center for Database Marketing with a marketing officer from a medium-sized bank. The management had come to realize how important it was to customer loyalty to have multiproduct customers. They offered a substantial bonus to all senior branch personnel in those branches that had a high percentage of 5+ customers—meaning customers who were using five or more of the bank's products. The policy was working: every branch was focused on this objective, but the results were far from what was intended. Many branches were turning down new accounts: they ruined the branch's 5+ percentage!

Many banks, however, have found a way to organize themselves to take advantage of their MCIF files and create profitable relationships with their customers. The key to their success was the analysis of profitability. There are three steps:

- Develop an accurate and credible system for determining the profitability of each customer on a periodic basis, preferably at least monthly, using day-to-day inputs on interest rates and costs.

- Develop segmentation schemes that divide customers into useful and actionable segments based on profitability.

- Develop and implement tactics, based on these segments, which are used to modify the behavior of employees and customers to increase sales, improve retention, lower costs, and improve profits.

Profitability Calculation

Profitability calculation is the heart of the system. It is defined as the total profit (less all expenses) earned each month by the products and services owned by a single customer. It is complex, but it is computed automatically by bank software for every product for every customer every month. To understand it, one must understand a few banking terms. It is worth taking the time, because profitability determination is the foundation for a number of very profitable and advanced database marketing segmentation and behavior modification techniques. One of the experts in the use of profitability analysis in banking is Robert James, who was Group Manager at the Centura Bank. Bob, a graduate of the Database Marketing Institute, had 24 years of banking experience at the time. Here is how he listed the concepts vital to understanding profitability:

Cost of funds. Banks obtain money from depositors and loan it out to borrowers. They make money on the difference in what they pay depositors and what they earn from borrowers. The Cost of Funds is the amount of interest expense paid for the funds used.

Funding credit. The amount earned by the bank on the deposits employed.

Margin. The difference between the interest earned and the interest expense.

Loan loss provision. All loans have risk and some loans never get repaid. The loan loss provision is a pool of dollars reserved by banks to cover expected loan losses.

Capital allocation. Capital is the equity of a company, the difference between assets and liabilities. Capital allocation is the amount of capital set aside for each product to cover unexpected losses and is based on the overall risk profile of the product.

Capital charge. The capital allocated multiplied by the bank's desired rate of return on the capital assigned to the product.

Overhead. The fixed and variable expenses associated with the product. These include origination expense, transaction expense, maintenance, and personnel expense. The cost of a customer visiting a branch to cash a check may amount to $1.65 per visit. This is part of overhead.

FDIC expense. The cost of providing deposit insurance through the Federal Deposit Insurance Corporation.

These are banking terms. But the concepts underlying profitability apply to any industry where detailed costs are available, such as insurance, and many service industries.

Using these terms, let us compute the monthly profitability for a typical customer product—an automobile loan. This four-year loan originated two years ago for $15,500 at a rate of 8.5 percent. At this point, the average outstanding balance is $9,806.66. The net profitability of this loan, last month, was $13.74. Here is how that profitability was calculated:

Automobile Loan

Average balance	$9,806.66
Capital allocated	$367.75
Interest income	$69.46
Less cost of funds	$46.50
Margin	$22.96
Fees	$0.00
Gross profit	**$22.96**
Less:	
Capital charge	$4.88
Loan loss provision	$3.27
Overhead	$1.07
Total costs	**$9.22**
Net product value	**$13.74**

This says that for this product for this customer last month, the bank made a profit of $13.74 after all costs related to the product were deducted from the revenue.

For comparison, here is the profitability calculation for a checking account:

Non-Interest-Bearing Checking Account

Average balance	$1,184.84
Capital allocated	$2.96
Funding credit	$5.24
Fees (service charge)	$6.50
Gross profit	$11.74

Less:

Capital charge	$0.04
FDIC expense	$0.03
Overhead	$15.17
Total costs	$15.24
Net product value	–$3.49

In this case, the bank lost $3.49 on this account last month. The gross monthly profit of $11.74 from the average balance of $1,184 was overwhelmed by the high overhead costs of $15.17. The overhead includes the fact that this customer visited the branch several times last month to make deposits or cash checks. At $1.65 expense per visit, his branch visits wiped out the profitability of this particular product. By comparing these two calculations, you will note that the capital allocation for a checking account is significantly less than for a loan. This is because, for a bank, loans are more risky than checking accounts.

The same process is repeated each month for every product owned by every customer with the bank. Once completed, a customer's household profitability is computed by summing the net product values for all products owned by the household. It looks something like this:

Customer J. Smith Monthly Profitability Measurement (Figure 15-2).
This customer's total monthly profit to the bank is $101.51.

Creating Profitability Segments

After computing every customer's monthly profitability, you group them into customer profitability segments. Figure 15-3 is an actual example of the way one bank grouped its customers into profitability segments. They created five groups.

This can be graphed as a now familiar chart (Figure 15-4).

	Average Balance	Profit
Automobile Loan	$9,806.66	$13.74
Checking Account	$1,184.84	($3.49)
Certificate of Deposit	$15,000.00	$27.05
Credit Card	$2,917.66	$8.11
Home equity loan	$20,420.90	$56.10
Total Profit		**$101.51**

Figure 15-2. Monthly profitability calculation.

Monthly Profit from All Customers				
Segment	Households	% Households	Total Profit	% Profits
5	20,126	5%	$11,180,791	79.67%
4	46,706	11%	$3,483,724	24.82%
3	118,273	28%	$2,221,018	15.83%
2	119,804	28%	$212,669	1.52%
1	118,394	28%	-$3,063,817	-21.83%
Total	423,303	100%	$14,034,385	100%

Figure 15-3. Bank customers segmented by profitability.

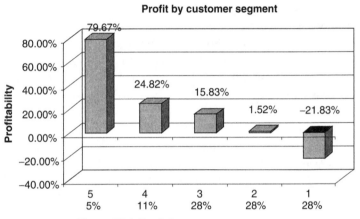

Figure 15-4. Profit by customer segment.

Every customer in the bank was classified as a 5, 4, 3, 2, or 1, where 5 represents most profitable customer and 1 represents the least profitable customers. What this chart shows is that the top group, representing only 5 percent of the bank's customers, was responsible for almost 80 percent of the bank's total profit. The bottom group, consisting of 28 percent of the bank customers, was responsible for a loss of almost 22 percent of the bank's profit. This is amazing and insightful information. Until the creation of MCIFs and monthly profitability analysis, no bank in America had this kind of information. Most banks still lack it today.

Once a bank has done this calculation, the profitability segment designation is stored in each customer's database file every month. A personal profile of each bank customer is made available to all customer contact personnel at each point of contact with the customer, including teller lines, service desks, or branch manager's offices. The profile can include:

- addresses and phones numbers;
- birth dates, and social security numbers;
- home ownership with date at present address;
- occupation and employer;
- other financial institutions where the person banks;
- the bank officer assigned and the branch;
- whether the customer has filed a financial statement;
- all accounts with their current balances, line amounts, and amount owed;
- the profitability segment to which the customer belongs;
- suggested next best product for the customer.

Turning Knowledge into Action

Statistical analysts at the bank use these data to build models to predict the lifetime value of each customer, which products a customer is most likely to need next, and which behavior change will improve the customer's profitability. These solutions are shown on the customer's database record screen. Customer contact personnel then utilize the knowledge to improve cross-sell and up-sell opportunities, to make better decisions regarding pricing and fee waivers, and to suggest alternative channels for certain types of transactions.

Each of the five profitability segments has different customer behavior goals:

- For 5s—the Gold customers—and 4s, the goal is to retain them, acquire more like them, and expand their purchase of bank products. Since the profit segments, 5s and 4s, represent only 16 percent of the customer households, but up to 105 percent of the monthly profit, the bank will want to allocate substantial human and marketing resources toward retaining these customers. And, since human resources are limited, particularly those resources devoted to sales, the bank should attempt to direct the acquisition activities of their calling officers to prospects who have the potential to be profit segment 5s or 4s.

- For 3s the goal is simply to get them to expand their use of products.
- For 1s and 2s the goals are to re-price their unprofitable products such as loans or certificates of deposit as they mature or are renewed. Concerted efforts are used to migrate these customers' routine transactions to less expensive alternative channels of delivery, such as ATMs, and call centers.

Gold Customer Programs

Once you know who the Gold customers are, what can you do to be sure you retain them? Banks are using such tactics as:

- identifying and assigning Personal Bankers to them;
- making sure that they get the best service including:
  - priority problem resolution;
  - priority telephone response;
  - discretionary pricing initiatives.
- providing special communications strategies including:
  - outbound calls from their Personal Banker;
  - special mailings and product offers;
  - annual thank you mailings;
  - reward programs.

One bank has the profitability segment built into the software that controls their customer service call director. Gold customers' calls are identified before they are answered and are picked up on the first ring. Unprofitable customers may have to wait for five or six rings before anyone answers, and even then, it is likely to be a voice or touch tone activated machine.

Analysis of Behavior by Profitability Segment

Beyond identifying profitability segments is the analysis to determine why some customers are so profitable or so unprofitable. For example, one bank divided their entire customer base into 50 segments, from most profitable to least, each representing 2 percent of all customers, and ranked them by the number of bank products that they were using

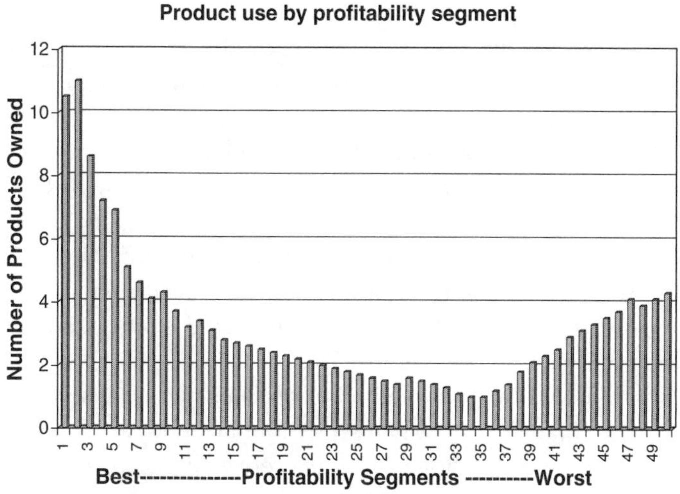

Figure 15-5. Product use by profitability segment.

(Figure 15-5). We have already established that the more products a customer uses, the higher is their retention rate. But how does their profitability vary by product usage?

What the bank learned from this analysis was that both the best and the worst customers used a lot of bank products. The average customers used only a few. This suggests that while high product use leads to high retention, it does not necessarily lead to high profits.

A similar analysis was done of the same bank customers ranked by the number of times they visited bank branches. This also showed that both the best and the worst visited bank branches a lot. The average customer banked by mail or at an ATM. *Any policy designed to discourage expensive branch visits would seriously threaten the bank's very best customers who bring in 80 percent of the bank's profits.*

Computing Lifetime Value and Potential Lifetime Profitability

It is not enough to know the current profitability of a customer. You need to be able to predict the future by making accurate forecasts of each customer's potential lifetime profitability. To forecast the future, you determine for each customer the likelihood of your being able to sell them additional profitable products and the expected net revenue from usage of those products minus the promotional expense involved in the sale of the products. This forecast is added to current profitability to create a reasonably reliable lifetime profitability forecast which can drive bank marketing strategy and tactics.

Fleet developed a bank-wide MCIF originally maintained with an external vendor. Once it was up and running, they took their first measure of customer value by simply adding up all non-mortgage deposit and loan balances for each customer. This was a beginning. Next they created the software necessary to determine the Net Income after deduction of the Cost of Capital (NIACC) for all retail customers. For a typical customer, it looked something like Figure 15-6.

This is a slightly different method of profitability calculation from that shown earlier. It arrives at the same basic number, however. In this annual calculation for a typical customer, the net profitability is $63, due principally to the fact that the customer invested in mutual funds. Without this investment, the customer would have represented a loss of $166 to the bank.

As a second step, Fleet extended this system to its commercial customers. They were using industry benchmark costs for computing profitability. When these processes were working properly, the bank created an in-house data warehouse, which enabled them to keep all of this data current and use actual Fleet activity based costs, rather than industry benchmark numbers.

At their PC workstations, power users including both marketing and business analysts accessed the data on each customer, did analytical work and modeling, and developed marketing initiatives. The analysis server,

	Check & Savings	Home Equity	Credit Card	Mutual Funds	Total
Revenue					
Net interest	$210	$248	–$280	$0	$178
Fees	$18	$18	$396	$1,500	$1,932
Total Revenue	$228	$266	$116	$1,500	$2,110
Expenses					
Amort.Sales Costs	$20	$120	$67	$75	$282
Acc. Maint.	$30	$75	$40	$900	$1,045
Transact Cost	$193	$21	$0	$30	$244
Allocated Overhead	$0	$0	$0	$0	$0
Total Expenses	$243	$216	$107	$1,005	$1,571
Loss Provision	$0	$23	$160	$0	$183
Net Income	–$15	$27	–$151	$495	$356
Taxes	–$6	$11	–$60	$198	$143
NI After Taxes	–$9	$16	–$91	$297	$213
Cost of Capital	$1	$49	$32	$68	$150
NIACC	–$10	–$33	–$123	$229	$63

Figure 15-6. Alternate method of profitability calculation.

for example, provided for statistical analysis, neural networks, ad hoc query and analysis, and geodemographic analysis. The data mart provided summarized, preformatted data for promotion design, tracking, and analysis, and enabled the users to do point and click, drill down analysis. The management-reporting server provided on-demand reports which could be modified by the users.

Preliminary Lessons Learned

The new system enabled Fleet bank management, for the first time, to really understand their customer profitability and to do something about it. As Randall Grossman, Senior Vice President and Director of Customer Data Management and Analysis at Fleet Financial Group, explained, the data showed that:

- Half of all customers were unprofitable.
- 20 percent were very unprofitable.
- The balances that people maintained were only loosely correlated with profitability.
- Demographics were even more poorly correlated with profitability.
- Half of the new accounts being currently sold would never be profitable.
- The bank staff was working hard every day to retain customers who would destroy customer value.

Even though half of all customers were considered unprofitable, the marketing staff realized that they could not simply walk away from half of their customer base. Further analysis showed that:

- It was almost impossible profitably to cross-sell the most profitable customers. Most of these sales cannibalized existing profitable products. For these Gold customers, it was determined that marketing should focus on retention, not cross or up selling.
- Some customer profits and losses were temporary, not permanent.
- Some low-profit customers had great potential, sometimes because their assets were elsewhere and they were, in fact, Gold customers at another bank.
- Some unprofitable customers could be nudged into profitability if they were offered the right products at the right prices.
- There were, however, many customers for whom there was very little potential for profit.

What to Do with the Information?

Faced with these sobering facts, the Grossman's marketing staff decided to figure out ways to use the database that they had created to turn the situation around. The key to their strategy was to develop three measures of customer value:

- Lifetime profitability,
- Potential profitability,
- Potential customer value.

Lifetime Profitability

Lifetime profitability is the net present value of the expected future stream of net income after the cost of capital, discounted at the corporate hurdle rate. It is calculated based on the current products that the customer is now using, including planned re-pricing. The corporate hurdle rate is that required rate of return in a discounted cash flow analysis, above which an investment makes sense and below which it does not. Discounted cash flow is a method of evaluating an investment by estimating future cash flows and taking into consideration the time value of money (the discount rate). As calculated by the bank, customer profitability differed from organizational or product profitability for several reasons.

Many customers' business with the bank cut across business lines, whereas organizational profitability was computed by adding up the profits from each line of business. Some costs in the Fleet system, such as overhead, were not allocated to each customer, since the methods for doing this involved arbitrary decisions which Fleet managers thought might distort the real profitability of the customer to the bank.

For those costs that were allocated to the customer, the allocation had, of necessity, to use standard cost factors (such as the cost of a branch visit, telephone call, or product sale) for which it was not cost effective to determine accurately based on each specific event. Customer profitability did not "roll up." If two customers shared the same account, the bank gave full credit to both (which one is the decision maker?). For this reason, you could not add up each customer's profitability to get total bank profitability. Organizationally, of course, the account was only counted once, not twice, so product profitability did add up to a bank total.

Given these qualifications, lifetime customer profitability was calculated for each bank customer and stored in the customer's database record each month. Customers were then ranked and segmented. It was possible to pick out the Gold customers, those just below Gold, the average customers, and the unprofitable customers. Each customer's profitability status was flagged in each customer record so that marketers and branch personnel could recognize the customer's value to the bank and develop appropriate strategies and tactics.

Potential Profitability

Potential Profitability carried the Fleet analysis one step further. A typical customer had a limited number of bank products. There were usually many other bank products that the customer could be using. The probability of a given customer purchasing an additional product was determined using CHAID analysis (see Chapter 9). For example, if a customer owned a home with a mortgage of W, had a checking account with an average balance of X, a savings account with an average balance of Y, and a monthly credit card usage rate of Z, an age of 44 years, and two children in college, CHAID was used to predict the likelihood of him purchasing:

	Probability (%)
An auto loan	12
A home equity loan	16
A personal loan	12
Mutual Funds	21
A Certificate of Deposit	3

CHAID was also used to predict the average balance that he would maintain on each of the possible additional products. Logistic regressions were then used to determine the expected NIACC that the bank would realize from the possible sale of each of these products to the customer. In each case, an estimate was made of the promotional expense involved in getting him to purchase the product. The potential profitability was then calculated for each product as the:

$$\text{Probability of purchase} \times \text{Expected NIACC from}$$
$$\text{usage} - \text{Promotional expense}$$

The profitability calculation software then added up each of the products for this customer with a positive NIACC to get the potential profit.

Potential Customer Value was then determined for each customer by adding together the lifetime profitability (with current products) and the potential profitability (from possible new products). This value was stored in every customer's database record and used to select the most likely candidates for promotion for each product in direct mail or e-mail promotions. It was also used to suggest the next best product when branch personnel were talking to the customer or customer service had them on the line.

Customer Retention Tactics

Knowing who is profitable and who is not is important. But eventually, you have to come down to tactics: how do you persuade a customer to do what you want them to do? How do you keep customers from defecting? Credit card managers have to deal with defections on a daily basis. They call it "churn." A high percentage of the American public received competing credit card offers every week. Some of them accepted the offers and dropped cards, which their banks had spent more than $80 to get them to accept. How can you get customers to keep their cards?

As already explained, the best method is to sell them another product. The more products the bank customers have from a particular bank, the less likely they are to drop any particular product. But, ultimately, we will have to do something directly for the credit card customers who are likely to drop their cards. There is, by now, a fairly straightforward method of churn reduction, which combines lifetime value and probability modeling to achieve satisfactory results. Here is the way it works.

Let us consider a typical bank that has 369,502 credit card customers, with an annual churn rate of about 18 percent. If it costs the bank $80 to acquire a credit card customer, the annual loss of the acquisition costs due to churn is about $5,320,829—a tidy sum. Something has to be done. Most banks with a large number of credit card holders allocate an annual retention budget to be spent on projects aimed at getting these defectors to change their minds. Let us suppose that the bank management has set up a retention budget of $700,000. They want to make the best use of this fund. If they allocate it equally to all cardholders, it will amount to $1.89 per cardholder per year. They are not going to change many minds for $1.89 each. Either the budget must be increased or it must be allocated in a much more intelligent way than spending it equally on all cardholders.

The intelligent way to begin is to build a statistical model of all card-holders to determine which customers are most likely to drop their cards. Such a model can be based on experience over the last several years. From these years, we know who dropped the card. The model can include such factors as:

- average amount charged per year,
- average unpaid balance each month,
- number of other bank products owned,
- number of other cards owned,
- income of the card holder,
- number of years with the bank and with the card,
- balances maintained on other product accounts.

A regression model or a neural network (see Chapter 9) can be run, using these and other factors, to develop a score for all cardholders. The score indicates who is most likely to drop the card in the near future. A score of 95 indicates that the cardholder is 95 percent likely to drop the card in the next six months. A very low score predicts that this customer will probably keep his card. Figure 15-7 shows what the model could predict.

To be sure that our retention budget does the most good, we should ignore those loyal customers who are unlikely to drop their card. In this illustration, we are going to concentrate on all customers who have a score of 60 percent or better. There are 276,560 of these customers. We have safely cut 92,942 customers from our retention program, which gives us more money to spend on the more likely droppers.

Next, we want to consider lifetime value. We can compute the lifetime value of card holders based on methods developed throughout this book.

Figure 15-8 shows how the bank determined the lifetime value of a group of customers who were using its credit cards. This segment of customers had an annual profitability of $241. It cost $80 to acquire them. Their retention rate was about 85 percent. The bank spent about $8 each year in retention programs. In the third year, the lifetime value of the customers in this segment was about $451. If you compare this lifetime value chart to those in Chapter 3, you will notice that the costs are computed differently. That is because bank profitability includes all costs except acquisition and marketing costs. As you can see, the retention rate of loyal customers goes up and their profitability goes up as

Cardholders Ranked By Likelihood to Churn				
A	B	C	D	E
Score	Total Base	Actual Attrition	Percent Attrition	Cumulative Base
95	3,315	1,619	48.84	3,315
90	15,014	3,974	26.47	18,329
85	26,378	4,858	18.42	44,707
80	39,923	7,139	17.88	84,630
75	32,874	5,226	15.90	117,504
70	33,926	6,182	18.22	151,430
65	53,536	6,992	13.06	204,966
60	71,594	9,274	12.95	276,560
55	34,870	2,709	7.77	311,430
50	18,733	907	4.84	330,163
45	12,844	412	3.21	343,007
40	9,833	513	5.22	352,840
35	7,400	223	3.02	360,240
30	6,411	205	3.20	366,651
25	2,355	74	3.16	369,006
20	464	0	0.00	369,470
15	32	0	0.00	369,502
Totals	369,502	56,672	11.28	369,502

Figure 15-7. Selection of credit card customers by likelihood to churn.

	Acquisition Year	Second Year	Third Year
Card Members	13,433	11,418	10,048
Retention Rate	85.00%	88.00%	92.00%
Annual Profitability	$241	$248	$255
Total Revenue	$3,237,353	$2,831,676	$2,562,210
Acquisition Cost $80	$1,074,640	$0	$0
Marketing Costs $8	$107,464	$91,344	$80,383
Total Costs	$1,182,104	$91,344	$80,383
Profit	$2,055,249	$2,740,332	$2,481,827
Discount Rate	1.00	1.20	1.44
Net Present Value Profit	$2,055,249	$2,283,610	$1,723,491
Cumulative NPV Profit	$2,055,249	$4,338,859	$6,062,350
Lifetime Value	$153.00	$323.00	$451.30

Figure 15-8. Lifetime value of credit card customers based on profitability.

well. The actual computation of lifetime value for bank customers is more complicated than this chart appears to show because of the fact that most bank customers tend to have more than one bank product. Their retention rate and lifetime value tends, therefore, to be higher than those who have only one product.

This type of lifetime value is computed for all credit card customers. They are ranked in lifetime value groups for the purpose of allocating the credit card retention budget. The ranking looks like that shown in Figure 15-9.

As you look at this chart, you can see that some customers are more valuable than others. What is the point of working to retain customers with a low lifetime value? Once you know their lifetime value, you can spend your retention budget on those who have the highest lifetime value. In this case, the bank decided to make a major effort to retain those 55,323 likely droppers who have a lifetime value of $450 or more. What can we do to retain these people? You can, of course, sell them additional products. That is the first step. A second step would be to provide some inducements. There are many possibilities. Here are seven typical inducements:

- Increase the credit line.

- Upgrade the card to Gold status.

- Provide cash advance checks.

- Reduce the interest rate.

- Reduce the annual fee.

- Waive the annual fee.

- Provide air miles for every dollar spent.

Each inducement had a cost to the bank. Each inducement also was more or less effective in reducing attrition. The average attrition was

Lifetime Value of 276,560 Cardholders Most Likely To Churn				
A	B	C	D	E
Average Lifetime Value	Number Members	Cumulative Members	Cumulative Percent Members	Total Lifetime Value
$637.24	17,723	17,723	6.41%	$11,293,805
$550.00	11,334	29,057	10.51%	$6,233,700
$500.00	12,833	41,890	15.15%	$6,416,500
$450.00	13,433	55,323	20.00%	$6,044,850
$400.00	15,534	70,857	25.62%	$6,213,600
$350.00	18,556	89,413	32.33%	$6,494,600
$300.00	20,356	109,769	39.69%	$6,106,800
$250.00	25,543	135,312	48.93%	$6,385,750
$200.00	31,456	166,768	60.30%	$6,291,200
$150.00	35,993	202,761	73.32%	$5,398,950
$100.00	41,789	244,550	88.43%	$4,178,900
$50.00	26,578	271,128	98.04%	$1,328,900
$0.00	5,432	276,560	100.00%	$0

Figure 15-9. Credit card customers arranged by lifetime value.

	C	D	E	F	G	H	I	J
Inducements	Members	Dollars	Dollars	Attrition	Est.	Est.	Total	Gained/
Average LTV $531	Selected	Budgeted	Per	Red.	Attrition	Red.	LTV Gain	$ Spent
	(Max 20K	(Col C	Member	Percent	(18%	(Col G	(Col H	(Col I
	/ Line	* Col E)			of Col C)	* Col F)	* $531	/ Col D)
Increased Credit Line	20,000	$157,600	$7.88	14.00%	3,600	504	$267,624	$1.70
Upgrade to Gold	2,000	$25,040	$12.52	21.00%	360	76	$40,144	$1.60
Cash Advance Checks	20,000	$70,000	$3.50	6.50%	3,600	234	$124,254	$1.78
Reduce Interest Rate	7,323	$204,971	$27.99	49.00%	1,318	646	$342,967	$1.67
Reduce Annual Fee	2,000	$70,000	$35.00	60.00%	360	216	$114,696	$1.64
Waive Annual Fee	2,000	$80,000	$40.00	69.00%	360	248	$131,900	$1.65
Provide Air Miles	2,000	$90,000	$45.00	72.00%	360	259	$137,635	$1.53
Total	55,323	$697,611			9,958	2,183	$1,159,220	$1.66

Credit Card Retention Budget Calculation Chart

Figure 15-10. Calculation of the ideal allocation of a credit card holder retention budget.

18 percent per year. Figure 15-10 shows how a budget of about $700,000 could be spent most efficiently in reducing churn among the 55,323 people most likely to drop the card who had an average lifetime value of $450 or more. We are making an assumption here that the management has limited us to a budget of $700,000, and further required that we not include more than 20,000 customers in any one inducement, with a minimum of 2,000 in each inducement as a test of its effectiveness.

What the chart shows is that since the average lifetime value of these 55,323 customers is $531, we can save that amount by preventing the attrition of some of these cardholders. We know that 18 percent of them were going to leave us if we do nothing about it. By using these inducements, we can persuade 2,183 cardholders to stay. Their lifetime value is $1,159,220. We have spent $697,611 to keep these cardholders, a return of $1.66 for every $1 spent.

The mathematics of this chart is tricky, since we want to stay within the budget, provide some inducement for all 55,323 cardholders, stay within management's arbitrary limitations, and maximize the lifetime value gain. The reader may enjoy working with this chart in the software that is available to readers of this book. The free software is at www.dbmarketing.com.

Prospecting Using E-mails

Kestler Financial Group, Inc. (KFG) is a national field marketing organization serving over 5,500 independent insurance brokers. KFG specializes in annuities, life insurance, long-term care insurance, and seminars selling systems and securities. When they began, KFG sent plain text e-mails to their brokers asking them to e-mail or call KFG with data on quotes. These e-mails did not contain a way to gather data directly from the e-mail, so response rates were low.

By shifting to a system developed by ExactTarget, KFG increased the impact of their e-mails and made the creation process easier. The surveys let KFG gather information directly from each e-mail, making it easy for agents in different time zones or on tight schedules to contact them. They sent bi-monthly e-mails that let a broker request an immediate annuity quote. The new e-mails included sales information, personal incentives, and selling tools. For example, one e-mail included 20 free prospecting letters to send to clients. The system permitted KFG to connect with an agent while he or she was still browsing through the letters.

The return on investment from the new e-mail system proved to be $4,400 for every dollar spent on the ExactTarget software. In a single month, quotes increased by over 12 million, 5.5 million of which were converted to sales. Click-through rates to e-mails were as high as 24 percent and open rates were around 50 percent. When open rates and click-through rates dropped from time to time, KFG used the system to find out what topics were currently of interest to their agents. This information was included in their next e-communication.

Credit Card Case Study

A bank sought to reduce defections and increase the use of its card. They asked KnowledgeBase Marketing to develop models to identify those highly profitable customers who were most likely to drop their credit cards. These customers were then treated with targeted personalized communications.

To determine profitability, they developed an algorithm that was applied to all of the bank's credit card customers:

Profitability score = Interchange income + Finance Charges + Fees
and Charges – Cost of Funds – Delinquency costs.

To determine the likelihood to defect, a series of neural network models were applied to 953 voluntary defectors and 9,520 randomly selected active accounts. After review of the results, the best of four neural networks were chosen along with two regression models.

Attribute	Tendency
Balance Carried	Defection as revolving balance goes up
Disputes & CS Communications	Retained as contacts go up
Reissue Flag	Retained when not up for reissue
Credit Bureau Score	Defection as score goes up
Trend on Purchase Activity	Retained when increasing

Figure 15-11. Indicators of potential churn.

The models showed the indicators of potential churn given in Figure 15-11.

Once the bank was able to identify those high-value customers most likely to defect, they began a proactive campaign to communicate with them to prevent them from leaving and to increase their appreciation of and use of their credit cards. After six months, the level of churn in the targeted groups had dropped by 73 percent compared to the controls which did not get personalized attention. The level of spending by these same groups had increased by 42 percent as compared to the controls.

Age and Income Are Not Enough

A major brokerage firm had been using age and income-based list selections to target their direct mail to prospective mutual fund buyers. Analysis showed that even though the "over 30 years old, $100,000+ income" segment was more likely than the general population to respond, over 90 percent of their buyers were not coming from this segment. In other words, targeting this group would provide a lift over random selection, but would also exclude the vast majority of likely responders. To understand what was going on, they built a model using financial and demographic data. The model showed them how to select prospects so that they could effectively reach over 75 percent of likely buyers instead of 10 percent—a huge improvement over their age and income selection strategy. The model illustrated that buyers of investment products today can no longer be effectively targeted just by age and income. With so many investors in the market, net worth, risk preferences, and attitudes are becoming important in defining customer segments.

In another case, a major mutual fund company marketed a complete line of different funds by direct mail and telemarketing. They were using just age and income to select prospects from compiled lists. They wondered if perhaps they were missing the mark by not selecting different lists based upon their prospects' expected tolerances for risk and their fund preferences. A consultant took a sample of their investor files across several of their different funds, overlaid demographic information, and developed segment profiles. It was clear that they were indeed selling their different funds to markedly different segments; in fact, in several cases, the segments buying conservative funds were mutually exclusive from those investing in aggressive funds. Their marketing plan that had tried to target both types of funds with the same lists could not possibly reach both types of buyers and would actually do a poor job of reaching either group. Based upon the model results, they revamped their entire strategy to target their funds to specific segments.

Executive Quiz 15

Answers to quiz questions (Figure 15-12) can be found in Appendix B.

Put the appropriate letter before each definition		
	Term to be defined	Definition
a	Ad hoc queries	% customers who drop a product in a time period
b	Capital allocation	Access tools that permit answers to any question
c	Capital charge	Amount earned by the bank on the deposits employed
d	CHAID	Analytic tools permitting users to view details behind any query.
e	Churn rate	Capital set aside to cover unexpected losses
f	Corporate Hurdle Rate	Chi-square Automatic Interaction Detection
g	Cost of funds	Cost deposit insurance
h	Drill Down Analysis	Customer Profitability if she were to buy all likely products
i	FDIC Expense	Desired rate of return on capital assigned to the product.
j	Funding credit	Difference between interest earned and interest expense
k	Lifetime Value	Dollars to cover expected loan losses.
l	Loan Loss Provision	Fixed and variable expense of a product
m	Margin	Interest expense paid for the funds used
n	MCIF	Manipulation of data in a database using a mouse
o	Neural Networks	Marketing Customer Information File
p	NIACC	Monthly profit (less all expenses) provided by a single customer
q	Overhead	Net Income after deduction of the Cost of Capital
r	Point and Click	NPV of future profits from a single customer
s	Potential Lifetime Profitability	ROI above which the investment makes sense
t	Profitability	Software combining multiple multiple regressions

Figure 15-12. Quiz 15.

16

Why Databases Fail

Database marketing, properly conceived and executed, can bring your company customer loyalty, repeat sales, reduced costs, cross sales, improved identification of prospects, and a continuing boost to your bottom line. But if you go about it in the wrong way, it will not bring you any of these things—and it could be a costly failure. In this chapter, we present the nine most common errors that lead to database failure.

Mistake 1: Lack of Marketing Strategy

Database marketing has at last caught on. There is not a major corporation that does not have a director of database marketing with a customer marketing database of some sort. All over America, marketers are collecting names of people who have bought their products. "When we get enough," they say, "We will have a marketing database!" But what they seldom think through is what they are going to do with the names once they have them. How can they turn a list of names and transactions into profits? That is a tough question to answer.

A marketing plan using a database aims at building a relationship with each customer—making her feel recognized and special. You become an old friend. You give her things that she wants: recognition, information and service, and she gives you what you want: loyalty and repeat sales.

But how are you going to do that? To go from a list of names and addresses to building a relationship is a giant leap. Somewhere in your plan there must be a practical program for using the names, which accomplishes a definite objective. You will need:

- Some benefit that the customer will gain by being on the database

- A control group that does not get special attention so you can measure whether your relationship building really pays off

- An achievable numeric goal which can be translated into profits

- A series of practical steps, which modify customer and company behavior to reach the goal

- A segmentation system that separates profitable customers from unprofitable customers, and treats them differently

- A long-range (three year) plan with a budget that lasts long enough so that it is possible to show results

The list of possible steps might contain:

- Membership cards with points and credits
- Newsletters with coupons
- Surveys and responses
- Personal letters, e-mails, and telephone calls
- Recognition and special services

Many, many database projects have been undertaken without spelling out the goals, having the budget, or having worked out what the practical steps should be.

Constructors and Creators

There are the two general types of people who are interested in database marketing.

A *constructor* is someone who is interested in building a database: collecting and cleaning the names, designing the computer access, planning instant retrieval and segmentation.

A *creator* is someone who figures out how to make money with the database by designing practical relationship and sales building programs.

You need both kinds to have a successful database. The creators are the hardest to find. Without them, you are doomed to failure.

A major national corporation collected the names of seven million of their customers as a result of a number of promotional activities with baby food, pet food, and adult food products. Marketing executives decided that this pool of names constituted an important corporate asset. The money was found to merge/purge these names, and to put them into a common format. NCOA^{LINK} was applied to update the addresses. A database was created.

The only problem was that no one knew what to do with the names once they were ready. None of the brand managers had any promotions planned, which could use the names. There was no newsletter, or other vehicle in the works. As a result, the seven million names hung on a tape rack for three years, while the names got stale.

No one was willing to admit it, but every penny spent on this database was totally wasted.

Here is a simple recipe for database marketing strategy.

1. Decide what you want the customers to do. Do you want to retain them, sell them second products, buy upgrades, provide referrals, or renew their subscriptions or policies?

2. When you have defined the goal, quantify it. By how much and within what time frame? Compare that with what is happening now. If, for example, 43 percent are renewing their policies every year, then set your goal for some other level: 50 percent by the end of next year.

3. Determine how you are going to modify the customer's current behavior. Will you use communications, rewards, or points? Will you use newsletters, e-mails, policy reviews, or sales calls? Will you try to get customers to shift to automatic monthly renewals unless cancelled? Come up with some examples from your experience or industry case studies that show that your method has worked.

4. When you have determined the mix of methods, determine how much you are prepared to spend on achieving your goal. This will require building two lifetime tables that show the current situation, and the achievement of your goal. Put into the table the costs of the behavior modification projects. These tables are very, very helpful. Once you have created them, you may find that your methods may not work, or are too expensive.

Mistake 2: Focus on Price instead of Service

What do you offer a customer to build a relationship? A discount is the last thing you should consider. Before neighborhood stores went out of business people kept coming back to them because they liked the owner, they liked his employees, and the friendly atmosphere at his store. His store was convenient. The owner recognized you and did favors for you. You would not think of asking him to cut his price. The relationship was built on trust and service.

That is not true today. Mass marketing stores are based on price, not on relationships. Databases are built on relationships. Once you begin talking discount, it sends the wrong message. A discount is what everyone else offers. Discounts do not build loyalty or relationships. They make people forget about quality, service or loyalty, and think about the price.

If all you can think of to do with your database is to use it as a channel for offering discounts, your database will fail. Why? Because a database costs money. There are a lot cheaper ways of providing discounts, particularly coupons. Once you begin to play the discount game, any competitor with a deeper discount can rob you of your customers.

The Quaker Oats Company launched a major national database program built on that idea. Quaker Oats began a major database marketing effort called Quaker Direct. After a test mailing, with a budget of $18 million, Quaker Direct sent co-op mailings of coupons to 20 million households carefully selected from Computerized Marketing Technology's compiled database *Select and Save*. Unlike FSI coupons found in newspapers or magazines, the Quaker coupons were bar-coded with a Quaker household number so that data could be collected on the response of each of the 20 million households.

The central idea in the promotion, according to Dan Strunk, the director of the Quaker program, was to gain knowledge of the market, and to begin a dialogue with a select group of confirmed Quaker users, thereby building brand loyalty.

Although the program cost approximately four times as much as the cost of sending the same coupons in a Sunday newspaper, and twice as much as the cost of the Carol Wright co-op program, Quaker Direct reasoned that because of the correct targeting, the redemption rates would be much higher. The net effect, therefore, would be a reduction in overall costs by "mailing smarter." Another means of reducing the cost of the promotion was enlisting national advertisers who paid to share the mailing with Quaker.

Quaker hoped to achieve a real "one-to-one bonding" with the consumers of their brands, through the dialogue created by the receiving and redemption of coupons. After the first mailing, however, the entire project was canceled, and the director was terminated. Quaker did not comment on the reasons.

Quaker Oats is a household word in America, with an excellent reputation with the public. Why did their database project fail?

First, they did not get as many co-op advertisers as they had hoped to get, so the program was more expensive than they had assumed. Their failure to get other co-op partners stemmed from the second problem.

Second, coupons do not build a relationship. People love Quaker because of the wonderful wholesome food that Quaker is famous for, not because they discount their products. No one will love Quaker more because they got a coupon in the mail giving them 50 cents off. The entire basis for the Quaker program was mistaken. They were smart to stop it before more money was wasted.

Contrast the Quaker fiasco with what Kraft General Foods did with the Crystal Light program. John Kuendig, Director of Direct Marketing created the Crystal Light Lightstyle Club. Crystal Light is a low-calorie artificially sweetened drink powder, selling for about $3 per box. Heavy users buy 10 or more boxes during the summer.

There were about a million members in the club at any given time. These were medium-to-heavy users of the product. The goal was to preserve this group and increase their usage.

Members received a package that contained a club newsletter on diet and fitness, discount coupons for General Foods products, a cover letter, and a catalog. The catalog was part of the club image, because it offered watches, mugs, jogging suits, and other gear that bore the Crystal Light emblem. Catalog items could be purchased with cash plus proof of purchase seals from Crystal Light boxes.

Each year, market research was used to measure the effectiveness of the program in building and maintaining sales of the product.

How did this program differ from the ill-fated Quaker Direct? It was built upon three key concepts all of which were missing from Quaker:

- A theme (fitness, exercise, weight loss, diet).

- A club (with a logo, clothing, a newsletter).

- Exclusivity (a very focused narrow group of consumers interested in the club and the theme).

Of course Crystal Light used discount coupons, but it was not *based* on the coupons. They were not the main idea. They were a sweetener, which supported the program and facilitated the dialog. I would venture to say that if Kraft simply mailed out coupons alone, the program would have quickly died.

Where mailing programs are built on discount coupons as the core, instead of building a relationship focused on the product or the manufacturer's established name and reputation, they are doomed to failure. So what is wrong with discounts?

- A discount, of course, erodes your margin.

- A discount tells customers that your product is over-priced. They know that you are making a profit at the discounted price. So you must be ripping them off if you charge the regular price.

- A discount makes people think about how much they are paying instead of how much they are getting. You want them to think about the value of the product and the service, and the relationship you have created, not about the price.

- Any competitor can match your discount. No one can match the relationship you have built up with your customers.

Solid relationships built through database marketing are immune to discounts. Your customers prefer you because you are an old friend who recognizes them, who provides personal services, and delivers a well-known quality product. You would be insulted if a friend gave you money for doing them a favor. A database should aim at that same kind of friendship.

Mistake 3: Getting the Economics Wrong

What could you do with a clean list of all the households in America that buy Del Monte canned peas? Mail letters to them to sell them more canned vegetables or some similar product? Wrong! What you could do is to lose a lot of money. The margin on such products is so pathetically thin, that there is no way you could communicate with these households by mail, fax, e-mail, or phone and have the incremental profit pay even for the cost of the communication. The economics just are not there. That is true of most packaged goods. Who wants to get letters from the people that make our English muffins? Life is just too short to spend it corresponding with the makers of all the products and services that we use every day. There are plenty of situations in which database marketing just is not going to work. We have to get the economics right.

On the other hand, if you sell automobiles, rental cars, insurance, power tools, vacation cruises, software or computers, your customer list could be turned into a valuable database.

Big-ticket items, repeat sales items, cross-brand possibilities: these are the lifeblood of marketing databases. Too many companies rush into building a database without thinking about the economics. Say to yourself: "How am I going to make money with these names?" Your answer must be simple and practical—something that you can explain to your mother so she can understand it.

Citicorp, one of the nation's largest banks, became a major entrant into the database marketing field for retailers a while ago. Their idea, called "Reward America," was to help grocery chains build up a valued customer database, with each customer having a family membership card. When the family came to shop, they would bring their card and present it for scanning while their shopping cart contents were rung up. As a result, the computers in each cash register would have a record of all the purchases made by that family: the date, the time of day, the SKU, the quantity, the price.

The idea caught on fast. Several chains were signed up and the software was installed. Every night, the cash registers were electronically polled. The data on the day's transactions were fed over the telephone lines to each chain's central computer. From there, on a weekly basis, Citicorp retrieved each member household's purchasing data for storage on their mainframe in Connecticut.

With detailed information on the shopping habits of millions of Americans, Citicorp figured it would be able to realize a profit from the sale of this household data to manufacturers: such as Camay, Pampers, Crest, or Del Monte.

It was a great idea. The stores would use the data to learn more about their customers: where they lived, when they shopped, what they bought. They could use the data to pursue members who stopped buying, and to reward loyal member customers with daily specials and premiums.

There were many different types of discount arrangements made by the different chains who installed the system. For example, in some systems, members using their card to purchase goods which were "on special" would receive $2.00 for buying eight cans of this juice, or $1.00 for buying three boxes of that cereal. The system would keep track of purchases, so the products did not have to be bought on the same visit. Each month, members could receive a mailing including a purchase summary and a certificate for the amount they had earned so far. In other systems, the reward would be instant—with a discount for special items with each visit, and no retention of credits.

Citicorp made retailers a deal that the supermarkets could not refuse: free. They planned to make their money on the other end, by selling the purchase data to manufacturers. They hoped to build a database of 40 million households.

Most of the dozen chains that signed up for the system did so because the program was free and offered a way to learn about frequent shopper programs. Unfortunately for Citicorp, many things went wrong. What did go wrong?

1. *Rewards must be instant.* The concept of rewarding customers three months down the road for purchases just did not go over. If you are going to give grocery shoppers money, they want it now, which explains the success of the instant discounts and electronic coupon programs—such as those run by Catalina marketing. Catalina is the company that makes the systems in supermarkets that generate coupons during the checkout process. If you bought one brand of Yogurt, the Catalina coupon generated might offer you a discount on a rival brand.

2. *The data problems were immense.* Citicorp's central computer choked on the data. They did not realize how huge the volume of grocery chain purchase data could be. They did not have adequate software in place. After the program was canceled, they had thousands of tapes stored in their computer center, unprocessed and gathering dust. What can anyone do with the information that on August 3 at 3:40 p.m. Arthur Hughes bought 6 pounds of potatoes? Nothing profitable! Add to that tens of millions of other transactions that take place every day in American supermarkets and you will soon bring any computer to its knees.

3. *Few companies wanted the names.* Manufacturers did not jump at the chance to buy the names of their customers, as Citicorp expected they would. The fact is that names and addresses of purchasers of package goods are almost worthless. What can you do with data about someone who has bought frozen spinach? Spam? Clorox? Cool Whip? Think about it. You cannot make any money with these names.

4. *Costs exceeded revenues.* The program cost too much to support. They spent $200 million, and generated about $20 million in revenue. After three years they canceled the program and fired the 174 employees, leaving many retail chains with no way to maintain a system that they had been promoting to their customers.

Looking at the broad picture, what lessons can we draw from the Citicorp experience?

- *Test first.* Before you do something big in the database field, you should test, test, test. Citicorp, a very large and successful bank, approached this project the same way they successfully approached credit cards and other projects: pour in money, get a national foothold before the competitors know what is going on. It paid off in credit card acquisitions, but it certainly did not work in retailing. If they had been prepared to start on a small scale with one or two chains, experimenting and learning (with just a few employees on the project), they could have gotten the bugs out of the concept at a modest cost—such as $10 million. Then they would have been ready for a successful national rollout in two or three years.

- *Compute the costs.* Do not underestimate the data processing aspects of database marketing. When you compute the data on one household's grocery purchases in a year, you may be talking 6,000 or more items purchased by a family of four. Multiply that by 40 million households and you have 240 billion transactions in one year alone. Without really efficient software, the costs and time consumed will bring even the most powerful data center to serious grief and high costs.

- *Work out lifetime value.* Put yourself in the customer's shoes. Successful database marketing is relationship building: one on one with the customer. Some marketers might be thinking "How can we make money selling data about these rubes?"—instead of saying, "Why would anyone want to join a frequent shopper club?" You have to start with the basics. Profits should be created by having built a relationship with the customer that is satisfying to all concerned.

- *Know your market.* The economics were wrong for the product manufacturers. Few package goods manufacturers today know what to do with a database of their own customers. Most of them have millions of names stored in their data centers from previous promotions. They have not yet figured out how to turn these names into relationships, loyalty, repeat sales, cross sales, and profits. If that is the case, why would they go out and pay money for more customer names?

If there were a demand for the names because the manufacturers had a way of making money from them, the profits would have solved all of the other problems. But, alas, the demand was not there.

A satisfactory economic solution to database marketing will not come looking for you. You have to find it. And if you cannot, maybe it is not there!

The Reward America fiasco does not invalidate the idea of frequent shopper cards for supermarkets. Since that time, scores of supermarket chains have created their own frequent shopper cards and used them quite successfully. Brian Woolf's excellent books: *Customer Specific Marketing* and *Loyalty Marketing—The Second Act* provide details on how to go about such programs. The benefits of these cards are explained in Chapter 13 of this book.

Mistake 4: Failure to Link Your Database to the Web

Database marketing began because computers and software became quite sophisticated and economical. It was possible to store information about customers, and use the information to build lasting relationships with them. As a result, it was possible to increase sales and profits by

- changing customer buying behavior
- promoting cross sales, repeat sales, and upgrades
- computing customer lifetime value and using it in strategy evaluation
- creating referrals and customer loyalty

Don Peppers and Martha Rogers created industry buzz by taking database marketing one step further to one-to-one marketing. The only trouble was that very few companies ever achieved one-to-one marketing. They used models to create customer profiles, segmenting customers into profitability or preference groups, and developed a different strategy for each group. But, to devise a different strategy for each person was really beyond the capability of any marketer.

Then along came the Internet. It took several years before most marketers realized the potential of the Web, but when they did they saw that the Internet is the greatest database marketing vehicle ever invented. Using the Internet, it is possible to do things that we only dreamed about in the old database marketing days.

For example, using cookies, you can recognize a customer whenever she returns to your Web site, and greet her by name: "Welcome back, Susan." Would not you love to do this whenever a customer walks into your store? This recognition opens a whole new world of relationship-building possibilities.

For example, some companies today customize or personalize their Web sites for each customer. Since they know what Susan has bought, or even better, what she is interested in (as a result of an on-line survey) they can spruce up the first page that Susan sees with items of interest to her. How do they know that this will increase sales? Here again, the Web offers tremendous opportunities for tests and controls that provide real proof.

A company that has 100,000 customers who visit their Web site, for example, can deliberately create a control group for 20,000 of them. This control group will not have a personalized Web page. Visitors will see the same Web page that everyone else sees. Only the 80,000 in their test group will have personalized pages. If the personalization is doing any good, the sales to the test group will be greater than those to the control group. The exact value of the personalization can be learned in a week or so, depending on how often people typically visit the Web site. This increased value can be measured against the cost of the programming to create the personalization, resulting in a sound return on investment calculation (Figure 16-1).

The theory of control groups is basic to database marketing, but is very seldom rigorously followed either there or on the Web. There are a couple of good reasons. In the first place, marketers and their management are always interested in meeting some sort of a sales quota for the season in question. Setting aside 20,000 customers does not fit into a marketing marathon. The other problem is that most marketers are simultaneously testing five or six different marketing ideas at once. A database system has to be quite complex to manage six tests and six control groups at once. The Web simplifies all of this, however. Since the results of tests in the Web are often known within a week or two, it is possible to conduct far more tests than in the old direct mail database days.

Of course, one of the most impressive changes has occurred in customer communications. In the old days, the best that a marketer could do was to send out an occasional "Thank you" letter to his best

	Number	Sales	Sales/Customer
Test	80,000	$2,272,000	$28.40
Control	20,000	$469,000	$23.45
Total	100,000	$2,741,000	$27.41
Cost of Personalization		$45,000	$0.45
Gain from Personalization			$4.95

Figure 16-1. Gain from Web site personalization.

customers. Today there has evolved a very efficient group of communications concerning each sale. There is no cost at all for e-mails sent by a company's database to its customers.

Companies are learning that the response to any advertisement or offer should include both a toll free number and a Web response option. There are several important reasons for this. Customers

- never get put on hold
- can log on at any hour of the day or night
- can print out a confirmation of their order
- get an e-mail confirmation

Customers enter their data directly into the Web which can be (and should be) directly connected to the customer database. This means that your reaction to their response can be instant: an e-mail thank you, and a shipment within a few hours. That cannot happen with any of the other response mechanisms.

- Probably the greatest change in database marketing due to the Web is in the area of customer service.

Unfortunately, despite the tremendous advantages of the Web, most companies are not there yet. If you call a catalog company, the toll free sales representative can tell you that the item you want is out of stock. If you click the same item on the company's Web site, more than likely the Web will take your order and notify you in a few days that the item is not available. What a pity! For the Web to succeed it must be good, very good. It must have up to the minute information, and must be smart enough to do what a phone operator does—suggest an alternative right then and there. This requires very sophisticated software—but the costs are not astronomical. Marketers cannot let IT manage the Web site. It must be designed and managed by marketers who understand the thinking of customers.

Some companies are using collaborative filtering from companies like NetPerceptions.com to make product suggestions to their customers both on the phone and on the Web. This software, linked to your customer database, figures out what kind of items you like based on your preferences or previous purchases. That is how Amazon.com is able to make profitable book and CD recommendations whenever you come to their site.

Rules for Web Success

Despite the obvious benefits of the Web, most companies have not yet figured out how to use the Web in their sales and relationships with customers. Catalogers, for example, find that 10 percent to 35 percent of their sales come through the Web. What are the rules for success in this field?

- The Web is a very powerful channel for customer communications and sales, but it should not be the only channel. Do not put all your eggs in one basket.

- Companies that have an established business (warehouses, delivery systems, stores, business contacts, and customers) can increase their business with Web contacts and sales. Few Web-only companies will survive.

- Collecting e-mails with permission to use them is one of the most valuable activities you can engage in. You should collect them using all possible customer contacts.

- Web response is so much less expensive than phone response that you absolutely must provide this option in all cases. Give them an 800 number and a www.yoursite on every form, catalog, product, and communication.

- Web sites must be managed by marketing and not by IT if you are going to be successful in e-commerce and customer relationships. If IT is running it now, go to top management and show them this book.

- The Web is an ordering medium not primarily a sales medium. It will never replace printed catalogs, direct mail offers, radio, TV, print ads, stores, malls, newspapers, magazines, or books. Give them a catalog, but put your Web site at the bottom of each page to receive their orders.

- Use cookies to recognize your customers when they come to your site. Greet them by name. Personalize their Web experience.

- Use tests and controls to prove that what you are doing is profitable.

If you are not linking your database to the Web, using customer profiles and cookies to personalize your Web site and e-mails, you are not getting the value you need from your database. Your competitors have already learned how to do this. Your database, in the long run, will operate at a disadvantage, and will fail.

Mistake 5: Building the Database In-House

Many companies believe that they have to build their marketing database in-house on their own mainframe. Some have been successful. Kraft General Foods, for example, built their huge customer base on their internal mainframe. The majority of large corporations, however, have outsourced their customer database, and even Kraft finally realized their mistake, and turned to outsourcing. Why is that?

- Few company computer systems are built for marketing. They exist for payroll, inventory, billing, or manufacturing. These operations pay the bills, and control the data processing priorities of the company. Marketing must sit in the dugout when these heavy hitters step up to the plate. Marketers will soon find that they cannot get the priority attention to their functions that they need to do their job.

- In-house MIS staffs seldom have the specialized software and experience needed to do database marketing. Merge/Purge, geocoding, statistical modeling, on-line access, ad hoc counting and selecting are a few of the skills that are needed for database marketing, and seldom available on in-house company computers.

- Most computer operations, like payroll or inventory, are stable systems that run for years without change. Marketing is dynamic. The software requires constant testing, modification, retesting, and shifts in approach. MIS will not understand having to devote hundreds of hours of program development time on a monthly basis to your marketing database. "Why cannot you guys make up your mind?" is the MIS refrain.

- As a result, it will take you much longer to get your database up and running, *and cost you much more* to build your system in-house. Finally: you probably will not be able to do most of the profit making things recommended in this book.

The solution, of course, is to find an external experienced service bureau to build your marketing database. If you get the right one, they will have built databases for many others, and can bring a wealth of experience to the table. Develop a tight contract that puts you, as the marketer, in control. You will be able to specify and hold your contractor to timetables and quality standards that you could never do with your in-house MIS staff.

Once your database is successfully built and running, it can always be migrated to your in-house computer. But in the crucial formative years, you cannot afford to rely on a part-time pick-up job done by an inexperienced in-house crew.

An Outsource Example

The marketing staff of a large telephone company wanted to build a database of its one million yellow page advertisers. The plan was to have the database up and running in six months so that they could use it as a lead generating and tracking system for their sales force. The marketing staff received funding approval for a pilot test of the idea. The database was built by an outside service bureau in a three-month period. It enabled the marketers, for the first time, to know who their most profitable customers were, and to compare the level of advertising by different industrial classifications. It worked and provided the marketing staff with exactly what they wanted.

The next step was a long-term contract to keep the database updated on a monthly basis using a tape from the MIS billing file as the key input. Seeing a reduction in their key role in the company, the in-house MIS group said they could build such a database themselves, and what is more, do it cheaper. The external contract was canceled.

To build the database in-house, MIS had to install new and unfamiliar database software, new merge/purge software, and postal pre-sort software. They had to create a new on-line access system so that users could work directly with the database. Millions of dollars were spent on acquiring this new software and learning how to use it. The work went slowly, because MIS had many other more high-priority projects which took programmer time and funding away from the marketing database. Four years later the database had not been built. The key individuals in the marketing staff who had initiated the program had left the company. The project was canceled.

This experience is not at all unique. Contrast this story with the database experience of companies like Microsoft, Pizza Hut, Western Union, or Nestle. All of them have large mainframes, yet they have elected to have their *marketing databases* built and maintained at outside database service bureaus.

Mistake 6: Treating All Customers alike

Everyone says that companies should organize themselves around customers: to become customer centric. Database marketing was sometimes
called customer relationship management (CRM) as a result. But if you
look around, you see that little has really changed. Brand or product
managers are still in charge. What is the evidence that customer centric
marketing is profitable?

- Eighty percent (or some very large percentage) of every company
  revenue or profits comes from the top 20 percent of the customers.

- The bottom 20 percent of customers is usually unprofitable. In some
  companies the losses from this bottom group are very substantial.

- Long-term customers have higher retention rates, higher spending
  rates, higher referral rates, and are less expensive to serve than new
  customers.

- Marketing dollars spent on upselling, cross-selling, or retention building programs focused on existing customers produce more revenue
  than the same dollars spent on new customer acquisition.

- A small percent increase in the retention rate will produce a very
  significant increase in company profits.

- The more different products or categories that a customer buys from
  a firm greatly increases the likelihood that the customer will become
  loyal, long term, and profitable.

These beliefs underlie database marketing: the idea that marketing
activities should be focused on increasing customer lifetime value. To
achieve LTV increase, the company has to create customer segments, and
develop customer segment managers who develop customer-focused programs based on these beliefs. Yet, most corporations are not organized in
this way. Their compensation systems work to frustrate customer relationship building activities. Look at the typical bank organization.

In Chapter 15, we learned that in a typical bank, there are vice presidents for each major product: credit cards, home equity loans, retail
(checking and savings accounts), insurance, etc. The credit card manager receives no bonus or special recognition if some of his credit card
customers take sign up for checking account. The Retail Vice President
gets no special reward if some of his customers apply for a credit card.
Yet any analysis of bank customers will show that the more different

bank products that the average customer has, the higher will be that customer's loyalty to and profits for the bank. The organization and compensation system does not reflect the theory of database marketing.

What Does It Take to Change an Organization to Begin to Focus on the Customer?

- Information: group all household purchases on one record so that you can understand what a customer is doing and what she wants.
- Determine customer profitability and lifetime value.
- Create a chart that shows customer retention and profitability based on the number of different products owned.
- Group customers into marketing segments.
- Develop different strategies for each segment: service strategies, marketing strategies, reward strategies, migration strategies, and management strategies.
- Look at these strategies to determine whether the present organization and compensation system permits you to carry them out.
- Change your organization and compensation system to assure that you become customer centric.

Banks who have built a marketing customer information file (MCIF) have proved to themselves that customer retention is a function of the number of products owned. This fact indicates that the best thing that the VP for one bank product can do to improve retention of his customers is to sell his customers additional products from some other department of the bank. But few banks are set up to do that. The VPs compete with one another. The compensation system has to be changed or the organization will never truly focus on the customer.

How Sears Canada Became Customer Focused

In Chapter 13, we learned how Sears Canada used their database to target their customers. Sears Canada was the largest general retailer in Canada with sales of more than $5 billion. A few years ago, Sears Canada had more than 110 full line retail stores, eight whole home furniture stores, eight outlet clearance stores, 79 dealer stores, and 2,000 catalog agents. Their big book catalog reached five million households in Canada every year. Two thirds of all sales in both catalog and retail were done on the Sears Credit Card. After a lot of hard work, Sears Canada gained a new insight into their customer base by putting data from catalog and retail sales, for the first time, on the same household record. It was an eye opener.

At the time the database was built, there was a Senior Vice President (SVP) for retail stores and an SVP for catalog operations. These two channels competed with each other openly. Their rivalry went back a long way. In early Canadian retailing history, the Sears Canada pioneers were the catalogers. They built a strong base in rural Canada. Once this base was established, Sears would open retail stores based on the growth of the catalog. To the company it was profitable. But to the catalogers, it created a sense of perceived cannibalization. The catalog merchants who had previously owned these markets saw sales attrition due to the stores. They saw it as channel competition. Over the years, the competition became quite heated.

The competition reflected where the catalog operation was located in the typical Sears retail store. In Canada, as well as in the United States Sears stores put the catalog office way back in the store, where you have to walk through the whole store to get there. It was viewed as an overhead to the selling operation, taking up valuable space that should be used for merchandise. The catalog desk was put as far as possible from the entrance to the store to generate store traffic. Customers coming in to pick up a catalog item would have to walk past aisle after aisle of merchandise. It was not designed for customer convenience—just the opposite, in fact.

Once the database was built, Sears was able to measure the performance of catalog customers vs. retail customers. The data was very revealing. They found that the average catalog customer spent $492 dollars per year. The average retail customer spent $1,102 dollars per year.

What about customers who were shopping both channels? These customers bought more than the average in both channels. When Bruce Clarkson, General Manager of Relationship Marketing looked at these cross shoppers, he found that the average cross shopping customer spent $584 on catalog items *and* $1,299 in retail stores. Leaving these cross shoppers out of the total figures, the customers who only shopped one channel spent $409 on catalog items, or spent $994 in retail stores. Cross shoppers were spending $1,883 per year with Sears, compared to half that or less spent by single channel shoppers.

The facts were staggering. The marketing staff provided their findings to top management. Management could clearly see that the way the business was being managed was inconsistent with customer behavior. The leadership said things like, "I knew it, but we did not have the numbers to prove it!" "We have to do something to encourage cross channel shopping."

Once top management saw what was happening, Sears began to make major changes. No longer were Catalog and Retail each under a competing SVP. Instead, Sears Canada shifted to have three major divisions:

- Executive Vice President (EVP) for Marketing
- EVP for Sales and Service
- EVP for Merchandising

Each EVP worked across all channels: retail, catalog, and several other channels including the credit card, long distance services, gift registries, etc. Marketing did branding, advertising, TV, preprint, catalog production, in-store marketing, the look and feel of the store, the arrangement of the store, customer relationship marketing and e-commerce. Sales and Service delivered service excellence through all the channels.

One of the first fruits of the reorganization was the change in the location of the catalog desk in the retail stores. Stores began to look contemporary: bright, functional, and convenient. The catalog desks were put at the most used entrance of each store. Throughout the retail store, Sears created outposts where they put copies of the catalog. At each outpost, there were telephones for immediate access to the call centers. The catalog was positioned as an extension to the retail store. Selected catalog pages were displayed throughout the store, so if you were in the footwear division, you would find catalog pages laminated in the footwear department. If you could not find the size or style you want, you could pick up a phone and order it. It was not promoted as being a catalog order. It was just another way of shopping at Sears.

To promote telephone shopping, Sears developed 48-hour national service on most orders. No matter where you were in Canada, Sears could arrange delivery for you to a convenient location near your home within 48 hours. Plus, they did not charge for shipping or handling. With 2,000 locations throughout Canada, goods could be shipped free to nearby locations. The whole idea was to increase the number of cross shoppers, who Sears recognized as being their most valuable customers.

What was the result of this? Before Sears provided the catalog and telephone service in the store, clerks would say, if they did not have what the customer wanted, "Gosh I am sorry. Maybe they have it at so and so down the mall." With the new system, Sears in their first year with the new system saved sales that were equivalent to adding another mid-sized store to their 110 store chain with no bricks and mortar—essentially at almost no cost. That virtual store became the largest single store in the Sears Canada chain.

But the database and the reorganization did not stop at integrating catalogs with retail. Marketing moved towards the goals of retention, acquisition, and purchase stimulation. Clarkson developed customer attrition models. His first effort was to find out why some people were not shopping through the catalog. What he discovered was that the strongest predictive variable for not shopping the catalog was exposure to bad service: out of stock, or merchandise that was not satisfactory. He proved that money spent on improved service would increase customer retention. The performance of the EVP for Sales and Service was measured based on a customer loyalty index.

Sears experience shows how a company can become truly customer centric. But it took a massive reorganization to do it. How many other companies are willing to make the changes in organization and compensation needed to achieve profitable database marketing?

Mistake 7: Failure to Use Tests and Controls

As pointed out in Chapter 11, it is absolutely essential that you use control groups to measure the success of any database marketing strategy. Many new marketing strategies take a long time from the original idea to the actual execution. Once permission and budget is available, there is a rush to get the project out the door before someone changes their mind. At that point, the idea of setting up a control group often goes by the board. If the program is a success, it may be that no one notices the control group absence. But if the program does not seem to be a success, the failure to use a control group may cost the marketer his job. It could be that business during that quarter is down everywhere. Those who were exposed to your new strategy might be the only bright spot in an otherwise dismal situation (their purchases went down less). Without a control, you will not know that. Your failure to use tests and controls could doom not only your job, but the entire database marketing program.

Many marketers have had difficulties setting up control groups. It is not difficult to select the customers to be in the group. The difficulty is making sure that their performance is not adulterated by some other marketing program which stimulates them to greater activity than a regular customer. There must be discipline in the organization to assure that everyone treats the control groups as regular customers, without special programs.

Once you have set up a control group, there are many valuable things that you can learn from them. A couple of case studies will show what I mean.

PreVision helped Stride Rite to fill their 135 retail stores with customers in the spring, using a personalized direct mail program to their customer database. They set aside no-contact control groups that matched the audience selection criteria of the mailed households, but did not get any of the communications. The control group showed a 15 percent lift in sales. Because of the success of this program, PreVision conducted similar communication strategies for Stride Rite.

An insurance company had a 43% renewal rate on their property insurance policies. Industry statistics show that when agents perform a personal review with the policyholder, renewal rates go up. Most of their agents concentrated on new business. To get them to do the personal reviews, they decided to incentivize them with a $30 payment for one personal visit per client. Using tests and controls, they were able to prove that payments reduced customer lifetime value. The increased retention did not justify the additional expense.

Mistake 8: Lack of a Retention Program

Most companies are set up for customer acquisition rather than retention. As we have already explained there are several reasons for this:

- Every company needs to acquire new customers. That is why you have a sales staff.
- Many companies are opposed to paying significant sales commissions for renewals. They assume that the renewals will come in automatically. Paying a commission is just throwing money away. Make them go out and get us some new business.
- You can count the number of new customers acquired each year.
- It is more difficult to count the number of customers that did not leave because of your retention program.

- Many companies assume that retention is based largely on good customer service, good products and services, and speedy deliveries, and they are right. So why do we need a retention program?

Answer: because it will improve your bottom line. Many industry reports show that $100 spent on retention programs has a higher payoff in terms of profit than $100 spent on new acquisitions. That does not mean that you can stop acquiring customers, of course. What it means is that you should devote some effort at keeping customers.

To decide whether to create a retention program, you have to first learn what your current retention rate is. If your retention rate is 95 percent or better, you probably do not need a program. But if your retention rate is like everyone else's where you lose 50 percent or some other large percent of your customers every year, you need to do something.

Increasing retention is, of course the main reason why anyone does database marketing in the first place. Simply having a customer marketing database, however, will not improve retention unless you create many of the programs outlined in this book. There are many companies that have gone to the work of creating a customer marketing database, and then never use it to improve retention. In my career in database marketing I built and maintained several marketing databases for large corporations that did not use them for retention. They used them for product design, or customer profiling, or marketing research. These are useful projects, but hardly sufficient to justify the cost of maintaining a database. To drive the point home, let us look at the effect of a retention program already outlined in this book. In the beginning of Chapter 6 on Customer Communications, we presented the results of an experiment with customers of a lighting manufacturer. As you recall, by having a two person staff make phone calls to 600 customers over a six-month period they increased the retention rate by 3 percent.

Mistake 9: Lack of a Forceful Leader

Too many databases fail through the lack of a strong leader to head the project. Leadership is vital: there is much work to be coordinated within the company and with the outside suppliers if a database marketing program is going to produce long-term profit gains. Successful databases usually have outside telemarketers, a service bureau, a creative agency, a fulfillment house; inside they need the coordination of marketing, market research, sales, billing, customer service and MIS. Pulling the team together requires a forceful leader. The committee system will never work here. Decisions are needed on a daily basis to keep the database going, responsive, dynamic, building customer relationships, and making sales.

If you are planning a database in your company, be sure you have found a strong leader and that he or she has been delegated the responsibilities and authority to make it work. Without this, your database will never get off the ground.

How to Do Things Right

What should you do to avoid these mistakes? There are a few simple steps that you can take to be sure that you go about building your database properly:

Put Yourself in Your Customer's Shoes. Do not think of what you want to sell, think of what you, as a customer, would want from your company. It may not be primarily a product at all—it may be recognition, attention, information, helpfulness, service, or friendship. If you can deliver on these things, the sales will follow. A database may be the best way to provide these things.

Build a Database Team. Successful databases have a strong, creative, imaginative leader who has pulled together a team composed of marketing, sales, the service bureau, the creative agency, MIS, customer service, outside telemarketers, brand managers, fulfillment and billing.

Think Small and Think Fast. Start your database with a small elite group of customers. Start soon. Make every action a test. Conduct your test, and evaluate your results. Build bigger as you accumulate experience.

Keep Your Eye on the Bottom Line. Database marketing is supposed to make money. Plan your economics. Calculate lifetime value. If you cannot quite see how what you are doing will be profitable, then do not do it! Rack your brains and find a way to turn your customer relationship into a profitable customer relationship.

Summary

1. You can easily go wrong in database marketing. There are nine deadly mistakes enumerated in this chapter:

- Lack of a marketing strategy
- Focus on price instead of service

- Getting the economics wrong
- Failure to link your database to the web
- Building the database in house
- Treating all customers alike
- Failure to use tests and controls
- Lack of a retention program
- Lack of a forceful leader

2. To be successful you need to

- Put yourself in your customer's shoes
- Build a database team
- Think small and think fast
- Keep your eye on the bottom line

Executive Quiz 16

Answers to quiz questions (Figure 16-2) can be found in Appendix B.

Put the appropriate letter before each answer	
Questions	**Answers**
a Why did Sears Canada reorganize?	Cost, experience, speed, expertise.
b Why did Quaker Direct fail?	Coupons do not build loyalty
c Why did Reward America fail?	Cross shoppers spent more than others
d How long should building a DB take?	Few companies wanted the names
e Why are most large databases outsourced?	Fifteen percent
f Why did Chrystal Light succeed?	It had a theme, not based on discounts
g What is a "Creator" in DB jargon	Lifetime Value went down
h What proved that $30 per visit was not good	Marketing Customer Information File
i The value of personalized communications	Sales are higher to those who get them
j Collaborative filtering software	Selling names to manufacturers
k An ordering medium, not mainly a sales medium	Six months or less
l MCIF	Someone who creates profit with a DB
m Stride Rite's lift in sales from personalization	Tells you what to offer to customers
n To where did Sears move the catalog desk?	The internet
o The central idea behind Reward America	The most traveled entrance

Figure 16-2. Quiz 16.

17

Database Types that Succeed

The U.S. version of the Air Miles loyalty program came crashing to earth a year later, although the more successful Canadian and British programs continued uninterrupted. The US program had 40 corporate sponsors and 2.2 million members, less than half of whom actively collected Air Miles. The Canadian program had 56 corporate sponsors and about four million consumers signed up.

The differences: in the U.S. program, consumers had to clip out proofs-of-purchase and mail them in to receive credit. In Canada, a mag stripe, UPC code, and embossing on the Air Miles membership card allows members purchases to be tracked the same way credit card purchases are tracked. "In Canada, we created a card that makes collecting easy", said Joanna Fuke, Loyalty Management Group Canada's director of consumer marketing. "In the U.S. they took a packaged goods strategy and had a clip-and-snip program...That probably made it a little tougher for consumers to play the game, and depressed the activation rate."

STEPHEN P. LLOYD
Canadian Direct Marketing News

By now, you are aware that database marketing and the Web are zooming ahead in some areas, and failing in others. It is not all win–win. Some marketers have lost their jobs by betting on database marketing or the Web in areas where they did not work. Before you risk your career, let us see if there are some rules that will guide us to success, and steer us away from failure in this new marketing mode. To begin with, you must pick the product situation where database marketing is likely to work.

Picking the Right Product Situation

There are really two separate (but related) forms of database marketing:

a. Relationship building with current customers and
b. Marketing to prospects selected by developing profiles of the most profitable customers.

This second activity is much easier to succeed in than the first. Marketing to prospects, when done right, always involves a test. Before a rollout of one million, you do a 20,000 test, study the results to determine the factors leading to response, and mail smarter on the rollout. If you follow the rules, you cannot fail. There is no problem in this area.

Relationship building database marketing or Web site construction is the area where most mistakes are made. Why? Because you are supposed to treat customers differently from unknown prospects. You must recognize them and remember what they have bought, and what they have told you. It is much harder to see the immediate results when dealing with customers. You can count the number of customers that you have acquired. How do you count the number that you have not lost through attrition? It may take months or years before relationship building begins to pay off. By the time you discover that it does not pay off, millions of dollars may have been wasted. That is why this chapter is so important.

Relationship Marketing

The principle underlying relationship marketing is the same as that of any free market transaction: both parties make a profit. Why would I want to have a relationship with the makers of my shirts, shoes, or soap? I really do not. I do not care enough about these products to want to waste time corresponding with their manufacturers. But, at heart, the main reason that I do not want to be on their databases is that I cannot visualize any particular benefit to me in the relationship.

Relationship marketing is like courtship and marriage. In the beginning, there is often unfamiliarity or indifference. There are plenty of courtships that begin when an unlikely boy forces his attentions on an indifferent girl; the girl discovers some good features in the boy that she had not noticed before. They fall in love, get married and live happily ever after. Most successful databases begin like that.

But not all marriages or Web site relationships are successful. For a marketing relationship or a marriage to last, both parties have to want the relationship and want it to last. They have to see some value in staying together. Both parties have to make a profit from the exchange of communications, services or products.

Database marketing designed to maintain a relationship works wonderfully in some areas, and does not work at all in others. Let us take a few examples and see how they illustrate our general principles.

Where Relationship Marketing Works if Done Correctly
Figure 17-1

Where It Is Harder to Make Relationship Marketing Work
Underlying these two lists is a general principle: Relationship marketing works when the provider can supply sufficient benefits to the customer

Products	Services
Automobiles	Auto Service
Baby Products	Banks & Financial Services
Books, Records, Video	Business to Business
Business to Business	Communications
Children's Food Products	Credit Cards
Computers	Diet and Health Centers
Department Stores	Doctors & Dentists
Diet food products	Entertainment
Drug Stores	Home Maintenance Services
Florists	Hospitals & Physicians
Fuels and Utilities	Insurance
Gasoline & Car Care	Lawyers
Gardening Supplies	Medical care and glasses
Heating and Air Conditioning	Membership & Non-Profits
Lumber and Hardware	Sporting events
Magazines	Travel & Related Services
Pharmaceuticals	TV and Radio
Sewing and Knitting Supplies	Restaurants
Supermarkets	

Figure 17-1. Products and services where database marketing may succeed.

Products	Services
Apparel and Upkeep	Contractors
Appliances & Electronics	Electricians
Building supplies	Home remodeling & additions
Carpets	Locksmiths
Food (exceptions)	Movers
Furniture & home furnishings	Painters
Glass and Mirrors	Paving
Linen and draperies	Pest Control
Office Supplies & Equipment	Real Estate
Packaged goods (exceptions)	Roofers
Toys & Sporting goods	Towing
Water treatment	Wallpaper

Figure 17-2. Difficult relationship marketing situations.

to make it worth the customer's while to read the provider's communications and to modify her behavior (Figure 17-2). At the same time, the average customer has to be in a position to modify her behavior in ways that benefit the provider and which exceed the provider's costs in creating and maintaining the relationship.

To explain this in my case, I will be willing to play my part in a relationship with a supplier of products and services if I can see some benefit to me which is greater than the work I have to do or the money I have to pay: filling out survey forms, reading e-mails, answering the telephone, buying products, etc. As a customer, I have to make a profit from the relationship, or I will not play.

The supplier, on the other hand, has to be able to increase the lifetime value of his customers by means of the relationship building activity. Let us take a specific case: my Swingline Stapler.

I have had this stapler on my desk for more than 10 years. It is a heavy, solidly built excellent product that is still working as well as when I bought it at an office supply store. It probably cost about $25.00. Swingline, as far as I know, does not have a database, and if they do, I am not on it. I do not need another stapler. I need staples occasionally, which I buy from Office Depot. Would I buy them direct from Swingline if they wrote to me? Perhaps. But I buy them less than once a year, and spend less than $5. Their profit on the sale would not justify the cost of the database, or the communication costs.

The people that should be on the Swingline database are Office Depot and Staples and many small office supply chains. These chains, more than I, are responsible for this piece of equipment on my desk.

I bought the best thing that my office supply store had. If they had featured some other brand at the time, I would have bought that.

The conclusion: there are thousands of products that find their way into consumer's hands, for which the manufacturer should not create a consumer marketing database because the consumer cannot profit by being on the database. Since that is so, neither can the manufacturer profit by maintaining it. The same thing applies to a Web site. Why would I want to check out the Swingline Web site? What would be in it for me?

Alternate Database Uses

On the other hand, there are circumstances in which the customer database or Web site for such mundane objects as a high-quality stapler might be profitable after all. Swingline has an excellent Web page. It has a lot of interesting information about their products and their company. They have a product registration page. If I were the purchasing manager of a company, I could click on any of the store names on the where to buy it page and be transported directly to sites where I could order a Swingline stapler or a thousand other products. This is good for Swingline and good for the retailers. Through the registration process, Swingline is capturing names for their customer marketing database. They have a policy that they will not rent these names and addresses to anyone. They will correspond only with their registered customers. If my business had lots of employees, it might be worth my while to register, and Swingline's while to correspond with me. Since I do not have any employees, however, a relationship building consumer database will probably never have any economic value to either Swingline or to me.

Further Criteria for Success

Just being on the "might work" list does not guarantee that Web sites and customer databases will be profitable. There are other criteria. Databases and Web sites for relationship building purposes are more likely to be profitable if some or all of the following are true:

■ The provider has a well thought through database marketing program. Such programs are hard to think up. There must be a creative marketing director who has designed a program that will return real benefits to the customer in exchange for which the customer will furnish real benefits to the provider: loyalty and repeat business resulting in increasing long-term value.

■ There must be a payment system for the product or service that makes it easy to get names, addresses, and purchase behavior. This is true in utilities, transportation, communications, banks and financial services, insurance, magazines, credit and gasoline cards, etc. The providers of these products and services have to have the name and address of the customer to provide the service in the first place. Many of them mail monthly statements. This type of activity leads very easily into the building and maintenance of a customer database. Unfortunately, with most products, purchase behavior is much more difficult to capture.

■ The product or service involves periodic repeat purchases plus name capture at point of sale. This is true for automobiles, automobile servicing, medical care, pharmaceuticals, diet and health centers, home services (such as heating and air conditioning, plumbing, lawn care).

■ There is a definite affinity group from which a database can be constructed. This applies to parents of new babies, sports enthusiasts, non-profits, gardening supplies, knitting, sewing, music, etc.

■ The provider can construct a frequency reward system with significant benefits for both parties. This applies, of course to the travel industry, to department stores, supermarkets, and the entertainment industry.

Why the "Will Not Work" List Exists

What is wrong with the products and services on the second list that makes them unlikely candidates for relationship building database marketing? There are a couple of factors that apply to most of these products and services:

1. The product is a commodity with a markup that is too narrow to finance relationship-building activity

2. The purchase is made seldom and unpredictably. Furniture is a good example. A family pays $2,000 for dining room furniture. It may last 5 years, 10 years, or even 20 years. Furniture is usually purchased from a dealer that displays the products of many different manufacturers in one location. Can a relationship be developed by the manufacturer of one specific brand of furniture and the customer that will assure that your furniture is considered when the next major purchase takes place? It seems like a long shot to me.

The furniture manufacturer's database should be a business-to-business one which he uses to market to furniture dealers. On the other hand, furniture retailers (not manufacturers) can use a consumer prospect database to good advantage (see below).

In the case of lumber and hardware, there exists the handyman who spends his life puttering and fixing up his house or boat or car. If the retailer can locate such people and build a database of them, a profitable relationship can ensue. Can the manufacturer of these products profit from building a relationship? In some cases, yes. Black and Decker, or Skilcraft with a wide line of power tools could build a relationship by using surveys combined with catalogs, a Web site or a newsletter on carpentry. There are always new tools coming out which handymen want to learn about. A few years ago, one company made a good business of selling nuts, bolts and screws by direct mail to handymen. From what I could tell, no attempt was made to build this into a database. Could Armstrong develop a relationship with someone who bought floor covering once, which would lead to them buying floor covering a second time? Who knows? It seems unlikely to me.

To illustrate why the second list is a something to worry about, let us see whether Hoover, or Oreck could profit from building a customer database of vacuum cleaner customers and doing relationship marketing with them.

They could get the customer's name from a registration form inside the shipping container, and could initiate a direct mail program, selling replacement bags and attachments, leading to announcement of new models when they become available. Would such a database be successful? The analysis which follows applies to any household appliance, such as a dishwasher, washer, dryer, refrigerator, lawn mower, room air conditioner, television, or computer.

One characteristic of such appliances is that they are seldom purchased every year. Some appliances last for 20 years or more. Few of them, nowadays, wear out rapidly. Customers buy new ones most often when they move or remodel, or purchase a second home. To begin our analysis, we have to make some assumptions about customer purchase of replacements. We are making these numbers up, but a vacuum cleaner company can estimate the actual numbers by consulting a customer database. Let us follow the purchase decisions of 400,000 new vacuum purchasers in their first six years. We assume that:

- In the first year, 5 percent buy a replacement vacuum, and thereafter 10 percent of those still owning the original machines buy a replacement.

- 40 percent of those who make a purchase buy the same make of cleaner.

- 16 percent of those owning the original machines buy parts and service per year.

Here is the lifetime value of these customers in the sixth year after purchase (Figure 17-3).

Now let us do a little customer relationship marketing. We will create a Web site with information on spare parts and new models with a dealer lookup. We will concentrate on relationship building, friendship, and communication. We will encourage the direct sale of filter bags, motor belts and attachments. We will send occasional direct mail and e-mails to our customers. Let us see what happens to lifetime value with these customer relationship management programs in place. We are going to

	Vacuum Cleaner Customer LTV without DB Marketing Acquisition			
	Year	Year 2	Year 4	Year 6
Products Owned	400,000	380,000	307,800	249,318
% Replaced	5%	10%	10%	10%
Number Replaced	20,000	38,000	30,780	24,932
Buy Same Make	40%	40%	40%	40%
Same make bought	8,000	15,200	12,312	9,973
Average Price	$200	$205	$220	$230
New Sales	$80,000,000			
Replacement Sales	$1,600,000	$3,116,000	$2,708,640	$2,293,726
Parts & Service	$100	$105	$115	$125
% Buying P&S	16%	16%	16%	16%
Parts & Service	$6,400,000	$6,384,000	$5,663,520	$4,986,360
Revenue	$88,000,000	$9,500,000	$8,372,160	$7,280,086
Costs	60.00%	58.00%	58.00%	58.00%
Total Costs	$52,800,000	$5,510,000	$4,855,853	$4,222,450
Profit	$35,200,000	$3,990,000	$3,516,307	$3,057,636
Discount Rate	1	1.2	1.6	2.1
NPV Profit	$35,200,000	$3,990,000	$3,516,307	$3,057,636
Cum NPV Profit	$35,200,000	$39,190,000	$46,440,947	$52,779,608
Lifetime Value	$88.00	$97.98	$116.10	$131.95

Figure 17-3. Lifetime value of vacuum cleaner customers before database. This chart covers six years. To simplify it for reading purposes I have left out years 3 and 5. These years continue the same actions, but do not change the trend. The full chart can be downloaded from www.dbmarketing.com.

spend \$500,000 on building the database system in the first year, and
\$200,000 each year thereafter.

As a result of these programs, we have gained the following benefits:

- The number replacing their vacuum has increased from 10 percent
  per year to 11 percent (a 10 percent increase).

- The percent who purchase our make when they buy goes up from
  40 percent to 50 percent.

- Parts and service purchases go up from 16 percent to 20 percent.

Here is the resulting lifetime value (Figure 17-4).

	VC Customer LTV showing new DB Marketing Strategies Acquisition			
Year	Year	Year 2	Year 4	Year 6
Products Owned	400,000	380,000	300,998	238,421
% Replaced	5%	11%	11%	11%
Number Replaced	20,000	41,800	33,110	26,226
Buy Same Make	50%	50%	50%	50%
Same make bought	10,000	20,900	16,555	13,113
Average Price	$200	$205	$220	$230
New Sales	80,000,000			
Replacement Sales	$2,000,000	$4,284,500	$3,642,076	$3,016,020
Parts & Service	$100	$105	$115	$125
% Buying P&S	16%	17%	17%	17%
Parts & Service	$6,400,000	$6,783,000	$5,884,511	$5,066,436
Revenue	$88,400,000	$11,067,500	$9,526,587	$8,082,455
Costs	60.00%	58.00%	58.00%	58.00%
Direct Costs	$53,040,000	$6,419,150	$5,525,420	$4,687,824
Database Cost	$500,000	$200,000	$200,000	$200,000
Communiications ($3)	$1,200,000	$1,140,000	$902,994	$715,262
Web Site	$400,000	$100,000	$100,000	$100,000
Total Costs	$55,140,000	$7,859,150	$6,728,414	$5,703,086
Profit	$33,260,000	$3,208,350	$2,798,172	$2,379,370
Discount Rate	1	1.2	1.6	2.1
NPV Profit	$33,260,000	$3,208,350	$2,798,172	$2,379,370
Cum NPV Profit	$33,260,000	$36,468,350	$42,248,753	$47,212,074
Lifetime Value	$83.15	$91.17	$105.62	$118.03

Figure 17-4. Lifetime value with retention programs. This chart covers six years.
To simplify it for reading purposes I have left out years 3 and 5. These years
continue the same actions, but do not change the trend. The full chart can be
downloaded from www.dbmarketing.com.

	Acquisition	Year 2	Year 3	Year 4	Year 5	Year 6
Old LTV	$88.00	$97.98	$107.31	$116.10	$124.30	$131.95
New LTV	$83.15	$91.17	$98.63	$105.62	$112.08	$118.03
Difference	($4.85)	($6.80)	($8.69)	($10.48)	($12.22)	($13.92)
With 400,000	($1,940,000)	($2,721,650)	($3,474,059)	($4,192,194)	($4,889,268)	($5,567,534)

Figure 17-5. Score card on vacuum cleaner database.

As you can see, the increased sales are not enough to pay for the cost of the database and the relationship building program. The lifetime value has gone down from $131.95 to $118.03. Look at the final score card (Figure 17-5).

We just get deeper and deeper in the red. This is the usual situation with such products. The Web site undoubtedly will work and produce benefits, but the database and communications will not.

These charts, unlike the others in this book, are based on surveys and speculation. There is no way that a manufacturer of appliances can obtain such data. Consumers normally do not register their purchases, and certainly do not tell you when they have discarded your product and bought something else. I built a database for a major automobile manufacturer. Unlike appliances, automobiles must be registered. But the automobile manufacturer could keep accurate track only of new vehicles purchased from his dealers. He could not know when one of his customer's vehicles was sold to buy another make. With appliances, the data is even more difficult to collect.

Therefore, there is no way that I can see that database marketing can work with rarely purchased appliances or packaged goods. I would love to say that it works, but it just does not. The connection is too indirect. The benefits to the customer are too small. People are just not interested enough to correspond with their vacuum cleaner or dishwasher manufacturer. If the appliance works OK, most people are not willing to go the expense and trouble of buying a new one, based on direct mail messages. They will buy a new one when the old one breaks down, or when they move, but not when they get a nice folksy letter or email. Too bad.

The database that the vacuum cleaner company should be counting on is the retail store database. They are the ones that tell their customers, "You know, there are a lot of good ones out there, but nothing beats a Hoover." That sentence alone can make or break the company's future. How do you get the dealer to say that? Database marketing can work with appliance dealers. Let us not get too optimistic about what it can accomplish with consumers.

I think that the reader can see that there are no definite firm lines that can be drawn. For any product which you select, it is possible to visualize how a profitable relationship building database might be constructed. Whether it can be constructed depends on the economics of the product and the creativity of the marketers involved.

How to Determine the Return on Investment

Before you create any marketing database, you have to compute the return on investment. To illustrate how return on investment for a database project can be calculated, let us look at a case study. The company was a major ski resort. Although the company had been in business for many years with two million skiers per year, they did not have a marketing database, and were seeking to justify creating one. Customers were sold an admission which permitted unlimited visits during the year. The goal of the customer marketing database was to increase company profits by

- increasing renewals of existing customers
- increasing reactivation of lapsed customers
- increasing visits by customers
- reducing costs by better targeting of communications to customers

Before the database was created, out of approximately two million customers in the previous year, 30 percent or about 600,000 normally renewed their registration for the next year. Each registrant made an average of 1.3 visits to one of the company's locations per year. The value of a renewal to the company was $216 broken down as follows (Figure 17-6).

The value of the expected renewals for the company each year was about $129 million (Figure 17-7).

Value of One Renewal			
	Dollars	Number	Totals
Admission	$60	1	$60
Lodging & Food	$120	1.3	$156
Total			$216

Figure 17-6. Value of one renewal.

Customers	Number	Renew Rate	Renewals	Value	Total
Customers	2,000,000	30.0%	600,000	$216	$129,600,000

Figure 17-7. Value of annual renewals.

What Could the Database Do to Improve This Situation?

It was assumed that better information would permit the company to send personalized and targeted communications, rather than the mass messages they had been using. These should increase the number of visits. The planners assumed that the communications could increase the number of visits per year from 1.3 to 1.4 (an increase of 7.7 percent). The new picture would look like Figure 17-8.

The gain in the number of visits would represent an increase of $7.2 million per year (Figure 17-9).

About half of the outgoing communications were by e-mail. The rest were by direct mail. The database planners assumed that the database would permit the company to send personalized communications, both e-mail and direct mail, rather than mass marketing communications. Case studies in other industries show that personalized communications have a greater response (sales) rate than non-personalized communications. They assumed that as a result of better information and better communications, the renewal rate could be increased from 30 percent to 31 percent (an increase of 3.3 percent). Here was the resulting revenue gain (Figure 17-10).

Value of One Renewal			
	Dollars	Number	Totals
Admission	$60	1.0	$60
Lodging & Food	$120	1.4	$168
Total			$228

Figure 17-8. Value with increased visits.

	Number	Renew Rate	Renewals	Value	Total
Customers	2,000,000	30.0%	600,000	$216	$129,600,000
Customers	2,000,000	30.0%	600,000	$228	$136,800,000
Increase					$7,200,000

Figure 17-9. Annual revenue increase.

	Number	Renew Rate	Renewals	Value	Total
Customers	2,000,000	30.0%	600,000	$216	$129,600,000
Customers	2,000,000	31.0%	620,000	$228	$141,360,000
Increase					$11,760,000

Figure 17-10. Annual revenue increase from both visits and renewals.

What these charts show is that it could be possible to increase revenue by more than $11 million through communications based on the new database.

Increased Reactivations

The company had a file of over five million lapsed customers, of whom approximately one million were reactivated every year through communications and mass media. Once the database was created, it was possible to model these lapsed customers and do a better job of reactivating them. How many additional could be reactivated with the database, scoring with a model and targeted communications? The answer was estimated as follows (Figure 17-11):

For their projections, the planners assumed that they could induce three tenths of one percent additional lapsed customers (above the previous two percent rate) to become reactivated through their new program. The revenue gain would be $3,420,000. They also assumed that the cost of the data appending, scoring and additional reactivation communications could be conducted for about $420,000. The new database cost the company about $400,000 per year. Here is the resulting ROI calculation (Figure 17-12).

The formula for return on investment is

$$ROI = (total\ revenue\ gain/total\ database\ cost) - 1$$

Lapsed Customers	Additional Reactivation Rate	Additional Customers Reactivated	Revenue Each	Total Increased Revenue
5,000,000	0.60%	30,000	$228	$6,840,000
5,000,000	0.50%	25,000	$228	$5,700,000
5,000,000	0.40%	20,000	$228	$4,560,000
5,000,000	0.30%	15,000	$228	$3,420,000
5,000,000	0.20%	10,000	$228	$2,280,000

Figure 17-11. Possible results of increased reactivation.

Return on Investment	
Renewals	$11,760,000
Reactivation	$3,420,000
Total	$15,180,000
Database Cost	$400,000
New Messages	$420,000
Total new costs	$820,000
Net DB Gain	$14,360,000
ROI per $1.00	$16.51

Figure 17-12. Return on investment.

In summary, the database would have a return on investment of more than $16 for every $1 invested. Note that we are not including new communications here. We are assuming that the existing communications would get better results through better targeting and personalization. Neither targeting nor personalization would be costly to the company once they had a consumer marketing database.

Can a Return on Investment Be Rewarded with a Bonus?

We are all familiar with sales force compensation arrangements. A salesman has an annual quota. If he makes it his compensation is specified in an annual contract. If his sales are 20 percent more than his quota, his bonus reflects that. Some salesmen have become very rich as a result of such bonus arrangements.

The same arrangement is usually not possible in marketing. This is why database marketing may be difficult to implement in your company. For example, suppose that an outside partner has proposed a new strategy: they will build a database and create automated communications to customer segments which will increase company profits by $X as measured against a control group that does not get the communications. Their compensation is based on a bargain: if they achieve $X in profits, they receive $Y as their fee. If they achieve 110 percent of $X, they receive 110 percent of $Y, etc. There can be compensating penalties if they fail to achieve $X. This is a good bargain for the company and for the outside partner. But marketing may not be able to sign such an agreement. Why not?

Because in most companies, marketing operates on a fixed budget approved in an annual plan. The revenue from sales or profits does not come to the marketing department. So if the database increases company profits by 20 percent, for example, the marketing budget remains the same. There is no account from which the marketing department may draw funds to compensate the outside partner. This situation probably applies in your company. What can you do?

In such a situation, the database contract with a bonus plan has to be approved at a high level within the company, particularly by the CFO and the SVP of Sales. These executives may have the power and budget authority to implement a bonus plan. It is possible to use LTV projections for both the marketing chief and the outside partner to predict the success of a database marketing initiative. If you want to get a significant return on investment from database marketing, you may have to find a way to implement such a bonus arrangement.

Summary

1. Using database marketing to find new prospects is relatively easy. Building a profitable long-term relationship with existing customers is often rather difficult.

2. In some product situations, relationship marketing may not be possible at all. A list of the easy and difficult products is presented, knowing that the list is probably full of holes, but may be helpful as a starting point.

3. To be successful, relationship building requires a well thought through marketing program, an easy way to get names, addresses and purchase behavior, and repeat purchases with name capture at the point of sale, an affinity group, and some sort of system that benefits both parties.

4. Even the best database program can be defeated by mistakes in execution, which occur all too often.

5. Seldom purchased appliances may not be profitable candidates for database marketing, although a Web site would not be inappropriate. It is possible to use lifetime value analysis to determine whether database marketing would work before serious money is expended on building a database.

6. Before you start any project, compute your return on investment.

7. Before you sign a pay per performance contract with a database providing partner, make sure you can honor your agreement.

Executive Quiz 17

Answers to quiz questions (Figures 17-13 and 17-14) can be found in Appendix B.

Fill in the blanks below:

Quiz 17-9 Chart	Current	With DB
Annual Customers	1,500,000	1,500,000
Renewal rate	25%	26%
Renewals		
Renewal Payment	$40.00	$40.00
Visits per year	2.5	2.6
Spending per Visit	$38.00	$39.00
Spend per renewal		
Annual Renewal Spend	$0	$0
Lapsed customers	3,000,000	3,000,000
Reactivation Rate	10%	11%
Reactivated Customers		
Reactivated Spending		
Renewal + Reactivate Spending		
Total Increase		
Database Plus Comm Costs		$1,000,000
Net Increase		
Return on Investment		

Figure 17-13. Quiz 17A.

Put the appropriate letter before each answer	
Questions	**Answers**
a US Air Miles Program drawback	1
b Why relationship building mistakes often not realized	Apparel manufacturing
c Success in relationship marketing requires	Buyer make a profit
d Unlikely area for successful relationship marketing	Consumers
e Who not to keep on DB of medical thermometer manufacturer	Data impossible to get
f Makes for unsuccessful database marketing	Dining Room Furniture
g Why pay per performance may not work	Home maintenance services
h Dining room furniture consumer database	LTV usually goes down
i Why consumer DB does not work for appliances	Marketing lacks the budget
j Better response rate than many communications	Personalized messages
k Product unlikely to be successful with database marketing	Proof of purchase clipping
l Product likely to succeed with database marketing	Purchase behavior by individuals
m Needed for database marketing	Results take longer to see
n Result of database marketing for appliances	Unlikely to succeed
o ROI = (total revenue gain / total increased costs) minus ?	Unpredictable purchase date

Figure 17-14. Quiz 17B.

18

Choosing Business Partners

> *"...Partnership produces a long array of benefits in the management of change...State Farm refers to its agents as marketing partners, and that's more than just a pretty phrase. Neither agent nor company can survive without the other; for either to prosper, both must meet their separate responsibilities with energy and skill...By structuring partnerships with the right value-sharing incentives, the company has managed to thrive for more than seventy years, creating the largest network of independent business locations in North America—half again as many as McDonald's or 7-11."*
>
> FREDERICK REICHHELD
> *The loyalty effect*

Why Outsource?

If you have been to one of the National Center for Database Marketing's conferences, you will notice that most of the success stories involve outsourcing to external partners. While anyone can do some form of database marketing, those who are most successful seek outside help. What functions can you outsource?

- Strategy development
- Designing and building a database
- Customer service and communications

- Telesales
- Building a Web site
- Maintaining a database and a Web site
- Fulfillment

Why would you want to outsource functions to external partners? There are a number of important reasons:

- *Experience.* Many service bureaus have designed, built, and maintained databases for other companies in the past. If you get them to help you, you will get the benefit of their experience: the mistakes they have made in the past which they will try not to repeat and the new ideas that others have thought up, that you may pick up from them.

- *Expertise.* Some companies have achieved unique knowledge of particular fields such as financial services, pharmaceutical direct to consumer, business to business, loyalty programs, direct response TV, or Web advertising that you simply could not replicate in-house in a short time.

- *Speed.* If you are going to set up a database, a Web site, or a teleservices operation inside your company, it will take a lot longer to do it internally than if you go to an outside experienced provider. Internally, you will have to hire skilled people, and train them. This takes time and money. Outsourced functions can usually get started in half the time.

- *Economy.* If you compare the cost of doing these functions inside with doing them at an outside source, you will find that in many cases, you can save money. To do database marketing, there is a lot of software to be purchased, and people to be trained to use it. This is expensive.

- *Entrepreneurship.* Building inside usually involves full time people. They may not all work for the marketing department. Typically, your MIS department may want to build the Web site or maintain the database. When you need something done now, and not a month from now, your MIS director may say, "I have two programmers out sick, and a four month backlog of regular work. You will just have to wait." And she is probably right. But, if you tell your external service bureau partner to undertake a new project, she is likely to say, "Great! When do I start?" Why the difference? For the service bureau, this is money. She is maintaining four other databases right now. She can divert other people, or take on additional contract programmers to meet your needs. That is not so easy inside. It is easy to throw your weight around with a contract service bureau. It is not as easy to do that inside your company.

To outsource a function, you have to find someone to do business with, and that is where you need a Request for Proposals, or an RFP. In this chapter, we will give you some suggestions on how to write such a document. First, however, you might want to consider outsourcing the RFP function as well.

Outsourcing the RFP Function

There are consultants who write RFPs for other companies. Using such consultants can save you many weeks of one-time-only learning which you may not need to use again. Using the skills and resources of someone who has done the same function two or three times for other companies can save you time and money.

Creating an RFP Committee

Any significant RFP will require some sort of internal committee to prepare it, and to select the winners. Typically, a committee will consist of people from marketing, MIS, sales, customer service, contracting, and, if available, your direct agency. Marketing should chair the committee to keep it focused on the marketing goals.

Qualifying the Participants

Your first job is to decide whom to send the RFP to. You can solve this problem by calling people you know in the industry and asking them. Attend the National Center for Database Marketing where you can meet with a dozen companies over a couple of days. It is important to pre-qualify the participants so as not to waste your time and those of unqualified firms. You might consider sending out a one-page e-mail or letter survey form, which would ask some key questions to determine if the recipient companies have the skills and the interest in your project. For those who respond positively, you might follow up with the confidentiality agreement, getting this signed before you send out the RFP. Don Hinman of Acxiom suggests that this letter should contain a précis of your situation and ask each respondent to provide a two-page description of a possible solution to your requirements. This would not be a statement of how wonderful they think they are, but how they would go about solving your problems.

Do not send out too many RFPs. Four is plenty. What is wrong with sending out 10 or 15 or more? Two things: you will be wasting the time of scores of people in answering your RFP. And you will be wasting possibly weeks of time of your committee members reviewing thick responses from far too many companies. Trim the project down to size before you send anything out. Do your homework in advance, not afterwards.

Writing the Scope of Work

The first step in an RFP is a definition of the work to be done. A well-developed scope of work will guide your thinking and actions, and help your prospective partners understand what is required. There are several parts to a scope of work.

- *Background.* You need to describe your company, its products and its customers. Start a few years ago, and tell how you got to where you are today. Explain whether you are in a growth phase or a mature phase. Talk about how products are sold. Is there a channel of distributors and retailers? Are there independent or company-owned dealers or agents? How are you organized to sell? Describe the marketing staff and the sales staff. If there is a database already, describe it. How big is it? What data is in it? How is it updated and maintained? Who uses it, and what for? What is the culture of your company, and where is it going?

- *The Problem.* You would not be writing this RFP today if there were not some problem to be solved. How did the problem come about? Is it caused by external competition, by a change in the market? What steps have already been made to solve this problem, and why did they not work out?

- *The Solution.* Describe how you think that the problem can be solved by using external resources. What do you think that outsiders can do to help? Explain what changes in the database, or the Web site, or customer service, or inside sales, or sales force automation you think would lead to a satisfactory solution to the problem. Give your ideal answer.

- *The Goal.* You need a one-paragraph statement of the goal of your database marketing program. Examples:

  □ Reducing attrition by five percent within the next year.

  □ Increasing customer lifetime value by 10 percent in the next year.

  □ Increasing our customer base by 20 percent per year for the next three years.

  This goal should give a meaning and purpose to your entire scope of work.

- *Your strategy.* To support your goal, the scope of work must spell out an overall strategy, outlining how you are going to get from here to there. The specific project for which you are seeking assistance may be as mundane as "producing thank you letters" or "responding to DRTV advertisements." The strategy indicates how this particular activity is aimed at achieving the specified goal. Without this strategy statement, your outsource partners may not see the real purpose in what they are doing. You may miss your objective because the implementers do not have the full picture. There is a second reason why this strategy statement is important. By putting it in writing, you may realize that what you are asking the outsourcers to do cannot achieve the goals you have set. You may have to change the scope of work before you issue the RFP.

- *The customers.* Provide a description of your customers. What are they like? What problems have they had in working with your company? What do they want from your company that they are not getting? Why are the defectors leaving? What would you like to do in the way of communications with customers that would be better than what you are doing right now?

- *The size of the work.* How big a solution are you looking for right now? Some companies make the mistake of thinking too big. They look for some huge comprehensive solution that will take several years to implement, and could pose great funding difficulties. You are much better off coming up with a master design that begins with only one small step for mankind. Database marketing is best accomplished by a series of small successes, rather than massive reorganizations. Lay out a series of small improvements that you think that an outside firm can undertake within a few months, which will demonstrate to your management that real progress is being made. In the course of implementing these small improvements, you will undoubtedly see new projects that should be carried out. These could be amendments to the original contract.

■ *Break the job down into phases.* If the project is very large, it is better to break it down into phases. You can scope out Phase 1 in great detail, and list what will happen in Phases 2 and 3 in less detail, since you will get separate bids on them later. The winner of Phase 1 will probably get Phases 2 and 3 as well, but that is off in the future. If the winner of Phase 1 does not work out, you can bid out the other phases. It gives you much more flexibility than bidding the whole thing out at once. Once you get started on database projects, you will be learning a lot, and changing your strategy and direction, based on what you learn. So the phase idea may make very good business sense.

■ *Quantitative measures.* You have to give your prospective partners some idea of the numbers they are dealing with. If you are thinking of a call center, estimate the number of calls per day, per week, per year. If it is a database, tell how many records are in the database now and how many will be added each month. Provide a sample of the data, on a CD that you provide to each bidder so that they can get a feel of what you are talking about.

■ *Organizational location.* Who is going to use the data? Describe the divisions of your company, and what they will do with the data. If possible, provide a flow chart that explains where the data comes from, who works on it, and where it goes. Explain the mission of each group: "Inquiries go to the telemarketers who qualify them and set up appointments for the sales force. They enter data into the database, which is used by the fulfillment staff to send out brochures. The data generates an automatic e-mail or fax that thanks the inquirer for the call and reminds him of the appointment."

■ *The timing.* When do you plan to begin the project, and when do you expect to see the first results? Lay out a time line that covers the first year of the project, so the bidders will see what resources they have to commit, and when.

■ *The pricing scheme.* This is a most difficult requirement. You will be getting bids from several possible partners. You want to be able to compare apples to apples. It would be helpful, therefore, for you to give them some sort of numerical measurements to price out.

You might ask the bidders how they prefer to submit the prices: answer your questions, submit their own price section, or to fill in a spreadsheet or table. To be sure that the prices are comparable, each bidder should submit one table that shows the total amount to be spent in Year 1 and Year 2. That will help you to understand what each is suggesting.

Examples of individual price comparisons might be:

☐ *Database updating.* Based on the number of records involved.

☐ *Web site creation and maintenance.*

☐ *Fulfillment costs per piece.*

☐ *Modeling costs per hour.*

- **The budget.** You probably should not announce this in the RFP, but you have to have agreement from management of the amount of money that is budgeted for this project before you send anything out. If there is no budget, do not send out the RFP. The size of the budget will affect the scope of work. You simply cannot create a practical RFP without a budget. If asked by the bidders, it is helpful to tell them a range. "We expect to spend between $300,000 and $500,000 on this project during this next year." If you say that, you will eliminate bids in the $1+ million range, which are far beyond your budget. It will also encourage some bidders to think of creative ways to end up in the low end of your range.

- **Competition is a good idea.** If the project involves cleaning your records, and providing access using the bidder's system, you might create a file of 25,000 of your customers (complete with all the messiness and duplications that currently exist), and give the same file to each of the bidders, asking them to show you what they can do with your actual data. A competition like this can really separate the sheep from the goats.

- **Evaluation criteria.** Tell the prospective partners how you will go about evaluating their responses, including any weighting that you want to include: "Innovation 40 percent, Experience 30 percent, Price 30 percent," etc. Tell them how long you will take to review their RFP and when you expect to announce a winner.

- **A confidentiality requirement.** If your scope of work is any good, it will contain proprietary information about your company. Before the bidders are allowed to see it, they should have signed a confidentiality agreement). Your RFP simply refers to this agreement.

Rules of the RFP

- *Due date.* Specify specifically when the responses are due including date and time of day. Be sure to give them at least 30 days from the date you sent out the RFP. This is important. Never make the time less than 30 days. You will get slipshod responses as a result.

- *Questions.* Announce when you send out the RFP whether questions will be permitted (you should), and how they can ask the questions and of whom, and whether they may be in writing or at a meeting or by phone. Unless your project is very large (and we do not recommend large projects—see below), you should entertain telephone or e-mail questions, with a cutoff date. By that date, you should send out an e-mail letter to all the bidders with a summary of the questions and the answers. It is important that you be fair to everyone, and that you appear to be fair. You will want to do business with these people in the future.

- *Digital submission.* In the old days, responses to RFPs arrived at the last minute by Fedex, with 10 or more copies. That was before the days of the Internet. Today, companies accept proposals by e-mail or through a Web response device. We are getting very digital these days. The advantage in a digital submission is that you can easily put several proposals on a spreadsheet to compare them. We are database marketers. Let us be up to date. You may want to have the responses in two separate reports: the work proposal and the pricing. Sometimes it is useful to decide on the proposal without being influenced by the prices.

- *Where to send?* If you do insist on hard copy proposals (which is very old fashioned) tell them where to send the proposal, providing a Fed-Ex compatible address (not a post office box), since many of them will come in at the very last minute.

- *Extensions.* Provide in the rules of the road whether extensions of time will be permitted, and how to go about getting an extension. You may not think that this is important, but it almost always comes up, so think it through in advance.

- *Bidders list.* Decide whether you will release a list of the bidders to the bidders. I think that it is a good idea, and could help in the bidding process. I would issue the list early enough so that all bidders can know what they are up against before they bid. It will help you to get relevant and comparable offers.

Your Partners

If you are going to accomplish the objectives spelled out in the scope of work, you will need your contractors to become your partners. Too many inexperienced marketers look on their outside help as "vendors." They tell them as little as possible about the overall project, saying, in effect, "Don't ask too many questions. Just do what I tell you, and shut up."

You will not get their hearts and minds involved in your database project if you treat them as vendors. Without their hearts and minds, you may miss some vital ideas about improving your customer relationships, which may make your project less effective than it could be, or could even get you into real trouble.

Partner Example. A partner maintained the database for a Fortune 500 company that was doing DRTV. The program got one million responses in the first six months, for which the partner did the fulfillment. It was great business and highly profitable. There was only one problem. The people answering the advertisements were the wrong people. They were not buying the product. No one at the company asked the partner about this. The partner's dilemma: Should we tell them about it? The partner decided that they had to. Some of the company's marketing staff were thankful for the information. But others thought that the partner had exceeded their charter, which was to do the fulfillment, and shut up. What do you think?

Vendor Example. Another company asked their vendor to select a group of preferred customers, who were to receive special recognition and benefits. The vendor was not asked to set up a control group. They were not told what was to be done with the preferred customers, but they thought the absence of a control group was bad database practice. On the other hand, pointing this out might anger the direct agency which had set up the program, and considered the partner a mere vendor. The vendor decided to keep quiet. Later, the direct agency was fired when the absence of a control group was shown to undermine the validity of their results. What should the vendor have done?

Your objective in the RFP, therefore, is to find a partner who feels as involved in the success of your database marketing or Web site project as you do. How can you do that? The psychology of management tells us that your effectiveness as a manager is determined by the extent that you allow your employees to influence you. If you listen to what your employees say, and use your influence to carry out the good suggestions that they make, then they will feel that they are an important part of the company. They will put their hearts and minds into the work. You will be successful as a supervisor. The same principles apply to outsourcing functions. Treat these companies as partners, and you will reap significant benefits.

Key Questions

How can you find out if the people bidding on your job have the imagination, drive, resources, skills, and chemistry necessary to become your partners? There is a simple answer: treat them as professionals. Ask them these questions:

■ *Company history.* Who are they? What have they done in the past? What is their company philosophy? Provide references.

■ *Their solution to the problem.* Have them describe in their own words, how they propose to go about carrying out the scope of work.

■ *The training involved.* Most database or Internet projects involve training for company employees in the new system. The response should describe this training and provide the pricing for it.

■ *Who owns the software?* Since there is usually proprietary software involved, the response should indicate what that software is, and who owns it. The proposal should spell out how the updates to the software will be provided, and who is supporting the software.

■ *Innovative ideas.* Ask them to describe some innovative ideas that they have for your project, or that they have introduced in working with other clients.

■ *Biographies of the leaders.* Have them tell you about one or two of the key people whom you will be working with and what their background is. There is a caution here. If you have a big project, the partner will have to hire additional workers. Few firms have enough employees sitting around doing nothing waiting to see if they win a contract with you. Do not insist, therefore, that you know, in advance, all the people that will be working on your job. If they are able to tell you, it will probably be a lie anyway.

■ *References.* You absolutely must have a list of names and telephone numbers from companies that have used your prospective partner's services in the past. Call these people up, and ask them what it is like working with this partner.

- *Executive summary.* Tell them to write a one-page summary listing the key benefits of the system they propose.

- *Project costs.* They should use the scheme that you have laid out for the project. However, by all means, if they request it, permit them to give you their pricing in addition on some other basis that they feel more comfortable with.

What Not to Do

RFPs can become very deadly bores for everyone involved. In 25 years of direct marketing, I have seen some really horrible examples. Here is what to avoid:

- *Too many questions.* Many RFPs are designed by a committee. Twenty people throw in anything that they can think of. The questions go on for 10 pages or more. To get good results to an RFP, keep the questions to a minimum: one page or less.

- *Too many pages.* Many RFPs are up to 100 pages in length. They include all sorts of legal restrictions such as anti-discrimination, environmental protection, etc. A good solution to this problem is to have your legal team draft up a separate document containing all of the legal restrictions that they want. Ask the bidders to sign this document. Then put a clause in the RFP referring to the fact that the document is signed, and covers the work to be done under this RFP.

- *Cover too much in one document.* As I already pointed out, successful database marketing consists of a number of small successes, which lead up to a great overall success. If you make the project too big and comprehensive at the beginning, you may have trouble getting the money for it, or finding one external supplier who can do everything that is required. You should break the work down into phases.

- *Not enough time to fill it out.* Many RFPs require that the responses come in within two weeks. That is not enough time. For a good RFP you should allow at least 30 days. You will then have solid, well thought through responses. Some companies just do not bid on documents where the time line is too short. They may be your best partners.

- *Boring.* Database marketing should be fun for the marketer and for the customer. We are going to use the data in our database to delight the customer with unexpected recognition and relationships. Our employees will be happy with the system because they will feel the good will coming to them from the delighted customers. Your RFP should reflect the joy and enthusiasm that comes from successful database marketing. If your document is boring and puts people to sleep, your partners may get the wrong idea about your company or your project. If your RFP is boring, rewrite it before it goes anywhere.

■ *No money.* Some companies make the mistake of issuing an RFP before there is any approved budget within the company for the activities to be covered under the RFP. This is a terrible waste of time within your company, and in the many partners who you get to bid on your project. Some marketers think, apparently, that the RFP process will jump-start their marketing program. The winning partner will be so impressive that management will cough up the money. This seldom happens. Why not? Because RFPs that have no budget, soon get out of control. Everyone on the committee puts anything into it that they can dream up. Since there is no budget, there is little reason for leaving anything out. The final monstrosity looks exciting to outside partners, but it is all a sham. It will hurt the reputation of your company in the database marketing community, and make it more difficult later to get good partners to pay attention to you.

■ *Scam RFP.* Sometimes a company has decided to build their database inside with MIS. To be sure that the project is well designed and cost effective, they issue an RFP, getting outside prospective partners to bid, hoping that they can come up with some innovative ideas. The marketing staff has no intention of awarding the project to anyone outside, since it is already "wired" for MIS. This is a fraud and a deception. If you are a self-respecting database marketer, you should have nothing to do with such a deceitful scheme.

■ *Gullibility.* The RFP process can generate lies, mistruths, and exaggerations. Take everything you are told with a pound or two of salt. Question the references closely, and get to the bottom of any claim. If it sounds too good to be true, it probably is.

Evaluating the Results

If you have drafted a long, boring RFP with too many questions and legal paragraphs, now is when you will pay for it. You will have to review six or eight thick and equally boring responses. Every member of your committee will have to read through hundreds of pages of tedious text. You will have to use a spreadsheet to compare the results. This may take you a couple of weeks if your documents are too voluminous. Finally, you get your committee together, and pick out the finalists.

Try to stick to your schedule. Most companies fail to do this. They get the responses in by October 15, announcing that they will make a decision by November 1. In fact, the evaluation process is much more complicated than they thought. There is no decision until late January. By this time, they have missed the schedule for the early spring launch. The winner will have to race to get going, skipping several important steps. The project will be in trouble from the start.

Meeting with the Finalists

The last step is a half-day session with each of the finalists. Before these sessions, your committee should agree on a simple list of evaluation criteria, based on what they have seen in the RFP responses. Do not pay the expenses of the bidders who come to your meeting. Let them get there on their own. The atmosphere should be cheerful, not formal. After all, these may be your partners for years to come. See how you relate to them. See how interesting and innovative they are. Let them do any kind of presentation they want. Have a nice long question and answer session after their presentation.

Before the meeting, let everyone know how much time is available for the meeting. The time should be the same for all the bidders. Let them know what you want them to do at the meeting (one hour presentation, one hour questions). Let them know what is available for them to use such as a PC projector or monitor, or outside telephone line.

When the last presentation is over, have your committee meeting right away. If possible have the interviews in the first part of a week, and the committee meeting in the last part of the same week when everything is fresh in everyone's mind. Make a decision. Announce it. Get started.

The Contract

When you have selected a partner, that is not the end of the process, it is the beginning of a process. You need to draw up a contract that incorporates all of the concepts of the winning partner's proposal. That may take some time. It is a good idea to begin work immediately based on a Purchase Order from your company, so valuable time is not lost while the lawyers fight over detailed provisions. Time is of the essence. You are not building relationships with your customers while you haggle over contract wording.

The Transition Team

To hit the ground running, you need a single point of contact in both companies. It should be someone who has authority to make decisions and to get answers. One of the first problems will be to get MIS to provide the essential data: the customer database and the definitions of the fields. Sometimes that takes *months!* Knowing that you will have this problem, you should begin to plan for the transition long before you have finally selected a partner. MIS may drag their feet because they wanted the project in the first place, and are unwilling to help the partner. You may have to go to a higher level to get this problem resolved. In the early weeks, you will be inundated with detailed questions:

"What is the format for the product codes?"

"How can you tell which region a customer is in?"

"The format for the customer data changed last year. Where is the format for the old data?"

These questions have never come up before. You do not know the answers, *and nobody else does either!* Your business partner will have to get these answers, or the project will never get off the ground. Be prepared for the questions and figure out a way to get rapid answers.

Summary

1. Successful database marketing makes use of external business partners who do a variety of outsourced functions, such as building and maintaining the database or Web page, customer service, and fulfillment. These companies should be partners, not vendors.
2. Outsourcing contributes experience, speed, economy, and entrepreneurship.
3. The scope of work of the RFP should contain a definition of the problem, goals, strategy, quantitative measures, timing, and pricing.
4. You should have a budget for the RFP, sending it out to no more than six recipients, whom you narrow to two or three after the review.

5. Do not make the RFP too long, ask too many questions, make it too comprehensive.

6. Give people enough time to fill out the response. Do not make it boring. Make sure that you have enough money to pay for it.

7. When you have narrowed your search to two or three firms, have them come in for a presentation, pick one, and move ahead rapidly.

Executive Quiz 18

Answers to quiz questions (Figure 18-1) can be found in Appendix B.

Put the appropriate letter before each answer		
Questions		**Answers**
a	When should you not send an RFP	Ask them how they would do it
b	Maximum number of RFPs to send out	Boring
c	If the project is very large	Built faster
d	Outsourced database can be	Don't send out an RFP
e	If it is wired for internal IT	Experience and speed
f	How do you know you can handle your data	Four
g	What is the minimum time for response	In digital form
h	What should an RFP not be	No budget for the project
i	How to see if they have good ideas	Send them a CD with data
j	How the responses should arrive	Split into phases
k	Why you should outsource	Thirty days

Figure 18-1. Quiz 18.

19

Database Marketing and the Internal Struggle for Power

In a market economy at any given time, an enormous amount of ignorance stands in the way of the complete coordination of the actions and decisions of the many market participants. Innumerable opportunities for mutually beneficial exchange...are likely to exist unperceived. Each of these opportunities also offers an opportunity for entrepreneurial profit. Each of the potential parties to each of these unexploited exchange opportunities is, as a result of the imperfection of knowledge, losing some possible benefit through the absence of coordination represented by this situation.

ISRAEL KIRZNER
Competition and Entrepreneurship (Chicago 1973)

Losing Your Champion

In our business, you have to have a champion at the top, or there will be no database marketing program. In most industries, database marketing is not the main marketing vehicle. It is something new and additional to whatever was already in place. Often it is viewed with suspicion or fear by other units in the same company. These rival units often include sales, advertising, dealers, agents, or top management. If your program works well, you might make them look bad. You might steal their customers, or commissions, bonuses, or budgets. It is dog eat dog in the corporate world.

377

To illustrate these principles, here is the story of a couple of guys who developed a highly successful database marketing program, only to have it killed in its fourth year by a new executive who had other ideas. It is a fable of modern corporate life.

A few years ago, David Christensen was Director of Marketing of the Outboard Marine Corporation, manufacturer of the Johnson and Evinrude outboard motors. OMC had a 50 percent brand penetration in a very stable industry that had about 4,000 independent dealers nationwide. There were only two big domestic manufacturers, OMC and Mercury. Yamaha led the growing foreign competition.

David realized that database marketing was ideal for his industry. There was a finite, identifiable market of about 10 million U.S. households who owned an outboard powered boat. OMC had a database of two million customers who had filled out warranty cards. OMC decided to launch a new series of products to meet the Yamaha intrusion into the U.S. market. David called on Stanton Lewin to help him. Stanton was the Director of Client Services at LKHS, a direct response advertising agency in Chicago specializing in database marketing. Together, they were to make database marketing history.

They decided to build a database of boat owners and use that database to drive customers to dealers. They were looking for those customers most likely to buy a new outboard in the near future. They decided to focus on saltwater boaters, because saltwater was very corrosive to outboard motors. It destroyed most of them in three or four years. The new motor that OMC was launching was highly superior to any other motor in the market at that time. It was built with many stainless steel parts, which were impervious to the eating away of saltwater.

The Florida Test

They began with a major test in Florida, which had a very large number of saltwater outboarders, with 750,000 boats registered in the state. Their goal was to create a Florida Boater's Database that would identify exactly those boaters who needed a new motor in the near future. Secondly, they wanted to do research to determine the right message and the right offer.

The database was built by combining the 750,000 registered boats in Florida with the two-million-name OMC customer database. The data included the size, type, age, and propulsion system of the boat. From the data, they were able to pinpoint 250,000 Florida households that owned a boat that was at least three years old, used in saltwater, and the right size for the type of outboards that they were selling. They divided the group into OMC customers and prospects.

The next step was to create an offer. David and Stanton tested seven different messages each in seven creative executions. The message positions were:

- reliability,
- durability,
- technology,
- warranty,
- corrosion resistance,
- made in America,
- price.

They tested the messages in focus groups in three cities in Florida. The winning message was Technology. The new engine had more stainless steel, and hence would last longer in saltwater. Their slogan was: "Their warranty is written on paper. Ours is written on stainless steel." After several tests, their stroke of genius was a free gallon of oil for anyone who would bring the coupon to a dealer to check out the new motor. Outboarders use a lot of oil.

To get the program launched, they had to get the support of dealers throughout the state. If the field sales force was not on line, such a program would not happen. They visited dealers from one end of Florida to the other to sell the idea. The dealers had to understand the program and stock plenty of oil, which was paid for by OMC. The dealer message was reinforced with trade advertising to communicate the battle cry and rally the members. Before the campaign began, they launched a dealer communications package reminding them of their commitment to stock up on oil, and to reiterate their role in the program.

The direct mail pieces and the fulfillment to TV and print respondents contained local dealer names. If someone called in, they were asked five questions, including when they planned to purchase. Hot leads were sent daily to the dealers, many of whom followed up by phone. The media was highly integrated. Even though they used consumer advertisements, direct mail, television, in store materials, and fulfillment, all media had the same look and feel.

As a part of the 250,000 selected for the mailing, 20,000 were set aside as a control group. This group received no mailing, but was tracked in their purchases. The control groups permitted OMC to learn the effectiveness of their entire program.

The results were dramatic. Over a 16-week period:

- they stunned the competition with OMC's most dynamic product launch ever;
- their efforts directly increased OMC's market share for this segment by 17 points;
- for every dollar spent on the program, they increased gross incremental profits by $1.21.

The National Rollout

Throughout the Florida test, David and Stanton kept the CFO of OMC fully informed of their efforts. It was the OMC accountants who confirmed the fact that every $1 produced $1.21. With this type of proof, they had no trouble in getting the budget necessary for a national rollout. In the second year, their marketing budget was increased by 400 percent to multi-million dollar size. They used this to create a mega database.

Their new national database was the largest database of registered boaters in the United States. It combined 46 different sources of legacy data:

- 39 state registrations;
- two million customers;
- subscribers to publications;
- show attendees;
- demographic data from Polk.

The database included 30 key element fields in all seven million records, including:

- type of water craft and year;
- type of propulsion and year;
- recency and frequency responder data;
- type of boating application;

- age, income, education;
- spending indexes.

The database became a shared corporate resource. They did 32 mailings a year, setting aside 32 control groups to validate their results. They used it to sell not only the new motors, but also their parts and accessories. The result: they sold 24 percent more parts to the test groups than to the controls. They sent videos to dealers to educate them on the program.

Eight hundred dealers nationwide participated in the program. This group comprised the largest boat dealers in the United States. OMC mailed two million pieces a year for the next three years. Some dealers experienced an 8 percent response to the mailings. The average response rate was 2.83 percent. In subsequent years, the saltwater program was broadened to bass boats, fresh water fishing, and performance outboards. It was a highly successful program, well researched and tested. David and Stanton knew what they were doing, and really made database marketing history. Then it all came to an end.

They lost their champion. When the original VP for Marketing left, his replacement supported their efforts, once he understood what they were doing. Two years later, he was replaced with a new man who was totally hostile to database marketing. One of his first questions was, "What idiot came up with the oil thing?" The database project was abandoned. OMC went back to traditional marketing such as advertising in the swimsuit edition of Sports Illustrated, plus advertisements in enthusiast publications and sponsoring fishing tournaments. David and Stanton went on to other projects in other companies.

This is the story of corporate America. You lose your champion, you lose your program.

The Budget Battle

Inside every company there are always contests being waged between different individuals and units seeking larger budgets, personnel, programs, and power. There is only so much money to go around at any given time, and each unit believes that it needs more to accomplish its vital functions.

For many years, marketing—particularly database marketing—had a real struggle to get any funding at all. Sales and advertising were usually much more successful in their efforts. Sales could point to the revenue they generated. The results of advertising can be seen by everyone in the company when they look at magazines, newspapers, and television or the Web. Database marketers, on the other hand, operate out of limelight on obscure programs that many people do not understand.

The money for any new program—like a Web site or a marketing database—has to be taken out of someone else's budget. Those who stand to lose seldom take a cut lying down. Only when the CEO gets religion and decides to make the customer the focus of the company's marketing strategy will database marketing or e-commerce get a chance to show what they can do. When that happens, the marketers have to quickly produce something useful, or they will be swept aside. The attention span of top management for any new program seldom exceeds 12 months.

Database marketing is faced with a Catch 22 problem—database marketing cannot prove itself unless it receives:

- enough funding over a three-year period to permit the building of the database and a functioning Web site,
- the launching of a group of relationship-building programs,
- the establishment of control groups, and
- the measurement of lifetime value change during those three years to prove the long-run effect.

No one is going to give them sufficient funding for all of these steps unless the marketers can first prove that it works. How do you do that?

There are really two ways that database marketers can get the resources they need to begin their work: by educating top management and by demonstrating results through successful experiments. Successful experiments are described throughout this book. Let us concentrate here on educating management.

Educating Management

It is a common place of economics that the most successful production techniques are usually the most roundabout. For a primitive man to be successful at hunting, he had to first build a bow and arrow that usually involved much experimentation with different types of wood and different materials for the cord. To an outsider, such a primitive man would not look as if he were engaged in hunting, but he really was going about it in a very intelligent and roundabout way. Database marketing is also very round about.

To be successful at building customer loyalty and repeat sales, we must first build a marketing database which involves much experimentation with lists, software, data cleaning and correction, construction of reports and customer profiles. We must build a customer Web site. None of this looks to the outsiders as if it were connected with the generation of customer loyalty or repeat sales—but it really is an intelligent way of beginning the process.

Early man probably had a wife and children who were demanding that he bring home some food and asking him why, instead of attempting to catch an animal for supper, he was experimenting with pieces of wood and cord. Database marketers have the same type of disbelievers looking over their shoulders wondering what all this data processing and Web site creation activity has to do with the generation of profitable sales.

Because database marketing is so roundabout, marketers have to conduct a major educational campaign within the company. Such campaigns are really directed at influencing the top management, even though they begin by educating people at lower levels.

Management involvement is necessary because management has to understand the process before it will be willing to commit the funds necessary to make it a reality. How do you educate management?

a. You can send top management executives to conferences on database management and e-commerce.

b. You can recruit one or more experienced database marketers who know how to build a database, and create profits by using it.

c. You can sign up a direct response consultant or agency with database experience to advise you and brief the top management.

d. You can form a Web site and database marketing planning committee that meets regularly to lay out the groundwork for a comprehensive relationship-building system, providing regular progress reports to the top management.

All of these methods are useful and, in most cases, all of them should be attempted.

Database Conferences

It is amazing how much progress is made at national database conferences. I have been to almost a hundred such meetings in the last 20 years. I learn a great deal from each one. The speakers are usually executives from direct response agencies, service bureaus, or marketing departments of companies. Many of the exhibits enable you to get a good idea of what is available. There is no better way to learn the state of the art. The conferences not only educate, but also bring marketers into direct contact with service providers. The National Center for Database Marketing devotes a considerable effort to networking: getting people together. I had a very interesting experience at one of their conferences in Orlando.

In the opening session, the conference chairman, Skip Andrew, asked all 700 attendees to stand up, introduce themselves, and shake hands with the person behind them. I did so, meeting a woman from Michigan, an account executive from a small direct response agency. She had come to the conference seeking help in building a database for one of her clients, a large pharmaceutical firm. I had come to the conference to speak and to find account executives just like this delightful woman. In the 60 seconds that Skip Andrew gave us to talk, we found out about each other, and arranged to meet for breakfast the next day.

At the "all you can eat" buffet breakfast the next day, she and I spent two hours together. I ate six scrambled eggs, 14 sausages, French toast, and mounds of rolls. I also persuaded her to visit us in Reston to meet our staff, and discuss the pharmaceutical database. A month later, we had a signed contract, and were happily creating a fascinating marketing database, which is described elsewhere in this book. I have had other equally rewarding conferences, but this was the one at which I gained the most weight.

This conference, which is held twice a year, is probably the best single event for finding out about the science and practice of database marketing and e-commerce. If you can get your senior executives to go to such an event, you are half-way on your journey to introduce database marketing to your company.

Enlisting Outside Help in Your Struggle

The hardest part of database marketing is developing an intelligent and productive strategy, which uses the database. Building a database is comparatively easy. Making money with one is the real trick.

The famous economist Joseph Schumpeter drew an important distinction between an invention and an innovation. Inventions, he pointed out, are really not worth very much unless someone has invested some capital in their development. Once money has been invested in them, inventions become innovations; they change the course of human events. Leonardo da Vinci invented the airplane and a great many other things, which were, essentially, ahead of his time. Nothing much came of them. They came long before the industrial revolution. Capitalists were not available to take advantage of them.

Today many companies are resting on their past laurels, and simply will not go out on a limb for some new marketing idea. There are others, however, that are still struggling to get to the top, that are looking for ideas which they can turn into successful innovations. For database marketing or e-commerce to be converted from an invention to an innovation requires these two ingredients: a profit-making idea and a company with the capital resources and the entrepreneurial spirit needed to take advantage of the idea. Where do such ideas come from?

Ideas, of course, can come from anywhere. Many people have the ability to think up a better way to do the job that fate has assigned to them. With any luck you, the reader, will hit on a winning concept that will enable your company to make its customer happy, and build the bottom line with database marketing.

There are powerful reasons for believing that the best place to look for profit-making database ideas that can lead to successful innovations is on the payroll of direct response service bureaus and consultants. These reasons are:

- Direct response service bureaus have usually helped several companies to build successful (or unsuccessful) databases already. Either way, they have learned something valuable, which you do not know, and which can help to make your company's road to profitable database marketing a little easier.

- Such service bureaus and consultants must live by their wits. Lose an account; they may lose their jobs. The entrepreneurial spirit is strong. In large corporations, on the other hand, marketing employees are just that: employees who can count on a pay check whether they win or lose. The entrepreneurial spirit is weak or non-existent. Large corporations tend to stifle innovators, and reward people who go along.

- Outsiders, like external database marketing providers and consultants, can often go right to the top with an idea. Top corporate managers often listen to ideas from a consultant or executive from a database marketing service bureau.

For these reasons, you should have the assistance of an experienced outside database marketing service bureau or strategy agency in building your program and selling it to the top.

Forming an In-House Team

Database marketing is different from any other marketing program. It requires building a lasting relationship with your customers. They will come to see your company as a friend who listens to them, asks their opinions, and reacts to what they say. How can you deliver on that concept?

The only way is to get a large number of internal groups actively involved in the relationship building:

- customer service,
- your Web designer,
- technical support,
- sales,
- dealer support,
- advertising,
- corporate communications,
- fulfillment and delivery,
- accounts receivable,
- MIS,
- marketing research,
- your outside direct response agency,
- your outside database service bureau,
- your outside telemarketers at your 800 number,
- your outside data entry and fulfillment house,
- your outside list manager,
- representatives of your branches, dealers, or independent agents.

Few companies have all of these groups, but all companies have some of them. Your job, as a marketer, is to pull all of these units together as a working team, which coordinates policies and activities relating to the customer. For example:

- If you classify customers into Silver, Gold, and Platinum, how are you going to assure that the appropriate groups within your organization work to treat these different levels differently, recognizing the privileges of the Gold and Platinum customers?

- If you promise 24-hour turnaround, how are you going to assure that this happens?

- If you ask people to bring one of your promotional letters in to your branches, how are you going to assure that the branch personnel react properly to the letter, and let you know that they have received it, noting the customer's ID number?

- If you have a customer with a 10-year buying history and a lifetime value of $2,000, how are you going to assure that Accounts Receivable takes that into consideration when they fall 60 days behind in payments because they are traveling in Europe?

Looking at the above. You can see that you, as a marketer, must become the leader of a relationship-building team that completely restructures the communications between your customers and your internal units.

Getting these in-house and outside people lined up in support of the plan is a major job. But it is also a source of your strength. If and when you form such a team, they will see the value of what you are doing. They will appreciate the importance of customer lifetime value, and the part that they can play in making it grow. Once they have gotten religion, they will be your key allies in selling your program to top management, and getting the multi-year funding that you require.

Knowledge of the Market

How can you learn what is in your customer's minds, and what your competition is doing? Economists who assume that all knowledge of the market is shared by the participants just do not understand the market. The fundamental problem that all marketers face is ignorance: lack of knowledge of what is out there, of what customers want, of how to let them know what we have to offer. Every piece of knowledge about the market, about how to price our products, about what the customer is thinking, is valuable, and can be converted, by alert marketers, into profit opportunities.

The difference between those who are successful marketers and those who fail can largely be attributed to the ability of the former to gain knowledge about the attitudes and plans of existing and possible customers and to put that knowledge to work in a productive way. Successful marketers are alert to opportunities; but they have also developed ways of making the opportunities turn up—by increasing their knowledge of the market.

Building a successful marketing database fed by a Web site is one of those ways. Just as a CFO can look at a balance sheet and an income statement and determine a profitable direction for company activity, so can an alert marketer look at the information stored in a customer database, and learn of profitable marketing opportunities. Such knowledge, in the hands of a skillful marketer, is market power. It is also internal power in the struggle for success within the corporate hierarchy.

The data in a customer database is still rarely understood. Database marketing is now taught in a number of universities, many of which are using this book as a text. But often, such courses are hard to find. Analysis of sales figures is well known and widely studied. Income and expense reports, inventory, stock prices, and balance sheets: these are all common management tools. They give the CFO his power and influence. He uses them to control the destinies of most units of the company.

Customer data, on the other hand, is an entirely new breed of information, which many on the corporate ladder do not yet understand. Certainly, what customers are saying and thinking about current products and services and their desire for changes can be, in the right hands, one of the most powerful marketing tools imaginable. Let us take an example from real life.

Knowledge of How to Bring in New Business

What inducements are needed to get existing customers to persuade a neighbor to become a customer as well? Of those new customers brought in by such a program, how long will they remain customers— what is their lifetime value? From the answers to these two questions, how much can the company afford to spend on such a program?

These are detailed questions. The answers are far from universal. Success depends a great deal on the specific product, the offer, the method of selection of the customers, and the timing. If the marketer is alert to opportunities, and able to experiment and test, the database can provide very useful answers to these questions. These answers, in the right hands, represent real market power. Larry Hawks of Marketing Communications, Inc., provided an interesting example.

> A major propane gas distribution firm with over 500 district offices nationwide, had a customer base of over 500,000 households and businesses, located mainly in rural areas.
>
> Several years ago, a marketing executive launched a referral program to generate new customers. The referral package offered either a $15 credit on the customer's next statement, or a flannel-lined jacket, as the premium. Existing customers were asked to supply three referral names, which were then followed up with personal sales calls by the district office. District managers loved the program because the conversion rate to customers was quite successful.
>
> The letters to customers inviting their participation were highly personalized, bearing the digitized signature of the local district manager. The envelopes containing the responses went directly to the local office, instead of to the headquarters that sent out the letters. The marketer believed that making the program appear to be a very local affair would improve the participation rate and hence the overall success.
>
> In the first year of operation, the program signed up 3,000 new customers who generated over $3 million of revenue. One year later, more than 80 percent were still buying gas at the same rate. The total cost of the program in terms of mailings and premiums was less than $350,000.

What does the knowledge of how to go about creating such a program mean to the propane gas company? Market power. What does the ability to use that knowledge to generate $3 million in increased revenue give to the marketer who possesses it: internal power—the same type of power possessed by a CFO whose authority comes largely from his ability to analyze the company income statement.

Is the propane gas company spending too much or too little to acquire new customers? How much should they spend? Lifetime value calculation will answer the question.

Uses for Market Knowledge

A marketer who has built a marketing database, and who knows how to use it, as in the case of the propane gas marketer, thus has very powerful knowledge in his possession. He can use it to win customers away from oil and electric heating in the marketplace. He can also use it to justify his marketing budget within the organization. Here, for the first time, is a chance to stand up to the CFO and argue for a higher allocation for marketing in terms that the CFO can understand. This is powerful. It is more than the advertising chief can do—yet, because of tradition; advertising budgets are always many times larger than direct marketing budgets.

In time, this type of market knowledge will make its mark within most companies. The logic and precision of this type of calculation is unassailable. But to get to a position where he has that knowledge, the marketer must first get the resources to build his database, and learn how to use it. There are many steps necessary to the position of power within the corporation that most database marketers will attain in the future.

Steps to Knowledge

To gain market knowledge, leading to market power, the database marketer must:

- Build a customer marketing database, complete with purchase history and demographics.
- Develop an active marketing program which uses the database to gain new customers, and to retain and increase sales to existing customers.
- Build a Web site that involves the customers in the activities of the company.
- Determine customer lifetime value.
- Use the database and the Web site to analyze his marketing activities with precision and predictive capability so that he becomes the master of his marketplace. And finally,
- Use the knowledge gained within his company to obtain sufficient resources for the database marketing program so that it becomes the most powerful marketing force in the organization.

Obstacles to Database Realization

These are exciting ideas. They are powerful ideas. But realization of the potential of database marketing is not going to be easy for anyone. Here are some of the obstacles:

- Brand managers and the advertising agencies that they work with are not going to roll over and play dead when a marketing database comes along. Every dollar for a database or the Web site is one dollar less for the advertising budget. It will be tough.

■ The CFO, and the MIS department that reports to him, are used to being the information resource for the company. A customer database or a Web site, they will begin to realize, will, in time, represent an independent source of knowledge and power. This independence will rival the power that the CFO has gained through cash flow reports and balance sheets.

Some CFOs have caught on to this and are requiring such information as customer visitation frequency and the retention rate in the monthly reporting system throughout the company.

Power within a corporation tends to be a zero sum game. For everyone who gains internal influence, the dominance of other groups tend to be lessened. Few leaders will take the loss of power lying down. To the extent that consumer databases and Web sites confer authority and influence on the marketing staff, there will be a counter reaction from other parts of the corporation who feel their position threatened by these new techniques. In many cases, there has been, and will continue to be active opposition to database marketing and the Internet as a threat to established centers of internal power. Ultimately, top management will have to intervene, or potentially potent sources of sales and profits will be sabotaged by internal bickering.

How does this opposition manifest itself? Let us look at a couple of additional examples of real situations in major companies.

> The product design department of a growing company began to pack registration cards inside every unit that they manufactured. The cards were quite detailed in the information they requested of the registrant. The idea was to figure out who was using the product, and what they were doing with it so that the product design department could anticipate market trends, and come up with features that were most in demand.
>
> The project was a great success. Thousands of cards were received and poured over by designers who soon learned a great many things that they had not known before. For example, they learned that large numbers of people went out and bought—from external vendors—hardware, which they plugged in to the product to make it more useful. In effect, this highly successful product was carrying a dozen other companies, like parasites, on its back, whose existence depended on inadequate product design! Gradually they redesigned the product to incorporate these features so that the profits from these extras came to the company, not to the outsiders. The existence of the built-in features also provided a very useful selling point, which contributed to the growth of overall sales.

So many cards were received that the product design team could not handle them all. After reviewing them, they shipped them in cardboard boxes to the company librarian. This enterprising woman knew a professor at a local university whose specialty was public opinion surveys. She persuaded him to take the cardboard boxes off her hands. A local data entry firm keypunched the cards into tapes, which were sent to the professor at the university computer department.

Within a few months, the professor was able to furnish the librarian with printed reports, which summarized the findings from the cards. The company library soon became a haven for internal researchers who wanted to learn more about the uses of their rapidly expanding product. There were several problems, however. The computer printouts were very bulky and hard to read, particularly the carbon copies. Even though the professor presented the information in a dozen different cross-tabs, it always happened that the exact relationship sought by the researchers was not on any of the cross-tabs. There was a demand for additional reports. The professor and the university programming staff soon grew months behind in their ability to keep the librarian satisfied.

The librarian drew up an RFP, which was sent to three service bureaus, one of which was selected to take over the growing database. The change in the library was dramatic. Reports were now printed on easy-to-read laser copies. There were 56 different cross-tabs for each of the new models, which came out four times a year. There was so much information, that the librarian became an essential resource in all company meetings involving the product or public reaction to it. Her growing status increased the power and prestige of her job, to which two assistants were soon added, and that of her supervisor who was given a substantial raise and a new title. In effect, without realizing it, they had created a powerful consumer database.

It was not long before the marketing department learned of this valuable resource. After studying the reports, they tried to get tapes from the system to do test mailings. They were firmly rebuffed; being told, "Our customers are not going to be bombarded with junk mail. If we did, the flow of customer cards would soon cease." The marketing department's pleas fell on deaf ears within the company, because for the next six years, the company had more orders for products than they could handle. Marketing was almost irrelevant, and database marketing was never attempted.

After a few years, intense competition in the industry brought this company its first loss after years of growth. New management determined that this would be "the year of the customer". The marketing department was told to begin active marketing operations. They began to rent outside lists of names from magazine subscribers and others. The one source they could not tap was the company's customer base, which by this time included more than a million names. These million people had each purchased a by-now obsolete model. Marketing wanted to get these customers to "trade up". Selling to satisfied customers is the easiest sell in the world, but the company did not attempt it. Why? The protection of the fiefdom of the database manager. As he saw it, if he gave up his database to the marketers, his monopoly of information would be at an end—and so would his power and position within the company. He successfully fought any use of the customer base for marketing, alluding to a "sacred understanding with the customers that we will not use their names".

Needless to say, this company, which had one of the finest and most comprehensive consumer databases in the world, did not do any database marketing. Internal opposition effectively killed this possible marketing route.

Later, a competitor developed a Web site that permitted customers to create their own personal products. The competitor, Dell Computer, became a major player almost overnight, stealing market share from everyone in the industry. The effort to compete with Dell in their Web site was sabotaged within the company we have been studying because of opposition from the division that managed the independent dealers. "They will drop us if we sell direct." So, another opportunity was passed up until it became too late to catch up.

Is this attitude unique? Not at all. It is quite common. The General Electric Answer Center received three million calls a year from customers from whom it usually obtained the name, address, and telephone number, and an interest in a specific GE product. Were these names placed into a marketing database? Absolutely not. They were destroyed 90 days after the telephone calls were made. Customer service, you see, considered itself as a higher calling than mere sales. Customers do not want to be bombarded with sales literature, just because they called to inquire about a GE product—that is the rationale for not turning these names over to the marketing department.

Conflicts between Marketing and Market Research or Customer Service are not rare at all. Market Research, in particular, is often staffed by statisticians whose interest is to discover "truth" rather than to increase sales. They see themselves as researchers not marketers, and resent the implication that they have a responsibility for the bottom line. They feel that the results of customer surveys should not be put into the database. Real database marketers, on the other hand, want to write to every customer who has filled out a survey and thank them for their help, starting a profitable dialog with them.

Sales organizations also oppose database marketing. Database marketers want to get their hands on the customer names to put them into the database. Once this happens, the next step, as sales sees it, is direct marketing to the customers, cutting the sales staff out of their commissions.

Database marketers find that the names of customers in many companies are denied to them.

The fact is that information is power in corporate America. Those who have gotten their hands on information, seldom like to give it up to others—else, where is their source of power?

> The XYZ Company maintained ongoing records of the monthly service use by their one million customers. Augmented by credit data compiled during the customer's application process, the database represented a tremendously valuable resource for marketing, market research, financial analysis, customer service, product design, technical support, and dealer relations. In the early days, no one knew how to get information out of the database. An enterprising researcher whom we will call "Phil" imported the software package FOCUS that enabled him to extract data and produce useful reports. His services were soon in great demand on all sides. His boss soon told Phil to drop all other work so that he could become an information resource to the entire company.
>
> Demand for reports led Phil to a much-deserved promotion, and the appointment of a full-time assistant. Two years later he hired another assistant. Despite the staff increase, the team consistently maintained a six-month's backlog of requests for reports and data.
>
> Realizing it was time that the company entered the database marketing world, top management approved an RFP for an outside service bureau. The choice was eventually narrowed down to two firms. The first one would collect the data on their server; transfer it regularly to the company's server where it could be used by Phil and his staff to service data requests much more rapidly than they had in the past. The second contender would also keep the data on their server, but provided Web access by PCs from all of the departments, which needed information, thus largely doing away with the need for Phil and his staff.
>
> The decision-making process was an agonizing one for the company. Phil maintained that giving users direct access to the data would be a disaster: inexperienced users would not know how to interpret their results correctly, leading to erroneous conclusions, disputes over data, and mistaken marketing decisions. Users argued that their programs were hampered by inability to get information. They had no faith that Phil's famous six-month backlog would be reduced by the new system, as it represented a cushion for Phil at budget time to assure him of continued support for his operation.

What can we conclude from this?

- Knowledge derived from a consumer database or Web site confers significant market power on the company that possesses it and uses it appropriately.
- Failure to use the knowledge confers no power at all.

- Ability to capture and use the knowledge also confers internal power in the quest for advancement inside the company.

- Companies that allow this knowledge to be centralized to a limited group—for their own advancement—are weakening their market power, and denying themselves the benefits that come from proper use of a consumer database.

- Every company should

  1. Assure that all relevant sections have access to the data.

  2. Build a strategy for its use.

Winning over Top Management

You want to build a marketing database. You need to convince top management. Here is a strategy that will work:

- Determine lifetime customer value using the present system.

- Create a picture of lifetime value with the database and the customer Web site.

- Show the effect on the bottom line.

A Final Example

Let us conclude the chapter with a final example of the way database marketing and the Internet can be linked to changing strategies, organization, and to building profits.

A health information company produced a monthly wellness newsletter, suggesting the use of vitamins, hormones, enzymes, and various herbs designed to deal with arthritis, aging, prostate problems, etc. In this analysis we will call them vitamin pills, but of course, there were more than 200 different products involved. The newsletter provided valuable information on health subjects and products. After a year's worth of these monthly wellness newsletters, most people did not renew their subscriptions. Their renewal rate was 19 percent. As a separate business, the company sold bottles of pills containing the remedies recommended in the newsletter. When the Internet arrived, the company added a Web site that provided an additional way to order the pills. There were three vice presidents in charge of the three businesses: newsletter,

Newsletter Sales	Acquisition Year	Second Year	Third Year
Subscribers	300,000	57,000	22,800
Retention Rate	19.00%	40.00%	45.00%
Price Paid	$40.00	$40.00	$40.00
Subscription Revenue	$12,000,000	$2,280,000	$912,000
Costs			
Cost Each	$8	$8	$8
Direct Costs	$2,400,000	$456,000	$182,400
Acquisition Cost $33	$9,900,000	$-	$-
Renewal Costs $6	$-	$342,000	$136,800
Total Costs	$12,300,000	$798,000	$319,200
Profit	($300,000)	$1,482,000	$592,800
Discount Rate	1	1.2	1.44
NPV Profit	($300,000)	$1,235,000	$411,667
Cum. NVP Profit	($300,000)	$935,000	$1,346,667
Lifetime Value	($1.00)	$3.12	$4.49

Figure 19-1. Newsletter Subscriber LTV.

drug sales, and the Internet. They were highly competitive, and overall, the business was profitable.

The main problems occurred in the newsletter. Several million pieces of direct mail went out each year to generate the 300,000 subscriptions. The cost per acquired subscriber was $33. The subscription price was a nominal $70 per year, but everyone was given a discount to $40. On that basis, the newsletter never was profitable by itself. It was worthwhile only in combination with the vitamin business (Figure 19-1).

The pressure was always on the newsletter staff. "Why are your acquisition costs so high? Why do you have such a miserable renewal rate?" They tried everything they could think of, but the situation never got any better. Meanwhile, the vitamin business was very healthy. It depended on the newsletter for sales, so the acquisition cost was zero. Was this a great business, or what?

This chart (Figure 19-2) shows clearly that vitamin sales are a function of the newsletter subscribers. People ordered when they were prompted by the newsletter, and when they ran out, as shown by the increasing number of orders per year.

Meanwhile the Web site began to become profitable. The Web served mainly as an ordering vehicle for the vitamins. They published the previous month's articles from the newsletter and had the vast archives of

Vitamin Sales By Phone	Acquisition Year	Second Year	Third Year
Subscribers	300,000	57,000	22,800
Retention Rate	19.00%	40.00%	45.00%
% Order Vitamins	34.00%	40.00%	45.00%
Vitamin Customers	102,000	22,800	10,260
Avg. Vitamin Order Size	$72.00	$73.00	$81.00
Orders per year	1.5	1.8	2.4
Vitamin Spending	$11,016,000	$2,995,920	$1,994,544
Costs			
Cost Percentage	37.00%	34.00%	32.00%
Direct Costs	$4,075,920	$1,018,613	$638,254
Total Costs	$4,075,920	$1,018,613	$638,254
Profit	$6,463,800	$1,977,307	$1,356,290
Discount Rate	1	1.2	1.44
NPV Profit	$6,463,800	$1,647,756	$941,868
Cum. NVP Profit	$6,463,800	$8,111,556	$9,053,424
Lifetime Value	$63.37	$79.53	$88.76

Figure 19-2. Vitamin sales to newsletter subscribers.

past newsletter articles available. Their sales were only a fraction of the total vitamin sales, but they were growing steadily (Figure 19-3).

You can just skim over this chart, or you can study it carefully. It bears some close scrutiny. Web sites that sell products, like this one, have two sources of buyers: an outside source (such as the newsletter or a paper catalog) and Web visitors prompted by www.google.com or other search engines. In this chart we are just tracing the buyers that come from the newsletter. Why? Because we are trying to trace the value to the company of the original 300,000 subscriptions sold. We are not tracing the search engine buyers since that is a different acquisition stream which justifies a separate analysis. What this chart shows is that the future of the web site is heavily linked to the success of the newsletter. It costs approximately $100,000 per year to maintain the Web site. In the first year 18,000 people signed up to buy vitamins in response to the newsletter. The estimate was that six percent (10 and 12 percent) of newsletter subscribers used the Web to order. So the Web buyers in the second and third years are a function of the retention rate of newsletter subscribers. This means that the web site was dependent on a successful newsletter.

We can now add together the profits from the three business units: newsletter, phone vitamin sales, and Web vitamin sales from newsletter

Website Sales	Acquisition Year	Second Year	Third Year
Newsletter Subscribers	300,000	57,000	22,800
Percent Web Buyers	6.00%	10.00%	12.00%
Newsletter Buyers	18,000	5,700	2,736
Avg. Vitamin Order Size	$72.00	$73.00	$81.00
Orders per year	2.5	2.7	3.6
Total Revenue	$3,240,000	$1,123,470	$797,818
Costs			
Cost Percentage	37.00%	34.00%	32.00%
Direct Costs	$1,198,800	$381,980	$255,302
Website Costs	$100,000	$100,000	$100,000
Total Costs	$1,298,800	$481,980	$355,302
Profit	$1,941,200	$641,490	$442,516
Discount Rate	1	1.2	1.44
NPV Profit	$1,941,200	$534,575	$307,303
Cum. NVP Profit	$1,941,200	$2,475,775	$2,783,078
Lifetime Value	$107.84	$137.54	$154.62

Figure 19-3. Vitamin sales on the Web site due to the newsletter.

subscribers. (We can forget mail response in these charts. They represented only about two percent of the overall business) (Figure 19-4).

In summary, we have acquired 300,000 newsletter subscribers. The total profit from these 300,000 people directly attributed to the newsletter is $8 million in the acquisition year and over $3 million in each subsequent year. Remember, as you look at this chart, that we are tracing the value of these 300,000 customers acquired in one year. There will, undoubtedly, be 300,000 acquired in subsequent years which will have similar revenue streams. There are also Web customers acquired from search engines that are not shown here. Our goal is simply to trace the

All Sources Profits	Acquired Customers	Acquisition Year	Second Year	Third Year
Newsletter LTV	300,000	($1.00)	$3.12	$4.49
Newsletter Profits		($300,000)	$935,000	$1,346,667
Phone Vitamin LTV	102,000	$63.37	$79.53	$88.76
Phone Vitamin Profits		$6,463,800	$1,977,307	$1,356,290
Web Vitamin LTV	18,000	$107.84	$137.54	$154.62
Web Profits		$1,941,200	$641,490	$442,516
Total Profits		$8,105,000	$3,553,797	$3,145,473

Figure 19-4. Profit from all three units.

value of these 300,000 acquired newsletter subscribers during a three-year period.

A marketing expert was called in to look into the newsletter situation. He created the lifetime value tables shown here. For the first time, people began to see what was really happening. He made some recommendations:

- Combine all three businesses under one leader.

- Concentrate on the customer, not on the product lines.

- Build a database including information about the customer's preferences, age, lifestyle, and interests.

- Use RFM and direct mail to sell new products to existing customers—*result*: more orders per year.

- Personalize the Web by issuing each customer a PIN number, printed in the label for the newsletter. When they enter this PIN, the Web page will say, "Welcome back, Susan. Click Here to find out how to slash your risk of breast cancer by up to 80%... Jane Goodwell successfully got off heart drugs. Click here to find out how she did it."

- Feature the Web throughout the newsletter. After each article, say, for example, "To find out more about estrogen therapy, visit www.xxxxhealth.com and click on estrogen."

- Eliminate the subscription fees for the newsletter. The newsletter is a loser. Vitamins sales are the winners. Instead of a charge, have the subscribers fill out a questionnaire about their health, lifestyle and interests. Use that information to create a personalized newsletter and Web page. Have the newsletter subscription be a negative option decision. In other words, the newsletter comes automatically unless you cancel it. Result: the renewal problem largely goes away and we have much higher subscriber retention rates.

- Persuade 15 percent of customers to receive their newsletters by the Web, thus cutting newsletter costs still further.

The result of these changes in LTV is shown in Figure 19.5.

This chart, in a way, is a culmination of everything that you have learned in this book. We have used lifetime value analysis to make a significant organizational change in this company. The numbers show us that trying to squeeze subscription money out of vitamin buyers was a losing cause. The subscribers are simply an audience for the vitamin business. Using RFM we have nudged the orders per year up and the average order size up. In the first year, of course, our profits went down

Combined Operations	Acquisition Year	Second Year	Third Year
Subscribers	300,000	210,000	157,500
Retention Rate	70.00%	75.00%	80.00%
% Vitamin Phone Buyers	34%	41%	46%
Phone Vitamin Buyers	102,000	86,100	72,450
% Web Vitamin Buyers	7.00%	11.00%	13.00%
Web Vitamin Buyers	21,000	23,100	20,475
Total Vitamin Cust.	123,000	109,200	92,925
Avg. Vitamin Order Size	$74.00	$76.00	$83.00
Orders per year	2.60	2.80	3.70
Vitamin Purchases	$23,665,213	$23,237,783	$28,537,307
Costs			
Cost Percentage	37.00%	34.00%	32.00%
Direct Costs	$8,756,129	$7,900,846	$9,131,938
Newsletter Costs Each	$6.8	$6.8	$6.8
Newsletter Costs	$2,040,000	$1,428,000	$1,071,000
Customer Acquisition $33	$9,900,000		
RFM Mail $1 to top 20%	$60,000	$42,000	$31,500
Web Costs	$100,000	$100,000	$100,000
Total Costs	$20,796,129	$9,428,846	$10,302,938
Profit	$2,869,084	$13,808,937	$18,234,369
Discount Rate	1	1.2	1.44
NPV Profit	$2,869,084	$11,507,448	$12,662,756
Cum. NVP Profit	$2,869,084	$14,376,532	$27,039,288
Lifetime Value	$9.56	$47.92	$90.13
With 300,000 Customers	$2,869,084	$14,376,532	$27,039,288
Previous Profit	$8,105,000	$3,553,797	$3,145,473
Increase	($5,235,916)	$10,822,735	$23,893,816

Figure 19-5. Combined customer lifetime value.

because we did not have that subscription revenue. But by the third year, we have a profit increase of more than $23 million. This is modern database marketing using everything that we know: strategy, organization, use of RFM, use of the Web, and personalization to recreate the old family grocer. If you can create a chart like this for your company, you will be a database hero, and a success at your work.

Good luck.

Summary

1. Database marketing has a struggle to obtain funding. Programs take many years to show real results. The money must come from some other unit's budget. Programs can be funded only by persuading top management.

2. Methods include sending top management to database conferences, enlisting the help of a direct response agency, and forming an in-house database marketing planning committee.

3. Direct response agencies are essential because they usually have broad experience building databases for others, they have the entrepreneurial spirit, and they can gain access to your top management more easily than you can. In addition, they have large creative staffs that can really flesh out an idea.

4. An in-house team is essential for database marketing. There are a dozen different disciplines that are needed to craft a relationship-building program with customers. It is hard to get such a team together, but it is also a source of strength for the marketing staff.

5. In-house coordination is needed to assure that preferred customers get preferred treatment, that turnaround time is given as promised, that customer contacts are reported to the database.

6. Few company executives know how to compute customer lifetime value, and relate it to the bottom line, as they can analyze sales figures and corporate balance sheets. Marketers have to get on top of this discipline if they want to succeed.

7. Experience in database marketing, plus precise calculation of lifetime value can be powerful tools in getting database marketing budgets approved.

8. There are many obstacles: Brand managers and advertisement agencies will fight any cut in their budgets. MIS will fight marketers getting their own independent sources of information.

9. Information about the company's customers can provide market power. Too often, however, this information is locked away inside market research, customer service, or some other unit where it cannot be used to build market share. Companies that allow this to happen are throwing away money.

10. By combining database marketing and the Web, it is possible to change to a customer focus, from a product focus. The result can be a major increase in the bottom line.

Executive Quiz 19

	Put the appropriate letter before each answer	
	Questions	**Answers**
a	What was the secret of the OMC database program	A source of customer leads
b	How many annual mailings did OMC make?	A zero sum game
c	Joseph Schumpater discussed the difference between?	They are marketing vehicles
d	Israel Kirstner said enterpreneurial profit comes from	Built a marketing database
e	Best place to look for new ideas	Cookies
f	Larry Hawkes pioneered with	DBM Planning Committee
g	In Vitamin example, newsletter fees became?	DBM Service Bureaus
h	How can you say, "Welcome back Susan?"	Free Oil
i	How to be a database management leader	Ignorance
j	Where is the enterpreneurial spirit weak	Innovations and inventions
k	Fundamental problem all marketers face	Inside a large corporation
l	Power inside a large corporation tends to be	Lack of information
m	Why did the librarian get promoted	Reduced to zero
n	The General Electric Answer Center was not	Referral Programs
o	Why should websites not be managed by IT	The old family grocer
p	What is personalization trying to recreate?	Thirty two

Figure 19-6. Quiz 19.

20

A Farewell to the Reader

Congratulations on getting this far. You are a glutton for punishment! As we say farewell to each other, let us review the things that (I hope) you have learned:

- Database marketing and customized Web sites do not always work. They are generally quite useful in marketing to prospects, where they usually permit reduction in marketing costs and improvement in response and profits. They are most difficult to carry out successfully in marketing to existing customers. In the right situations they will create loyalty, reduce attrition and build your bottom line. There are some product and service situations, however, in which a database or personalized Web site may not be economically justified.

- The biggest difficulty in making database marketing or e-commerce work is the development of an effective and profitable marketing strategy. Too much attention is focused on hardware and software, and not enough on marketing.

- The way to estimate the possibilities of proposed database marketing and Internet strategies, and to evaluate the effectiveness of existing ones, is to create test and control groups and calculate the lifetime value of both groups. Lifetime value is the *net present value of future profits to be received from the average customer.*

- In free market transactions, both the buyer and the seller *always* make a profit. The way to increase your sales, therefore, is to find a way for the buyer to make a profit. In today's market situation, what the buyer sees as a profit may not necessarily be a low price. It may be recognition, helpfulness, service, information, convenience, and an opportunity to identify with a friendly and reliable organization: your

403

company. A customized Web site with an Extranet and a database program may be the ideal way to provide those things at the least cost.

Conclusion

Let us end with the words we started with in the Introduction: Database marketing and personalized Web sites are not just a way to increase profits by reducing costs and selling more products and services, although that is, and must be, one of their results. They are tools that provide management with customer information. That information is used in various ways to increase customer retention and increase customer acquisition rates—the essence of business strategy. The Web site and the database provide both the raw information you need, and a measurement device essential for the evaluation of strategy.

Looked at from the customers point of view, database marketing and customized Web sites are ways of making customers happy; of providing them recognition, service, friendship, and information for which, in return, they will reward you with loyalty, reduction in attrition, and increased sales. Genuine customer satisfaction is the goal and hallmark of satisfactory customized Web sites and database marketing. If you are doing things right, your customers will be *glad* that you have a Web site and a database which includes them. They will appreciate the things that you do for them. If you can develop and carry out strategies that bring this situation about, you are a master marketer. You will keep your customers for life, and be happy in your work. You will have made the world a better place to live in.

A

How to Keep up with Database Marketing and Commerce on the Web

To keep up with the many new innovations and developments in this field, you will have to read, talk to people, and attend conferences. During the last 15 years hundreds of readers have called me up to talk about their database marketing experiences. I have used much of the knowledge gained from these talks in the present book. As a reader, you should feel free to contact me if you think that the call would be useful for both of us. Send me an e-mail at Arthur.hughes@kbm1.com or call me at 954-767-4558 or visit the Database Marketing Institute's Web site www.dbmarketing.com.

Magazines

Magazines and newsletters that you should subscribe to are:

- *DM News*. Mill Hollow Corporation, 19 West 21st Street, New York 10010 (212) 741-2095, fax 212-633-9367 www.dmnews.com.
- *Direct*, Intertec Publishing, 11 River Bend Drive South, Stamford, CT 06907-203-358-9900 www.intertec.com.
- *Target Marketing*, 401 North Broad Street, Philadelphia, PA 19108 (215) 238-5300 www.targetonline.com.
- *Canadian Direct Marketing News*, 1200 Markham Road, Scarborough, Ontario M1H 3C3 (416) 439-4083 lloydmedia@compuserve.com.

■ *U.S. Banker*, Faulkner & Gray, 11 Penn Plaza, 17th Floor New York, NY 10001 Web site: www.electronicbanker.com.

■ *Bank Technology News*, Faulkner & Gray, 11 Penn Plaza, 17th Floor New York, NY 10001 Web site: www.electronicbanker.com.

■ *FutureBanker*, Thomson Information Services One State Street Plaza, New York, NY 10004 800-221-1809 sraeel@tfn.com.

■ *Financial Services Marketing*, Thomson Information Services One State Street Plaza, New York, NY 10004 800-221-1809 sraeel@tfn.com.

■ *Internet Telephony*, Technology Marketing Corporation, One Technology Plaza, Norwalk, CT 06854 203-295-2000 www.itmag.com.

Books about Database Marketing and the Web

All of the following books are reviewed and ordered at www.dbmarketing. com:

■ *The Customer Loyalty Solution, What works (and what doesn't) in Customer Loyalty Programs*, by Arthur Middleton Hughes New York: McGraw-Hill Publishing Company, 2003, 364 pp.

■ *The Complete Database Marketer 2nd Edition*, by Arthur M. Hughes Chicago: McGraw-Hill Publishing Company, 1996, 610 pp.

■ *The Loyalty Effect*, by Frederick Reichheld, Harvard Business School Press, 1996, 322 pp. A tremendously stimulating book full of good ideas.

■ *Customer Specific Marketing*, by Brian Woolf, Teal Books, 1996, 249 pp. The best book on retail customer card marketing ever written.

■ *Business@The Speed of Thought*, by Bill Gates Warner Books, 1999, 470 pp. Filled with very good ideas and case studies. You need this book.

■ *customers.com*, by Patricia Seybold Random House, 1998, 360 pages. An excellent introduction to customer relationship marketing on the Web.

■ *Permission Marketing*, by Seth Godin, Simon & Schuster, 1999, 255 pp. An excellent short study of the concepts espoused in the book you are reading now.

■ *2239 Tested Secrets for Direct Marketing Success*, by Denny Hatch and Don Jackson. NTC Business Books, 1997, 358 pp. The title says it all. Thousands of nuggets of profitable ideas.

- *Being Direct,* by Lester Wunderman. Random House, 1996. Lester is the man who invented Direct Marketing. In this fascinating history he explains how he did it.

Conventions & Seminars

The following events are probably the best two or three days you could possibly spend on learning about database marketing. The seminars include small groups of marketers from (mostly) household-word companies. There is a lot of interaction and networking. The NCDM conferences are held every six months in Chicago, Orlando, and other cities. The conferences are attended by over 1,200 people each time, with over 100 speakers. You will hear about new things and meet all sorts of people in our business:

- *National Center for Database Marketing Conference & Exhibition (NCDM)* www.the-dma.org.
- *Direct Marketing to Business* www.the-dma.org.
- *Annual Catalog Conference* www.the-dma.org.
- *The Net Marketing Conference* www.the-dma.org
- *The DMA Annual Conference* www.the-dma.org.

There are also other valuable database marketing conferences called from time to time by such institutions as *Canadian Direct Marketing News* (see above) and *Target Marketing* (also above).

Technical Assistance

If you want technical assistance in database marketing, you can contact me at Arthur.hughes@kbm1.com or 954-767-4558. I may be able to arrange assistance from KnowledgeBase Marketing where I am the Vice President/Solutions Architect. I can help you find the assistance you need in obtaining consumer data (AmeriLINK), database design building and maintenance, lifetime value and profitability calculation, analytics and modeling, data cleaning and correction, NCOA^{LINK}, merge purge, and all of the techniques covered in this book. More on KnowledgeBase Marketing can be found at www.kbm1.com.

The first edition of this book, which appeared in 1994, was the basis for a series of seven two-day seminars at York University in Toronto from 1993 to 1995. It was also the basis for 28 two-day seminars by The Database Marketing Institute held in Washington and San Francisco beginning in April 1994. More than 1600 marketers have been through these seminars. Many of them have contributed their ideas and case studies, many of which appear in this book. There has been a general clamor from these participants for technical assistance on the mathematics of lifetime value, RFM, Tests and Controls, etc. For this reason, the Institute has made available free software on its Web site www.dbmarketing.com. At that location, you will find many of the spreadsheet tables and formulas that are used in this book, plus *RFM for Windows*, a software package that has been used by scores of marketers in their work. By clicking on www.dbmarketing.com you can obtain:

- Books on database marketing and the Web.
- More than 140 published articles on database marketing and the Internet.
- Software with spreadsheet tables and formulas.
- *RFM for Windows*.
- Information on sources.
- Networking information to reach other database and Internet marketers.

APPENDIX

B

Answers to Quiz Questions

Executive Quiz 1—Overview

See Figure B-1.

Term to be defined			Correct Definition
a	LTV	u	Access to the database by many company units
b	RFM	p	Ad hoc back end analysis
c	Relational Database	t	Add age and income to a name file
d	Profitability	k	Affluent buy in several ways
e	Predictive Modeling	q	Customer learn about your company
f	Next Best Product	v	Customers like to build equity in your company
g	Caller ID	w	Don't waste resources trying to retain losers
h	Penetration Analysis	r	Instant customer contact
i	Cluster Coding	s	Main use for a database
j	Segmentation	l	Make sure mail gets delivered
k	Multi Channel Marketing	n	One purchase = ten catalogs
l	Address Correction	m	Plan and select for a mailing in an afternoon
m	Campaign Management Software	a	Predict future profits
n	Rented Lists	b	Predict who will respond
o	Tests and Controls	o	Prove that what you are doing is working
p	Analytical Software	j	Senior Citizens, College Students
q	Websites	i	Shotguns and Pickups; Furs and Station Wagons
r	Email	x	Silver, Platinum and Gold.
s	Customer Communications	g	Talk on the phone as if you really knew them
t	Appended Data	c	Unlimited storage of data about a customer
u	Web access	h	What percent of all law firms buy your product?
v	Loyalty Programs	f	What should we sell them today?
w	Treating Customers Differently	d	Which are the best customers today
x	Status Levels	e	Who is most likely to leave?

Figure B-1. Answers to Quiz 1.

Executive Quiz 2—The Vision Thing

See Figure B-2.

	Questions		Answers
a	The Left Brain	p	Amazon
b	Both buyers and sellers make a profit	j	August 18th
c	Stores in Germany	b	Basic principle of free market
d	Annual productivity gain 1700 BC - 1700 AD	o	Blocks of ice
e	Key reason for success of US economy	c	Close at 6:30 every night
f	Average income of Americans today	a	Computes Mathematics
g	Trade deficit with China	i	Determined by the customers
h	Why do customers buy products	l	Eighty six percent
i	Value of most products	f	Higher than their parents
j	When is Helena's Saint's Day?	g	Increases investment in US business
k	The source of our desire	n	The consumers
l	Middle class percent in 2005	e	The extent of our market
m	Profit = utility + brand − Cost − ?	k	The right brain
n	Who controls the US economy?	m	Time
o	Frederick Tudor	h	To reduce uneasiness
p	Jeff Bezos	d	Zero percent

Figure B-2. Answers to Quiz 2.

Executive Quiz 3—Lifetime Value

See Figure B-3.

Customers	Sample LVT Table Acquisition Year	Year2	
Referral Rate	3.00%	4.00%	
Referred Customers	0	510	a
Retention Rate	50.00%	60.00%	
Retained Customers	0	9,004	b
Total Customers	16,988	9,514	
Spending Rate	$200.00	$220.00	
Total Customer Revenue	$3,397,600	$2,093,080	c
Expenses			
Variable Cost Percentage	60.00%	55.00%	
Variable Costs	$2,038,560	$1,151,194	d
Acquisition Cost $40	$679,520	na	
New Strategy $15	$254,820	$142,710	e
Referral Incentive $20	0	$10,193	f
Total Costs	$2,972,900	$1,304,097	
Profits			
Gross Profit	$424,700	$788,983	
Discount Rate	1.00	1.20	
NPV Profit	$424,700	$657,486	g
Cum NPV Profit	$424,700	$1,082,186	h
Lifetime Value	$25.00	$63.70	I

Figure B-3. Answers to Quiz 3-1.

See Figure B-3.

	Questions		Answers
a	NPV of $4,000 in 3 years. int = 8%, rf = 1	e	53%
b	Int =14% Wait 4 years for money. Disc. Rate =	h	73.91%
c	Why include risk in the discount rate?	b	1.69
d	Retention Rate=Customers this year /	g	$6.10
e	2000 customers last year. 1060 today. RR=?	a	$3,175.33
f	Disc. Rate 1.8 Revenue $142,846 NPV=?	f	$79,359
g	80,000 cust yr 1. Cum NPV yr 4=$488,219 LTV=?	d	Customers last year
h	Cust buy cars every 3 years. RPR=40%. Annual RR=?	c	Obsolescence of product

Figure B-3. Answers to Quiz 3-2.

Executive Quiz 4—Customer Strategy

See Figure B-4.

Term		Definition
a	Why not market to gold customers?	h	A screen view
b	How AMEX helps magazines	i	A virtual table
c	Why cookies beat a PIN	j	Add fields without redoing the database
d	Getting subscribers to find others	b	Automatic billing
e	The value of a second product	k	Chief structure in a relational database
f	Globe and Mail renewal rate after	s	Customer Age
g	Personalized offers are better than?	p	Dictate data correctness
h	Dashboard	e	Higher loyalty to the first product
i	View	c	More like the Old Corner Grocer
j	Relational Database	r	Need only web access and a browser
k	Table	g	Offer of the month
l	Record	o	Primary key of another table
m	Field	f	Sixty nine percent
n	Primary Key	m	The atom of any database
o	Foreign Key	a	The sales will cannibalize existing business
p	Business Rules	l	Unique instances of a table subject
q	Event Driven Communications	n	Uniquely identifies a record within a table
r	Thin Client Application	d	Viral Marketing
s	Calculated Value	q	Your order has shipped

Figure B-4. Answers to Quiz 4.

Executive Quiz 5—RFM Analysis

See Figure B-5.

Questions		Answers	
a	Cost per piece = $0.72 Avg. Net Profit = $60 Break Even = ?	a	1.20%
b	Mail 30,000. Responders = 510. RR = ?	b	1.70%
c	Which produces best prediction: R, F, M, Demographics	f	219
d	Rollout response compared to test response is	k	31
e	Cust = 7,000 BE = 2.12 How may RFM cells can you make?	e	37
f	BE = 1.83% What is minimum test cell size	h	444
g	Best way to measure frequency	j	48
h	311, 444, 231, 211, 333. Which gives highest response?	g	Be creative
i	How to use RFM to increase the response rate	l	File fatigue
j	Divisions: R = 4, F = 3, M = 4 How many cells in all?	c	Recency
k	How many times sorts required to do RFM?	i	Skip low cells
l	Danger from overuse of RFM	d	Usually lower

Figure B-5. Answers to Quiz 5.

Executive Quiz 6—Communicating with Customers

See Figure B-6.

	Questions		Answers
a	Communicating with customers increases the?	l	38%
b	Needed to prove the value of a communication?	g	41.10%
c	In Travelers case, messages came from?	j	$2.54
d	In Lighting case, control group spent?	p	$2.69
e	Email messages compared to direct mail	m	$707
f	Ideal group to receive messages	n	1,500
g	How many birthday cards redeemed in case study	o	$50,000
h	Restaurant reactivation increased visits from 25 to	h	42
i	Which risk revenue cells should be mailed?	i	A and B
j	Travelers gain in ROI per dollar	c	Agents
k	How can Amazon say, "Welcome back Arthur"?	w	average order size
l	In telecom case, attrition rate reduced from 39.27% to	b	Control group
m	In telecom case, revenue per account increased to	k	Cookies
n	In telecom case, minutes used went from 1,300 to	r	Customer communications
o	Annual Indiana Health Care saving though emails	x	Failure to respond
p	Annual participating Travelers agent costs per customer	f	High LTV, High Churn
q	Who helped Dayton Hudson improve communications?	q	Hot line staff
r	Central idea in database marketing	d	Less than before
s	Result of giving customers access to a premier page	t	Lifetime Value
t	Risk revenue axes is likelihood of leaving versus	e	Lower response
u	The best time to sell a second product	a	Retention rate
v	Good way to assure envelopes get opened	v	Show accumulated points
w	Successful retention messages also increase	y	The next best product
x	What shatters the illusion of a close relationship?	u	The same day
y	Product path analysis helps to determine	s	They become addicted

Figure B-6. Answers to Quiz 6.

Executive Quiz 7—Customer Retention and Loyalty

See Figure B-7.

	Questions		Answers
a	Higher insurance customer retention	r	13 members in the program
b	Loyal Customers	l	About twenty percent.
c	Why insurance retention rate went up	e	Acquire loyal customers
d	Primary purpose of loyalty card	f	Affluent customers
e	Reichheld's Discovery about Loyalty	c	Agents sought better customers
f	Which customers like loyalty programs	b	Buy higher priced products
g	Why Helena & Arthur dropped MBNA	h	Cookies
h	Caller ID on the Web	i	Customer communications
i	Link between loyalty and database marketing	g	Didn't offer American Miles
j	How you measure loyalty	o	Don't answer the phone right away
k	Those who give you their preferences	q	Dropped 37.65% with communications
l	How many Americans move each year	d	Get information about customers
m	How to know if birthday cards work	p	High revenue high risk
n	Why the paint companies did not want paint	a	Increase commissions for renewals
o	How one bank discourages unprofitables	u	Long term loyal customers
p	Most important quadrant for retention	k	More loyal than those who don't
q	Cell Phone Loyalty #2 Gold Churn	t	One third
r	Hallmark Gold Crown after 3 years	m	Tests and controls
s	Very important names in a database	s	The defectors
t	How many Gold Crown dollars on the cards	j	The retention or renewal rate
u	A higher retention and referral rate	n	Their customers paid for it.

Figure B-7. Answers to Quiz 7.

Executive Quiz 8—Customer Segmentation

See Figure B-8.

	Definition		Term to be defined
a	Families with children	d	Anecdote
b	Gold, Silver	j	Automated Communication
c	On line database access	g	Behavioral Data
d	A strategy that worked elsewhere	q	Beltway Boomers
e	Aha! This will work for us.	m	Control Group
f	Age, Income	f	Demographic Data
g	Mail responsiveness	y	Gold Coaster
h	Points and Perks	u	High Flyers
i	First Class	r	Index of response
j	Happy Birthday	c	Infrastructure
k	High responding non profit cluster	e	Insight
l	I think these folks will respond	t	Length of Residence
m	Don't send them what others get	s	Long Form
n	Loyalty	o	Migration
o	Move up or down	v	Opt In Email Addresses
p	Percent spending in your category	i	Perk
q	A PRIZM NE Group Name	x	Quadrant Analysis
r	Response compared to cell population	n	Retention
s	US Census Data	h	Rewards
t	Long time no move	k	Rustic Elders
u	Airline Segment	a	Segment
v	You can send me commercials	l	Segment Hypothesis
w	Digital neighborhood cluster	p	Share of wallet
x	Income versus spending	b	Status Levels
y	Resort Chain Segment	w	Upscale Analogs

Figure B-8. Answers to Quiz 8.

Executive Quiz 9—Predictive Modeling

See Figure B-9.

	Questions		Answers
a	Helps to create marketing segments	c	−0.06
b	Not demographic data	n	500
c	Factor weight = − 0.5. More likely to respond than weight = ?	j	Addresses
d	Model works well with test, but not with validation. Problem?	k	Algorithm
e	Why do response rates go up when you use a model?	o	Behavioral Data
f	A hot line name	a	CHAID
g	Which predicts response better? RFM or a profile?	e	Don't mail low deciles
h	If customer income exceeds national average, response = ?	i	Faster, cheaper
i	Why should you outsource a model?	h	May not be related
j	NCOA^LINK may change some?	d	Model is bad.
k	A mathematical routine	l	Models
l	SAS or SPSS are used to run	m	Much bigger than average
m	Outliers	f	New Movers
n	Minimum sales for a model	p	Previous promotion
o	Mail Order Buyer	g	RFM
p	Needed for predictive model	b	Zip plus four

Figure B-9. Answers to Quiz 9.

Executive Quiz 10—Customer Acquisition

See Figure B-10.

	Term to be defined		Definition
a	CASS	c	Classifies an address as a business
b	DPV	b	Confirms that an address exists
c	DSF^2	d	Corrects for missing address elements
d	AEC	g	Don't mail these
e	LACS	m	Don't pay for duplicates
f	NCOA	f	Finds addresses of those who move
g	Nixie	j	Forecast results in a couple of weeks
h	Throwback	k	How did you do?
i	Drop	a	Improves Accuracy of Delivery Point Codes
j	Half Life Reports	h	Inaccurately Cased Mail
k	Back End Analysis	i	Mail delivered by in house staff
l	Third Class Mail	l	Undelivered mail is not returned
m	Net Names	e	Updates rural addresses

Figure B-10. Answers to Quiz 10.

Executive Quiz 11—Testing and Control Groups

See Figure B-11.

	Term		Definition
a	Early Promotion of Teaser Rates	l	35,714
b	Select a sample file just like main file	f	Attendance increase of 3%
c	What determines test group size	a	Capital One
d	Non Responders	k	Could lose your job
e	Sears Canada Catalog Half Life	e	Day 20
f	Dynamic emails before a race	i	Eight percent
g	Holy Grail of Direct Marketing	m	Five percent
h	How Travelers faked a control group	j	Home Equity Loan application
i	How high did boat dealer response rates go?	d	May buy more anyway
j	How did Chevy Chase know insurance levels	c	Minimum of 500 responders
k	Danger in not testing	g	Single Variable Test
l	Assumed Response Rate 1.4%. Test size?	b	Use an Nth
m	Travelers increased retention rate was:	h	Used non participating agents

Figure B-11. Answers to Quiz 11.

Executive Quiz 12—Internet Marketing

See Figure B-12.

	Term		Definition
a	Micro Site	o	Every night look for database changes
b	Viral Marketing	d	Find things inside a web site
c	Google	c	Find things rapidly on the web
d	Search Box	m	Five times a day
e	Search Engine	b	Get customers to refer others
f	Spider	i	Get help while on a website
g	Shopping Cart	h	Nuisance when visiting a newspaper website
h	Registration	a	Quicker to set up and change than a company website
i	LivePerson	l	Spend more than other customers
j	SPAM	g	Takes orders and credit cards
k	Personalization	j	Unexpected and unwelcome
l	Multi Channel Customers	f	Used by search engines to visit web sites
m	Incremental Updates	k	Welcome back, Arthur
n	URL	p	What to offer customers
o	Trawling	n	www.yoursite.com
p	Next Best Product	e	Yahoo and Google

Figure B-12. Answers to Quiz 12.

Executive Quiz 13—Retailing

See Figure B-13.

	Questions		Answers
a	Occasional Shoppers	c	189 Segments for all 13 catalogs
b	Silver Customers according to Safeway	h	A top retail store customer CHAID segment
c	Sears Canada RFM system	e	Best customers buy baby products
d	Free Turkey for Thanksgiving	g	Can't find out whether the customers are buying
e	Why 40 foot aisle of candies was changed	f	Capture thousands of customer names
f	Telephone numbers in POS	l	Card Holders pay less than occasional shoppers
g	Why packaged goods DB fail	p	Elimination of 10% duplicate names
h	Age 19 to 20 and >$164K Home Value	o	Fifty times as much
i	Promoters use your brand name	r	From two weeks to thirty seconds.
j	Why Customer Specific Marketing Fails	d	Increased sales 20% over the previous year
k	Sears Canada Half Life Day	n	Market share for went up from 25% to 29%
l	Straddle Pricing	q	Maxed out. Doing all their spending with you.
m	The effect of coupons on brand loyalty	a	Often have a negative lifetime value
n	How customer specific marketing helped Big Y	t	Register their credit cards with you
o	Spending difference top 20% vs bottom 20%	u	Send them birthday cards
p	How Sears Canada paid for their new database	b	The greatest potential for increased sales
q	Why Gold Customers should not be marketed	s	The majority defect within twelve months
r	Outsourcing cut selection time for 60,000 custs.	k	The twentieth day after the first order comes in.
s	Customers earned by deeply discounted prices	j	There are puny rewards
t	How to track customer sales	m	There has been serious erosion
u	How to build retention	i	Valuable profit & customer knowledge at no cost

Figure B-13. Answers to Quiz 13.

Executive Quiz 14—Business Customers

See Figure B-14.

Questions		Answers	
a	Least service pays highest price	b	5.82
b	Risk rate 1.6, Interest 8%, payment 80 days, 3 yr disc. Rate = ?	c	Advisory council
c	Builds customer loyalty	f	Bargain Hunters
d	Not prime candidates for b 2 b database marketing	d	Gold Customers
e	Shift from supplier to supplier	g	Price
f	Most service pays lowest price	a	Program Buyer
g	Most important to transaction buyers	h	Relationship buyers
h	Most important segment for any business	i	Talk price
i	How to ruin relationship buyers	e	Transaction Buyers

Figure B-14. Answers to Quiz 14.

Executive Quiz 15—Financial Services

See Figure B-15.

Term to be defined		Definition	
a	Ad hoc queries	e	% customers who drop a product in a time period
b	Capital allocation	a	Access tools that permit answers to any question
c	Capital charge	j	Amount earned by the bank on the deposits employed
d	CHAID	h	Analytic tools permitting users to view details behind any query.
e	Churn rate	b	Capital set aside to cover unexpected losses
f	Corporate Hurdle Rate	d	Chi-square Automatic Interaction Detection
g	Cost of funds	i	Cost deposit insurance
h	Drill Down Analysis	s	Customer Profitability if she were to buy all likely products
i	FDIC Expense	c	Desired rate of return on capital assigned to the product.
j	Funding credit	m	Difference between interest earned and interest expense
k	Lifetime Value	l	Dollars to cover expected loan losses.
l	Loan Loss Provision	q	Fixed and variable expense of a product
m	Margin	g	Interest expense paid for the funds used
n	MCIF	r	Manipulation of data in a database using a mouse
o	Neural Networks	n	Marketing Customer Information File
p	NIACC	t	Monthly profit (less all expenses) provided by a single customer
q	Overhead	p	Net Income after deduction of the Cost of Capital
r	Point and Click	k	NPV of future profits from a single customer
s	Potential Lifetime Profitability	f	ROI above which the investment makes sense
t	Profitability	o	Software combining multiple multiple regressions

Figure B-15. Answers to Quiz 15.

Executive Quiz 16—Why Databases Fail

See Figure B-16.

	Questions		Answers
a	Why did Sears Canada reorganize?	e	Cost, experience, speed, expertise.
b	Why did Quaker Direct fail?	b	Coupons do not build loyalty
c	Why did Reward America fail?	a	Cross shoppers spent more than others
d	How long should building a DB take?	c	Few companies wanted the names
e	Why are most large databases outsourced?	m	Fifteen percent
f	Why did Chrystal Light succeed?	f	It had a theme, not based on discounts
g	What is a "Creator" in DB jargon	h	Lifetime Value went down
h	What proved that $30 per visit was not good	l	Marketing Customer Information File
i	The value of personalized communications	i	Sales are higher to those who get them
j	Collaborative filtering software	o	Selling names to manufacturers
k	An ordering medium, not mainly a sales medium	d	Six months or less
l	MCIF	g	Someone who creates profit with a DB
m	Stride Rite's lift in sales from personalization	j	Tells you what to offer to customers
n	To where did Sears move the catalog desk?	k	The internet
o	The central idea behind Reward America	n	The most traveled entrance

Figure B-16. Answers to Quiz 16.

Executive Quiz 17—Database Types that Succeed

See Figure B-17A and B.

(A)

	Current	With DB
Annual Customers	1,500,000	1,500,000
Renewal rate	25%	26%
Renewals	375,000	390,000
Renewal Payment	$40.00	$40.00
Visits per year	2.5	2.6
Spending per Visit	$38.00	$39.00
Spend per renewal	$135.00	$141.40
Annual Renewal Spend	$50,625,000	$55,146,000
Lapsed customers	3,000,000	3,000,000
Reactivation Rate	10%	11%
Reactivated Customers	300,000	330,000
Reactivated Spending	$40,500,000	$46,662,000
Renewal + Reactivate Spending	$91,125,000	$101,808,000
Total Increase		$10,683,000
Database Plus Comm Costs		$1,000,000
Net Increase		$9,683,000
Return on Investment		$8.68

(B)

	Questions		Answers
a	US Air Miles Program drawback	o	1
b	Why relationship building mistakes often not realized	d	Apparel manufacturing
c	Success in relationship marketing requires	c	Buyer make a profit
d	Unlikely area for successful relationship marketing	e	Consumers
e	Who not to keep on DB of medical thermometer manufacturer	i	Data impossible to get
f	Makes for unsuccessful database marketing	k	Dining Room Furniture
g	Why pay per performance may not work	l	Home maintenance services
h	Dining room furniture consumer database	n	LTV usually goes down
i	Why consumer DB does not work for appliances	g	Marketing lacks the budget
j	Better response rate than many communications	j	Personalized messages
k	Product unlikely to be successful with database marketing	a	Proof of purchase clipping
l	Product likely to succeed with database marketing	m	Purchase behavior by individuals
m	Needed for database marketing	b	Results take longer to see
n	Result of database marketing for appliances	h	Unlikely to succeed
o	ROI = (total revenue gain / total increased costs) minus ?	f	Unpredictable purchase date

Figure B-17. (A) Answers to Quiz 17A. (B) Answers to Quiz 17B.

Executive Quiz 18—Choosing Business Partners

See Figure B-18.

	Questions		Answers
a	When should you not send an RFP	i	Ask them how they would do it
b	Maximum number of RFPs to send out	h	Boring
c	If the project is very large	d	Built faster
d	Outsourced database can be	e	Don't send out an RFP
e	If it is wired for internal IT	k	Experience and speed
f	How do you know you can handle your data	b	Four
g	What is the minimum time for response	j	In digital form
h	What should an RFP not be	a	No budget for the project
i	How to see if they have good ideas	f	Send them a CD with data
j	How the responses should arrive	c	Split into phases
k	Why you should outsource	g	Thirty days

Figure B-18. Answers to Quiz 18.

Executive Quiz 19—Internal Struggle for Power

See Figure B-19.

	Questions		Answers
a	What was the secret of the OMC database program	n	A source of customer leads
b	How many annual mailings did OMC make?	l	A zero sum game
c	Joseph Schumpater discussed the difference between?	o	They are marketing vehicles
d	Israel Kirstner said enterpreneurial profit comes from	m	Built a marketing database
e	Best place to look for new ideas	h	Cookies
f	Larry Hawkes pioneered with	i	DBM Planning Committee
g	In Vitamin example, newsletter fees became?	e	DBM Service Bureaus
h	How can you say, "Welcome back Susan?"	a	Free Oil
i	How to be a database management leader	d	Ignorance
j	Where is the enterpreneurial spirit weak	c	Innovations and inventions
k	Fundamental problem all marketers face	j	Inside a large corporation
l	Power inside a large corporation tends to be	k	Lack of information
m	Why did the librarian get promoted	g	Reduced to zero
n	The General Electric Answer Center was not	f	Referral Programs
o	Why should websites not be managed by IT	p	The old family grocer
p	What is personalization trying to recreate?	b	Thirty two

Figure B-19. Answers to Quiz 19.

C

Glossary of Terms Used in Strategic Database Marketing

1:1 Marketing. A marketing system in which each customer gets marketing messages specifically tailored for her, based on information about her preferences and purchases contained in her database record.

Acquisition. Most companies are set up to acquire new customers, rather than to retain existing ones. Acquisition programs are seldom profitable, but must be continued to balance the constant loss of customers.

Ad hoc Query. Modern database marketing access tools permit you to ask questions like: How may women over 60 have bought more than $200 from us in the last four months?

Affinity Groups. Customer or product groups. Customer groups would include parents of new babies, sports enthusiasts, people who like to travel. Product groups would include categories such as financial service products, women's clothing, automotive.

Attrition Rate. The opposite of retention rate. The percentage of customers this year who would no longer buy next year.

Autocad. Computer aided design programs used by surveyors and others.

Average Pricing. A system in which all customers in a retail store pay the same price, regardless of the volume of their purchases.

Back End. As in phrase "back end analysis" refers to the results of actions with people who have responded to your initial offer.

Banner Advertisements. Small advertisements inserted on Web sites. If a viewer clicks on a banner, she is transported to the Web site of the advertiser paying for the banner. There she can register and purchase products. Banner advertising was supposed to be a highly successful way of reaching customers. Banners still work, but not as well as previously anticipated. The advertisements can be very scientifically calculated.

Behavioral Data. Customer responses, purchases, store visits, etc. Behavior is usually more powerful in predicting response than demographics.

Brand Loyalty. Loyalty to a brand, such as Hertz or amazon.com is valuable both to the advertiser and to the customer. The advertiser spends a lot of money to build up a brand image in the minds of millions of people. This helps to acquire and retain customers. The customers benefit because they enjoy shopping for well-known name products.

Break-Even. An RFM cell breaks even on a test or a rollout if the net profits from sales to the cell exactly equals the cost of mailing to or telephoning to the cell. The formula for the break-even rate is: BE = (cost per piece) / (net profit from the average sale).

CASS. See Coding Accuracy Support System.

Call Me Button. A button on a Web site that, when clicked, will initiate a text chat or a live phone call between the customer and an agent at the Web site. Call me buttons are becoming more and more popular as more people use the Web.

Caller Id. A feature of telephone systems whereby the call receiver knows the number of the calling party before she picks up the phone. Used by commercial customer services to get the customer's database record on the screen before the call is taken. It is very helpful and friendly for the customer.

Cardholders. People who own and use plastic cards issued by a retail store. Use of this card permits the retailer to know who is shopping and what they are buying. A powerful marketing tool.

Cell Code. After completing RFM analysis or traditional merge purge for a mailing, every customer is assigned a Cell Code that identifies her recency, frequency, and monetary level of buying (or the list from which her name was selected). Sometimes used interchangeably with the terms Source Code or Mail Code.

CHAID. Chi-square Automatic Interaction Detection. CHAID is a classification tree technique in modeling that displays the modeling results in an easy-to-interpret tree diagram going from top down instead of from the bottom up.

Churn. Customers may switch to a different service provider (of phone service, credit cards, etc.) due to a better price, quality of service, quality of customer care, equipment and technology, billing issues or simply more effective marketing campaigns. The percentage of customers who churn in a particular time period is defined as the churn rate.

Coding Accuracy Support System (CASS). An USPS certified system that improves the accuracy of delivery point codes, ZIP + 4 codes, 5-digit ZIP Codes, and carrier route codes on mail pieces. CASS provides a common platform to measure the quality of address matching software and to diagnose and correct software problems. It appends address quality and type codes to each record.

Continuity. Products or services bought as a series of small purchases, rather than all at one time. Book of The Month Club, or other products shipped on a regular schedule.

Control Group. Every database promotion should include a control group of customers who are not exposed to the promotion. The success of the promotion is measured by the difference in response of the promoted group compared to the control group (after subtracting the cost of the promotion).

Conversion Rate. The percentage of responders who become customers.

Copy. The text of your direct mail piece.

CPI. Cost per inquiry.

CPM. Cost per thousand records. Rental names are usually purchased on a CPM basis.

Cross-Selling. Encouraging customers to buy products from other departments or categories.

Deciles. A method of dividing customers into ten groups based on their spending or response. Very common in marketing research. Too numerous for RFM.

De Dupe. Identifying and consolidating duplicate names usually done in a merge/purge operation.

Delivery Point Validation (DPV). Contains all delivery point addresses serviced by the U.S. Postal Service. The software confirms that an address actually exists, allowing users of this service to avoid mailing to an invalid address.

Delivery Sequence File (DSF)—Second Generation. DSF^2 is an address hygiene tool that provides additional address information about a DPV-verified address to minimize address delivery errors not detected by NCOA^{LINK} or CASS-certified processing. DSF^2 processing further classifies an address as business, residential, vacant, seasonal, or throwback (i.e., rerouted), and it also identifies the mail delivery method—curbside delivery, door slot, neighborhood delivery and collection box unit (NDCBU), or central delivery.

Demographic Data. Information about customers or prospects, such as age, income, presence of children, home value, own vs. rent, etc. can be purchased for appending to a customer database or mailing file from such companies as Experian, KnowledgeBase Marketing, or Equifax. Contrast with Behavioral Data.

Dynamic Change of Address (DCOA). Over 30 percent of people who move never submit a change of address with the USPS. The DCOA file retains records of address changes for more than seven years, including multiple moves and forwarding addresses.

Direct Marketing. Any marketing system in which the customer is expected to respond directly to the advertiser (rather than going to a store). Direct marketing can use advertising, mail, phone, or the Internet.

Discount Rate. In lifetime value calculation, it is necessary to determine the net present value of future revenue or profits. The discount rate is divided into future dollar amounts to calculate the net present value. The formula for the discount rate is $D = (1 + i)^n$ where i is the rate of interest including risk, and n the number of years you have to wait to receive the money.

Discounts. If database marketing is done properly, it is not necessary to give discounts to customers, since they value the relationship with their supplier more than the discount. Discounts reduce the perceived value of the product and the relationship, and erode margin. If you have to give something, give points or premium, not discounts.

Drill Down Analysis. Analytic tools that permit users to view the details behind any query. Example: Query: customers buying more than $1,200 this year. Drill Down: break this down by product categories bought.

E-mail. Fast becoming the most popular method of communication between customers and suppliers, electronic mail is rapidly replacing fax and regular postal mail. Companies are being flooded with e-mail from customers, which they must answer rapidly. E-mail response is becoming a new business.

Employee Loyalty. Frederick Reichheld in The Loyalty Effect pointed out that the best way to assure customer loyalty is to have loyal employees, since many customers build relationships with the sales and customer service personnel.

Enhancement. Appending demographic or lifestyle data to a database or a list.

Entrepreneurship. To be successful in marketing, it is useful to outsource as much as you can to specialists who are entrepreneurs. Entrepreneurs have the freedom to be creative and the financial incentive to be successful. The opposite of an entrepreneur is an employee working for a regular salary that does not go up even if she does a very good job.

Event Driven Programs. Database programs which are triggered to produce output (usually communications) based on events: a birthday letter, anniversary letter, thank you letter, etc.

Extranet. A system whereby your best customers are given their own private page on your Web site which they reach through a password (PIN) or cookie. There they see messages, products, services, and prices just for them. Extranets build customer loyalty.

File Fatigue. Sending too many unwelcome messages to your customers produces file fatigue whereby they cease to read or be interested in your communications.

Format. The way data (name and address and other fields) are organized on a disk or tape. There is no standard format. Every company has its own.

Frequency. The number of times that a customer has made a purchase from you, such as orders per month, phone calls per month, checks and deposits per month, items per month. A part of RFM analysis, frequent buyers respond better than infrequent buyers.

Frequency Programs. Programs designed to increase the frequency of purchase by customers by rewarding them in some way. Frequency programs often work quite well.

Frequent Shopper Cards. Supermarkets issue these cards to give customers special benefits when they shop using the cards. The cards enable the supermarket to know who is buying what and when, and to reward desired shopping behavior. These cards are scanned at POS terminals when the shopper goes through the checkout lines.

Fulfillment. The process of sending goods or literature to a prospect or customer. Fast fulfillment is essential to successful database marketing.

Gains Chart. The segments in a CHAID tree diagram can be shown in a gains chart which shows how "deep" into a file one must go to select prospects that have the results you are looking for in terms of dollar value or response rate.

Geocoding. A system for assigning a census code to any name and address. Once a file is geocoded, you can append census data (income, race, etc.) to the records and assign cluster codes.

Geodemographics. Customers can be grouped by geodemographics such as zip code, age, income, presence of children, type of home, etc. In some cases geodemographics are very useful in segmenting prospects and customers. In many cases, they do not work at all.

Gift Certificates. A highbrow name for a coupon. In Gold Customer programs, customers are rewarded with gift certificates that they can exchange for products and services.

Gold Customers. A very small percentage of all customers is always responsible for a very large percentage of revenue and profits. The top group are the Gold customers. Special programs are developed to reward and retail these valuable customers. In some cases, it is not possible to market to them, because they are already giving you their entire purchases in your category. You give them super services.

Graphical User Interface (GUI). Software that permits users to access their data by manipulating a mouse.

Half Life. When you send out an offer or catalog, it may take months until the last sale has been registered from the offer. On one day, half of the dollars or responses would have come in. This is your half-life day. Once you know what that day is, you multiply by two and you will know the eventual success of the offer. Half life permits rapid tests. Free software is available at www.dbmarketing.com.

Hardware. Computers and disks, tape drives, printers, and other gear that are plugged into computers.

Householding. A process in which all people and their accounts are grouped by the house that they live in so that they only get one letter per house in a promotion.

Impression. A measure of Web advertising. Every time a viewer clicks on a Web site that includes your banner advertisement that counts as an impression. You pay the Web site $X per thousand impressions (CPM).

Integrated Account Management. A system developed by Hunter Business Direct in which a central telemarketer supervises a customer account team including customer service and a field sales force.

Internet. A modern system that links computers all over the world including e-mail and access to Web sites. The Internet has a lookup system so that you can find and view any Web site if you know its name (URL).

Lead. In business to business, a prospect that has expressed interest in your product and has supplied his name and address is considered a lead.

Lead Tracking. The process of keeping up with what has happened to a lead (prospect who has expressed an interest in your product or service). Lead tracking is very difficult because salesmen hate to report on the status of leads.

Lettershop. An independent company that handles all the details of printing and mailing letters. Also called a mail shop.

Lifestyle. Each consumer has his own unique lifestyle, which may resemble that of millions of others. A wealthy senior citizen may have a very different lifestyle from a young unmarried hospital nurse. Each may be interested in buying different products and services. Once you understand their lifestyle, you can market differently to them.

Lifetime Value. The net present value of the profit to be realized on the average new customer during a given number of years. Lifetime value is used to measure the success of various marketing strategies including retention, referrals, acquisition, reactivation, etc.

Lift. The improvement in response from a mailing due to modeling, segmentation, or some other change in the mailing preparation. Divide the response from a segment by the overall response, subtract 1 and multiply by 100.

List broker. A service which brings list owners and prospective list renters (users) together.

List maintenance. Keeping a mailing list current through correcting and updating the addresses and other data.

List Rental. The process of renting (for onetime use, or other periods) a list of names of customers owned by some organization for an agreed upon cost per thousand (CPM).

Locatable Address Conversion System (LACS). LACS enables companies to update their mailing lists when addresses have been converted by local authorities from rural to city style address.

Losers. Customers who cost you more in expenses than they deliver in profits. Every company has losers, but few have figured out what to do about them.

Loyalty. Customer loyalty is usually measured by the retention, renewal, or repurchase rate. Loyalty can be increased or decreased by things that you do for customers. Loyalty is easier to achieve if you recruit loyal customers to begin with. Loyalty is seldom increased by discounts.

Loyalty Programs. Programs designed to increase customer loyalty. The term also applies to points programs, whereby customers earn credits for purchases.

LTV. see Lifetime Value.

Marginal Utility. The extra value you get by acquiring one more unit of a product or service. Typically, marginal utility decreases with each additional unit acquired.

Market Rate of Interest. The interest rate paid for waiting to receive future sums of money.

Market Research. A scientific method of determining what products and services people want and are willing to pay for. Uses surveys, focus groups, and modeling. Differs from database marketing, which is designed to build relationships with customers.

Mass Marketing. A highly successful method of reaching millions of people to tell them about available products and services. Uses TV, Radio, Print advertisements, and the Internet. It will never be replaced by direct or database marketing. It works best for packaged goods and services that are sold through channels, rather than directly.

MCIF. Marketing Customer Information File, a system used by banks to view the entire bank services used by a household. MCIF is an essential first step for banks wishing to do database marketing.

Merge/Purge. A software system used to merge many different input tapes in differing formats and put them into a common format for a mailing. Merge/Purge detects duplicates.

Migration. Customers can be encouraged to migrate from standard to deluxe products, from a few products to many products, from small balances to large balances. Customer migration is a valid marketing technique.

Minimum Test Cell Size. How few people can be included in a test for the results to be valid? There is a formula, which is used for test cells within a larger test. It is: Minimum test cell size = 4/(break even rate).

MIS. Management Information Services. A shorthand way of naming the central data processing staff of a company. Often called IT or DP.

Modeling. Market research uses models to predict customer behavior based on past behavior plus demographics. Models use CHAID or multiple regressions. They usually require appending demographic data and are costly to run. In some cases they can accurately predict churn or identify customer segments most likely to purchase a product.

Monetary Analysis. Part of RFM analysis. Monetary analysis involves categorizing all customers by the total amount that they have purchased (per month, year, etc.) and sorting all customers by that amount. The resulting file is divided into quintiles. The top quintile (highest spenders) usually responds better than lower quintiles.

Multi-buyer. A person who crops up on two or more independent rented lists. Multi-buyers usually respond better to a direct offer than other buyers.

Multiple Regression. A statistical technique used in modeling whereby you develop a formula which explains the relationship between several variables in explaining behavior.

NCDM. The National Center for Database Marketing, a convention held twice a year by the Direct Marketing Association. The best place, other than this book, to find out about database marketing.

NCOA^{LINK} National Change of Address, a U.S. Postal Service system under which about 20 service bureaus nationwide have exclusive use of the change of address forms filed by persons or businesses who are moving. These forms are keypunched, and can be used by the service bureau to update your file of prospects or customers to obtain their correct current address. A worthwhile service for database marketers.

Negative Option. A system in which products or services come automatically, charged to a credit card, unless the customer specifically requests that they be stopped. It is a wonderful system that is not used often enough.

Net Present Value (NPV). The present value of money to be received in the future. It is equal to the future money divided by the discount rate.

Net Names. The actual names used in a mailing, after removing the duplicates and matches to your customer list. In some cases, you can rent names on a net-name basis.

Next Best Product. The results of an analysis of many customer purchase behaviors plus demographics that selects for each customer the next best cross-sell product for each customer based on profit to the company, needs of the customer, likelihood of sale, cost of marketing, etc. The NBP is put into each customer record on the database.

NIACC. Net Income after capital charges. A banking term used in determining customer profitability.

Nixies. USPS provides a Nixie Elimination Service as an addition to NCOA^{LINK}. This service provides footnotes as to why an address match could not be found. This service is very useful in correcting bad addresses.

NPV. Net Present Value.

Nth. A system whereby a small test group is selected from a large database. Using an Nth, the test group is an exact statistical replica of the larger database. To get an Nth, divide the desired size of the test group into the size of the database. For example, 40,000 in a test group and 400,000 in the database. Result is 10.

An Nth would be the result from putting every tenth record into the test group.

One-to-One Marketing.   1:1 marketing.

Outsource.   The process of hiring expert companies and consultants to perform marketing functions such as building databases, telesales, fulfillment, market research. Outsourcing is usually more cost effective and efficient than building up in-house staff.

Overlaid Data.   To any consumer or business-to-business file it is possible to find data providers who will overlay data to enrich your knowledge of your customers or prospects. Overlaid data can include SIC codes, income, age, presence of children, etc. Only use overlaid data if they improve your marketing success.

Package.   The envelope or container or look of your outgoing direct mail piece.

Packaged Goods.   Products sold in retail stores. Database marketing seldom works with packaged goods because you cannot tell who is buying your products, and the margin on each sale is too small to finance the relationship building involved.

Penetration.   Your customers as a percentage of the universe that defines your customer's type of household or business. "We had a penetration ratio in that zip code of 8 percent."

Personalization.   The process of including personal references in an outgoing mail piece such as "Thank you for your order of Feb. 23 for six boxes of hard candy, Mrs. Williams." With a database, personalization can be achieved very inexpensively. The lift is usually enough to pay the extra cost.

Points Programs.   A method of rewarding customers for their purchases, and thereby helping them to build up equity in the relationship. Airline miles programs are the most successful points programs. There are other similar successful programs in both consumer and business-to-business marketing.

POS System.   Point of Sale System. A system whereby goods are bar coded and scanned at the time of checkout. In some cases, consumers have frequent shopper cards that can be scanned at the same time, so that the retailer can learn what each customer is buying. POS systems are a major breakthrough in database marketing in retail situations.

Postal Pre-sort.   Sorting outgoing letters in a special way to take advantage of postal discounts.

Predictive Model.   An analytical technique that ranks all customers or prospects by their likelihood to do something (respond, buy, cancel service, etc.) It is useful in acquisition and in reducing churn.

Premiums.   What you give customers in lieu of discounts. Premiums are better than discounts because they do not appear to reduce your price point or margin. They build loyalty, whereas discounts do not.

Present Discounted Value.   A financial process for calculating the present value of an amount of money to be received or paid in the future. The formula is $PDV = V/(1 + i)^n$ where V is the future value, i the market rate of interest, and n the time in years.

President's Club.   Many companies create President's Clubs or Advisory Panels for their best customers. It is a way of recognizing the rewarding your best customers. It helps to keep them for a lifetime.

Profiles.   A method of understanding large groups of customers by segmenting them into groups with similar lifestyles and purchasing habits. A retail store may identify profiles as Gold, Regular, or Occasional shoppers.

Profitability.   Banks have developed a system using their MCIF where the profitability of each household is measured every month. Customers are segmented in to profitability groups. The profitability of a household adds all revenue received during the month, and subtracts all costs and interest paid.

Program Buyers.   Types of business-to-business buyers for whom their purchasing manual or buying schedule is more important than price or marketing messages. Many government agencies are program buyers.

Query. A question designed to retrieve information from a database. The result can be a count, a cross tab or a report. See ad hoc query.

Quintiles. A method of dividing customers into five equal groups based on spending or response. Quintiles are more useful for RFM than Deciles which are used in marketing research.

Reactivation. A program that encourages lapsed customers to start buying again.

Recency. The most powerful single factor affecting customer repurchase. The customer most likely to buy from you again is the customer who bought from you most recently. A basic factor in RFM analysis.

Reference Accounts. Business accounts that may not be profitable in themselves, but may bring in a lot of other business because the account is prestigious or well known.

Referral Programs. Programs designed to foster referrals by rewarding those who refer people who become customers. Can be more cost effective than almost any other database marketing program.

Referrals. Referred customers have a higher retention rate and spending rate then the average newly acquired customers. For that reason, it is vital that you keep track of both referred people and those who refer them in your database.

Reformatting. Changing the format of a rented list to a new record format that matches a desired arrangement. This is done in traditional merge purge. It is not a complicated process.

Regression Analysis. A statistical method used in modeling. Using a regression, the influence of various variable factors is assigned a weight in their ability to predict a known outcome, such as a purchase or a response.

Relationship Buyers. The best kind of customers. People who want to do business with you because they like your products, your employees, or your brand. The opposite is transaction buyers who are interested only in price.

Relationship Marketing. The process of building a relationship with customers which results in the customers becoming more loyal, buying more, and staying as customers. Another word for Database Marketing.

Relational Database. A relational database is what is needed for database marketing. Such a database is kept on disk and consists of related files (name and address, orders), which are related to each other by ID numbers and accessed by indexes.

Renewal Rate. The percentage of current subscribers or customers who sign up for service when their current contract has expired.

Repurchase Rate. Used particularly in automobiles. The percentage of current customers who will buy your brand again when they make their next purchase in your category. For U.S. automobiles, the satisfaction rate is about 90 percent. The repurchase rate is about 35 percent.

Response. The people who respond to your advertisements or direct marketing appeals. In the Internet, a response is someone who has clicked on your banner advertisement or the "click here" in your email newsletter or web site.

Response Device. On every outgoing direct mail piece, there is included a response device that usually shows up in the "window" in the envelope to provide the name and address. The response device is an order or donation form. It is important because it always contains the prospect number and a source code that identifies the offer, package, list, segment, etc.

Response Rate. The percentage of people who received your direct marketing offer who responded to it by a further inquiry or a sale. In the Internet, it is the percentage of impressions that resulted in a response.

Retention Rate. The percentage of customers who made a purchase from you last year who have made a purchase from you this year. This is the most important single number in a lifetime value table.

Return on Investment (ROI). A key measure of the success of any direct marketing activity. It is the total net profit from a direct marketing initiative, divided by the total cost of the entire operation. ROI from an initial offer is often negative. But when customer lifetime value is taken into account, it often becomes positive.

Rewards. Something that you give customers besides the product or service to thank them for their patronage. Rewards can be premiums or points or status symbols. An important database marketing tool.

RFM. Recency, Frequency, Monetary Analysis. A very old and very powerful method of coding existing customers. Used to predict response, average order size, and other factors. The most powerful predictive system available in database marketing.

RFP. Request for proposals. The first step in outsourcing to database partners.

Risk Revenue Matrix. A simple matrix with likelihood of churn is on one axis and lifetime value or revenue is on the other. The matrix is used to focus attention on those customers who have the highest lifetime value and the highest likelihood of leaving. You save your retention program dollars by concentrating on these rather than on all customers.

Rollout. After a successful test in direct marketing, you expose a much larger group to your offer. This called a rollout.

RON. Run of Network. An Internet advertising term. Advertisers who place a RON advertisement with a large number of sites simultaneously get instant feedback as to which sites are giving them the best response. RON is the cheapest form of Internet advertising, and may be the best.

Saturated Market. A situation in which everyone has the product, and the market is essentially a replacement market. For example, tires, batteries, PCs, television.

Segments. A group of customers that you have identified as having similar purchase patterns. Creating and using segments is essential to successful database marketing.

Sic Code or NAICS. Coding systems designed by the U.S. Department of Commerce for classifying the products and services produced by companies.

SKU. Stock Keeping Unit: a warehouse term for the products that a company produces. Each different product has its own SKU number.

Source Codes. Codes of letters or numbers used to identify a particular offer on a particular date. The codes are stored in the customer's database record so you have a promotion history.

Spending Rate. The amount that a customer spends with you in a month or a year.

SQL. A query language used with the IBM software DB2. Often pronounced "sequal."

Straddle Pricing. A retail pricing method in which prices for occasional shoppers are set higher than the competition, whereas prices for regular customers are set lower than the competition.

Strategy Development. Database marketing is only successful if it is accompanied by a winning marketing strategy. No single system works universally. Strategies are always being upset by the market competition.

Suppression Files. Using names on one file (a customer file) to suppress or drop names from another tape (a prospect file). Examples: the DNC (do not call) file, the DMA (do not mail) file, a deceased or prison file.

Surrogate Measurements. In marketing, the success of an offer is often measured indirectly by awareness, focus groups, Neilson ratings, etc. In direct marketing and Internet marketing, success is measured directly by responses and sales.

Sweepstakes. An offer promising a randomly drawn prize to all respondents, regardless of whether they buy your product. Those who do not buy, but still respond to the sweepstakes may be valuable names for rental or for other offers. In comparison to buyers, sweepstakes respondents are generally much less valuable.

Targeting. The system in which a specific group of prospects is selected for marketing, based on assumptions about their interest in the product or ability to purchase.

Teaser Rates. Introductory very low credit card interest rates which are then raised to normal high levels after the introductory period of a few months has passed.

Telesales. Sales persons who talk on the telephone to prospects and customers. In business to business, telesales is preferred by many customers over sales force visits. In consumer situations, outbound telesales is often resented. Inbound telesales (where customers call a toll-free number) is preferred.

Test Groups. Groups of customers selected by an Nth who are made an offer to test the validity of the offer. If the response is good, the marketer will go to a rollout.

Third Class Mail. Over 85 percent of all mail carrying advertising or promotion is sent by third class. It is much less costly than first class. It usually requires postal pre-sort. If it is not delivered for some reason (bad address, person no longer there), this mail is thrown into the trash by the USPS, and the sender will not know this.

Touches. A customer contact through personal visit, phone, letter, e-mail, or fax. Customers like to hear from their suppliers. Touches should be planned in advance.

Trade Deficit. The difference between what we sell to foreigners and what they buy from us in a year. A high trade deficit is not necessarily bad for U.S. consumers or businesses.

Transaction Buyers. Customers who are only interested in price, not in quality or service. They have no loyalty, and will leave you for a better offer at any time. It is hard to make money from transaction buyers.

Two-Step Offer. A promotion system in which you get responders to call in for a brochure or catalog, or salesman's visit, which then makes the sale.

Update. To modify a database record to insert new information into it, or to delete it. Updating is either done in batch mode (fast and cheap) or online (slow and costly). Usually done once a month. Some companies can do this several times a day.

Up Selling. Prompting customers to buy upgraded products when they had intended to buy something of lower value.

Virtual Distributors. Distributors have warehouses and stock a limited number of products. Virtual distributors have a Web site and may have no warehouse at all. They arrange shipment to customers directly from the manufacturers.

Web Advertising. Advertisements on web sites were once thought to be a successful method of reaching new customers. Experience has shown that they may be less profitable than TV, Radio, or Print. Why? Because most people who visit the web are already looking for something, and find the web ads a distraction.

Web Site. Every company in the world will soon have its own Web site on the Internet, advertising its products and services. An increasing percentage of business, particularly business-to-business commerce will take place through Web sites. Best customers are given personal pages on company Web sites.

White Mail. Mail received from a buyer or donor who has not included the response device, so you cannot determine the source code of the offer which promoted his purchase or gift.

World Wide Web (www). Another name for the Internet. Company Web sites names (URLs) usually begin with www: www.dbmarketing.com.

Index

436

Index